Homily Grits 5 Snack Food for the Soul
Copyright © 2006 Robert W. VanHoose

Library of Congress Control Number: *2006930661*

ISBN: *0-9742612-8-9*
Published by Homily Grits Publishing Co.

Homily Grits 5

Snack Food for the Soul

A One Year Feast of
Daily Devotions and Prayer

By Robert W. VanHoose

Homily Grits Publishing Co.
Ocala, Florida
www.homilygrits.com
RVanHoose@homilygrits.com

Other Books by Robert VanHoose
Homily Grits (2003)
Homily Grits 2 (2003)
Homily Grits Daily Devotions and Proactive Prayer (2004)
Homily Grits 4 (2005)
Homily Grits 5 (2006)

Advocate
All in All
All Knowing God
All Sufficient God
Almighty God
Anchor
Anointed One
Author & Perfecter
Avenger
Best Friend
Blessed Assurance
Bread of Life
Bright Shining Star
Burden Bearer
Cleanser
Companion
Conformer
Conscience
Consuming Fire
Cornerstone
Counselor
Creator
Defender
Empower
Encourager
Equipper
Eternal God
Everlasting Father
Everpresent God
Fair
Forgiver
Fount of Blessings
Giver of Good Gifts
God of All
God of My Tomorrows
Good Shepherd
Good
Great God

Great I AM
Guarantor
Guide
Healer
Helper
Hiding Place
High Tower
Holy God
Hope of Glory
Joy

"Devote yourselves to prayer with an alert mind and a thankful heart".
Colossians 4:2 NLT

Prayer Template
Lord, You Are_____
Forgive Me For _____
Thank You For _____
Needs of Others _____
Personal Needs _____
Answered Prayers _____

Many people have found this little format to be helpful in getting them to focus and better concentrate on their prayers.

Judge
Keeper
King of Kings
Lily of the Valley
Lord of Lords
Lamb of God
Living Lord
Merciful God
Most High God
Fulfiller
Potter

Peace
Prince of Peace
Perfect Sacrifice
Promise Keeper
Protector
Provider
Reconciler
Redeemer
Refuge
Reinforcer
Renewer
Rest
Restorer
Revealer
Righteousness
Righteous
Risen Lord
Rock
Safety Net
Sanctifier
Savior
Security
Shelter
Shield
Sin Bearer
Sovereign
Strength
Stronghold
Substitute
Supplier
Sustainer
Transformer
Trust
Validator
Wisdom
Wonderful
Worthy God
Victorious

Forward

"Because the Teacher was wise, he taught the people everything he knew. He collected proverbs and classified them. Indeed, the Teacher taught the plain truth, and he did so in an interesting way."
Ecclesiastes 12:9 NLT

We are blessed to be able to share these spiritual insights from God's Word with you. This little faith based ministry of the Word has been blessed to go into some 50 countries via our web site and email.

We pray that these devotions will prove to be a channel of God's grace to you as you hear God's Word applied in everyday situations of life through them.

As in most teachings, the writer ends up being blessed more than the readers because of the time and study involved.

It is my sincere prayer that you will be as blessed in reading these as I have in writing them, and that these meditations will be pleasing in God's sight.

In His Love,

Robert W. VanHoose

Colossians 1:9-11

Our Special Thanks to
Elizabeth Bone
for our cover design
and my <u>very dear</u> granddaughter
Stacey Hudson
for proof reading

Dedication

This book is dedicated in loving memory of my sister, Martha Jewel Corbitt, whose unconditional love and ever positive reinforcement when I needed it most made a big difference in my life.

Putting on the New

"Through the LORD's mercies we are not consumed, because His compassions fail not. They are new every morning; great is Your faithfulness." Lamentations 3:22, 23

The baggage of the past holds many of us back too many times and in too many areas of our lives.

"Create in me a clean heart, O God. Renew a right spirit within me."
Psalm 51:10 NLT

When we get "burnt" by relationships, failed efforts, and reverse fortunes of any kind, we too often withdraw and lick our wounds instead of confessing, forgiving, being forgiven, forgetting, and moving on.

Hopefully we will learn something every time we get burnt and will not make the same mistake again, but we must never let burnings defeat us as we seek to live life to the fullest in Christ.

As we start a new year, it is a good time to be reminded that we were made new when we received Jesus Christ as our Savior, and we are continually being renewed by daily confession and repentance as we put off the sins of our old nature and put on the righteousness of Christ.

We need to remind ourselves daily that our new birth means that sin no longer has dominion over us, and there is absolutely no reason why we have to continue sinning.

When we put on the new, we need to remember that we are new creations in Christ, and we are actually set free from the control of sin so that we can become slaves to Christ and His righteousness.

"And that you put on the new man which was created according to God, in true righteousness and holiness."
Ephesians 4:20

When we appropriate by faith whom we have become in Jesus Christ, we will receive resurrection power and strength from the Holy Spirit to begin living like the new creation Christ has made us to be.

If there is no change in our conduct, attitudes, and perspectives, we must question the reality of our conversion and go back to the well of confession and true repentance until the evidence of Christ living in us becomes manifest.

Father, as You came to make all things new, let me live daily in newness of life I have found in You. Amen.

Lord, You Are _____

Forgive Me For _____

Thank You For _____

Needs of Others _____

Personal Needs _____

Answered Prayers _____

What Will We Leave Behind?

"The wise shall inherit glory, but shame shall be the legacy of fools."
Proverbs 3:35

Sometimes it is good to look ahead to the end of our time on this earth. We are all going to leave a legacy to someone. It may just be a memory or sometimes a tangible material blessing, but hopefully it will be eternal life itself as a conduit of God's grace in leading someone to saving faith in Jesus Christ.

"The end of a thing is better than its beginning; the patient in spirit is better than the proud in spirit."
Ecclesiastes 7:8

Some will leave a legacy of broken promises, broken homes, selfishness, and shame. Others will leave many toys that offer no pleasure at all when they are no longer able to be used or enjoyed. Many of the pursuits for which we had such passion will turn out to be so trivial that they will be long forgotten.

We need to be ever mindful that the way we live today may well determine the legacy we will leave tomorrow. All of the great plans God made for us before we were even born should become the legacy of a life well lived, fruitful and pleasing to God. This can never happen if we insist on living our lives controlled by our flesh and self centeredness in willful disobedience and separation from God.

The only legacy worth leaving is the legacy of love. How sweet it will be to be remembered as a loving spouse, parent, or friend!

"By doing this they will be storing up their treasure as a good foundation for the future so that they may take hold of real life."
1 Timothy 6:19 NLT

When we truly love God, we will leave a legacy of good works that will be remembered not only by others, but by Jesus Himself. Could anything be sweeter than hearing "well done, thou good and faithful servant"?

It may be later than we think, but it is never too late to come to God's throne of grace with godly sorrow and true repentance over our past. There our crooked paths can be straightened as we submit to the Lordship of Jesus Christ and live in freedom from our bondage to sin.

Father, may the legacy I received as a child of God be the legacy I leave to those I love in this life, and take with me when I go to meet You face to face. Amen.

Lord, You Are _____

Forgive Me For _____

Thank You For _____

Needs of Others _____

Personal Needs _____

Answered Prayers _____

OJT

"God is educating you; that's why you must never drop out. He's treating you as dear children. This trouble you're in isn't punishment; it's training." Hebrews 12:7 MSG

Most of us have gone through some sort of on the job training sometime. All of us need to go through what a friend of mine called "own the job training."

"Be blessed, GOD; train me in Your ways of wise living. I'll transfer to my lips all the counsel that comes from your mouth." Psalm 119:12 MSG

What a difference there is when we go to work, school, or through our daily life with an "own the job training" attitude.

When we take ownership of our position on a team and train accordingly, we are going to be better players.

When we get up in the morning and do life with the understanding that we own our jobs as followers of Christ and children of God, we begin doing life God's way by the transforming power of the Holy Spirit.

When we own up to the fact that God is serious about us taking ownership of our salvation through faith in Jesus, we will also have to own up to the fact that He takes sin seriously. His command to not only be a disciple but to make others disciples is not just a suggestion but a command.

"Spend your time and energy in training yourself for spiritual fitness." 1 Timothy 4:17b NLT

Our own the job training in becoming imitators of Christ and growing into His fullness involves growing inwardly as we learn to trust and obey God through reading, hearing, and inwardly digesting His Word.

We are also called to own the job training out in the world of everyday life, where we learn to love people because God loves them. We should be ever mindful of others need for a Savior and should help and encourage them to find Jesus.

Father, help me to grow into the image of Your Son through daily own the job training. Amen.

Lord, You Are _____
Forgive Me For _____
Thank You For _____
Needs of Others _____
Personal Needs _____
Answered Prayers _____

Caring by Sharing

"Don't forget to do good and to share what you have with those in need, for such sacrifices are very pleasing to God." Hebrews 11:16 NLT

When it comes to showing that we care, we need to be generous, sharing people.

"Everyone will share the story of your wonderful goodness; they will sing with joy of your righteousness." Psalm 145:7 NLT

We usually think of sharing in terms of physical things such as food, money, or other possessions. These are all good things to share, but they are not always what are needed most.

What the world needs most is the "love sweet love" which we have gained by receiving God's love through faith in Jesus Christ and sharing this love with others.

When we spread this love in a caring way by sharing how the Good News has changed our life and blessed us so richly, we are caring for the souls of people and the needs of their souls.

When we visit the sick or those in prison, we are caring by sharing God's love through comforting and encouraging them.

We can care for others by sharing our time or talents with them in a way that ministers to them and serves them.

Sharing is a great antidote for selfishness or greed. It is living out the love of Christ by being other-centered instead of self-centered.

We all too often like to share our complaints and prejudices as a means of validating or justifying them. There is generally not a lot of caring shown in these pursuits.

"Love each other with genuine affection, and take delight in honoring each other." Romans 12:10 NLT

Jesus reminds, "If anyone desires to be first, he shall be last of all and servant of all" *(Mark 9:35b)*. This should be the guiding principle for all to show their caring by sharing.

Father, help me to be a carer and sharer, just like Jesus. Amen.

Lord, You Are _____
Forgive Me For _____
Thank You For _____
Needs of Others _____
Personal Needs _____
Answered Prayers _____

Holy Transformation

"And do not be conformed to this world, but be transformed by the renewing of your mind, that you may prove what is that good and acceptable and perfect will of God." Romans 12:2

The good work of salvation that has been done for us by faith in Jesus Christ as our Savior is only the beginning.

"You have turned my mourning into joyful dancing. You have taken away my clothes of mourning and clothed me with joy,"
Psalm 30:11 NLT

The good work of sanctification is the ongoing process whereby the Holy Spirit empowers us to replace our natural life with a spiritual life through daily obedience, confession, and repentance.

We are to be transformed by our new birth in every area of our lives wherein we are to become the righteous ones naturally as we have already been made righteous spiritually in God's sight the hour we first believed.

When we really understand and accept the significance that our bodies have become the temple of the Holy Spirit, we must understand the importance of keeping the temple clean through fleeing temptation and daily cleansing through confession and repentance.

In addition to being ever mindful that our bodies are temples of the Holy Spirit and should be lived in as such, we must cooperate with the Holy Spirit in the transformation process by harnessing the power of God's grace through feeding frequently on the Word and by celebrating, remembering, and proclaiming the Lord's death until He comes through the Lord's Supper.

"And as the Spirit of the Lord works within us, we become more and more like Him and reflect His glory even more."
2 Corinthians 3:18b

The fact that we are never going to achieve the natural holiness and righteousness of Christ on this earth should never discourage or dissuade us from surrendering and growing into His fullness as we do life under the direction of and by the power of the Holy Spirit. The Holy Spirit has been given as a deposit and guarantee that Christ in us is our hope of glory.

Father, help me to become more like You in every area of my life by the sanctifying power of the Holy Spirit. Amen.

Lord, You Are _____

Forgive Me For _____

Thank You For _____

Needs of Others _____

Personal Needs _____

Answered Prayers _____

January 6   Read Romans 5, Psalm 36
Our Highest Privilege
"All honor to the God and Father of our Lord Jesus Christ, for it is by His boundless mercy that God has given us the privilege of being born again. Now we live with a wonderful expectation because Jesus Christ rose again from the dead." 1 Peter 1:3

There are many blessings from God. Many are given unconditionally to everyone whether just or unjust. The sun shines on all, the rain falls for all, and the breath of physical life is given freely.

"For You are the fountain of life, the light by which we see." Psalm 36:9 NLT

Many blessings are conditional. God's Old Testament covenants provide blessings based on obedience. "He is the faithful God who keeps His covenant for a thousand generations and constantly loves those who love Him and obey His commands" (Deuteronomy 7:9b).

We receive many blessings by simply asking for them. God loves to give good gifts to those who ask. "If you then, being evil, know how to give good gifts to your children, how much more will your Father who is in heaven give good things to those who ask Him!" (Matthew 7:11)

The greatest blessing of all is the high privilege we have of friendship with God through faith in Jesus Christ.

When we view loving and serving others as a privilege instead of a burden God is able to live in and work through us in accomplishing the purposes for which He created us.

"Because of our faith, Christ has brought us into this place of highest privilege where we now stand, and we confidently and joyfully look forward to sharing God's glory." Romans 5:2 NLT

Too many of us abuse our great privilege too many times. We "forsake the assembling of ourselves together," neglect growing in the Word, and slip back into the slavery of our old sin nature too easily.

The grace that made possible our high privilege is the grace that will keep us there and lead us safely home if we will confess, repent, and let the Spirit have control over our flesh.

Father, thank you for the privilege of being one of Your redeemed. Amen.

Lord, You Are _____
Forgive Me For _____
Thank You For _____
Needs of Others _____
Personal Needs _____
Answered Prayers _____

Who Do You Look Up To?

"Looking unto Jesus, the author and finisher of our faith, who for the joy that was set before Him endured the cross, despising the shame, and has sat down at the right hand of the throne of God." Hebrews 12:2

It is good to have people to look up to especially when they are good examples of being sermons in shoes that we can learn from and try to emulate. We thrive on encouragement we receive from others.

"I was looking the other way, looking up to the people at the top, envying the wicked who have it made,"
Psalm 73:3 MSG

If we look, we can see Jesus all around us, living in and through those He has called into a personal abiding relationship of faith.

The more important question is can people look up to us? Are we bearing the fruit of "love, joy, peace, longsuffering, kindness, goodness, faithfulness, gentleness, and self-control" (Galatians 5:22)? Can others see Jesus living in us?

It is a sad thing indeed when those who claim the name of Christ cause people to look down on Him because they shame His name by hypocrisy, pride, greed, envy, or other moral melt downs.

We are called to be building blocks instead of stumbling blocks. We are to be beacons of light in a dark and sinful world.

We all too often fall into the trap of looking down on others as a means of making ourselves look better. How much better it is to make ourselves look better by looking up to others who are reflecting the love of Christ in the way they are living their lives.

"Therefore be imitators of God as dear children. And walk in love, as Christ also has loved us and given Himself for us, an offering and a sacrifice to God for a sweet-smelling aroma."
Ephesians 5:1

When we look up to Jesus we will find the perfect example worth imitating. When we compare ourselves to Him, we will find how short we fall of His glory and will never again seek the hypocritical glory of looking down on others.

Father, help me to look up to You, the perfect example I should be imitating in every area of my life. Amen.

Lord, You Are _____

Forgive Me For _____

Thank You For _____

Needs of Others _____

Personal Needs _____

Answered Prayers _____

January 8   Read 2 Peter 1:4-6, Psalm 17
Applied Divinity
"May you always be filled with the fruit of your salvation – those good things that are produced in your life by Jesus Christ – for this will bring much glory and praise to God." Philippians 1:11 NLT

The divine character and nature of God was made manifest in Jesus Christ. It took every bit of this divine nature and character to live in a sin-sick world and remain pure and spotless through great trials and temptations of living in the humanity of man.

"As for me, I will see Your face in righteousness; I shall be satisfied when I awake to Your likeness." Psalm 17:15

God knows full well the weakness of the flesh of man and how to overcome it. He cleansed us by washing away all our sin with the divine blood of Jesus, which was shed so that we may receive His righteousness.

God cleanses us in His sight the minute we receive Jesus as our Savior. He also sends the Holy Spirit to continue cleansing and conforming us into the likeness of Christ daily until we achieve the perfection of Christ in heaven.

Applied divinity is the ongoing process through which holy transformation takes place.

Our freedom and power to become bearers of the fruit of the Spirit grows as we grow in our relationship with Christ through the Word.

Colleges and seminaries award Master of Divinity and Doctor of Divinity degrees to those who complete the required courses. The Holy Spirit comes to help us receive our "Master's Divinity" as we receive the supernatural power to know Christ in us— our hope of everlasting

"And by that same mighty power, He has given us all of His rich and wonderful promises. He has promised that you will escape the decadence all around you caused by evil desires and that you will share in His divine nature." 2 Peter 1:4 NLT

glory. When we learn what Jesus did, we will also learn what He would do in any given situation. This is the way we apply the divinity of Christ in our everyday life.

Father, in Your mercy help me appropriate the divinity of Christ through the power of the Holy Spirit. Amen.

Lord, You Are _____
Forgive Me For _____
Thank You For _____
Needs of Others _____
Personal Needs _____
Answered Prayers _____

What Were We Not Thinking?

"There is more hope for a fool than for someone who speaks without thinking." Proverbs 29:20 NLT

Most of us often have cause to ponder mistakes. Hopefully we learn from and don't repeat them. From the perfect 20/20 vision of hindsight, we often wonder what in the world we were thinking when the problem is that we were not thinking.

"Clean the slate, God, so we can start the day fresh! Keep me from stupid sins, from thinking I can take over your work," Psalm 19:13 MSG

Flying off the handle without thinking about the consequences for ourselves or others often does a lot of damage and leads to a lifetime of regret.

Being overcome by lust can lead to sins of the flesh that can break up families and marriages and has consequences that would never have happened if we had been thinking.

Sometimes our problems stem from thinking too much with earthly wisdom instead of seeking wisdom and spiritual discernment from God, whose thoughts are different and so much higher than ours.

Sometimes we find ourselves over our heads trying to solve problems beyond the scope of our experience or abilities and create more problems instead of solving anything. I have broken watches, computers, and other items sometimes beyond repair by not realizing that I didn't know what I was doing. Unfortunately, I have the sadness of some broken relationships from the same problem.

"Whoever knows what you're thinking and planning except you yourself? The same with God—except that He not only knows what He's thinking, but He lets us in on it." 1 Corinthians 2:11 MSG

When we think we are better than others, that we are invincible, that failure can never happen to us, that God does not take our sins seriously, we will sooner or later find out that we were not thinking rightly.

May God forbid that we ever take our self-centered thinking so seriously that we are blinded and never find the wisdom and spiritual discernment God wants to give all His children.

Father, help me to think with the wisdom from on high. Amen.

Lord, You Are _____

Forgive Me For _____

Thank You For _____

Needs of Others _____

Personal Needs _____

Answered Prayers _____

We'll Never Have to Walk Alone
"Teaching them to observe all things that I have commanded you; and lo, I am with you always, even to the end of the age." Matthew 28:20

When the grace of God comes upon us and we receive the marvelous gift of eternal life, we also receive the eternal presence of the Holy Spirit who comes to live in our hearts forever. Loved ones are not always going to be with us. Through all the loneliness this brings, we have the comfort of the Holy Spirit filling the emptiness with that all-sufficient security of God's love.

"For the LORD loves justice, and does not forsake His saints; they are preserved forever, but the descendants of the wicked shall be cut off."
Psalm 37:28

We may often find ourselves abandoned and forsaken by others. We should not be surprised. We must realize that all people are born sinners, and many will disappoint us. This is why we should never worship the ground any human stands on, but rather we should keep our faith and trust anchored in the One who has promised never to leave or forsake us.

No one ever experienced more loneliness and abandonment than Jesus. He was the only one ever forsaken by God. He who committed no sin had to suffer the agony of hell alone and forsaken so that we would never have to experience it.

That "peace that surpasses all understanding," which is promised to every believer, is the peace that will sustain us through times of loneliness or feeling forsaken.

"And I will ask the Father, and He will give you another Counselor, who will never leave you."
John 14:16 NLT

When we allow the love of God to fill us with the security of knowing that we are unconditionally loved, forever forgiven, and totally righteous in God's sight through the imputed righteousness of Christ, we can rejoice even through times of loneliness or abandonment by others.

God will never let us walk alone when we walk in faith. He will even pick us up and carry us when the walk gets too hard for us.

Father, keep me ever mindful that I am never alone when I have You in my life. Amen.

Lord, You Are _____

Forgive Me For _____

Thank You For _____

Needs of Others _____

Personal Needs _____

Answered Prayers _____

Have You Been Tenderized?

"My child, don't ignore it when the LORD disciplines you, and don't be discouraged when He corrects you. For the LORD corrects those He loves, just as a father corrects a child in whom he delights." Proverbs 11:12 NLT

Meat tenderizers have been around for a long time. When the powder fails, a meat cleaver will soften the toughest of steaks.

"But you, O God, are both tender and kind, not easily angered, immense in love, and you never, never quit." Psalm 86:15 MSG

God is the Master Chef when it comes to using tenderizers as He molds and melds us into the image of Christ.

Brokenness is the tenderizer for our salvation. Until we are broken and admit that we are sinners who need a Savior, the hardness of our hearts and gristle of our flesh will make it impossible to experience the tenderness of Christ's love.

When we go through God's tenderizing process, it may involve relational, physical, financial, emotional, or spiritual problems. We can take comfort in knowing that God will provide His strength and sustaining grace throughout the tenderizing process.

Once we are saved, God will do whatever it takes to keep us in the security of His grace. He will let nothing separate us from His love that is ours in Christ.

If our pride, unrepented sin, or other outrageous conduct calls for it, He will not hesitate to use a cleaver on us to bring us back into the circle of His will.

God hates sin, but He loves us more than He hates our sins. Forgiveness and restoration is always as near as a broken spirit and contrite heart that confesses and repents.

"No discipline is enjoyable while it is happening—it is painful! But afterward there will be a quiet harvest of right living for those who are trained in this way." Hebrews 12:11 NLT

As God's character-development program tenderizes our hearts with the Master's touch and turns our "won'ts into wills," "can'ts into cans," and "shouldn'ts into shoulds," we trade our sorrows and shame for the peace and joy of the Lord. We become an offering fit for the King.

Father, thank you for tenderizing me to draw me closer to You. Amen.

Lord, You Are _____

Forgive Me For _____

Thank You For _____

Needs of Others _____

Personal Needs _____

Answered Prayers _____

Going My Way?

"You have shown me the way of life, and You will give me wonderful joy in Your presence." Psalm 16:11 NLT

This question begs serious and honest answering daily as we have to make a choice about what way or whose way we are going today. We can choose to go the way of the world, our flesh, the devil, or the cross every day.

"There is a way that seems right to a man, but its end is the way of death."
Proverbs 14:12

Going the world's way involves going with the flow and prevailing standards of conduct. It involves finding satisfaction of needs in worldliness.

Going the way of the flesh involves living in bondage to our sin and finding need's satisfaction in pleasure.

Going the way of the devil involves both of the above plus being deceived, depressed, and devoured by the forces of evil all around us.

Going the way of the cross is the only way that leads to true happiness, peace, and joy, which we can only find at the cross of Jesus, who is the Way, the Truth, and the Life.

Jesus came that we may have life to the fullest both now and forever. As we grow in our personal relationship with Him through the power of the Holy Spirit, we will become more like Him every day in every way.

When we go with The Way we are going with His presence and resurrection power. We are going with the promises of His all-sufficient grace, friendship, and fellowship. He becomes our refuge and strength in times of trouble, our comforter, our protector, our peace, our joy, and our happiness.

"Jesus told him, 'I am the way, the truth, and the life. No one can come to the Father except through Me.'"
John 14:6 NLT

When we choose to pick up our cross and follow Jesus, we find the power to live our new life in Christ and His fullness. We have the power to die to the lures, guilt, shame, and bondage to the wrong ways we may have been traveling. Whose way are you going?

Father, may I always be found fruitful and faithful as I walk in and with the Way of the cross. Amen.

Lord, You Are _____
Forgive Me For _____
Thank You For _____
Needs of Others _____
Personal Needs _____
Answered Prayers _____

Does the One with the Most Toys Really Win?

"I have God's more-than-enough, more joy in one ordinary day than they get in all their shopping sprees. At day's end I'm ready for sound sleep, for you, GOD, have put my life back together." Psalm 4:7 MSG

If we were to believe bumper stickers and the prevailing thought of many, life is summed up as "the one with the most toys wins."

"But let all who take refuge in you rejoice; let them sing joyful praises forever. Protect them, so all who love Your name may be filled with joy." Psalm 5:7 NLT

This begs the question: "win what"? What toy or idol will not be left behind? What pleasure is there in possessions that possess us? When the driving force of our life is to get more "toys," and we define our success in terms of how many "toys" we accumulate, we are going to experience the poverty of the soul.

How much better to make seeking Jesus' joy the driving force of our lives! How much better to know that "the one with the most joys wins"!

We have been created by God for His pleasure and to bring joy to His heart by being imitators of Jesus, whose number-one priority was to bring God joy by His "obedience even unto death."

Praise the Lord! God is not calling us to die to anything but sin. Rather, He is calling us to live in the fullness of Jesus' joy as we become more and more like Him by abiding in the Word and seeking to live fruitful lives fully pleasing to Him.

There are no joys to compare with the joys that are ours through faith in Jesus Christ. We have the joy of our salvation, the joy of friendship with Jesus, son ship with God, the joy of the presence of the Holy Spirit living within us, and the peace and joy of the Lord that surpasses all understanding.

The only real winners are those who experience the joys of winning the crown of everlasting life through a personal relationship with Jesus.

"And now I am coming to you. I have told them many things while I was with them so they would be filled with My joy." John 17:13

Father, thank you for making me a winner through Jesus. Amen.

Lord, You Are _____

Forgive Me For _____

Thank You For _____

Needs of Others _____

Personal Needs _____

Answered Prayers _____

January 14 — Read Romans 10:6-13, Deuteronomy 30:12-20

The Big Move

"I've banked Your promises in the vault of my heart so I won't sin myself bankrupt." Psalm 119:11 MSG

We have become a transient society. No longer does a vast majority grow up and live their entire lives within 30 miles of where they were born.

"The message is very close at hand; it is on your lips and in your heart so that you can obey it." Deuteronomy 30:12

Moving is usually a tedious and stressful chore which no one relishes. It is generally a time for discarding excess items that we no longer use or can no longer accommodate.

There is a spiritual move that is sometimes the hardest and most stressful move of all, and it is also the biggest move that anyone can ever make. Although the distance is short, sometimes the price is higher than many are willing to pay.

Holy transformation can only take place when God moves from our head to our heart, and Jesus moves from being not only our Savior, but also the Lord of our life by the power of the Holy Spirit.

The gift of eternal life through faith in Jesus is not just the end of sin's dominion and its power to kill us. It is the beginning of a new and vibrant life in Christ when we allow the Holy Spirit to move into our hearts and take control of our lives.

When Jesus moves from our heads to our hearts the excess baggage of guilt and shame is left behind. We become disciples and followers in spirit and in truth.

We are filled with the love of Jesus which makes us want to do the things that please and honor Him.

Although the move is only about 18 inches, the distance is too far for many who try to travel it in their own strength.

"For it is by believing in your heart that you are made right with God, and it is by confessing with your mouth that you are saved." Romans 10:10 NLT

We must become crucified with Christ and rise in newness of life with Him living in and through us. Only then can we begin the life-long sanctifying process of becoming the righteous children of God as we become imitators of Christ by the resurrection power of the Holy Spirit.

Father, thank you for helping me make the "big move." Amen.

Lord, You Are _____

Forgive Me For _____

Thank You For _____

Needs of Others _____

Personal Needs _____

Answered Prayers _____

Read Romans 3:10-27, Isaiah 45:18-25   January 15
How Good Do We Have to Be?
"We are all infected and impure with sin. When we proudly display our righteous deeds, we find they are but filthy rags. Like autumn leaves, we wither and fall. And our sins, like the wind, sweep us away." Isaiah 64:6 NLT

There is something within us that makes us love to compare ourselves with others who are worse sinners than us. *"At least I*

"Look to Me, and be saved, all you ends of the earth! For I am God, and there is no other."
Isaiah 45:22

don't _____ like _____" is one of the great tools of deceit used by the Devil. This makes us feel good, diminishes our guilt, and allows us to live life on our standards instead of God's standards.

Preaching about sin is not fashionable these days among many churches and amidst many professing believers. It's almost as if we ignore it, it won't harm us.

We need to know that God takes sin very seriously. There is nothing casual about it in His sight. He tells it like it is and calls abominations abominations, and the people can't handle it just like the Scribes and Pharisees couldn't handle it when Jesus told it like it was.

For the "salad-bar believers," who pick and choose what sins they will and will not believe are sins, the truth that God's commandments are not suggestions but commandments fall on ears that have become dull of hearing.

The tragedy of failing to take sin seriously is that we go through life with a false hope of heaven thinking that we are going to get there because of our goodness.

The truth is that Jesus Christ is the only human who ever lived that met God's holy standard of perfect righteousness. The good news is that He was good enough to take the wrath of God for our sins with Him to the cross and set us free from having to be good enough to get to heaven.

Only when our hope is built on nothing less than Jesus blood and righteousness, and we trust in Christ's goodness instead of our own can we ever hope to enjoy life forever in heaven.

"For all have sinned and fall short of the glory of God,"
Romans 3:23

Father, I thank Jesus for being good enough so that I don't have to be. Amen.

Lord, You Are _____
Forgive Me For _____
Thank You For _____
Needs of Others _____
Personal Needs _____
Answered Prayers _____

The Long and the Short of It

"As far as the east is from the west, so far has He removed our transgressions from us." Psalm 103:12

If we are to grow into the fullness of Christ, we need to acquire the grace of the long and the short-term memory.

"May He remember all your gifts and look favorably on your burnt offerings." Psalm 20:3 NLT

How great it is to know that God remembers our good deeds forever, yet He remembers our sins no more when we confess and repent.

When we know that we will stand before the throne of God boldly trusting that the blood of Jesus has made us righteous in God's sight, we marvel again at how amazing "amazing grace" really is.

Scripture after scripture confirms that God does not only remember but rewards our good works done out of our love for Him in response to His love for us.

The truth of the matter is that God never asks any of us to do anything that Jesus didn't do in living the life of perfect performance that fulfilled God's requirement for righteousness under the law.

If Jesus could forgive and forget those who crucified Him and beg God to forgive them, how can we dare not do the same and expect to be forgiven and have our sins forgotten?

We don't need to spend our energy carrying grudges and desiring vengeance even for those who are not repentant, because we can turn them over to God, secure in the knowledge that He can and will deal with them much better than we could.

As we seek to see and remember the good in others instead of finding fault, we are doing to others exactly as Jesus does to us.

"Then He adds, 'Their sins and their lawless deeds I will remember no more.'" Hebrews 10:17

Remembering the good and forgetting the bad is the long and the short term of being imitators of Christ.

Father, give me the grace and strength to "forgive and forget." Amen.

Lord, You Are _____

Forgive Me For _____

Thank You For _____

Needs of Others _____

Personal Needs _____

Answered Prayers _____

Are We Worth Imitating?

"Beloved, do not imitate what is evil, but what is good. He who does good is of God, but he who does evil has not seen God." 3 John 1:11

It should be a sobering thought that someone might be imitating us.

"Do not envy violent people; don't copy their ways,"
Proverbs 3:31 NLT

As parents, we can be sure that our attitudes and conduct will be imitated by our children in some way. We are all preaching "sermons in shoes" to our family and those with whom we come in contact in everyday life.

Hero worship and role models are a zillion dollar industry in sports and entertainment circles. It is sickening to see some of the role models young and old alike have chosen to glorify and try to emulate.

As believers, we are held to a high standard of being role models worth imitating. Others should know that we are Christians by our love, our speech, and our conduct.

The light of the gospel should be shining brightly in us and through us. The question of whether others can see Jesus in us should give us all cause to honestly ponder the answer to this question: "Are we worth imitating?"

Even more importantly, we need to judge ourselves and see what we need to do to become worth imitating. We need to earnestly seek the power of the Holy Spirit to change the things in our conduct and attitudes that need to be changed so that we do not bring shame to the name of Christ in our everyday life.

Scripture commands us to be imitators of Christ. He is the Way, the Truth, and the Life and came to earth as the Word incarnate to teach us how we should follow Him and imitate His life.

Our aim should always be to be building blocks and never stumbling blocks for the cause of Christ for our children, family, friends, fellow believers, and especially those who don't know the love of God because they have never seen it modeled.

"Therefore be imitators of God as dear children."
Ephesians 5:1

Father, by the power of Your Spirit, help me to be worth imitating. Amen.

Lord, You Are _____

Forgive Me For _____

Thank You For _____

Needs of Others _____

Personal Needs _____

Answered Prayers _____

What Will We Leave Behind?

"You didn't choose me. I chose you. I appointed you to go and produce fruit that will last, so that the Father will give you whatever you ask for, using my name." John 15:16. NLT

Sooner or later we are going to leave this world and move onward and upward if we have faith in Jesus. The bright future we have in Christ and His promises should cause us all to rejoice.

"They can't take it with them; fame and fortune all get left behind." Psalm 49:17 MSG

We should all be striving to leave something behind. Instead of immediately thinking of possessions and to whom we will leave them, we need to think about leaving fruit that will last in a legacy of love.

Jesus left us His whole life bound between the covers of a book as a legacy of love. He spent His life loving and serving others and calling them into a personal relationship with God. He died that we may live forever with Him in heaven.

If we have been blessed with children, we are going to leave behind a genetic legacy of inherited physical and temperamental traits that will live on through succeeding generations.

Too often we leave children "stuff" to fight over instead of memories to cherish and rejoice over as they share their heritage with each other and their children.

Our family fortune that we should be thinking about leaving behind should not be the inheritance of material wealth but the riches of God's grace exemplified by a fruitful life well lived and shoes of faith worth filling.

We need to invest our time, talents, and treasures into being fruitful in good works that bless the lives of others by loving, serving, and encouraging them, just as Jesus has loved, served, and encouraged us.

"There are three things that will endure—faith, hope, and love—and the greatest of these is love." 1 Corinthians 13:13 NLT

We should seek to leave behind added value to every person God has placed in our lives by being conduits of His love, grace, and kindness.

Father, help me to leave behind a legacy of love that will endure in others long after I'm gone. Amen.

Lord, You Are _____
Forgive Me For _____
Thank You For _____
Needs of Others _____
Personal Needs _____
Answered Prayers _____

The "Esau Syndrome"

"For what profit is it to a man if he gains the whole world and loses his own soul? Or what will a man give in exchange for his soul?" Matthew 16:26

Before we think too harshly and belittle Esau too strongly for selling his

> **"Then Jacob gave Esau some bread and lentil stew. Esau ate and drank and went on about his business, indifferent to the fact that he had given up his birthright."**
> **Genesis 25:34 NLT**

birthright for a bowl of soup, we need to think of how often we have devalued our birthright as sons and daughters of God and heirs to His covenants through faith in Jesus Christ.

Esau's sin was indifference. He could not care less about being the heir of the promises of God.

Many have come into the family of God through God's covenant of grace extended to generations of believers in a family only to disavow their birthright.

What joy there is in receiving this legacy of faith and passing it on to our children and our children's children.

How sad it is to see children of the promise disregard the clear teaching of Scripture and devalue their birthright by getting yoked to an unbelieving spouse, just like Esau. How sad it is to be indifferent to the promises and commands of God and to devalue our blessings as brothers and sisters of Christ for pleasures, possessions, and approval of others.

Indifference, like all sins, is serious and has severe consequences. It is akin to lukewarm, and God says that He will spit the lukewarm out on the Day of Judgment.

> **"Watch out for the Esau syndrome: trading away God's lifelong gift in order to satisfy a short-term appetite. You well know how Esau later regretted that impulsive act and wanted God's blessing—but by then it was too late, tears or no tears."**
> **Hebrews 12:16 MSG**

From God's perspective, God, parents, and others is the "blue chip" priority of values we should all be maintaining if we are serious about doing life God's Way.

Are there any unholy values that are compromising your life and witness?

Father, may I never be indifferent to Your promises or Your commands. Amen.

Lord, You Are _____

Forgive Me For _____

Thank You For _____

Needs of Others _____

Personal Needs _____

Answered Prayers _____

What Time Is It?

"For God says, 'At just the right time, I heard you. On the day of salvation, I helped you.' Indeed, God is ready to help you right now. Today is the day of salvation." 2 Corinthians 6:2 NLT

We all ask or think this question often in the course of a day or night, and the answer depends on where we are physically as relating to Eastern, Standard, Daylight, or universal Greenwich Mean Time.

"God has made everything beautiful for its own time. He has planted eternity in the human heart, but even so, people cannot see the whole scope of God's work from beginning to end."
Ecclesiastes 3:11

Time is also used in terms of seasons, stages of life, and history. The railroads used to pride themselves upon running on time. Airlines used to stress on-time arrival until they got so bad that they quit bringing it up.

We all need to understand and strive to live on Heavenly Standard Time. God has put us here for purposes for which He created us. He will hold us all accountable for our faithfulness and our fruitfulness in using the time He gives us.

We have a timeless God who has prepared a timeless eternity for us in heaven and a timely process through which we will grow into the image of Christ during our presence on this earth.

When we run on Heavenly Standard Time, we run life powered by the Holy Spirit who has been given as a guarantee that we will win the race and receive not only the gift of eternal life but the prizes that await all who have managed the Lord's business well.

"But you must not forget, dear friends, that a day is like a thousand years to the Lord, and a thousand years is like a day."
2 Peter 3:8 NLT

When we live by God's standards, controlled by the Spirit, we will no longer be held captive to our flesh and the consequences of living in the sin and corruption of the world.

When Jesus' ways become our ways by faith as we grow and abide in Him, we are going to have the time of our life living on Heavenly Standard Time.

Father, keep me ever mindful that my time is in Your hands and help me to make the most of it by glorifying You in all that I do. Amen.

Lord, You Are _____

Forgive Me For _____

Thank You For _____

Needs of Others _____

Personal Needs _____

Answered Prayers _____

A Major Character Flaw

"But when the Holy Spirit controls our lives, He will produce this kind of fruit in us: love, joy, peace, patience, kindness, goodness, faithfulness," Galatians 5:22 NLT

What is probably the #1 cause of traffic accidents? What causes many problems in homes, work places, and relationships? I believe that you will agree that impatience is a major character flaw with which we all struggle at some time. When we get in too big a hurry about anything, we often find that the "haste made waste" principle kicks in to haunt us.

> **"A man's wisdom gives him patience; it is to his glory to overlook an offense." Proverbs 19:11 NIV**

Impatience is usually the driving force of a quick trigger that leads to a lot of unnecessary strife. It causes us to try to speed up any recovery process and as a result sets back our healing.

Impatience is often the root cause of people falling into bondage to debt. It causes moral purity to be sacrificed and many to give up too soon on jobs, marriages, and relationships.

It is good to step back and put time into perspective. Let's take a measuring tape and circumscribe all 26,000 miles of the earth. When we put a stamp on the tape and let that represent our entire life on this earth, we will get some grasp of eternity where we will be living forever.

> **"So make every effort to apply the benefits of these promises to your life. Then your faith will produce a life of moral excellence. A life of moral excellence leads to knowing God better." 1 Peter 1:5 NLT**

The only things we should be impatient about are seeking the kingdom of God and His righteousness. When we do this, we will discover the patience that is part of the moral excellence of every believer.

In His mercy, God grants us His all-sufficient grace to persevere and endure as the Holy Spirit produces patience in us, along with the other fruit of the Spirit, as we are conformed into the image of Christ.

Father, may I grow in patience without which I can never hope to grow into the fullness of Your Son. Amen.

Lord, You Are _____

Forgive Me For _____

Thank You For _____

Needs of Others _____

Personal Needs _____

Answered Prayers _____

The Joy of the Lord

"Do not grieve, for the joy of the LORD is your strength." Nehemiah 8:10b NIV

When it comes to finding strength, we need to revel in the joy of our salvation. When we rejoice in what God has done for us through Christ, we can find strength to stand firm in times of trouble through the joy that is set before us by faith in Jesus.

"O LORD, the king rejoices in Your strength. How great is his joy in the victories You give." Psalm 21:1 NIV

There is great joy and strength in God's presence. When Jesus becomes the friend that sticks closer than a brother, we harness the resurrection power of the Holy Spirit that makes Christ living in us a reality in our lives.

When we live in the joy of the Lord, we are strengthened to become contagious conduits of God's love to others. We will discover the joy of trading God's strength for our weakness. We find ourselves being able to do those things through Christ— who strengthens us— that we could never do on our own.

Without the energizing strength of God that we find expressed through our joy and "our peace that surpasses all understanding," we are prone to give in to temptation and often become worry-prone and depression-plagued people.

The truth is that we are never going to be able to enjoy life to the fullest in our own strength.

We can have it all and yet have nothing if we do not have the love of God that can only be experienced through a faith relationship with Jesus Christ. Idols, pride, and toys are all going to pass away.

"About midnight Paul and Silas were praying and singing hymns to God, and the other prisoners were listening to them." Acts 16:25 NIV

The Good News was given that we might be filled with the joy of the Lord and strengthened by the wonder-working power of His love.

Father, may my joy always be full in You. Amen.

Lord, You Are _____

Forgive Me For _____

Thank You For _____

Needs of Others _____

Personal Needs _____

Answered Prayers _____

Do You Know a "Fanatic"?

"Because you have not served the LORD your God with joy and enthusiasm for the abundant benefits you have received," Deuteronomy 28:47

Someone once defined a fanatic as someone who loves Jesus more than you love Jesus.

"My zeal has consumed me, because my enemies have forgotten Your words." Psalm 139:139

When we think of religious fanatics, we too often think of misguided zealots who kill people and commit all sorts of sin in the name of religion or of confrontational Christians who come on too strong and too self righteous.

From a scriptural perspective, we all should be fanatics in terms of having "unbridled enthusiasm and intense uncritical devotion" if we have experienced the new birth in Christ.

We should be the contagious Christians who let the light of God's love shine in and through us, drawing others into a faith relationship with Jesus like flies to honey.

"For I bear them witness that they have a zeal for God, but not according to knowledge." Romans 10:2

We can become too religious by exalting ourselves in hypocritical glory and having disdain instead of love for sinners. We can make religion our God by dancing through the hoops of legalism and never have God in our religion because we miss out on the fact that Jesus is the perfect fulfillment of the law.

The difference between a legalistic and a grace-oriented faith is all about motivation. When we think we <u>have</u> to perform to somehow add to our salvation, we are missing the joy which comes from a grace-oriented faith that makes us <u>want</u> to do the things that glorify and please God because of the great thing He has done for us in Christ.

When we want to glorify God by living fruitful lives, fully pleasing to Him, it should be an honor to be called a fanatic.

Father, help me to be the kind of fanatic that You will not be ashamed to call one of Your very own. Amen.

Lord, You Are _____

Forgive Me For _____

Thank You For _____

Needs of Others _____

Personal Needs _____

Answered Prayers _____

Guarding Our Hearts

"Be on guard. Stand true to what you believe. Be courageous. Be strong. And everything you do must be done with love." 1 Corinthians 16:13 NLT

To know that God judges our hearts is a comfort and a concern.

"Wait on the LORD; be of good courage, and He shall strengthen your heart; wait, I say, on the LORD!" Psalm 27:14

When our conscience dictates going against the flow of popular opinion, peer pressure, and the ways of the world, it is comforting to know that God does not judge by outward appearances or by the world's standards but that He judges our hearts.

Knowing that God knows every thought, word, and deed that comes out of our hearts should also give us great concern and determination to guard our hearts.

Maintaining a pure heart means that we allow no impure or unkind thought to take root and that we seek and pursue holiness and moral excellence in every area of our life.

We must be on guard against the forces of evil and our old sin nature, which seek to create doubt, disbelief, anger, rebellion, lust, pride, or envy.

Hardness of heart is one of the worst results of failing to guard our hearts. It dulls our conscience, shuts off the flow of God's grace, and makes it impossible for us to grow into the fullness of Christ.

God has given us the tools for cleansing and maintaining a pure heart. When we confess and repent, instantly we get rid of the sin that should not be lingering there, and we allow the Holy Spirit to create a clean heart and renew a right spirit within us.

What comfort there is in knowing that we can also claim the peace of the Lord by rejoicing in and through all our circumstances!

When we come to the Lord with praise on our lips and thanks in our hearts, we are promised the power of the Holy Spirit to guard our hearts and minds as we grow into the fullness of Christ.

"And the peace of God, which surpasses all understanding, will guard your hearts and minds through Christ Jesus." Philippians 4:7 NLT

Father, keep me with a heart and mind stayed on You and Your glory. Amen.

Lord, You Are _____

Forgive Me For _____

Thank You For _____

Needs of Others _____

Personal Needs _____

Answered Prayers _____

What Price Glory?

"God purchased you at a high price. Don't be enslaved by the world."
1 Corinthians 7:23 NLT

It has been said that every one has their price. Scripture abounds with examples of those who sold out cheap and paid dearly.

"For you made us only a little lower than God, and you crowned us with glory and honor." Psalm 8:5 NLT

Esau sold his birthright and the glory of being God's chosen vessel for a pot of soup. Judas sold out Jesus for 30 pieces of silver.

Before we get filled with hypocritical glory and self righteous indignation at these examples, we might well examine our own records and see how many times we have sold out to sin.

Some have sold out sexual purity for the pleasure of the moment or addiction to pornography.

Some have sold out moral excellence by cutting corners on the truth and losing personal integrity in pursuit of material, political, and relational agendas.

Some have robbed God by withholding the first fruits of what is rightfully His and never experience the glory of the Lord as He reveals it to those who let His generosity flow through them.

The sad truth is that "all have sinned and fall short of the glory of God" (Romans 3:23). When we put any person or any thing above God, we are robbing God of the glory due Him, and we are wasting it upon the quicksand of idolatry.

God put a price on the glory that is ours as the redeemed children of God. It took the death of God's only Son on the cross at Calvary. Jesus paid the price for our glory with His blood. We dare not sell out or give this glory to a lesser God.

"For what profit is it to a man if he gains the whole world, and loses his own soul? Or what will a man give in exchange for his soul?" Matthew 16:23

Father, remind me daily that although I can never be worthy of the price of Your glory, I can always be thankful and live out my thanks by responding to Your love with my love expressed in obeying and glorifying You in every area of my life. Amen.

Lord, You Are _____
Forgive Me For _____
Thank You For _____
Needs of Others _____
Personal Needs _____
Answered Prayers _____

Living it Up

"This Book of the Law shall not depart from your mouth, but you shall meditate in it day and night, that you may observe to do according to all that is written in it. For then you will make your way prosperous, and then you will have good success." Joshua 1:8

"Living it up" is all about perspective. For some, it's all about fun and games and eating, drinking, and making merry before we die. For others it's living an upscale life of prosperity in accumulating possessions and status as upwardly mobile citizens.

"Cause me to hear Your loving kindness in the morning, for in You do I trust; cause me to know the way in which I should walk, for I lift up my soul to You."
Psalm 143:8

When we make our goal to live life growing up into the fullness of Christ, God promises prosperity and good success.

When we seek to "live it up" to God's standards, we receive the transforming power of the Holy Spirit to live with God's strength in a life that we can never live in our own strength.

We are living up to our high calling in Christ when we bear the fruit of the Spirit in our relationship with others and when we live to serve rather than be served.

When we "live it up" by allowing ourselves to be conformed into the image of Christ, we are going to experience the joy of having Jesus come down to live in us and manifest His glory through us as we live lives fully pleasing to Him and fruitful in every good work.

"You also, as living stones, are being built up a spiritual house, a holy priesthood, to offer up spiritual sacrifices acceptable to God through Jesus Christ."
1 Peter 2:5

When we "live it up" in Christ, we are going to enjoy the prosperity of richness in our relationship with God and with others as we receive the peace and security that only a right relationship with God through faith in Jesus can give.

When we "live it up" in the security of this "born again" relationship, we are free to be all that God has created us to be in Christ, which is to be light bearers in the world in which we live.

Sin has no power over those who are "living it up" in the fullness of Christ.

Father, help me to "live it up" as one who is upward bound. Amen.

Lord, You Are _____
Forgive Me For _____
Thank You For _____
Needs of Others _____
Personal Needs _____
Answered Prayers _____

God's Reprimands

"All Scripture is given by inspiration of God, and is profitable for doctrine, for reproof, for correction, for instruction in righteousness," 2 Timothy 3:16

"Let the godly strike me! It will be a kindness! If they reprove me, it is soothing medicine. Don't let me refuse it."

Psalm 141:5 NLT

Sin is serious to God. He does not sugar coat or ignore it. Both the Old and New Testaments are filled with God's reproofs or reprimands for sin.

We would do well to learn from God's reprimands regarding idolatry, hypocrisy, rebellion, pride, physical and spiritual adultery, unfaithfulness, greed, and all other sins.

It is not only important to learn the conduct and attitudes that God rebukes but also to confess, repent, and correct our failures and shortcomings in these areas of our lives.

As much as God hates sin, He loves us even more. He takes no pleasure in meting out punishment, but, in His love, He will do whatever it takes to correct us and to perfect us into the image of Christ.

Jesus died to earn perfection in God's sight for us by covering us with His righteousness. He sent the Holy Spirit to produce the fruits of righteousness within us that we might receive conviction of our sins, receive the power to overcome, and live free from bondage to them.

The key to receiving this supernatural strength and power is to abide in Christ through abiding in His Word.

God's grace is poured down from on high through the living water of a living faith fed and nourished by Jesus, the Word made flesh, who is our Bread of Life.

"Then Jesus spoke to them again, saying, 'I am the light of the world. He who follows Me shall not walk in darkness, but have the light of life.'"

John 8:12

When we learn from Scripture what God rebukes and commends and live accordingly, we will be on our way to enjoying the profits of living an abundant life here while we move towards the inexpressible joy and total abundance of heaven.

Father, help me to take sin as seriously as You do and to use your reproofs as springboards to repentance and holiness. Amen.

Lord, You Are _____

Forgive Me For _____

Thank You For _____

Needs of Others _____

Personal Needs _____

Answered Prayers _____

Looking Too Far Forward

"But exhort one another daily, while it is called "Today," *lest any of you be hardened through the deceitfulness of sin." Hebrews 3:13*

There's a lot to be said for delayed gratification and waiting upon the Lord and His time table. It never pays to get in too big a hurry except maybe to die to sin and get rid of all the garbage in our lives through confession and repentance.

"So teach us to number our days, that we may gain a heart of wisdom." Psalm 90:12

We should never forget that each day is a present from God, and we should live each one in the fullness of Christ and His joy. It is good to begin each day with praise on our lips and love in our hearts.

When we look too far forward, we tend to forget to take the time to "smell the roses" and enjoy the blessings of this day. Do we really appreciate our good health and the daily blessings we enjoy, or do we tend to take them for granted and only appreciate them when we lose them?

Instead of "sufficient to the day is the evil thereof," we should be thinking of the abundance of God's goodness and grace that He pours out each day to those who love Him and call upon His name. We should not get so engrossed in big dreams and plans for the future that we fail to grow in godly wisdom day by day.

We all have a big future and a hope in an eternity of sinless perfection with Christ in heaven. We can only imagine how wonderful this will be.

"But remember that the temptations that come into your life are no different from what others experience." 1 Corinthians 10:13 NLT

In the meantime, we have the "first day of the rest of our lives" to do the Lord's business until He comes, for which He purposed for us before we were ever born.

Who needs the blessing of our love and encouragement? What can we do "as unto the Lord" this day? How can we become more like Jesus this day? What blessings should we be especially thankful for this day?

We are living in the present. We should be growing more like Christ day by day and living for Him and letting Him live through us each day that He privileges us to be about His business on this earth.

Lord, may I ask, seek, and find You and Your love one day at a time. Amen.

Lord, You Are _____

Forgive Me For _____

Thank You For _____

Needs of Others _____

Personal Needs _____

Answered Prayers _____

Mowing Therapy

"So don't get ahead of the Master and jump to conclusions with your judgments before all the evidence is in. When He comes, He will bring out in the open and place in evidence all kinds of things we never even dreamed of—inner motives and purposes and prayers. Only then will any one of us get to hear the 'Well done!' of God." 1 Corinthians 4:5 MSG

Anyone who has not had the pleasure of mowing a lawn or pasture does not know what they've missed! To be able to look back upon an effort where you can see the results is a real blessing, especially when sometimes our best efforts seem to gain no measurable results.

"The LORD rewarded me for doing right; he compensated me because of my innocence." Psalm 18:20

We often just spin our wheels on trivial pursuits that go no where and are left with frustration and lack of fulfillment.

At these times, it is so good to know that God is alive, well, and in control. He is a *"rewarder of those who seek him."* He is working all things for our good when we love Him and are seeking to find and fulfill His purposes for our lives.

During times of scourging, which are often a part of God's character-development program in conforming us to Christ's image, we must allow God's strength to cover our weaknesses as we persevere through His mowing process.

The pleasure of looking back on a yard well mowed is nothing compared to the joy of looking back on a life well lived under the control of and by the transforming power of the Holy Spirit.

"But there is going to come a time of testing at the judgment day to see what kind of work each builder has done. Everyone's work will be put through the fire to see whether or not it keeps its value." 1 Corinthians 3:13 NLT

A day is coming when all of the wood, hay, and stubble of our trivial pursuits is going to be burned from our lawn of life.

When fruits of righteousness remain we are going to have the great joy of hearing our Savior say, *"Well done, thou good and faithful servant,"* as He looks back on lives richly lived in abiding and abounding in the Lord. May we all be found ever faithful to our calling to live lives *"fully pleasing to God and fruitful in every good work."*

Father, may I live to earn your approval for a life well done. Amen.

Lord, You Are _____

Forgive Me For _____

Thank You For _____

Needs of Others _____

Personal Needs _____

Answered Prayers _____

Selling Short

"For you have no place of refuge—the bed you have made is too short to lie on. The blankets are too narrow to cover you." Isaiah 28:20 NLT

A lot of people have made fortunes in the stock market "selling short." Selling short, simply put, is borrowing on a stock at the present price, betting it will go down in price, and betting that you will be able to replace it at the lower price. When you bet on a team to lose, you are "selling short."

"It is possible to give freely and become more wealthy, but those who are stingy will lose everything."
Proverbs 11:24

Any time we fail to believe that God is who He says He is and does what He says He can or will do, we are selling God short.

Esau was a real "short seller." The Scribes and Pharisees, who should have known better, sold Jesus short and missed the wedding feast.

Judas was perhaps the biggest "short seller" in the history of man. He sold Jesus for 30 pieces of silver, obviously failing to believe Jesus was the true Messiah.

Even as born again believers, we often "sell God short" by taking control in our own flesh rather than living under the control of God through the Holy Spirit.

"Look after each other so that none of you will miss out on the special favor of God. Watch out that no bitter root of unbelief rises up among you, for whenever it springs up, many are corrupted by its poison."
Hebrews 12:15 NLT

When we are stingy with God, we are really "selling short." We are essentially betting that we can out give God and that He does not do as He promises for those who are generous to Him.

We too often "sell God short" by giving in to fear and worry instead of giving out thanksgiving and praise and rejoicing in every circumstance as we are commanded to do.

Before "selling God short" we need to go back and reread the rest of the Book of Life. We must never bet on God to lose and become lost in the process.

Father, I know that I often fall short, but never let me sell You and Your wonderful gift of eternal life short. Amen.

Lord, You Are _____
Forgive Me For _____
Thank You For _____
Needs of Others _____
Personal Needs _____
Answered Prayers _____

Doing Without

"Those in frequent contact with the things of the world should make good use of them without becoming attached to them, for this world and all it contains will pass away." 1 Corinthians 7:31 NLT

There are many things that we can very well do without. We often fail to make the distinction between wants and needs, and needs and "greeds." The advertising industry is dedicated to creating wants and making us think that we just "gotta have" what they are trying to sell.

"I'm asking GOD for one thing, only one thing,"
Psalm 27:4 MSG

There is a big difference between holy and unholy discontent. When we are never satisfied and dwell on the pursuit of things to make us happy, doing without is a real downer.

Everyone of us have basic material needs for food, clothing, and shelter. We can only eat so much, wear so much, live in one house, and drive one car at a time.

The world seems to measure prosperity by how much more than basic needs we can accumulate and enjoy. "The one with the most toys wins" is the credo of the world.

It is quite a paradox that we think we cannot do without a cell phone, cable connection, new car, bigger home, or fancier clothes, but we have no problem at all doing without a daily feeding on the Bread of Life.

It is sad to see the pockets of physical poverty around the world, where people are dying for lack of the basic physical needs.

It is even sadder to see all of the people wandering aimlessly lost in a desert of doom because they refuse to drink the life-giving water of eternal life by receiving Jesus Christ as Savior and Lord.

"No, dear brothers and sisters, I am still not all I should be, but I am focusing all my energies on this one thing."
Philippians 3:13 NLT

When we find the holy contentment of peace and joy in Jesus, we will find that this is really the only thing that we cannot do without, and we will want to nourish it and have it grow within us as we feed on the Word by meditation, prayer, and waiting upon God.

Father, help me to find my contentment in You. Amen.

Lord, You Are _____

Forgive Me For _____

Thank You For _____

Needs of Others _____

Personal Needs _____

Answered Prayers _____

Round Up Time

"He is ready to separate the chaff from the grain with his winnowing fork. Then he will clean up the threshing area, storing the grain in his barn but burning the chaff with never-ending fire." Matthew 3:12 NLT

When we think of round up, we usually conjure up visions of the old west and cowboys rounding up cattle, but we are talking about another kind of round up.

"Then let thistles grow instead of wheat, and weeds instead of barley." Job 31:40

Chemical round up has proven a safe and effective product for killing weeds wherever they spring up from the ground. It is widely used in yards, on farms, roads, and wherever weed control is needed.

The weeds of sin threaten to choke us to death before we receive eternal life through faith in Jesus Christ. They come back time and time again trying to crowd God out of our lives and smother the peace and joy of our faith.

The war for the souls of men, women, and children has been won for us by Jesus' death on the cross. Unfortunately, this good news is often choked out by the enticements and temptations of sin all around us.

Even believers who have come to know and put their trust in God to save them by the blood of Jesus find sin trying to take root and destroy their witness and effectiveness as believers.

The competition is fierce as the forces of evil have taken control of TV, movies, internet, government, and schools to try to choke God out of the hearts and minds of believers and their children.

"And the seed that fell in the weeds—well, these are the ones who hear, but then the seed is crowded out and nothing comes of it as they go about their lives worrying about tomorrow, making money and having fun." Mark 4:18 MSG

The Word of God is sharper than any weed cutter. It's the most powerful sin controller ever known. When used daily, no weeds of sin can take root or grow within us.

We can be sure of being part of the great roundup in heaven when we let abiding in God's Word daily control the weeds of sin in our life.

Father, help me to use Your word to control sin that I might bear a great harvest of your righteousness. Amen.

Lord, You Are _____

Forgive Me For _____

Thank You For _____

Needs of Others _____

Personal Needs _____

Answered Prayers _____

Where's Your Treasure?

"For where your treasure is, there your heart will be also." Matthew 6:21

God not only deserves but demands that He be first in our lives. One of the best barometers for evaluating our hearts is where and how we spend God's time, talents, and treasures that He entrusts to us.

> "Above all else, guard your heart, for it affects everything you do," Proverbs 4:23 NLT

It is a sad commentary that a vast majority of us carry mixed up priorities and come up short in putting God first in every area of our lives.

When we do a time study of how we are spending our lives, we will all too often find that time spent with God in church, devotions, and prayer don't even come close to the time spent on TV, internet, movies, hobbies, or other recreational pursuits.

Everyone of us has been talented with certain gifts that should play a role in building up Christ's body through building up our body of believers. Some have the gift of encouragement, leadership, giving, mercy, teaching, prophecy or service. Others have musical talents or the gift of evangelizing, preaching, or intercessory prayer. The bottom line is that we are to use the talents God has given us for His glory and for the building up of His kingdom.

It is all too often true that the last thing to get saved is our pocketbooks. When we plug our weekly, monthly, or annual giving into our overall spending, many of us will find that we have put God near the bottom instead of at the top. If Detroit, the internet and TV cable provider, or cell phone company, etc., are getting more of our money than God, we most likely have a serious heart condition.

> "For God is not unfair. He will not forget how hard you have worked for Him and how you have shown your love to Him by caring for others." Hebrews 6:10 NLT

If we are treasuring the wood, hay, and stubble of this life above the greater everlasting joy of being found faithful servants on the day we must give account of the stewardship of our lives to Christ, we are going to miss out on a lot of the joy that Christ has gone on ahead to prepare for us in heaven.

Father, help me to guard my heart that I keep you first in every area of my life on this earth. Amen.

Lord, You Are _____
Forgive Me For _____
Thank You For _____
Needs of Others _____
Personal Needs _____
Answered Prayers _____

Why Choose to Lose?
"That is why they must eat the bitter fruit of living their own way. They must experience the full terror of the path they have chosen."
Proverbs 1:31 NLT

The dark side of freedom is the freedom to choose to lose. God gave us all a free will to live out our lives in the darkness of the sin with which we were born or to live in the wonderful light of our salvation by choosing to receive Jesus Christ by the call of the Holy Spirit.

"There is a way that seems right to a man, but its end is the way of death."
Proverbs 14:12

God will not force Himself or His way on anyone. We, like Adam and Eve, are free to choose to disobey God and live in bondage to sin, death, and decay, or we can choose to be set free from bondage to sin and death by receiving the new birth of freedom by receiving Jesus Christ as our Savior.

When we insist on exercising our free will as a license to sin and live our lives controlled by our flesh, we are choosing to lose our birth right as sons and daughters of God and all of the rights and privileges this affords.

We can choose to validate our lives in the quicksand of living for self-gratification and the approval of others. Or, we can validate our lives by choosing to live lives fully pleasing to God and filled with His blessings now and forever.

Solomon, the wisest man who ever lived, tried finding happiness and fulfillment in every worldly manner imaginable to no avail. The prodigal son chose to end up eating with the pigs before choosing to return to the outstretched arms of his father he should never have left.

"But now God has shown us a different way of being right in His sight—not by obeying the law but by the way promised in the Scriptures long ago."
Romans 3:21 NLT

The cry of Lazarus to be allowed to go back and warn his brothers of the torments of hell went unheeded, just as he had unheeded God's calls to repentance and faith through His prophets.

God's promises to those who love and obey Him are too good to lose through choosing willful disobedience and eternal separation from God.

Father, thank you for leading me to choose to receive You and make room for You in my heart by the power of the Holy Spirit. Amen.

Lord, You Are _____

Forgive Me For _____

Thank You For _____

Needs of Others _____

Personal Needs _____

Answered Prayers _____

Surround Sound

"For you are my hiding place; you protect me from trouble. You surround me with songs of victory." Psalm 32:7

Surround sound systems have become a multi-million-dollar business in our homes and cars as we seek to add another dimension to our listening or viewing enjoyment.

"Dreadful sounds are in his ears; in prosperity the destroyer comes upon him." Job 15:21

The quality of the sounds being transmitted often leaves a lot to be desired with regards to what sounds we should be surrounding ourselves with.

The vast wasteland of TV and the banal, blasphemous, and vile lyrics of many top songs have turned our hearts and minds into a garbage dump as we get filled with garbage that will sooner or later come out in some other than edifying fashion.

If we choose to continually surround ourselves with the sound of unholy songs, ungodly shows, or foul-mouthed people, we are going to become spiritually deaf to that still, small voice calling us to draw closer into a relationship with Jesus Christ.

If we are ever to grow into the fullness of Christ, we must surround ourselves with the sounds that stimulate our worship and praise of God. We listen to the pure spiritual milk of the Word and let it become the solid Bread of Life that sustains and nourishes our souls.

With all of the great Bible teachers and great hymns of praise on radio, TV, and the internet, we have no excuse for not surrounding ourselves in the wonderful power and glory of the sounds of God's love, grace, and mercy.

"And suddenly there came a sound from heaven, as of a rushing mighty wind, and it filled the whole house where they were sitting." Acts 2:2

Personally, the greatest surround sound I have ever heard was hearing praises to God being sung by 50,000 brothers in Christ surrounding me at a Promise Keepers stadium event.

Father may I never surround myself with the sound of garbage of any kind. Amen.

Lord, You Are _____

Forgive Me For _____

Thank You For _____

Needs of Others _____

Personal Needs _____

Answered Prayers _____

February 5   Read Matthew 6:19-24, Deuteronomy 30

The Key to Abounding

"Yes, a person is a fool to store up earthly wealth but not have a rich relationship with God." Luke 12:21NLT

Down through the ages, many of God's children have had difficulty handling prosperity. The children of Israel were blessed in every way, but they would time and time again desert God and go chasing after idols.

"The LORD your God will delight in you if you obey His voice and keep the commands and laws written in this Book of the Law, and if you turn to the LORD your God with all your heart and soul." Deuteronomy 30:10

There are well-documented stories about the misery and brokenness that followed lottery winners who could not handle abundance of wealth.

Many will never have the opportunity to abound in a lot of wealth because they have not been able to handle what little they have been given.

There is absolutely nothing wrong with having a lot of money. The key to abounding is not to let a lot of money have you. The rich fool never lived to enjoy his extra barns full of wealth.

The prodigal son found that all his fair-weather friends disappeared after his inheritance was all spent.

The key to abounding in material prosperity is to know Who it comes from and what He wants us to do with it. Scripture after scripture encourages us to let God's generosity flow through us, that God has given us an abundance so that we can be generous on every occasion, and even to test Him by trying to out give Him.

When we keep God first and let His generosity flow through us, we will never have to worry about the love of money becoming a root of evil even in our financial prosperity.

"Wherever your treasure is, there your heart and thoughts will also be." Matthew 6:21 NLT

Money is really a minor currency in God's economy. The prosperity of our souls that comes from abounding in good works that glorify God and finding godly peace and contentment in a close, personal, and shared relationship with Jesus Christ are the assets that will never leave us bankrupt.

Father, may I find joy in abounding beyond my pocket book. Amen.

Lord, You Are _____
Forgive Me For _____
Thank You For _____
Needs of Others _____
Personal Needs _____
Answered Prayers _____

Is It Worth It?

"And how do you benefit if you gain the whole world but lose your own soul in the process? Is anything worth more than your soul?" Matthew 16:26

It is not always easy to be a Christian. Although our victory over sin and death has been won on the cross, the battles continue to rage, and we don't always win.

"Great is the LORD! He is most worthy of praise! He is to be revered above all gods."
1 Chronicles 15:25 NLT

God's character-development program for us includes many tests. Although enduring persecution for most of us is nothing like it was for the martyrs of the faith over the centuries, it is still brutal in many parts of the world, and we are seeing more and more ridicule of Christians and Christian values in the media and in everyday life.

There are so many other fun things to do on Sunday mornings and throughout the week that compete for our time and attention for God, and time for God too often loses.

The world, the flesh, and the devil often attack our church and bring much strife and conflict within a body of believers. Even pastors stumble and fall, people lash out instead of love out, and the cause of Christ and the reason for our coming together gets lost amidst the turmoil.

People, pride, possessions, and circumstances will often disappoint us. God at work in us to perfect us into the image of Christ is not always easy. Our limited, self-centered perspective and understanding leads us to walk by sight and not by faith as we go through some of the deep waters through which we must sometimes sink or swim.

"There is a great irony here: proclaiming so much love, experiencing so much hate! But don't quit. Don't cave in. It is all well worth it in the end."
Matthew 10:21b MSG

"Is it worth it?" is not the best question. Asking "Was I worth it?" in terms of Christ dying to set us free from sin and death should give us all cause to believe that anything we may have to endure for the cause of Christ is more than worth it for the peace and joy that is ours in Him alone.

Father, I'm not worth it, but You are. Let nothing separate me from Your love that is mine in Christ. Amen.

Lord, You Are _____
Forgive Me For _____
Thank You For _____
Needs of Others _____
Personal Needs _____
Answered Prayers _____

The Waiting Game

"And remember, the Lord is waiting so that people have time to be saved. This is just as our beloved brother Paul wrote to you with the wisdom God gave him." 1 Peter 3:15 NLT

We all seem to be in too big a hurry in playing the game of life. "I can't wait until..." usually expresses hope, "I won't wait for..." usually expresses rebellion, and "I didn't wait for..." often expresses regret.

"But those who wait on the LORD will find new strength. They will fly high on wings like eagles. They will run and not grow weary. They will walk and not faint." Isaiah 40:31 NLT

We hold the present so close to our eyes that we too often fail to see the big picture. We too often trade instant gratification for high-priced future consequences like guilt, bondage to debt, and falling short of the glory of God and all of the blessings He wants to give us.

When we pursue the plan of man instead of trusting in the wisdom and promises of God, we are most often going to reap a bitter harvest of brokenness and disappointment.

It is paradoxical that those who can't wait for everything else often seem to think they can wait until they have "lived it up" in the world before inviting Jesus into their hearts and receiving the wonderful, instant, and eternal gratification that only the all-surpassing peace of God can provide.

We are so blessed to have a longsuffering God who has been waiting patiently for 20 centuries to give a chance for everyone in the world to hear the Good News and respond to His call to salvation.

We must never make the mistake of confusing God's patience with His coming judgment and think that we can play a waiting game with Him regarding our salvation.

"Live in such a way that God's love can bless you as you wait for the eternal life that our Lord Jesus Christ in His mercy is going to give you." Jude 1:21 NLT

The promises of God to those who come unto Him and seek His good and gracious will in true faith and obedience are much more gratifying and longer lasting than any temporary or fleeting pleasure. We should never try to have it our way contrary to His way.

Father, may I never get in too big a hurry except to flee to You. Amen.

Lord, You Are _____

Forgive Me For _____

Thank You For _____

Needs of Others _____

Personal Needs _____

Answered Prayers _____

Forget Not!

"In everything give thanks; for this is the will of God in Christ Jesus for you." 1 Thessalonians 5:18

The children of Israel were some of the biggest babies, whiners, and complainers in the history of mankind. In spite of the miraculous deliverance and physical manifestation of God for all to see, they continued to fall back into fear, whining, and idol worship at the slightest whim.

"Bless the LORD, O my soul, and forget not all His benefits."
Psalm 103:2

As bad as the children of Israel were, we are all probably as bad or worse from time to time. When our comfort zones get squeezed in any area, we tend to forget all of our benefits God has lavished upon us, and we dwell on what we perceive to be his failure to meet our present expectations.

The devil is continually trying to create doubt and despair in us. When he can get us to forget all that God has done and continues to do for us, he is setting us up for a fall into disappointment, disbelief, or depression.

Scripture clearly teaches that if we are to share in Christ's glory, we must be prepared to share in His suffering. Our bed of roses contains some thorns through which God inspects, corrects, and perfects us as he conforms us into the image of Christ.

It is through these times that we must never forget all of the blessings that God has poured upon us through Christ and has promised to pour out upon us forever.

Our God is a good God who delights in us and who is committed to working all things for our good and His glory. No matter what deep waters we go through because of our sins or the sin of the world, we can be sure that our rivers of eternal life will not overflow.

"My brethren, count it all joy when you fall into various trials, knowing that the testing of your faith produces patience."
James 1:2, 3

God gives us His all-sufficient grace to rejoice and be glad in our sufferings and disappointments. When we put our mind's attention and heart's affection on our Problem Solver instead of whining and complaining about our problems, we receive His grace and strength to "count it all joy."

Father, keep me ever mindful and thankful for all Your benefits. Amen.

Lord, You Are _____

Forgive Me For _____

Thank You For _____

Needs of Others _____

Personal Needs _____

Answered Prayers _____

'Tis More Blessed

"You're blessed when you follow His directions, doing your best to find Him." Psalm 119:2 MSG

There is a very important but often ignored and all too often forgotten principle at work in the Kingdom of God. We all need to understand that the best way to be blessed is to be a blessing!

"Blessed are you who give yourselves over to GOD, turn your backs on the world's 'sure thing,' ignore what the world worships."
Psalm 40:4 MSG

When we sincerely love and seek to help others, we will find that we are often helping ourselves even more.

Anyone who has ever taught a Bible class will find that they have learned more by preparing to teach than those being taught.

The millions of people who have found that they can't out give God financially provide a compelling testimony to this truth.

The challenge for all believers is to try the impossible task of out loving God. When we realize that we will never come across anyone that God does not love, we realize the impossibility of meeting this challenge in our own strength.

The same grace that allowed God to love us even when we were unlovable is ours to appropriate by faith, and it allows us to love the "unlovables" in our lives. We need to remember that God hates sin, but He loves us sinners so much that He sent His Son to die on the cross so that we would not have to die for our sins.

"Let your light so shine before men, that they may see your good works and glorify your Father in heaven."
Matthew 5:16

It all comes down to begetting. Kindness begets kindness, love begets love, and generosity begets generosity. This principle is true in most of our relationships with others and is always true in our relationship with God.

True joy comes when we appropriate the principle that the giver is most often blessed more than the receiver in the kingdom of God now and forever.

Father, keep me ever mindful of the blessing of being a blessing. Amen.

Lord, You Are _____

Forgive Me For _____

Thank You For _____

Needs of Others _____

Personal Needs _____

Answered Prayers _____

Added Value Options

"May you have more and more of God's special favor and wonderful peace." 1 Peter 1:2b NLT

Added value options have been one of the most successful marketing tools in the automotive industry for many years. They group a number of optional extras into one package and add them to your car for a special price usually much lower than the individual prices of the options.

"Your law is more valuable to me than millions in gold and silver!" Psalm 119:72 NLT

God gives us all any number of "added value" options that are designed to improve the quality of our lives in Christ forever.

When we receive Jesus Christ as Lord and Savior, we have the added value of having the Holy Spirit come to live within us and transform our bodies into temples where we receive the power from on high to live fruitful lives fully pleasing to God, which we can never live on our own.

Obedience is one of the biggest added value options in the life of any believer. Blessing upon blessing is promised and delivered when we obey God's commands, especially when they involve carrying out the Great Commandment and Great Commission.

Abiding in Jesus through abiding in the Word is perhaps the greatest added value option of all. Through this one simple practice, we are promised answered prayers, friendship with Jesus, awareness of the love of God and of others, joy, and the privilege of being used to glorify God.

There are too many references in Scripture to ignore the fact that we have added value options to the free gift of salvation consisting of rewards in heaven.

When we choose the added value options available, we not only add value and happiness to our own lives but to the lives of those around us.

"But also for this very reason, giving all diligence, add to your faith virtue, to virtue knowledge, to knowledge self-control, to self-control perseverance, to perseverance godliness, to godliness brotherly kindness, and to brotherly kindness love." 2 Peter 1:5-7 NLT

Father, let me enjoy added value in my life and the lives of those around me as I grow in faith, obedience, and love. Amen.

Lord, You Are _____

Forgive Me For _____

Thank You For _____

Needs of Others _____

Personal Needs _____

Answered Prayers _____

No Advisory Capacities Open

"'My thoughts are completely different from yours,' says the LORD. 'And My ways are far beyond anything you could imagine. For just as the heavens are higher than the earth, so are My ways higher than your ways and My thoughts higher than your thoughts.'" Isaiah 55:8

There are always plenty of jobs open in the Kingdom of God, because there is always much work to be done.

**"Who is able to advise the Spirit of the LORD? Who knows enough to be His teacher or counselor?"
Isaiah 40:13 NLT**

Unfortunately, too many of us, from time to time, seem to think that we are serving as advisors instead of servants as if God needed our advice.

We need to be very careful about presuming to serve God in an advisory capacity. As the all-powerful, all-knowing, majestic, everlasting, and ever-loving Creator and Sustainer of the universe, God does not need or want our advice. He wants our love, praise, and worship through obedience!

Instead of presuming to tell God what He should do, we should always be asking and seeking what we should do in accordance with His will for how we should live our lives in a manner fully pleasing to Him.

We too often try to put conditions on our relationship with God. It's not about us blessing and serving God if He blesses and answers our prayers. It's all about loving, serving, and obeying God because He first loved us enough to send His Son to die for us so that we may be redeemed and reconciled to Him and His unconditional love.

**"Let nothing be done through selfish ambition or conceit, but in lowliness of mind let each esteem others better than himself."
Philippians 2:3**

God's thoughts and ways are so much higher than ours; it is utter conceit to even think of telling Him what He should do or should have done. We need to listen, to learn, and to serve instead being served so that we will come to appreciate that God desires our obedience instead of our advice.

Father, let me abide in the assurance that You are all knowing and ever loving and that You do work all things for my good and Your glory. Amen.

Lord, You Are _____

Forgive Me For _____

Thank You For _____

Needs of Others _____

Personal Needs _____

Answered Prayers _____

The State of Our Union

"I don't want to hear any of you bragging about yourself or anyone else. Everything is already yours as a gift—Paul, Apollos, Peter, the world, life, death, the present, the future—all of it is yours, and you are privileged to be in union with Christ, who is in union with God." 1 Corinthians 3:21 MSG

The president of the United States has been giving annual State of the Union addresses either in person or in writing since 1790. They have mostly been a laundry list of things that have been done and need to be done in every area of government.

**"Behold, how good and how pleasant it is for brethren to dwell together in unity!"
Psalm 133:1**

We would all do well to often address the state of our union in every area of our lives and come up with our own laundry list of things be done.

What is the "state of our union" in holy matrimony? Is it holy? Is there that union of mind, body, and spirit that God had in mind when He instituted marriage? What do we need to do to improve this union?

How about the state of unity within our family? Are we bound together by love as well as by blood?

We are also called to be in union and communion with fellow believers for the mutual edification of all and the building up of the Kingdom of God. Are we assembling ourselves together as we should and celebrating our oneness in Christ with unity of the spirit and the bond of peace?

The most important union of all is our union with Christ through faith in His death on the cross for the forgiveness of our sins.

**"And you are complete through your union with Christ. He is the Lord over every ruler and authority in the universe."
Colossians 2:10 NLT**

We are like branches grafted into the vine where we are to grow and be fruitful in every good work for which we were created before we born.

When we become dead to sin and alive in Christ, our laundry list of things we should want to do for Him because of what He has done for us is one that we should use as guidelines for glory in being all that He has called us to be as the redeemed children of God.

Father, may I be ever mindful of the state of my union with You. Amen.

Lord, You Are _____
Forgive Me For _____
Thank You For _____
Needs of Others _____
Personal Needs _____
Answered Prayers _____

February 13   Read James 1:23-27, Psalm 90

Always a Vacancy!

"I know all the things you do—your love, your faith, your service, and your patient endurance. And I can see your constant improvement in all these things." Revelation 2:19 NLT

There is a room in every home, office, school, church, and work place that is always open. Sometimes the walls are thick and the doors are locked by stubbornness, laziness, self centeredness or pride, but there is always room for us all at the "room for improvement"!

"Teach us to make the most of our time, so that we may grow in wisdom." Psalm 90:12 NLT

All progress is dependent upon someone visiting the room for improvement to find new ideas for developing or improving products, procedures, programs, or practices.

Only within the mansions of our Father's houses in heaven will we find no room for improvement. When Jesus went there, He took perfection with Him and left us in a vacuum of sinful imperfection that will never be filled until He returns to take us home.

In the meantime, God's character-development program is all about our need to constantly dwell on our room for improvement in every area of our life.

We went from sinner to saint in God's eyes when we received Jesus as our Lord and Savior by faith spiritually.

Actually, we still have a lifetime to dwell in the room for improvement, living our lives "fully pleasing to God and fruitful in every good work," which is our reasonable and godly response to what He has done for us through Jesus' suffering and death for us on the cross.

"For if you just listen and don't obey, it is like looking at your face in a mirror but doing nothing to improve your appearance." James 1:23 NLT

When we daily ask God's help and abide in His Word, we receive the power of the Holy Spirit to become more like Jesus as we are "transformed by the renewing of our minds" into the image of Christ.

We should always remember that there is always room for improvement and room at the cross.

Father, help me to dwell in Your room for improvement. Amen.

Lord, You Are _____
Forgive Me For _____
Thank You For _____
Needs of Others _____
Personal Needs _____
Answered Prayers _____

Read Ephesians 1, Jeremiah 32   February 14
Signed, Sealed, and Delivered

"You are standing here today to enter into a covenant with the LORD your God. The LORD is making this covenant with you today, and he has sealed it with an oath." Deuteronomy 29:12 NLT

Any real estate broker or salesman can attest to the fact that no transaction is final until it is "signed, sealed, and delivered." A deal is not closed, and no commissions are paid until the purchase contract is signed, sealed with a deposit, and a clear title is delivered at closing. It is interesting to note that only 50 to 75 percent of real estate contracts written actually close.

"I signed and sealed the deed of purchase before witnesses, weighed out the silver, and paid him." Jeremiah 32:10 NLT

As believers in Jesus Christ, we have been "signed, sealed, and delivered." Our eternal destination should never be in doubt. It has been signed by the blood of Jesus on the cross and sealed by the indwelling of the Holy Spirit; we have been delivered from the death penalty of our sins and will be delivered into the presence of God and the eternal bliss of heaven.

If only we could be as satisfied with ourselves as God is satisfied with us! Because God sees the righteousness of Christ in us, we have nothing to fear but fear itself when it comes to standing before the judgment seat.

God's wonderful plan is that not only have we been made holy and justified in His sight by our faith in the blood of Jesus, but we are continually being made holy and more Christ like every day of our lives by the sanctifying power of the Holy Spirit living within us if we are truly saved.

Personal holiness is something that we can never achieve on our own. We all need the sanctifying grace of God to sustain us and cover our weaknesses with His strength.

We receive the motivation to holiness when we respond with thanksgiving and praise for the great thing God has done for us because of our faith in Jesus. We can accomplish

"It's in Christ that you, once you heard the truth and believed it (this Message of your salvation), found yourselves home free—signed, sealed, and delivered by the Holy Spirit." Ephesians 1:13a MSG

holiness only by the resurrection power of Christ living in us, which is our hope of glory and the evidence that we have been delivered.

Father, thank you for "signing, sealing, and delivering" me. Amen.

Lord, You Are _____
Forgive Me For _____
Thank You For _____
Needs of Others _____
Personal Needs _____
Answered Prayers _____

February 15   Read Hebrews 11, Isaiah 40:25-31

The Methodology of God

"Oh, what a wonderful God we have! How great are His riches and wisdom and knowledge! How impossible it is for us to understand His decisions and His methods!" Romans 11:33 NLT

"Have you never heard or understood? Don't you know that the LORD is the everlasting God, the Creator of all the earth? He never grows faint or weary. No one can measure the depths of His understanding."
Isaiah 40:28 NLT

God's methods for accomplishing extraordinary things through ordinary people are a great testimony to both the wonders of His love and His incredible power.

A background check of the Saints who have gone on before will reveal that God has given faith to murderers, prostitutes, persecutors, a rag tag bunch of fisherman, tax collectors, and uneducated and undistinguished people for accomplishing His purposes and His glory throughout the ages.

We are all without excuse and should never doubt the possibility of God's ability to accomplish what we consider impossibilities in and through us.

We should never let our weaknesses go uncovered by His strength, our fears overcome by His power, or our comfort zones unsqueezed by His call that we make God and His will the top priority in our lives.

By all human reason, the kingdom of God should have died on the cross with Jesus, but thanks to the methodology of God in rising from the dead and sending the power of the Holy Spirit to His disciples, the kingdom of God has spread through the entire world through all ages.

"But without faith it is impossible to please Him, for he who comes to God must believe that He is, and that He is a rewarder of those who diligently seek Him."
Hebrews 11:6

We need to know that God is sovereign, and He is Creator and Ruler of all things. He can do whatever He chooses whenever He chooses and through whomever He chooses. We must never question God's purposes or His methods in using us for our good and His glory as we put our trust in Him.

Father, may I always trust and obey no matter what method You choose to use me for accomplishing your purposes. Amen.

Lord, You Are _____
Forgive Me For _____
Thank You For _____
Needs of Others _____
Personal Needs _____
Answered Prayers _____

Read John 4:6-38. Proverbs 20   February 16

Digging Deeper

"But I called on Your name, LORD, from deep within the well, and You heard me! You listened to my pleading; You heard my weeping! Yes, You came at my despairing cry and told me, 'Do not fear.'" Lamentations 3:55-57 NLT

Wells sometimes have to be dug deeper and cased through bad water to get to the good. Sometimes the water level drops, and wells have to be dug deeper to tap into the life-giving liquid.

"Knowing what is right is like deep water in the heart; a wise person draws from the well within." Proverbs 20:5 MSG

God's character-development program for us sometimes involves digging deeper into His Word and our dependency upon Him as He causes us to go through the bad waters of bitterness, disappointment, pain, and suffering while conforming us into the image of Christ.

Just as many well diggers fail to find water because they don't dig deep enough, we fail to live in the fullness of Christ because we don't dig deep enough to get to know Him in a close and personal relationship.

When we dig deeper into God's Word, we will find the power for living today and forever as we experience the blessings of abiding in Him.

When inevitable troubles come we need to dig deeper to tap into God's all-sufficient and inexhaustible grace that He promises to all who call upon His name.

When we dig deeper in prayer we will find ourselves praying more fervent and effectual prayers that "availeth much."

"Jesus replied, 'If you only knew the gift God has for you and who I am, you would ask Me, and I would give you living water.'" John 4:10

As we experience God's pruning and sometimes even scourging, digging deeper with godly sorrow and true repentance is required to find the treasure that we seek which is true joy, peace, fulfillment, and completeness in Christ.

Above all, we need to dig deep enough to get through the polluted waters of self centeredness and sin, so we tap into the sweetness of living water which is "Christ in us, our hope of glory"!

Father, help me to "dig deep." Amen.

Lord, You Are _____
Forgive Me For _____
Thank You For _____
Needs of Others _____
Personal Needs _____
Answered Prayers _____

The Power of the Cross

"For the message of the cross is foolishness to those who are perishing, but to us who are being saved it is the power of God."
1 Corinthians 1:18 NLT

Catholics use the cross as a crucifix to remind them of Jesus dying there for us.

"Arise, O LORD, and enter your sanctuary, along with the Ark, the symbol of Your power."
Psalm 132:8 NLT

Protestants use the cross without Jesus on it to remind them that He has risen and is no longer there.

The cross of Calvary is much, much more than any ornament. It is an outward symbol and inward reminder of the strength and power we can find if only we will only take up this cross and follow Jesus.

The cross is the dumping station for our sins. We lay them there and receive the forgiveness for all of our sins and the wonderful joy of our salvation.

As we learn to lay our burdens at the foot of the cross, we have our burdens lightened so that we can rise above or bear up under them.

The power of the cross is our sure defense against the wiles of the world, our flesh, and the devil. When we remember that Jesus overcame our sin on the cross, we can find the power to live free from bondage to it.

When we appropriate the resurrection power of the cross through the new birth in Christ, we are enabled to grow into the fullness of His joy, His friendship, and His presence.

The power of the cross includes the power to trust, obey, and be secure in the love of Christ who died there so that we will never have to die.

"And by Him God reconciled everything to Himself. He made peace with everything in heaven and on earth by means of His blood on the cross."
Colossians 1:20 NLT

The power of the cross is not only the power for living richly, but it is also the power for dying well as ones who know that because Jesus rose, we shall rise also into the eternal bliss of heaven.

The power of the cross is transmitted by the Holy Spirit to all who call upon the name of the Lord to be saved.

Father, let the cross be a constant reminder of my power in You. Amen.

Lord, You Are _____
Forgive Me For _____
Thank You For _____
Needs of Others _____
Personal Needs _____
Answered Prayers _____

Read 1 Thessalonians 5:12-20, Psalm 112   **February 18**
Spheres of Influence
"The LORD replied, 'If you return to me, I will restore you so you can continue to serve Me. If you speak words that are worthy, you will be My spokesman. You are to influence them; do not let them influence you!'"
Jeremiah 15:19 NLT

"They give generously to those in need. Their good deeds will never be forgotten. They will have influence and honor."
Psalm 112:9 NLT

The world runs on spheres of influence. We all are one and are often parts of many. Our sphere may be just family and a few friends. We may become influential in our community or work place.

Every town, state, or country; sport, business, or church; or any other organization is controlled by the players with the greatest spheres of influence.

As Christians, we are called to be spheres of influence to the whole world spreading the gospel to everyone everywhere the Lord gives us influence. Scripture warns us time and time again about being a bad influence or stumbling block to others.

Falling under the influence of evil in an evil world has been the reality of life since the fall of man in the garden of evil. It is virtually impossible to live upright in a downright evil environment. Praise God that what is virtually impossible for man is more than possible for God.

No matter how low we sink or how far we succumb to the spheres of evil influences all around us, God is always ready, willing, and able to rescue, restore, and strengthen us.

"Dear brothers and sisters, honor those who are your leaders in the Lord's work. They work hard among you and warn you against all that is wrong."
1 Thessalonians 5:12-20 NLT

When Jesus sets us free, we are no longer controlled by sin but are transformed into the newness of life controlled and influenced by the Spirit of the Living Lord.

We are equipped with the full armor of God and endued with power from on high to become the sphere of influence to reconcile others to right standing with God through faith in Jesus Christ.

Father, let me be a sphere of influence for Christ wherever You might plant me. Amen.

Lord, You Are _____
Forgive Me For _____
Thank You For _____
Needs of Others _____
Personal Needs _____
Answered Prayers _____

Marriage for Misery?

"The LORD God said, 'It is not good for the man to be alone. I will make a helper suitable for him.'" Genesis 2:18 NIV

We have probably all heard about the evils of marrying for money and how you will earn every penny of it. We have never heard of anyone knowingly or intentionally marrying for misery.

"But you have been disloyal to her, though she remained your faithful companion, the wife of your marriage vows." Malachi 2:14b NLT

God established marriage as an integral part of His plan that we may be faithful, fruitful and blessed in joining our lives to establish a home of our own with a spouse of our own where we will be joined together in a oneness which only having Christ in our marriage affords.

When sin came into the world, it also came into marriages.

The misery of marriage can come from bringing baggage from the past. Old habits, old ways, and different upbringings can bring down a marriage. Problems of cleaving and becoming one are often present. Financial problems rank high on the misery list of most breakups.

Going in with the idea that we can always get out if things don't work out brings a lack of the real commitment and desire to work things out when inevitable problems and conflicts arise.

Failure to submit as unto the Lord and to love each other as Christ loved His bride (His church) brings the misery that always accompanies selfishness, pride, idolatry, and rebellion.

The failure to forgive and forget by either spouse will send the misery index through the roof.

When the Lord's admonition not to be yoked with unbelievers is ignored, marriage to an unbeliever is often a recipe for misery.

"Jesus replied, 'Moses permitted divorce as a concession to your hard-hearted wickedness, but it was not what God had originally intended.'" Matthew 19:8 NLT

Those who have suffered the misery of a failed marriage can take heart in knowing that God loves them more than He hates divorce and that He often can and will give us another chance to enjoy the bliss of marriage when we learn from our mistakes and commit to doing marriage God's way.

Father, in Your mercy, don't let me "miss the bliss." Amen.

Lord, You Are _____
Forgive Me For _____
Thank You For _____
Needs of Others _____
Personal Needs _____
Answered Prayers _____

"Been There Done That"

"But He was wounded for our transgressions, He was bruised for our iniquities; the chastisement for our peace was upon Him, and by His stripes we are healed." Isaiah 53:5 NLT

There is a lot of comfort and encouragement from someone who has "been there and done that." Only someone who has "been there and done that" can really know how we feel in times of trouble.

"My life is an example to many, because You have been my strength and protection." Psalm 71:7 NLT

It often seems that God lets bad things happen to good people so that they might be able to comfort and encourage others when they go through some of the troubled times of life in an imperfect, sinful world.

In Jesus, we all have a brother who has been tempted in every way and suffered more than we will ever be required to suffer. He not only knows our every weakness, but He can sympathize with us and supply the strength to overcome because He overcame.

Whether it is rejection, hatred, ridicule, abandonment, loneliness, disappointment, pain, or suffering, Jesus can sympathize with us and show us the way to live, learn, and grow from these troubles.

Jesus not only experienced and overcame temptations, but He also sent the Holy Spirit to give us the strength to do the same.

Even though Jesus never experienced addictions of any kind, He did endure and overcome the root causes. He can set addicts free by giving them the strength to root out and overcome the causes.

"This suffering is all part of what God has called you to. Christ, who suffered for you, is your example. Follow in His steps." 1 Peter 2:21

Although Jesus never sinned, He bore the pain and guilt of all of our sins and died to destroy their power to enslave and destroy us. Because He lives, we too can live in the assurance that we can live strengthened by the one who has "been there, done that" and will provide His all-sufficient grace to enable us to overcome.

Father, when troubles come, let me take heart in knowing that by the power of your Spirit, I can overcome. Amen.

Lord, You Are _____

Forgive Me For _____

Thank You For _____

Needs of Others _____

Personal Needs _____

Answered Prayers _____

Who Do You Trust?

"Oh, the joys of those who trust the LORD, who have no confidence in the proud, or in those who worship idols." Psalm 40:4

In our flesh, we are too often dwelling on discontent and how to overcome it. "I would be happy if" focuses our attention on perceptions of things that would make us more content with whom we are by what we have rather than Whom we have.

"But blessed are those who trust in the LORD and have made the LORD their hope and confidence." Jeremiah 17:7 NLT

Whether we place our trust in possessions, popularity, our own strength, talent, ability, or in a bottle, pill, powder, or other person, we are setting ourselves up for a big disappointment. None of these things can deliver true security, significance, godly peace and joy.

It is only when we can say "I am happy" because we have Jesus Christ as Savior and Lord of our life that we can know true inner peace and security and enjoy the abundance of blessings that only this trust promises.

When we seek first the kingdom of God and His righteousness, we are promised that everything we need for true peace and joy will be provided. "Eye has not seen, nor ear heard, nor have entered into the heart of man the things which God has prepared for those who love Him" (Isaiah 64:4, 1 Corinthians 2:9).

"There is no judgment awaiting those who trust Him. But those who do not trust Him have already been judged for not believing in the only Son of God." John 3:18

Why we would ever choose to build our lives and our hopes on the sinking sand of any other foundation apart from trust in the God who cannot fail, who does not lie, and who keeps all of His promises is beyond comprehension.

We see the signs of death and decay all around us as the world turns from trust in God to trust in man and the worship of intellect, science, and progress instead of the One who has come that we might have life abundantly in Him.

Father, may I never trust in anything or anyone above You. Amen.

Lord, You Are _____

Forgive Me For _____

Thank You For _____

Needs of Others _____

Personal Needs _____

Answered Prayers _____

We are Royal!

"But you are a chosen people, a royal priesthood, a holy nation, a people belonging to God, that you may declare the praises of Him who called you out of darkness into His wonderful light." 1 Peter 2:9 NIV

Queen Elizabeth and nobility have nothing on us! We are all royal!

"If your descendants obey the terms of My covenant and follow the decrees that I teach them, then your royal line will never end." Psalm 132:12 NLT

The hour we first believed and received Jesus as Lord and Savior we became members of the royal priesthood of believers with all the rights and privileges of royalty.

We were given a crown and robe of righteousness so that we can come before God as brothers and sisters of the Prince of Peace and joint heirs with Him in all of the rights and privileges of being subjects in the Kingdom of God.

As royalty, we are no longer subject to the rule of sin but are subject to the rule of God and His righteousness. We are able to offer sacrifices of praise and holy intercession for ourselves and others directly to God's throne of grace.

As members of this royal priesthood, we are given the King of King and Lord of Lord's grace, mercy, protection, abundance, strength and guidance.

As members of this royalty, we are set apart and given the high privilege of building up the Kingdom of God by producing fruits of righteousness and helping to spread the kingdom to the utmost corners of this world.

"You also, like living stones, are being built into a spiritual house to be a holy priesthood, offering spiritual sacrifices acceptable to God through Jesus Christ." 1 Peter 2:5 NIV

We are given not only the desire but the strength to keep our robes of righteousness spotless through the daily cleansing of the Holy Spirit.

With all of this being true (and it most certainly is), we can no longer avoid our responsibilities or depend on our pastors to do the priestly ministry to which we have all been called.

We all need to help the needy, comfort and encourage the weak and lonely, visit the sick, and help spread the Gospel by the witness of our lives and the testimony of our lips.

Father, help me to take my priestly duties seriously. Amen.

Lord, You Are _____
Forgive Me For _____
Thank You For _____
Needs of Others _____
Personal Needs _____
Answered Prayers _____

February 23   **Read Matthew 28:16-20, Isaiah 43:10-13**

The One That Got Away

"But sanctify the Lord God in your hearts, and always be ready to give a defense to everyone who asks you a reason for the hope that is in you, with meekness and fear." 1 Peter 3:15

It seems that about every conversation about fishing deals with that big one that got away. The size of the fish seems to grow with every retelling.

"'You are witnesses that I am the only God,' says the LORD." Isaiah 43:10b NLT

Whatever we are fishing for, we need to go where the fish are, use the right bait, and not let the one that got away deter us from "keepin' on, keepin' on."

We would never think of looking for a mate or a customer with a bad attitude or looking and acting our worst. We don't make many friends by being critical and negative, and we sure let a lot get away by neglect.

As believers commanded to be fishers of men, we need to know that God is continually arranging "divine appointments" to use us as "bait" to draw others to Him.

It may be a simple random act of kindness, a life lived modeling the love of Christ in us, or the opportunity to witness by presenting the good news with the power of God's Word.

In whatever way God chooses to use us, we must take advantage of the opportunity and be ever mindful of and sensitive to the importance of being God's conduit of saving faith to others.

We can all probably think of many times when we have let someone God has put in our path get away without hearing the Good News because we were too timid or too insensitive to recognize and take advantage of the opportunity when God arranged it for us.

"Therefore, go and make disciples of all the nations, baptizing them in the name of the Father and the Son and the Holy Spirit." Matthew 28:19 NLT

We are all great at inking what we could have or should have said after the fish has gotten away.

May heaven not be a lonely place because of the loved ones "we have let get away" by failing to do our part in fulfilling the Great Commission.

Father, let none get away because of my being a bad witness. Amen.

Lord, You Are _____

Forgive Me For _____

Thank You For _____

Needs of Others _____

Personal Needs _____

Answered Prayers _____

"Let's Make a Deal" Religion

"Nor should we put Christ to the test, as some of them did and then died from snakebites." 1 Corinthians 10:9

We have all probably tried to make some implied or concrete, conditional "deals" with God. We all have probably heard testimonies about how someone told God that if He would spare them or a loved one, they would serve Him…that if they won the lottery they would share with Him…or how if He were real to show them a sign.

"Deal bountifully with Your servant, that I may live and keep Your word." Psalm 119:17

As inspiring and sincere many of these testimonies are, Scripture gives no validation that we can "make a deal" with God. Outside of testing God in the area of giving tithes and offerings, we are specifically warned against testing God.

We need to know that God is always the "dealer," and we are the "dealee." To presume that the clay can tell the potter what to do or that we can make our faith or obedience conditional upon God meeting our conditions is the height of conceit, which shows utter ignorance of the knowledge or understanding of God.

How much better it is to understand the wonderful "deals" God has given us through His Old Testament covenants and especially through His New Covenant of grace through faith in Jesus Christ.

We do not enter into the Kingdom of God and His grace and mercy if He will do this or that. Rather, it is because we believe that He has done all that is necessary for us to be reconciled to Him by dying on the cross for our sins, and we receive His favor.

We do not put conditions on our response to God's wonderful gift of eternal life. We put our faith and trust in the fact that He has given it to us as a free gift and has promised to work all things for our good and His glory in this world and the next.

"Jesus responded, "The Scriptures also say, 'Do not test the Lord your God.'" Luke 4:12 NLT

Father, thank you for all the wonderful "deals" You have given me by Your grace, mercy, and loving kindness. Amen.

Lord, You Are _____

Forgive Me For _____

Thank You For _____

Needs of Others _____

Personal Needs _____

Answered Prayers _____

Who's in Charge?

"When we were controlled by our old nature, sinful desires were at work within us, and the law aroused these evil desires that produced sinful deeds, resulting in death." Romans 7:5 NLT

There is an inborn control instinct in the heart of many people. There is also the inclination for rebellion that resists any efforts to be controlled.

"Submit to God's royal son, or He will become angry, and you will be destroyed in the midst of your pursuits—for His anger can flare up in an instant. But what joy for all who find protection in Him!"
Psalm 12:2 NLT

We see this rebellious streak at an early age in most children. They seem to learn to disobey naturally without training of any kind. I have never heard of a child having to be taught to disobey.

Some children are allowed to grow up beyond the control of parents or any other authority and live undisciplined, unproductive, and destructive lives that end either in death or jail.

Pride often charges the ego to demand control of others as validation of our own power and significance. No one likes to lose a fight or argument. Everyone likes to be a winner, and we often equate winning with getting our way.

Our lives are battle grounds of control between our flesh and our spirit. We can choose to go through life in our free will of bondage to the flesh and all of the manifestations of the sins of pride, anger, envy, lust and other evils that accompany self-centered control.

God's call to salvation allows us to choose to receive a new life controlled by the Spirit of God living in us that will manifest the fruit of "love, joy, peace, longsuffering, kindness, goodness, faithfulness, gentleness, and self-control" (Galatians 5:22).

We can choose to live in our own strength or with the strength of God covering our weaknesses. We can harvest the fruits of righteousness through a new birth in Christ or harvest the consequences of living in rebellion against God. It's all a matter of who we allow to be in charge.

"Do not let sin control the way you live; do not give in to its lustful desires."
Romans 6:12 NLT

Father, take charge of my will and let my life be a celebration to You. Amen.

Lord, You Are _____

Forgive Me For _____

Thank You For _____

Needs of Others _____

Personal Needs _____

Answered Prayers _____

Wonder-Working Power

"But to those called by God to salvation, both Jews and Gentiles, Christ is the mighty power of God and the wonderful wisdom of God."
1 Corinthians 1:24

There is no power on this earth to match the power from on high that is promised to everyone who receives God's call to salvation by accepting Jesus Christ as the Lord and Savior of their life.

"Riches and honor come from You alone, for You rule over everything. Power and might are in Your hand, and it is at Your discretion that people are made great and given strength."
1 Chronicles 29:12 NLT

To go through life without appropriating this power by faith is to miss out on all of the incredible joy of growing into the fullness of Christ through this power supplied by the Holy Spirit living within us.

This is the power that raised Jesus from death to life. It transformed 11 fearful ragtag disciples into miracle workers and bold, fearless proclaimers of the Gospel.

The wonder-working power not only gives us the power to believe but also the power to overcome our weaknesses with God's strength. It provides all-sufficient grace for our every need. It heals us and frees from bondage to sin and death and gives us a new life.

This wonder-working power gives sight to the blind, help to the helpless and hope to the hopeless. When we allow it to work in and through us, God is able to accomplish more than we could ever hope or ask.

"And what is the exceeding greatness of His power toward us who believe, according to the working of His mighty power,"
Ephesians 1:19

The secret to appropriating this wonder-working power into our lives is found in allowing Christ to live in us by abiding in Him and growing in our knowledge of Him through His Word. As our love for Him grows through a real and personal relationship with Him, we discover more and more of the wonders of His love.

Father help me to grow into Your fullness by the wonder-working power of Your Spirit. Amen.

Lord, You Are _____

Forgive Me For _____

Thank You For _____

Needs of Others _____

Personal Needs _____

Answered Prayers _____

The Sweet Smell of Success

"Then Mary took a twelve-ounce jar of expensive perfume made from essence of nard, and she anointed Jesus' feet with it and wiped his feet with her hair. And the house was filled with fragrance." John 12:3 NLT

The multi-billion-dollar perfume and cosmetics industry is riding the sweet smell to success throughout the world.

"They are a stench in my nostrils, an acrid smell that never goes away." Isaiah 65:4b NLT

We are barraged daily with advertisements promoting a deodorant, perfume, or cosmetic that will provide a sweet smell.

While many prize perfumes, many enjoy that new car smell as their "sweet smell of success."

Sweet-smelling fragrances were expensive and highly treasured even in Jesus' day.

The stench of death and decay is very offensive and hard for anyone to endure. The stench of our sins is also offensive and hard for anyone to endure, especially God.

Jesus came to stop the stench of death and decay and replace it with the sweet fragrance of God's grace and love. The robe of righteousness with which He covers us when we receive Him through faith also covers the stench of our sins, and God remembers them no more.

The Holy Spirit comes as the deodorant for our sins. When we bathe daily in the cleansing waters of confession and repentance, we are refreshed and renewed. We are able to go forth daily with the "sweet smell of success" befitting one who has triumphed over sin, death, and the devil through the blood of Jesus.

"But thanks be to God, who made us His captives and leads us along in Christ's triumphal procession. Now wherever we go He uses us to tell others about the Lord and to spread the Good News like a sweet perfume." 2 Corinthians 2:14 NLT

As offensive as body odor may be to us, it is nothing compared to how offensive sin odor is to God.

Father, help me to live my life as a sweet fragrance unto You. Amen.

Lord, You Are _____

Forgive Me For _____

Thank You For _____

Needs of Others _____

Personal Needs _____

Answered Prayers _____

Do You Have a Sin License?

"O God, You take no pleasure in wickedness; You cannot tolerate the slightest sin." Psalm 5:4

Jesus Christ came to set us free from sin, not to free us to sin freely. While it is true that where sin abounds God's grace abounds even more, God's grace is the transforming power to die to sin and come alive to righteousness in Christ.

"Do not be like a senseless horse or mule that needs a bit and bridle to keep it under control." Psalm 32:9

This saving grace of God makes us righteous in His sight instantly by the imputed righteousness of Christ. The sanctifying grace of God gives us the strength and power to live free from dominion by sin and to live lives controlled by the Holy Spirit.

This sanctifying grace is an ongoing process where we grow into the fullness of Christ as we grow in the knowledge of God and His will for our lives as we grow in spiritual maturity by growing through His Word.

God knew that we could not become holy in our own strength or by our own power and that we would need help in breaking the power of the flesh to control us. He sent the Holy Spirit to live within us to guide, guard, and grow the fruits of righteousness within us as we surrender control to His power.

We dare not mock or make light of the wonderful freedom we have been given and the price that Christ paid for it. The idea that we can sin freely and willfully is a lie right out of hell designed to destroy the security, peace, and joy of our salvation. It seeks to destroy the blessings that only exercising our freedom to live lives in obedience to and fully pleasing to Christ can afford.

"Well then, if we emphasize faith, does this mean that we can forget about the law? Of course not! In fact, only when we have faith do we truly fulfill the law." Romans 3:31:NLT

God's law is still working to convict us of our sin and need for a Savior, to guide us into righteousness, and to curb sin so that all of the wonderful blessings He promises and showers upon obedience can be ours to appropriate by faith when we are born again.

Father, let me never misuse my wonderful security of Your unconditional love and forever forgiveness as a license to sin. Amen.

Lord, You Are _____

Forgive Me For _____

Thank You For _____

Needs of Others _____

Personal Needs _____

Answered Prayers _____

How Does Your Garden Grow?

"Finally, brethren, whatever things are true, whatever things are noble, whatever things are just, whatever things are pure, whatever things are lovely, whatever things are of good report, if there is any virtue and if there is anything praiseworthy—meditate on these things." Philippians 4:8

"The LORD will guide you continually, and satisfy your soul in drought, and strengthen your bones; you shall be like a watered garden, and like a spring of water, whose waters do not fail."
Isaiah 58:11

The concept of reaping what we sew is something we all need to understand and live by every day of our lives.

When we understand that kindness begets kindness, love begets love, and generosity begets generosity, we will understand how to receive more kindness, love, and generosity.

When we deal in discontent, anger, gossip, smut, or sin of any kind, we can be sure that it will ultimately come back to haunt us.

Our garden of life can be a garden of earthly heaven or hell depending upon what we grow in it and how well we irrigate it. When we plant God's love that He showers down on us, irrigate it with the living water of His Word, and weed it through daily confession and repentance, we are assured an abundant crop of fruit.

Our gardens will bear the fruit of the Spirit that gives us the love, joy, peace, patience, kindness, goodness, faithfulness, gentleness, and self-control that will nourish and sustain us so that we can live our lives to the fullest in Christ.

If we sew the seeds of selfishness, doubt, unbelief, unforgiveness, or disobedience, the roots of bitterness and weeds of discontent will grow. We will bear the guilt, shame, and consequences these seeds always produce.

"And let us not grow weary while doing good, for in due season we shall reap if we do not lose heart."
Galatians 6:9 NLT

When we treat others the way we would like to be treated, our gardens will produce a bumper crop of blessings. We will be on our way to growing into the fullness of Christ.

Father, fill my garden of life with an abundance of the fruit of Your Spirit. Amen.

Lord, You Are _____

Forgive Me For _____

Thank You For _____

Needs of Others _____

Personal Needs _____

Answered Prayers _____

Great Are Our Rewards

"But without faith it is impossible to please Him, for he who comes to God must believe that He is and that He is a rewarder of those who diligently seek Him." Hebrews 11:6

Eternal life is a gift which we receive by faith. Christ earned our salvation by dying as the perfect, unblemished sacrifice for our sins.

"You will keep him in perfect peace, whose mind is stayed on You, because he trusts in You." Isaiah 26:3

We should never try to take credit for earning this gift, thus robbing God of His glory and trivializing Christ's sacrifice for us.

The blessings of God's power, friendship, presence, peace, and joy are the rewards promised for trusting and obeying God and for abiding in a personal relationship with Jesus Christ. These are temporal blessings we don't have to wait to enjoy in heaven. They are ours to enjoy as we respond in love to what God has given us.

There is no pleasure or happiness we can find on our own that can begin to compare with the pleasure and treasure we will find when we seek to know God through the Son whom He has sent.

God is the "giver of every good and perfect gift," "the fountain of living waters", "our refuge and strength," and our "very present help in time of trouble."

"When you obey me, you remain in My love, just as I obey My Father and remain in His love. I have told you this so that you will be filled with My joy. Yes, your joy will overflow." John 15:10, 11 NLT

God's perfect gift to us is Jesus Christ. He came to die that we might live, and because He lives, we can live the abundant life in Him. We are promised answered prayers, His friendship, the fullness of His joy, His love, the love of the Father who sent Him, and the love of others.

The blessing of knowing and believing that God does work all things for the good of those who love Him and who are the called according to His purposes is one of the greatest rewards of all.

Father, thank you for being my "great rewarder." Amen.

Lord, You Are _____
Forgive Me For _____
Thank You For _____
Needs of Others _____
Personal Needs _____
Answered Prayers _____

The Jungle of Desire

"But one thing is needed, and Mary has chosen that good part, which will not be taken away from her." Luke 10:42

There is a jungle through which we all must travel if we are to truly "walk the walk."

"For the LORD God is a sun and shield; the LORD will give grace and glory; no good thing will He withhold from those who walk uprightly." Psalm 89:11

In order to reach our destination of peace and godly contentment, we need to acquire the wisdom of discernment between wants and needs.

The needs manufacturing industry is spending millions of dollars daily to try to create desires for products, goods, and services that we not only don't need but that can actually do us great harm.

The enticement to "buy now and pay later" has trapped millions into slavery to debt. The lure to be more important, attractive, popular, and happier by buying a bigger house, driving a better car, wearing designer clothes or shoes, etc., ad infinitum, ad nausea is the stock in trade of the needs manufacturing industry.

The truth is that most of us are living well beyond our needs and are pursuing the pleasures of obtaining our desires. We need to have a major "wanter adjustment" if we are going to have the true riches of life.

There is certainly nothing wrong with enjoying the fruits of our labors or the blessings of abundance which God often provides. The problem comes when we become slaves to debt and things instead of slaves to Christ and His righteousness.

God gives us an abundance of time, talents, and treasure so that we can be generous to Him and to others. When we squander them on selfish pursuits or for material things we don't really need, we are never going to know the true joy of the grace of giving in which we are commanded to excel.

"Yet true religion with contentment is great wealth." 1 Timothy 6:6 NLT

God has promised to supply our every need. He often supplies the desires of our hearts when our hearts are right with Him. We need to let the Holy Spirit be our "needs manufacturer."

Father, may my wants over my needs never consume me. Amen.

Lord, You Are _____

Forgive Me For _____

Thank You For _____

Needs of Others _____

Personal Needs _____

Answered Prayers _____

Who's Your Daddy?

"Anyone whose Father is God listens gladly to the words of God. Since you don't, it proves you aren't God's children." John 8:47

With more and more children being born out of wedlock every year and welfare roles packed with children abandoned by their fathers, it gets harder and harder for many to know just who their daddy is.

"For the word of the LORD holds true, and everything He does is worthy of our trust." Psalm 33:4 NLT

On a spiritual level, we must all deal with the reality that there is a father of lies seeking to keep us in the darkness of sin and death.

The devil seems to be the father of many who never come to know or have any relationship with the Heavenly Father who created us, loves us with an everlasting love, and calls us into a saving and sanctifying relationship with Him through faith in Jesus Christ.

We can only come to know God as our father through knowing the Son that He has sent. When we, by faith, receive Jesus Christ as our Lord and Savior by the power of the Holy Spirit, we become sons and daughters of God adopted into His household of faith.

It is only through this new birth that God truly becomes our father, and this new birth will be evidenced by obedience to Him.

Our Heavenly Father has brought us out of darkness into light, set us free from slavery to sin, and made us slaves to righteousness.

"So you should not be like cowering, fearful slaves. You should behave instead like God's very own children, adopted into his family—calling Him 'Father, dear Father.'" Romans 8:15 NLT

The holy transformation that takes place when God becomes our daddy in our hearts will leave no doubt that we are under the authority and control of the one who has called us into the light of His love, the control of His Spirit, and the incredible peace and joy of His salvation.

When we get to know who our Daddy is, we will choose to trust and obey Him and flourish in the security of His love.

Father by the power of Your Spirit, help me to live as one of Your children in every area of my life. Amen.

Lord, You Are _____
Forgive Me For _____
Thank You For _____
Needs of Others _____
Personal Needs _____
Answered Prayers _____

My Place or Yours?

"Surely goodness and mercy shall follow me all the days of my life; and I will dwell in the house of the LORD forever." Psalm 23:6

The question of where we will live our lives is one that we all have to answer for ourselves. God gives us a free will to choose whether to accept or reject His call to come live in His place.

"He who dwells in the secret place of the Most High shall abide under the shadow of the Almighty." Psalm 91:1

It is hard for anyone who has experienced the peace and joy of receiving Christ as their dwelling place to understand how anyone could choose to lose all of the incredible riches that God has stored up for those who place their trust in Him.

Our Father's place is a place of shelter, healing, rest, grace, mercy, peace, compassion, faith, hope, and love. To dwell in His presence, under the shelter of His wings, is to live life to the fullest now and forever. We have the only security that never fails.

When we choose to live in our place by doing life our way in our own flesh and strength, we are choosing a recipe for disaster.

We can acquire the grandest house ever built, succeed in any endeavor, and rise to incredible heights of fame and fortune only to see it all burnt up as wood, hay, and stubble as we burn with it in eternal torment.

The parable of the prodigal son serves as a stark reminder of the fate that ultimately awaits all who choose to lose by departing from the place God has prepared and desires for all who call upon His name.

"There are many rooms in my Father's home, and I am going to prepare a place for you. If this were not so, I would tell you plainly." John 14:2 NLT

Why, oh, why would anyone choose slopping with hogs when they have an invitation to a royal wedding banquet with a table of grace that satisfies every longing and every need?

May all of the goodness, grace, peace, and mercy of God be ours as we seek to dwell in the House of the Lord forever through faith in Jesus Christ.

Father, may I live in the peace and joy of the dwelling place You have prepared for me in Christ. Amen.

Lord, You Are _____
Forgive Me For _____
Thank You For _____
Needs of Others _____
Personal Needs _____
Answered Prayers _____

Read Colossians 3:9-17, Isaiah 57   **March 5**

Renewing a Right Spirit

"The sacrifices of God are a broken spirit, a broken and a contrite heart—these, O God, You will not despise." Psalm 51:17

Next to the gift of salvation, the grace of a renewed spirit is perhaps the greatest of the many wonderful gifts of God's grace.

"To revive the spirit of the humble, and to revive the heart of the contrite ones,"
Isaiah 57:15b

As pilgrims doing life in a sin-sick world, we can't help but pick up some of the road dirt of life that comes into our homes via TV, internet, or strife between spouses or other family members.

In schools, workplaces, churches, bars, or wherever relationships take place, forces of evil are at work seeking to divide, deceive, subdue, and tempt us to compromise our witness and personal holiness.

Since the struggle takes place on a daily basis, how important it is to seek the cleansing and renewal of confession and repentance on a daily basis.

God is faithful. His promises are sure. Whosoever comes to Him with a broken sprit and contrite heart will find the comfort of His love, the assurance of His forgiveness, the cleansing of conscience, and the renewal of a right spirit.

We were never meant to go through life in the weakness of the flesh without the strength of the Holy Spirit to renew, refresh, comfort, and sustain us.

"And have put on the new man who is renewed in knowledge according to the image of Him who created him."
Colossians 3:10

If we were created with the strength to overcome evil on our own, Christ would not have had to die to pay the price for our sins, and He would not have had to send the Holy Spirit to call, comfort, guide, guard, and supply us the supernatural strength to overcome our natural weaknesses of the flesh.

Father, thank you for sending Your Son to make all things new and Your Spirit to regenerate and renew us whenever we ask. Amen.

Lord, You Are _____
Forgive Me For _____
Thank You For _____
Needs of Others _____
Personal Needs _____
Answered Prayers _____

Where Are the Heroes?

"We do not want you to become lazy, but to imitate those who through faith and patience inherit what has been promised." Hebrews 6:12 NIV

We don't seem to have many role models of character to look up to these days. Our progress in human virtue has too often turned into a retreat as leaders in politics, religion, sports, and practically every other endeavor too often fail when their morality is put to the test.

"GOD's my strong champion; I flick off my enemies like flies. Far better to take refuge in GOD than trust in people." Psalm 118:7 MSG

As parents who are supposed to model who we want our children to become, we too often model and have our children imitate the worst of our qualities instead of the best.

Do we really want our children to grow up to be just like us? Do we really want them breaking the same promises we broke to our spouses, to them, and even to God?

The Good News is that God has given us a hero that we can always look up to.

This hero lived up to God's expectation of sinless perfection and died so that we would not have to die.

This hero came to not only model how we should live lives fully pleasing to God but sent the Holy Spirit to live within us and provide the power to do this.

Jesus Christ is the only hero we will ever need. He will never disappoint us or lie to us. He will never break a promise. He wants to be that "friend that sticks closer than a brother."

When our personal relationship with Jesus Christ grows not only into lordship but also friendship, we will find ourselves wanting to imitate Him and do the things that He teaches us, just as He did the things that His Father taught Him.

"Therefore be imitators of God as dear children." Ephesians 5:1 NLT

When the hero of God's heart becomes the hero of our heart, we won't have to ask where the heroes have gone. We will know where He is and will want to show others how to find Him.

Father, let Jesus be my hero in every area of my life. Amen.

Lord, You Are _____

Forgive Me For _____

Thank You For _____

Needs of Others _____

Personal Needs _____

Answered Prayers _____

The Poverty of Riches

"For what profit is it to a man if he gains the whole world, and loses his own soul? Or what will a man give in exchange for his soul?" Matthew 16:26

Money can buy many things and supply many needs and perceived needs, but a look at the lives and torments of many rich and famous will reveal the poverty of material riches.

"They trust in their wealth and boast of great riches. Yet they cannot redeem themselves from death by paying a ransom to God."
Psalm 49:6, 7 NLT

Winning the lottery or becoming wealthy has turned out to be a curse instead of a blessing for many people.

Some people go through life dirt poor but are rich. Others go through life on the lap of luxury but are miserable.

The bottom line is that riches without richness will never satisfy.

Richness cannot be measured by the car we drive, the house we live in, or the toys we own.

Richness should be measured by the fullness of joy we have in a real and personal relationship with God through faith in Jesus Christ that flows over into the richness of our relationships with others.

Richness should never be defined by what we possess but by Who possesses us. Only when we belong to God by virtue of a new birth through faith in Jesus do we become truly rich.

Money and riches can buy man's approval and acceptance, but it can never buy God's forgiveness, peace, and joy, which are free to all believers.

When we are filled with the richness of God's love as we grow in our relationship with Jesus through abiding in Him through His Word and growing more like Christ through the transforming power of the Holy Spirit, we will find out what real richness is all about.

"And the cares of this world, the deceitfulness of riches, and the desires for other things entering in choke the Word, and it becomes unfruitful."
Mark 4:19

Father, help me to seek and enjoy the true richness that only a right relationship with You affords. Amen.

Lord, You Are _____
Forgive Me For _____
Thank You For _____
Needs of Others _____
Personal Needs _____
Answered Prayers _____

What You Have Going For You

"And the joy of the LORD will fill you to overflowing. You will glory in the Holy One of Israel." Isaiah 41:16b NLT

When someone has looks, brains, athletic or artistic talents, we say they have a whole lot going for them. We have a tendency to look with envy on those who seemingly have so much more going for them than us.

"My heart is overflowing with a good theme; I recite my composition concerning the King; my tongue is the pen of a ready writer." Psalm 45:1

We sometimes are utterly amazed at how strong, how smart, how sweet, how talented or how much someone has going for them in a particular area in some other way.

How sad it is to see someone squander all that they had going for them through some bad choices or moral failures.

The truth is that as the redeemed children of God, we have a whole lot going for us. We have the priceless peace and security of knowing that we are unconditionally loved, forever forgiven, and are personal friends of Jesus.

Instead of thinking so much about what we have going for us, we need to think more of Who we have going with us as we travel as pilgrims in a barren land.

When we have Jesus as our Lord and Savior, we have "a friend who sticks closer than a brother," an advocate who pleads our case before the throne of God, a burden bearer, a lover of our souls, and the one and only beloved Son of God who came to die so that we would not have to die.

When we have Jesus going with us, we also have the Holy Spirit living in us to provide the resurrection power and strength we need to withstand the temptations of life that come our way in a sin-sick world.

When we have Jesus going with us, we know that our future is secure in the blessed assurance we have as the blood bought brothers and sisters of Christ.

"These things I have spoken to you, that in Me you may have peace. In the world you will have tribulation, but be of good cheer, I have overcome the world." John 16:33

If we don't have Jesus living within us by the power of the Holy Spirit, all that we have going for us is never going to be enough.

Father, keep me ever mindful and thankful of what I have going for me and living in me when I have You! Amen.

Lord, You Are _____

Forgive Me For _____

Thank You For _____

Needs of Others _____

Personal Needs _____

Answered Prayers _____

Transference

"The night is far spent, the day is at hand. Therefore let us cast off the works of darkness, and let us put on the armor of light." Romans 13:12

Transference is a tool psychologists use to replace bad attitudes and thoughts

"If you are willing and obedient, you shall eat the good of the land." Isaiah 1:19

with good as a means of treating mental illness. It is not a bad term to use in describing how Satan has used reverse transference to bring the world to the brink of destruction.

As God has been taken out of our schools, condoms, alternative life styles, sexual promiscuity, pornography, and drugs have been brought in to fill the void.

As God's truth and law have been taken out of the courtroom, relative truth and legal tricks have been brought in to often make a travesty of justice.

As God's order and prescriptions have been taken out of the home, they have all too often been replaced and attacked by the banalities and down right hostility towards God promoted on TV.

As scriptural authority has been diminished and redefined in many churches, licentiousness, blatant disobedience, and disregard for the commandments of God have become widespread.

The plain truth is that as God is moved out, sin and moral decay move in and the whole world is suffering the consequences.

There is a "holy transference" that must take place in the life of every true believer. We must die to sin and become alive in Christ by the power of the Holy Spirit if we are to be born again as redeemed children of the living Lord.

Our pride, anger, lust, envy, and any other sin that separates us from God will be replaced by love, joy, peace, longsuffering, kindness, goodness, faithfulness, gentleness, and self-control if we are the truly saved children of the living God.

"Humans can reproduce only human life, but the Holy Spirit gives new life from heaven. So don't be surprised at my statement that you must be born again." John 3:6

"Holy transference" is the only hope of the world. We need it now more than ever.

Father, bring holy transference back into the world, and let it begin with me. Amen.

Lord, You Are _____

Forgive Me For _____

Thank You For _____

Needs of Others _____

Personal Needs _____

Answered Prayers _____

What Price Progress?

"Nevertheless I have this against you, that you have left your first love."
Revelation 2:4

The World at large and America in particular has achieved the highest level of progress the world has ever known. Advancement in every technological and intellectual area has been unprecedented.

"The LORD says, 'O Israel, ever since that awful night in Gibeah, there has been only sin and more sin! You have made no progress whatsoever.'"
Hosea 10:9 NLT

The time involved in doing routine household chores has been cut by as much as 80 percent thanks to household appliances.

The abundance of leisure time now equals or surpasses the work time required to provide an abundant standard of life for many people.

All this being true, why is moral decadence surpassing the dark of the darkest ages? Why are divorces, addictions, teenage pregnancies, abortions, prison populations, national and personal debt, monetary and energy crises, and any number of other ills at all-time highs?

Somewhere along the yellow brick road of progress and advancement of civilization, virtue has all but disappeared. The God of the Bible has been replaced by the man-made gods of power, pleasure, prestige, and possessions.

The virtues of loving and serving God and loving and serving others have been replaced by the vices of loving ourselves and exploiting and using others.

We had better get back, and get back quickly, to that right relationship with God through faith in Jesus Christ and the virtues and values that this relationship imparts.

"Therefore, since we are surrounded by such a huge crowd of witnesses to the life of faith, let us strip off every weight that slows us down, especially the sin that so easily hinders our progress. And let us run with endurance the race that God has set before us."
Hebrews 12:1 NLT

Father, forgive our foolish ways and restore unto us and all the world the peace and joy of Your salvation. Amen.

Lord, You Are _____
Forgive Me For _____
Thank You For _____
Needs of Others _____
Personal Needs _____
Answered Prayers _____

Down Memory Lane

"Fix your thoughts on what is true and honorable and right. Think about things that are pure and lovely and admirable. Think about things that are excellent and worthy of praise." Philippians 4:8b NLT

We often think of special occasions and special scenes as "Kodak moments" and the perfect time to take a picture. We need to live our lives building "memory moments."

"They shall utter the memory of Your great goodness, and shall sing of Your righteousness." Psalm 145:7

Although it is not good to live in the past, it is certainly good to look back and learn from our mistakes and to enjoy the happy memories of a life well lived.

God has given each of us a film of life where our history is recorded, and we can rewind and recall.

As we climb the stairway to heaven through the seasons of life, we need to be mindful of what we will have to look down upon on memory lane.

Family or other reunions are mostly walks down memory lane where shared experiences are remembered and enjoyed. Treasured memories of growing up through childhood and adolescence include everything from sports to scouts, from learning to drive to graduation, and parents, teachers, and friends. As we get older, weddings, careers, children, and their lives continue to make deposits in our memory bank of life.

There are memories of mistakes made, sins committed, and opportunities lost that, although forgiven, will still cause us to have regret and godly sorrow. It is comforting to know that God remembers these confessed sins no more, and we should not fix our thoughts on them.

The fondest memories of all should be of falling in love with Jesus and remembering how He was always there for us, answered prayers, and continues to be not only our brother but our best friend. What joy there will be on memory lane when it has been walked with Jesus!

"For God is not unfair. He will not forget how hard you have worked for Him and how you have shown your love to Him by caring for other Christians, as you still do." Hebrews 6:10 NLT

Father, thank you for all the precious memories of "sacred delights" with which You have blessed my life. Amen.

Lord, You Are _____

Forgive Me For _____

Thank You For _____

Needs of Others _____

Personal Needs _____

Answered Prayers _____

Air Traffic Control

"Yes, and the Lord will deliver me from every evil attack and will bring me safely to His Heavenly Kingdom. To God be the glory forever and ever. Amen." 2 Timothy 4:18

The thousands of planes taking off and landing every day in most parts of the world submit to air traffic control to put them on a safe flight path and guide them to a safe landing.

"He makes me as surefooted as a deer, leading me safely along the mountain heights." Psalm 18:33 NLT

It would be utter chaos in the skies if someone were not directing traffic. How could the space flights operate without mission control at Houston?

Jesus knew that we would need a mission controller if we were ever going to arrive safely at our heavenly destination.

The friendly skies of life are not always so friendly. We have turbulence of every description that we must rise above, go around, or persevere through on the journey of life.

God knew that we not only needed a savior but also a traffic controller to guide and sustain us through the turmoil and strife of living as pilgrims in a sin-sick world.

He has given each of us the Holy Spirit to come live within us to guarantee a safe flight to our final and eternal destination.

The Holy Spirit comes not only to convict us of our sin and our need for a savior but to guide us into all truth and to conform us into the image of Christ.

He is the power from on high that covers our weaknesses with God's strength, which is the only way we can live in the freedom to grow into the fullness of Christ and become imitators of Him.

"Do not let sin control the way you live; do not give in to its lustful desires." Romans 6:12 NLT

Thank God we don't have to depend on our own sight to find the way home, but we can fly by faith with our personal flight controller.

Father, thank you for supplying my every need for eternal life now and forever. Amen.

Lord, You Are _____

Forgive Me For _____

Thank You For _____

Needs of Others _____

Personal Needs _____

Answered Prayers _____

Best Things That Never Happened

"For the angel of the LORD guards all who fear him, and he rescues them."
Psalm 34:7 NLT

The mysterious way in which God works His wonders is truly a wonder to behold. His ability to turn what we perceive to be bad into good is something we have all experienced and often to not realize until years after the fact or perhaps, even long after this life on earth is over.

"Your goodness is so great! You have stored up great blessings for those who honor You. You have done so much for those who come to You for protection." Psalm 31:19 NLT

What relationship breakup brought heart break at the time but turned out to be the best thing that never happened? What failed real estate purchase, job opportunity, or other deal has turned out to be the best thing that never happened?

I can personally attest to God watching over me and protecting me from many of my own impulsive, ill-advised pursuits that somehow fell through and turned out to be some of the best things that never happened in my life.

How many times have we been on the brink of succumbing to temptations of every description that turned out to be things that never happened thanks to the grace of God and the power to resist He gave by the power of the Holy Spirit?

God only knows how many times His angels have protected us from accidents and injuries that never happened.

We should never be surprised at the amazing grace of God and the truth that He really does work all things for our good and His glory. Scripture affirms that He turns what others meant for evil into good. When our ways are pleasing to Him, He makes even our enemies to be at peace with Him, and nothing can ever separate us from His love which is ours through faith in Jesus Christ.

"The eyes of the Lord watch over those who do right, and His ears are open to their prayers." 1 Peter 3:12 NLT

The next time one of your best laid plans doesn't work out, take comfort in knowing that your heavenly Father knows best, and that life is full of some of the "best things that never happen."

Father, thank you for Your divine protection and intervention. Amen.

Lord, You Are _____

Forgive Me For _____

Thank You For _____

Needs of Others _____

Personal Needs _____

Answered Prayers _____

The Energizer Bunny

"But you shouldn't be so concerned about perishable things like food. Spend your energy seeking the eternal life that I, the Son of Man, can give you. For God the Father has sent me for that very purpose." John 6:27

The energizer bunny has sold a lot of batteries but is not a good role model for living life to the fullest. Our spiritual batteries need constant charging to meet the peak power demands of life in today's world.

**"But as for me, I will sing about Your power.
I will shout with joy each morning because of Your unfailing love."
Psalm 59:16 NLT**

Our energy is being constantly drained trying to meet the demands and expectations of ourselves and others.

When we are driven by the pride, anger, greed, or lust of the flesh, we are going to experience severe power outages that will leave us burned out, used up, and totally drained of peace and joy.

When we pursue riches instead of richness, we are never going to get our batteries fully charged. The poverty of riches has ruined the lives of many wealthy people. The notion that "the one with the most toys wins" is a lie right out of the devil's handbook.

As believers, we need to know that "the one with the most joys wins." There can be no real joy without the peace of the Lord that surpasses all understanding.

When we use our energy to pursue the peace and joy of the Lord by growing in the knowledge and fullness of Christ, we are going to find our batteries fully charged by the power of the Word and through daily confession and repentance.

When we are driven by the desire to seek first the kingdom of God and His righteousness, we won't need the energizer bunny. We will have the inexhaustible and self-charging resurrection power of the Holy Spirit to supply our every need.

**"Do not waste time arguing over godless ideas and old wives' tales. Spend your time and energy in training yourself for spiritual fitness."
1 Timothy 4:7 NLT**

Father, let me find my security in knowing that You have promised the strength and power to meet my every need in Christ. Amen.

Lord, You Are _____

Forgive Me For _____

Thank You For _____

Needs of Others _____

Personal Needs _____

Answered Prayers _____

Read Matthew 16:24-28, Isaiah 1   March 15

When Giving Up is Easy

"The night is far spent, the day is at hand. Therefore let us cast off the works of darkness, and let us put on the armor of light." Romans 13:12

It is easy to give up things we never liked. I can think of all kinds of foods I can do without and not even miss. We can be very generous in giving away things that we no longer can use or things that cost us nothing.

"Wash yourselves and be clean! Let me no longer see your evil deeds. Give up your wicked ways." Isaiah 1:16 NLT

It's easy to give up sins that don't really beset us. The hard part is in giving up the things that we really enjoy or that we depend on for defining our self worth.

The rich young ruler went away very sad, because he couldn't bring himself to giving up his worship of wealth for worship of Jesus.

Millions of people who can't give up whatever it is that is more important to them than a right relationship with God die every day doomed to eternal torment.

The brush fires of the battle of the wills between our flesh and our Spirit will often continue even after we have spiritually died to sin and become alive in Christ .

The more control we surrender to the Lordship of Jesus Christ by the power of the Holy Spirit living within us, the easier it will become to give up the temptations of pride, anger, envy, lust, etc. that may remain in our flesh even after we have been born again.

Our sins will be easier to give up because we have the resurrection power and strength of the Holy Spirit to overcome our weaknesses.

When we sometimes lose a battle of the flesh, it is comforting to know that the war has been won on the cross of Calvary, and we can rise to fight and win with renewed strength and grace through sincere confession and repentance.

"If you try to keep your life for yourself, you will lose it. But if you give up your life for Me, you will find true life." Matthew 16:25 NLT

Giving up the things that are difficult to give up will never be easy when we depend on our own strength. When we learn to appropriate God's help by faith, we learn that things too difficult for us are easy for God.

Father, give me Your strength to overcome my weakness and make it easy for me to overcome the temptations that continue to come my way. Amen.

Lord, You Are _____
Forgive Me For _____
Thank You For _____
Needs of Others _____
Personal Needs _____
Answered Prayers _____

Read Colossians 3:1-10, Psalm 39

Getting Away From It All

"And when He had sent the multitudes away, He went up on the mountain by Himself to pray. Now when evening came, He was alone there." Matthew 14:23

For centuries holy people have chosen to get away from it all by going into monasteries and living lives of solitude and reflection.

"LORD, remind me how brief my time on earth will be. Remind me that my days are numbered, and that my life is fleeing away."
Psalm 39:4 NLT

We all have sins and temptations from which we need to get away and stay away. Whatever triggers or tempts us to sin needs to be avoided.

We are living in a stress-filled, energy-consuming world that will burn us out if we are not careful. It is all too easy to fall into the "toy trap" of pursuing possessions or standards of living that will impress instead of address, and we find ourselves being depressed and oppressed in the process.

The energy of life is not an inexhaustible resource. No matter how much mental, physical, emotional, or spiritual strength we may have, we can use it all up and burn out if we live at the max and beyond our capacity.

We need to get away from it all on a daily basis to recharge our spiritual batteries through devotion, prayer, and meditation with God. We need to get away from it all through rest and relaxation on a regular basis to avoid burn out and caving in to the pressures of living on the edge.

"In its place you have clothed yourselves with a brand-new nature that is continually being renewed as you learn more and more about Christ, who created this new nature within you."
Colossians 3:10 NLT

Jesus modeled the importance of getting away from it all. He often retreated to be alone with God and away from the cares of this world and the demands and expectations of people.

We must never let busyness take priority over growing in holiness as we live out our lives growing into the fullness of Christ.

Father, help me to get away from all of the things that are keeping me from growing into the fullness of Your Son. Amen.

Lord, You Are _____
Forgive Me For _____
Thank You For _____
Needs of Others _____
Personal Needs _____
Answered Prayers _____

Helping God Out

"Notice the way God does things; then fall into line. Don't fight the ways of God, for who can straighten out what He has made crooked?" Ecclesiastes 7:13

Of all the pursuits that require real spiritual wisdom and discernment, helping God has to be at the top of the list.

"Who has understood the mind of the LORD, or instructed him as his counselor?" Isaiah 40:13 NIV

While it is true that God is at work all around us and invites us to join Him in His work, we have to be very careful about confusing God's purposes and will with our human perception of His purposes and will.

Because we love God and want to live lives fully pleasing to Him and to be usable vessels in His service, it is only natural to let this love color our judgment at times and to make the wrong choice in some situations.

We can very easily thwart or complicate God's healing process for addictions and relationships by becoming enablers who prolong or prevent the "bottoming out process" God often uses to renew, restore, or prepare others to receive His wonderful gift of salvation.

We need to always cooperate with God, but we should never try to dictate what God should do based on what we would do or what we think He should do.

We should never let the devil's seeds of doubt and despair diminish our faith in the sovereignty of God and His faithfulness in keeping every promise He has ever made even through what we may perceive to be the worst of circumstances.

"I did this so that you might trust the power of God rather than human wisdom." 1 Corinthians 2:5 NLT

Jesus addressed this problem very well in His life and in the model prayer He gave us. When He was praying to escape the torment of separation from His Father during his descent into Hell, He prayed, "Nevertheless, not my will but thy will be done." He also taught us to pray: "Thy kingdom come, thy will be done on earth as it is in heaven."

It is through abiding in God's revelation of His will by living in and growing in His Word that we can discern how to really help God out.

Father, give me wisdom and spiritual discernment, patience, and faith to be a help and not a hindrance. Amen.

Lord, You Are _____
Forgive Me For _____
Thank You For _____
Needs of Others _____
Personal Needs _____
Answered Prayers _____

Going With the Flow

"Now it shall come to pass in the latter days that the mountain of the LORD's house shall be established on the top of the mountains, and shall be exalted above the hills, and all nations shall flow to it."
Isaiah 2:2

One of the basic laws of nature is that water flows down. This is also a basic law of human nature. On our own, we are bound to flow down to whatever level the lust of our flesh, the pride of our hearts, and the pressure of our peers takes us.

"He sends out His word and melts them; He causes His wind to blow, and the waters flow."
Psalm 147:8

The only water that flows upward is the living water that springs from the fountain of a new birth in Christ. The only thirst we will ever have when we are flowing with this water is for the kingdom of God and His righteousness.

This water will carry us upward and onward on our journey to our eternal home in heaven. We will be sustained by gushers of grace that will protect us from the currents of evil and rapids of destruction with which the world, the flesh, and the devil may try to pollute our streams of living water.

When it comes to going with the flow, we all have a choice to make. We can flow down the path of least resistance in the bondage of our will to the flesh and remain in bondage to sin and headed for sure destruction.

We can jump onto God's lifeboat of grace when He brings it, and begin flowing up into a new abundant life in Christ homeward bound to heaven as we grow into the fullness of Christ by riding the waves of His love, strength, and power to new heights of peace, joy, and security.

"If you believe in Me, come and drink! For the Scriptures declare that rivers of living water will flow out from within."
John 7:38 NLT

Instead of sinking deeper and deeper into sin and its consequences, we can rise in the resurrection power of the Spirit to live in freedom from the domination and condemnation of sin.

We all have a choice as with which flow we will go!

Father, may I always go with the flow of Your grace. Amen.

Lord, You Are _____

Forgive Me For _____

Thank You For _____

Needs of Others _____

Personal Needs _____

Answered Prayers _____

A Pillow to Lean On

"He grants a treasure of good sense to the godly. He is their shield, protecting those who walk with integrity." Proverbs 2:7 NLT

At some time or another, in some area or another, everyone is going to need a safety net or cushion.

**"I trust in the LORD for protection. So why do you say to me, 'Fly to the mountains for safety!'"
Psalm 7:1 NLT**

Our government provides benefits to cushion unemployment, retirement, and poverty problems.

Almost everyone gives thought to and makes provision for having a cushion to retire on in addition to social security benefits.

We take out auto and property insurance to cushion our loss from fire, theft, or other causes. We buy millions of dollars worth of extended warranties.

Every cruise ship has lifeboats, and every airplane has flotation devices and floating seat cushions to cushion the problem of disasters at sea.

The need for building a financial cushion through saving seems to have gone by the wayside as credit card debt soars into the trillions of dollars, and millions have no cushion to cover unexpected expenses or needs.

Everyone should keep in mind the distinction between making money and making a living. You only make over and above what you spend, and if you spend everything you make, you are barely making a living.

Whether it's spiritual, relational, financial, or physical, God is our best cushion in time of trouble. "He is our refuge and strength, our very present help" and is always only a prayer away.

When we put our trust in God and His promises, we are assured that He will work all things for our good and His glory. He will provide a means of escape for every temptation.

**"And He said to me, 'My grace is sufficient for you, for My strength is made perfect in weakness.'"
2 Corinthians 12:9**

We should all grow in our personal relationship with God through faith in Jesus Christ to where we know the blessed assurance that He has claimed us as His very own.

Father, may I always have the cushion of Your grace. Amen.

Lord, You Are _____
Forgive Me For _____
Thank You For _____
Needs of Others _____
Personal Needs _____
Answered Prayers _____

The Gift that Keeps on Giving

"The sin of this one man, Adam, caused death to rule over us, but all who receive God's wonderful, gracious gift of righteousness will live in triumph over sin and death through this one man, Jesus Christ." Romans 5:17 NLT

Diamonds may last forever, **but** many of today's presents will become tomorrow's trash. The only gift that really keeps on giving was the gift of eternal life given over 2,000 years ago on a cross at Calvary.

"He has given me a new song to sing, a hymn of praise to our God. Many will see what He has done and be astounded. They will put their trust in the LORD."
Psalm 40:3 NLT

This gift was not cheap. It cost God the life of His only begotten and dearly loved Son. We have only to receive it as graciously as it was given by admitting that we are sinners who need a Savior and that Jesus Christ is our Savior.

Salvation is a one-time gift that keeps on giving from now to eternity.

It gives us a new life of freedom from bondage to sin for now and forever. It is the wellspring from on high that pours out daily streams of grace, strength, and renewal.

This gift gives us the eternal security of God's unconditional love, forgiveness, and acceptance, not because we deserve it, but because Jesus Christ did and God accepted His perfect life and perfect sacrifice as payment in full for our sins.

"I am leaving you with a gift—peace of mind and heart. And the peace I give isn't like the peace the world gives. So don't be troubled or afraid."
John 14:17 NLT

This gift is self replenishing. No matter how many times we share this gift with others, we will have more than we originally received and always more than enough to share with others.

Because this gift is poured into corruptible containers, it must be continually replenished and refilled from the fountain of living water by daily confession and repentance. We dare not let the well run dry by ignoring or rejecting this greatest of all gifts.

Father, thank you for Your gift of salvation through Jesus. Amen.

Lord, You Are _____

Forgive Me For _____

Thank You For _____

Needs of Others _____

Personal Needs _____

Answered Prayers _____

Read Hebrews 12:14-28, Psalm 22   **March 21**
Be Careful What You Seek
"The LORD is wonderfully good to those who wait for Him and seek Him."
Lamentations 3:25 NLT

"Seek and you will find" is a truer phrase than most people realize, especially in a bad sense.

"The poor will eat and be satisfied. All who seek the LORD will praise Him. Their hearts will rejoice with everlasting joy." Psalm 22:26 NLT

When we go looking for trouble, we are sure to find it. When we are looking for faults, we will not be disappointed. When we are looking for reasons to get "bent out of shape," we will get bent.

God is the energy source for all life. Just as He breathed life into Adam, He gives us the energy of life and the free will to choose how to use it.

To waste our energy on seeking all the wrong things will leave little energy to seek and find the best that God desires for all and gives to all who will call upon His name in faith.

The prodigal son should remind us of the folly of seeking the pleasures of this world instead of finding the peace and joy that comes only from seeking the kingdom of God and His righteousness.

When we seek to know God better through a personal relationship with the Son that He has sent, we will find God's strength to cover our weaknesses and God's grace to sustain us and supply our every need. We will find that perfect peace and joy and all the good things that God desires to add to our lives.

"Try to live in peace with everyone, and seek to live a clean and holy life, for those who are not holy will not see the Lord." Hebrews 12:14 NLT

When we go through life in the energy of "love, joy, peace, patience, kindness, goodness, faithfulness, gentleness, and self-control," we will not have to worry about the energy that is our life being burned up and wasted in seeking all the wrong things in all the wrong places.

God is a rewarder of those who seek Him. He created us for His pleasure and His glory. These are the things we should be seeking,

Father, help me to be a seeker of You and Your righteousness. Amen.

Lord, You Are _____
Forgive Me For _____
Thank You For _____
Needs of Others _____
Personal Needs _____
Answered Prayers _____

Room at the Cross

"And anyone who calls on the name of the LORD will be saved." Joel 2:32a

Housing in many cities and countries is very scarce. We are running out of room. The Good News of the Gospel is that there is always room at the cross for all those who Jesus calls into saving faith by the power of the Holy Spirit.

"The LORD is near to all who call upon Him, to all who call upon Him in truth." Psalm 145:18

The garbage dumps are filled and out of room almost everywhere. Although the garbage of sin is accumulating more and more throughout the world, there is still plenty of room at the cross for dumping our sins and receiving freedom from guilt and bondage to them.

Garbage conversion technology is a big business as we seek to deal with waste management throughout the world. The cross is perhaps the greatest garbage converter ever invented as billions upon billions of people have laid down the burden of their sins and been converted through a new birth in Christ.

Scripture after scripture attests to the fact that there is room at the cross for everyone and anyone. Moses was a murderer, Paul was a persecutor of Christians, and David was an adulterer and murderer.

The cross has been open 24 hours a day, 7 days a week, 365 days a year for over 2,000 years. No one is ever too young or too old to find relief.

"Those who belong to Christ Jesus have nailed the passions and desires of their sinful nature to His cross and crucified them there." Galatians 5:24 NLT

When we die to our sin at the foot of the cross and pick up the cross of Jesus by following Him, we will find that He always has room for us in His Father's house.

Jesus not only has room; He takes the time to share our every burden, hear our every prayer, and make intercession for us to the Father that His righteousness will cover us that we may dwell in the House of the Lord forever.

Father, thank you for making room at the cross for me. Amen.

Lord, You Are _____

Forgive Me For _____

Thank You For _____

Needs of Others _____

Personal Needs _____

Answered Prayers _____

Redlining Life

"You put my feet in the stocks, and watch closely all my paths. You set a limit for the soles of my feet." Job 13:27

The importance of having a tachometer with the little red line at the maximum RPM's an engine can handle has doubtlessly saved many engines from burning up and prolonged the operating life of many others.

"When you go through deep waters and great trouble, I will be with you. When you go through rivers of difficulty, you will not drown! When you walk through the fire of oppression, you will not be burned up; the flames will not consume you."
Isaiah 43:2 NLT

All believers have a born in tachometer. It is better known as the Holy Spirit Who comes to make us aware that we have gone beyond the redline of sin and need a Savior. He then comes to live within us to serve as our conscience and pit mechanic on the raceway of life.

Growing into the fullness of Christ is a high-maintenance pursuit. The world is hell bent on self destruction as sin and depravity are out of control and are approaching the redline of God's coming judgment.

On a personal level, we are too often letting ambition, pride, greed, envy, lust, or other sins take us to and over the redline. When we let anything or anyone other than God control us, we are in mortal danger of burn out and burn up.

Just as engines thrive on good fuel, regular inspections, and oil changes, we need to thrive on the daily lubrication of God's grace, the attitude change brought by daily confession and repentance, and the high octane, uncontaminated fuel of God's Word.

"And I remind you of the angels who did not stay within the limits of authority God gave them but left the place where they belonged. God has kept them chained in prisons of darkness, waiting for the day of judgment."
Jude 1:6 NLT

There is no fast lane on the narrow road of eternal life for now or forever.

Father, keep me within your boundaries that I might not burn out or burn up. Amen.

Lord, You Are _____

Forgive Me For _____

Thank You For _____

Needs of Others _____

Personal Needs _____

Answered Prayers _____

What the World Needs Now

"Good counsel and common sense are my characteristics; I am both insight and the virtue to live it out." Proverbs 8:14 MSG

Once we have experienced the love of God and received eternal life through faith in Jesus Christ, what else could we possibly need?

"The LORD hates people with twisted hearts, but He delights in those who have integrity." Proverbs 11:20 NLT

Jesus has come to fill our every longing and has brought the grace of God through the indwelling of the Holy Spirit to supply our every need, whether physical, financial, relational, or spiritual.

It is great to have all the wisdom, knowledge, and faith in what great things God has done and has promised to do, but we need the virtue of godly character to go with our faith if we are to live our new life in Christ to the fullest.

Without the strength of character to persevere in our faith, we are never going to be all that we can be in Christ. Without giving evidence of our holy transformation in the way we live our lives, we must ask ourselves whether our conversion is real.

As works in progress, we all grow into spiritual maturity at a different pace determined to a great degree by how much we allow the grace of God to become manifest in us through growing and abiding in His Word, persevering through various trials, and bearing the fruit of the Spirit.

The Holy Spirit is determined to do whatever it takes to see that all true believers make it to heaven. If we insist on making bad choices and taking wrong turns, we can expect the consequences to be severe.

"But also for this very reason, giving all diligence, add to your faith virtue, to virtue knowledge, to knowledge self-control, to self-control perseverance, to perseverance godliness," 2 Peter 1:7

The more we cooperate with the leadings of the Holy Spirit and the teachings of God's Word, the less chastening and scourging we will need to be conformed into the image of Christ.

Father, help me to pursue personal holiness and righteousness worthy of my calling in Christ. Amen.

Lord, You Are _____

Forgive Me For _____

Thank You For _____

Needs of Others _____

Personal Needs _____

Answered Prayers _____

Futility of the Flesh

"Pursue a godly life, along with faith, love, perseverance, and gentleness."
1 Timothy 6:11b NLT

We spend wasted moments, hours, days, years, and even lifetimes living in the futility of our flesh.

"But as I looked at everything I had worked so hard to accomplish, it was all so meaningless. It was like chasing the wind. There was nothing really worthwhile anywhere." Ecclesiases 3:17 NLT

We are never going to find meaning and fulfillment for our lives on our own.

We pursue what we think will give us pleasure and make us happy only to find that there is no lasting pleasure or true happiness when we are separated from God.

As long as we persist in walking in the darkened understanding of the flesh and refuse to allow God to renew our minds by the power of the Holy Spirit, we can expect only to suffer the consequences of the corruption of our flesh and miss out on the fullness of peace and joy that can only be experienced by growing into the fullness of Christ.

Solomon was the wisest, richest, and one of the greatest and most powerful men who ever lived. He devoted most of his life to searching for understanding and contentment only to find that there was no such thing apart from God.

We are often so engrossed in chasing the rainbows of happiness as extolled by the world and pursued by our flesh that we never find the true happiness and joy that comes only when we find our validation and security through abiding in Christ.

"This I say, therefore, and testify in the Lord, that you should no longer walk as the rest of the Gentiles walk, in the futility of their mind," Ephesians 4:17 NLT

The incredible joy and blessings that come from abiding in Christ through abiding in the Word are never going to happen as long as we choose to feed the futility of the flesh by feeding on the fertilizer of the world as spread on TV, movies, porn, and by many peers and media pundits.

Father, help me to give up the trivial pursuits of the flesh and to pursue the righteousness and holiness of Christ in me as my hope of glory. Amen.

Lord, You Are _____
Forgive Me For _____
Thank You For _____
Needs of Others _____
Personal Needs _____
Answered Prayers _____

Is This the Thanks I Get?

"Therefore by Him let us continually offer the sacrifice of praise to God, that is, the fruit of our lips, giving thanks to His name." Hebrews 13:15

We all like to be appreciated. Spouses like to be appreciated by each other.

"Enter His gates with thanksgiving; go into His courts with praise. Give thanks to Him and bless His name." Psalm 100:4 NLT

Whether we are giving our time, treasures, talents or love to others, we appreciate it when those to whom we are giving express their appreciation.

The leprosy of ingratitude seems to be spreading all over the globe. The United States has been the most generous benefactor of every other country in the world, yet it is probably the most maligned.

When we experience the ingratitude of others, we should think of the ingratitude God has experienced since the beginning of time and the ingratitude Christ suffered throughout His life on this earth.

We were all created for God's pleasure and to glorify Him in all things. Scripture tells us that He inhabits the praises of His people and that we are to give thanks in all things.

God gives so much and asks so little in return. We ask so much and give so little in return.

We have received the wonderful gift of eternal life by merely believing in Jesus Christ. At the very least our lives should be lives of "thanksliving" to God for all the great things He has done for us. Living lives fully pleasing to Him and fruitful in every good work is the celebration of praise that God wants and the thanks that He should get daily from all of His children.

"And whatever you do or say, let it be as a representative of the Lord Jesus, all the while giving thanks through him to God the Father." Colossians 3:17 NLT

Father when I stand before You to give an account of the life You have given me, may You be pleased with the gratitude I have shown. Amen.

Lord, You Are _____
Forgive Me For _____
Thank You For _____
Needs of Others _____
Personal Needs _____
Answered Prayers _____

Let the Son Shine

"Don't hide your light under a basket! Instead, put it on a stand and let it shine for all." Matthew 5:15

When the Light of the World came into our darkness, He didn't come that we would hide His light under the darkness of joyless, self-centered lives that give no evidence that we are the redeemed children of God.

"Feed the hungry and help those in trouble. Then your light will shine out from the darkness, and the darkness around you will be as bright as day."
Isaiah 58:10 NLT

Jesus not only set us free from the bondage of sin but also set us free that He might freely live in and through us to accomplish the good and perfect will of God as we lead lives fully pleasing to Him and fruitful in every good work.

The secret that Christ living in us is our hope of glory should no longer be a secret, but it should be evidenced by the fruit of the Spirit that we bear in every area of our lives.

We should daily renew our power from the Spirit to overcome the weaknesses of our flesh by confession and repentance. We need to lay aside the encumbrances of pride, greed, anger, lust, critical or judgmental spirits, or anything else that beset us and keep us from being all that we are and can be in Christ.

Christ not only set us free, but He sent the Holy Spirit to live in us to guarantee that freedom and give us the grace and the power to live in it.

We can only become imitators of Christ by growing in a personal relationship with Him as we get to know Him through abiding in the Word and letting Him reveal Himself through it.

"But this precious treasure—this light and power that now shine within us—is held in perishable containers, that is, in our weak bodies. So everyone can see that our glorious power is from God and is not our own."
2 Corinthians 4:7 NLT

When we grow in our faith to the point that we truly believe who we are in Christ and start living like it, we will start letting the Son shine through us.

Father, help me to let Your love shine freely through me. Amen.

Lord, You Are _____
Forgive Me For _____
Thank You For _____
Needs of Others _____
Personal Needs _____
Answered Prayers _____

March 28 Read John 3:14-19, Psalm 116:13-19
How About a Faith Lift?
"Lift up your heads, O you gates! And be lifted up, you everlasting doors! And the King of Glory shall come in." Psalm 24:7

If the billions of dollars spent on face lifts were spent on faith lifts the world would be a better place.

"I will lift up a cup symbolizing his salvation; I will praise the LORD'S name for saving me." Psalm 116:13 NLT

Although outward appearances may be pleasing in our sight and many people may judge by them, it is good to always remember that God looks at our hearts.

There is nothing more beautiful in God's sight than a face lifted up to Him in praise, adoration, and obedience.

When our faith is lifted, we become partakers of the fullness of Christ's friendship, joy, and all of the blessings that obedience and faith provide.

We will all find ourselves down in the valleys of disappointments and discouragements that come from living in a sinful world among sinful people, including ourselves.

These are the times when we need a faith lift of God's grace that will lift us up above the suffering and doubt and sustain and strengthen us.

Daily abiding in God's Word and prayer will lift us up as we lift up Jesus. Corporate worship and fellowship with other believers will encourage and strengthen us as we lift up Jesus together.

Many find faith lifts in attending spiritual retreats, stadium events, and any number of Christian cruises offered each year.

Christian TV and radio are other good sources of faith lifts that will help us grow into the fullness of Christ.

"And as Moses lifted up the bronze snake on a pole in the wilderness, so I, the Son of Man, must be lifted up on a pole," John 3:14

There is no limit to the joy, peace, and security that are ours to claim by faith lifts.

Father, may I be lifted up as I lift You up in every area of my life. Amen.

Lord, You Are _____
Forgive Me For _____
Thank You For _____
Needs of Others _____
Personal Needs _____
Answered Prayers _____

Tears We Should Never Shed

"Let all bitterness, wrath, anger, clamor, and evil speaking be put away from you, with all malice." Ephesians 4:31

God has wired us all differently and made many of us more tender hearted and emotional than others. There are tears of sorrow, pain, and joy.

"The unfailing love of the LORD never ends! By His mercies we have been kept from complete destruction." Lamentations 3:15 NLT

The worst tears of all are the tears of bitterness, which we should never allow to take root in our souls.

When we consider all that we have been forgiven of and will have to be forgiven of, we absolutely cannot afford the tears of bitterness caused by an unforgiving heart. This root of bitterness is like a cancer that can rob us of our joy and even make us ill.

Tears of bitterness caused by anger at God are also tears that should never be shed. When tragedies or disappointments come, we should never fall into the trap of playing the blame game with God, because we are going to lose every time.

God is sovereign. He is in control of every situation. He can turn the worst of circumstances into the greatest of goods. We were created to worship, glorify, and fellowship with Him.

Just as Jesus submitted to the will of God in all things, including His persecution, torture, and unfair death, we too will be called to go through valleys of disappointments, losses, and other hurts.

"Therefore, since we are receiving a kingdom which cannot be shaken, let us have grace, by which we may serve God acceptably with reverence and godly fear." Hebrews 12:28

Scripture after scripture exhorts that we rejoice even in the bad circumstances of life and promises that we will be supplied with God's all-sufficient grace, comfort, and peace.

We are called to walk in faith in the belief that God works all things for our good and His glory.

It is good to grieve, to mourn, and to shed tears of regret with godly sorrow, but we must never allow ourselves to shed tears of bitterness.

Father, let no bitterness take root in my soul. Amen.

Lord, You Are _____

Forgive Me For _____

Thank You For _____

Needs of Others _____

Personal Needs _____

Answered Prayers _____

Don't Get Washed Away!

"For You have been a shelter for me, a strong tower from the enemy. I will abide in Your tabernacle forever; I will trust in the shelter of Your wings." Psalm 61:3, 4 NLT

We have probably all had the experience of getting caught in the rain and getting soaked in the process. We never seem to have an umbrella or rain coat when we need it most.

"And there will be a tabernacle for shade in the daytime from the heat, for a place of refuge, and for a shelter from storm and rain." Isaiah 4:6 NLT

There are also a lot of rain storms in life where we are continually going to get soaked and need to be under the shelter of God's wings in order to avoid getting washed away.

Just as plants need rain to grow, we need disappointments and adversities to grow through if we are ever going to grow into the fullness of Christ. This fact is often overlooked by proponents of the prosperity gospel who believe that faith promises a rose garden without any pruning or problems to encounter or endure.

In today's scripture, Paul makes it very clear that we are called not only to share in His glory but also to share in His suffering. It's part of God's character-development program He has designed to conform us into the image of Christ, Who is our only hope of real, everlasting glory.

When we daily put on the full armor of God, we can go through each day under the power of the Holy Spirit, Who supplies the umbrella of God's grace which will shelter and sustain us through every storm.

"And since we are His children, we will share His treasures—for everything God gives to His Son, Christ, is ours, too. But if we are to share His glory, we must also share His suffering." Romans 8:17 NLT

God has provided Jesus to save us and the Holy Spirit to keep us afloat when the rains turn into floods, and we are in danger of being washed away.

We can have peace and joy in and through every circumstance and shelter in every storm when we are anchored deep in promises and assurances of God's Word.

Father, by Your grace and the power of Your Spirit may I never be washed away. Amen.

Lord, You Are _____

Forgive Me For _____

Thank You For _____

Needs of Others _____

Personal Needs _____

Answered Prayers _____

Beware of Self Control

"Now you are free from sin, your old master, and you have become slaves to your new master, righteousness." Romans 6:18 NLT

When Scripture speaks of self control, it is not advocating that we live lives controlled by our flesh. It is talking about surrendering control of every area of our lives to the control of the Holy Spirit, Who has come to live within us when we receive Jesus Christ as Savior.

"Don't sin by letting anger gain control over you. Think about it overnight and remain silent." Psalm 4:4 NLT

Our flesh inherited every sinful inclination known to man. We are going to see these sins beset us in every area of our lives if we allow them to control us.

In our own strength we are no match for the wiles of the devil, the enticements of the world, and the weakness of our flesh. We need the resurrection power of God supplied through the Holy Spirit to cover our weaknesses with His strength and supply the all-sufficient, all-sustaining grace we need for living a Spirit-enriched and God-pleasing life.

If we insist on controlling our pocketbooks, we will miss out on the overflowing cup of material blessings God promises those who are generous to Him.

When we insist on controlling our sexuality by our biology instead of our theology, we are going to be partakers of the disasters that we see all around us that are the consequences of failing to give God control of this area of our lives.

"That's why those who are still under the control of their sinful nature can never please God." Romans 8:8 NLT

In our relationships with others, self control too often means selfish control that will make it virtually impossible to enjoy good fellowship and mutually beneficial relationships.

If we would think of God control when we think of what self control should really mean, we will have the proper control described as the fruit of the Spirit.

Father, help me to surrender to Your control in every area of my life. Amen.

Lord, You Are _____

Forgive Me For _____

Thank You For _____

Needs of Others _____

Personal Needs _____

Answered Prayers _____

Reactions
"For the Kingdom of God is not just fancy talk; it is living by God's power."
1 Corinthians 4:13 NLT

For every action, there is a reaction. We fight or flee, give in or hold out, react with joy or anger, with thanksgiving and praise, or cursing and withdrawal.

"Such people will not be overcome by evil circumstances. Those who are righteous will be long remembered." Psalm 112:6 NLT

Almost every medicine we take sometimes causes a side effect or more serious illness than what we are trying to treat.

The worst thing we can do in any situation is overreact. When we let our flesh control our reactions instead of our spirit, we will often find ourselves out of control which brings out our worst instead of our best.

We can diffuse many conflicts by taking proactive initiatives that will result in a favorable resolution of the conflict.

God calls us all to be proactive Christians. We are told to take the initiative in letting our lights shine so that others may be drawn out of darkness into light.

Whether we are reacting to sins against God or others, or the sins of others against us, we can often effect reconciliation by apologizing and reacting with the fruit of the Spirit.

We need to weigh our every action by the reaction or consequence.

Unconfessed and unrepented sins will usually trigger a downward spiral that will pull us down like millstones around our neck.

When we react to God's commands and calls with obedience, we will find ourselves lifted up and God glorified in all that we do and are.

God's grace is poured out in abundance as we react to His love for us. When we respond to God's love by loving Him and others with the love of Christ that is in us, we allow the Holy Spirit to fill us with the power from on high that will transform, renew, and conform us into Christ's image.

"Here is a simple rule of thumb for behavior: Ask yourself what you want people to do for you; then grab the initiative and do it for them!" Matthew 7:11 MSG

There are no harmful side effects to reacting to the love of God.

Father, help me to be a proactive Christian. Amen.

Lord, You Are _____
Forgive Me For _____
Thank You For _____
Needs of Others _____
Personal Needs _____
Answered Prayers _____

Cost Accounting

"Don't you see that you can't live however you please, squandering what God paid such a high price for?" 1 Corinthians 6:16 MSG

Knowing and counting costs is an essential for any business. To buy something that costs $50 and to sell it for $100 sounds good, but the real cost may well be over $100 by the time overhead expenses are factored.

"Ho! Everyone who thirsts come to the waters; and you who have no money, come, buy, and eat. Yes, come, buy wine and milk without money and without price."
Isaiah 55:1 NLT

On a personal basis, we too need to practice cost accounting. When we spend more than we earn and build up a huge credit card debt to cover the difference, we are going to learn what bondage to debt is all about.

It is a real mistake to confuse cost with value. Many spend their entire lives on trivial pursuits that have no real value and will not survive the fire of judgment that is going to test the value of everyone's spent lives.

We need to become more value conscious and less cost conscious in every area of our lives.

When we count the cost of selfishness, bitterness, pride, unforgiveness, lust, anger, jealousy, disobedience, or any other sin to ourselves and to others we will find that all of these things carry a high cost with no lasting value attached.

Although the cost of selling out to Jesus may seem high, and many may not be willing to give up their perceived sinful pleasures and flawed free will required, this price is nothing compared to the value received.

A friendly smile, encouraging word, or random act of kindness costs us little or nothing, but the value and benefits are high.

When we count what it cost God to reconcile us to Him, we should want to do everything with the freedom, power, and strength He gives us to give Him something of value in return by living lives fully pleasing to Him and fruitful in every good work.

"He paid for you with the precious life blood of Christ, the sinless, spotless Lamb of God."
1 Peter 1:19 NLT

Father, help me to daily count your cost in saving me. Amen.

Lord, You Are _____
Forgive Me For _____
Thank You For _____
Needs of Others _____
Personal Needs _____
Answered Prayers _____

April 3   Read Colossians 1:18-21, Psalm 71

How Far

"He says, 'You will do more than restore the people of Israel to Me. I will make you a light to the Gentiles, and you will bring My salvation to the ends of the earth.'" Isaiah 49:6 NLT

We all seem to be continually trying to extend our boundaries. As children we just naturally see how far we can go without being punished or corrected.

"My mouth shall tell of Your righteousness and Your salvation all the day, for I do not know their limits."
Psalm 71:15

As we grow older, we are often tested by people to see how far they can go in imposing their will or control over us, and we are continually seeing how far we can go in achieving our dreams or ambitions.

As believers, we should be ever mindful of how far we have come in our relationship with Christ since the hour we first believed and how far we have to go in being conformed in His image, which is God's desire for each of us.

The farther we go in growing in spiritual maturity, the more aware we become of how short we fall of God's glory. This awareness should fill us with the humility and graciousness of a true believer. The fuller we become in Christ, the less full of ourselves we will be.

When we see how far we can go in our own strength, we will sooner or later find out that apart from God we can do nothing that will please Him or bring us true peace and happiness.

We should be ever mindful of how far Jesus had to go in order to reconcile us with God and earn our forever life.

"This includes you who were once so far away from God. You were His enemies, separated from Him by your evil thoughts and actions,"
Colossians 1:21 NLT

When we think of how far God has removed our sins from us because of our faith in Jesus Christ, we should have no problem in going far on the road less traveled to love, honor, worship, and obey God and be faithful and fruitful in every good work for which He created us.

Our lives on this earth should not only be about how far but also about how well we travel as those who are "homeward bound"!

Father, keep me every mindful of how far Christ went for me. Amen.

Lord, You Are _____

Forgive Me For _____

Thank You For _____

Needs of Others _____

Personal Needs _____

Answered Prayers _____

Burning Bridges

"And when people escape from the wicked ways of the world by learning about our Lord and Savior Jesus Christ and then get tangled up with sin and become its slave again, they are worse off than before." 2 Peter 2:20 NLT

Someone once said, "Be kind to people on your way up so that they may be kind to you on your way down."

"I will hear what God the LORD will speak, for He will speak peace to His people and to His saints; but let them not turn back to folly."
Psalm 85:8

It is often easy to burn bridges with employers when we leave those with whom we have no further need or use.

People sometimes choose to walk out of churches, jobs, friendships, and even marriages instead of working out problems and disagreements and seeking reconciliation.

Sometimes our pride makes us want to "tell someone off," get in that last word, or win that argument and burn a bridge in the process. Our pride that will not allow us to admit a mistake or apologize even when we know we were wrong has probably burned more bridges than anything.

We need to burn our bridges to yesterday's sins and failures, repent instead of repeat, and move forward in our God-ordained purpose of growing into the fullness of Christ.

Jesus Christ lived and died to become our bridge to a right relationship with God through faith. The world, our flesh, and the devil are constantly igniting fires of doubt and despair trying to get us to burn this bridge by getting us to doubt our salvation and turn our backs on God.

"Live creatively, friends. If someone falls into sin, forgivingly restore him, saving your critical comments for yourself. You might be needing forgiveness before the day's out."
Galatians 6:1 MSG

We need to build stronger bridges of love, kindness, forgiveness, and patience with others so that we don't burn any bridges or become stumbling blocks to others.

Father, help me to be a bridge builder. Amen.

Lord, You Are _____

Forgive Me For _____

Thank You For _____

Needs of Others _____

Personal Needs _____

Answered Prayers _____

We Are All on Welfare

"He looked down on the Israelites and felt deep concern for their welfare."
Exodus 2:25 NLT

There is often a certain stigma and common attitude of looking down upon welfare recipients. Often this is based on St. Paul's admonition in 2 Thessalonians 3:10b, *"whoever does not work should not eat."*

"Whoever gives to the poor will lack nothing. But a curse will come upon those who close their eyes to poverty."
Proverbs 28:27 NLT

Before we get too critical and judgmental about the less fortunate, we need to be ever mindful that we are totally dependent upon God's grace and mercy as He provides.

We need to remember that everything we have comes from God and that we are all paupers save for the riches we have by His grace.

Unlike the welfare rights organizations that are always pushing for more and more handouts, we don't have to make demands for anything.

Our spiritual poverty qualifies us for God's welfare program the instant we realize our need for a Savior and ask for and receive the fullness of God's grace through faith in Jesus Christ.

We are transformed by the renewing of our minds through a new birth where we receive <u>G</u>od's <u>R</u>iches <u>A</u>t <u>C</u>hrist's <u>E</u>xpense a.k.a. GRACE!

"You know how full of love and kindness our Lord Jesus Christ was. Though He was very rich, yet for your sakes He became poor, so that by His poverty He could make you rich."
2 Corinthians 8:9 NLT

Our impoverished souls are set free from slavery to sin and are filled with power from on high to receive all of the riches of our inheritance as sons and daughters of the living Lord.

Our welfare is assured by the gift of the Holy Spirit who comes to live in us as a guarantee that all of the riches of eternal life are ours to enjoy forever.

Our welfare is second only to God's glory. He loves us unconditionally, forgives us forever, and accepts us just as we are. He begins working all things for our good and His glory as He begins conforming us into the image of Christ.

Father, thank you for putting me on Your welfare rolls. Amen.

Lord, You Are _____

Forgive Me For _____

Thank You For _____

Needs of Others _____

Personal Needs _____

Answered Prayers _____

Don't get Hooked!

"Moreover, no man knows when his hour will come: As fish are caught in a cruel net, or birds are taken in a snare, so men are trapped by evil times that fall unexpectedly upon them." Ecclesiastes 9:12 NIV

Scripture often speaks of people as fish. God called Peter, Andrew, and John from their fishing for fish to become fishers of men. Peter is still fondly referred to by many as "the big fisherman."

"The Sovereign LORD has sworn by His holiness: 'The time will surely come when you will be taken away with hooks, the last of you with fishhooks.'"
Amos 4:2 NIV

Fishing tackle stores have an astonishing assortment of lures, flies, and even live bait with which the angler is equipped to attract and hook any kind of fish, but these cannot compare with the lures used by the other "fisher of men."

Just as any successful fisherman knows when and where to fish and what kind of bait and tackle to use, the devil knows and exploits our every weakness and knows exactly when, where, and how to do it.

The devil often uses our biology to overcome our theology by exploiting basic sexual drives and instincts with a barrage of tantalizing temptations in TV shows, commercials, movies, and especially internet pornography that has hooked millions throughout the world.

Satan has used the deceptive and empty promises of feeling good or drowning sorrows to ruin the lives of millions through alcohol or drugs.

Others find themselves getting hooked on pride, possessions, power, or approval of peers where these become idols that keep them from "getting hooked" on the one thing needful for living life in the fullness of real joy and peace, now and forever.

"Once again, the kingdom of heaven is like a net that was let down into the lake and caught all kinds of fish."
Matthew 13:47 NIV

In our own strength, we cannot resist the lures through which "the other fisher of men" tempts us relentlessly. It is only through getting hooked on Jesus and receiving the incredible resurrection power of the Holy Spirit that we can escape the fire of the frying pan of the one who is always looking for more fish to fry.

Father, may I never get "hooked" by the evil one. Amen.

Lord, You Are _____
Forgive Me For _____
Thank You For _____
Needs of Others _____
Personal Needs _____
Answered Prayers _____

April 7   **Read 2 Timothy 2:15-19, Isaiah 43:1-7**
Are You Licensed?
"Giving thanks to the Father who has qualified us to be partakers of the inheritance of the saints in the light," Colossians 1:12

We live in an age of licenses. We need them to drive cars, fly planes, or pursue any number of professions or occupations.

"All who claim Me as their God will come, for I have made them for My glory. It was I Who created them." Isaiah 43:7 NLT

Most licenses require certain minimum qualifications for issuance. Many require the successful passing of a written or oral test and regular refresher courses in order to keep them.

Most of us would insist that our doctors and airline pilots be licensed for our protection.

Marriage licenses legalize sexual recreation and procreation with a seal of approval by both society and God.

Many occupations and practices have been characterized as having "a license to steal." The tax collectors of Jesus' day were characterized in this way.

Some people live their lives as though they have a license to sin, as though they can do whatever they want, whenever they want, with or to whomever they want without any consequences.

Circumcision was a form of licensing into the Old Testament household of faith. Holy Baptism should be viewed as our outward sign of our internal licensing as qualified, certified, bona fide, sanctified, and redeemed children of God and joint heirs with Christ.

As licensed believers, we have the privilege of practicing living at its best, free from bondage to sin and death. Our license will never expire if we keep it current and up to date through daily confession, repentance, and renewal.

"Nevertheless the solid foundation of God stands, having this seal: 'The Lord knows those who are His,' and, 'Let everyone who names the name of Christ depart from iniquity.'" 2 Timothy 2:19

While we may have a baptismal certificate to show as proof of licensing, the validation of our license will be in the transformed lives of faith, hope, and love we live by the power of the Holy Spirit, Who is our licensing authority.

Father may I never misuse Your license to love as a license to sin. Amen.

Lord, You Are _____
Forgive Me For _____
Thank You For _____
Needs of Others _____
Personal Needs _____
Answered Prayers _____

Keeping Up Appearances

"But the fruit of the Spirit is love, joy, peace, longsuffering, kindness, goodness, faithfulness, gentleness, self-control." Galatians 5:22, 23 NLT

The world seems to be obsessed with keeping up appearances. We spend billions on cosmetics, clothes, and even face lifts in order to project our image in what we believe to be a favorable light.

"That I may proclaim with the voice of thanksgiving, and tell of all Your wondrous works," Psalm 26:7

"Clothes make the man," and "you are what you eat," are just two of many slogans promoting appearance consciousness.

As believers we know that people look at outward appearances while God looks at the heart.

We need to be more mindful of keeping up appearances as we go out into a sin-sick world. We may very well be the only Jesus someone will see today or at least be the only one of His personal representatives with whom someone may come into contact.

When our hearts are right, our appearances are going to show it. We will be bearing the fruit of the Spirit in every area of our lives.

The world should see the difference God's extreme makeover has made in the way we talk, the way we walk, and the way we live. Others should be drawn to us like flies to honey wanting whatever it is that makes us so joyous, so content, so kind and loving.

"And whatever you do or say, let it be as a representative of the Lord Jesus, all the while giving thanks through Him to God the Father." Colossians 3:17 NLT

What kind of impression of Jesus will people see when they come in contact with us? Are grumpiness, irritability, and constant complaining and self seeking the appearances we want to project to others?

We are called to be not only believers but imitators of Jesus Christ. This means that we should be modeling His love, kindness, gentleness, humility, and compassion to others. This is what real "keeping up appearances" should be all about.

Father, keep me ever mindful of my need to "keep up appearances," glorify You, and let Your light shine through me. Amen.

Lord, You Are _____

Forgive Me For _____

Thank You For _____

Needs of Others _____

Personal Needs _____

Answered Prayers _____

Turning If Into Because

"I am praying to You because I know You will answer, O God. Bend down and listen as I pray." Psalm 17:6 NLT

Many of us spend too much time thinking about half-empty glasses instead of full glasses. We too often chase the rainbow of happiness as defined by the world and our flesh, and we miss the happiness that only godly contentment and security in Christ can provide.

"At midnight I will rise to give thanks to You, because of Your righteous judgments." Psalm 119:62

"I would be happy if" must be replaced by "I am happy because" if we are ever going to find the treasure for which we dig so diligently.

When we have Jesus in our hearts, we have all that we need to be happy. Because He lives, we have today's presents and tomorrow's promises.

Because we are unconditionally loved, forever forgiven, and totally acceptable by God by the righteousness of Christ, we have the security this love, forgiveness, and acceptance provides. We need not make our peace and joy dependent on the security of friends, possessions, power, or passions.

Not if, but when troubles and disappointments come as they most surely will, we can turn to the strength and power of God. Because God said it, we can believe that He does work all things to our good, that He will supply His all-sufficient grace, and that we can do all things through Christ.

"I counsel you to buy from Me gold refined in the fire, that you may be rich; and white garments, that you may be clothed, that the shame of your nakedness may not be revealed; and anoint your eyes with eye salve, that you may see." Revelation 3:18 NLT

Because He lives, we can live in the joy of today and the bright hope for tomorrow knowing that nothing can ever separate us from the love of God that is ours in Jesus Christ.

Because we can by faith rejoice and give thanks in all things, we receive that peace that surpasses all understanding. Happiness is not something to be longed for; it is something we have as sons and daughters of the living Lord.

Father, let me find my worth and happiness in my overflowing cup of blessings I have in Christ. Amen.

Lord, You Are _____

Forgive Me For _____

Thank You For _____

Needs of Others _____

Personal Needs _____

Answered Prayers _____

Freedom to Fail

"So I will restore to you the years that the swarming locust has eaten,"
Joel 2:25a

One of the downsides of our free will is the freedom to fail. Thank God, only our freedom to reject salvation through faith in Jesus Christ is fatal.

"Weeping may go on all night, but joy comes with the morning."
Psalm 30:5b NLT

All other failures may be painful, expensive, discouraging, depressing, and filled with consequences and regrets, but they are not fatal and are not final.

If we don't experience failures, we are not living to the maximum of our potential. God's grace and strength is at its best in our failures.

Peter failed miserably in denying Christ, but it was not fatal. Saul was a murderer and persecutor of Christians, but it was not fatal. Scripture is full of moral failures of every kind among God's elect.

The good news is that where sin and failures abound, God's grace abounds even more. There is no failure that God will not forgive when we confess with a contrite spirit and repentant heart. There is no failure that God's grace cannot turn into a learning and faith-building experience as we persevere and grow through it.

The old saying "no pain – no gain" is truer in more ways than we might think. When we fail, we need to acknowledge it, make restitution where necessary, learn from it, and continue growing into the fullness of Christ.

God is more willing to forgive and restore than we are to be forgiven and restored. Others may not be as forgiving and gracious, and we may well experience many painful alienations in our families, relationships, careers, and other areas of life.

"Who shall separate us from the love of Christ? Shall tribulation, or distress, or persecution, or famine, or nakedness, or peril, or sword?"
Romans 8:35

When we base our security and peace on the unconditional love and forever forgiveness of God that we have through faith in Jesus Christ, we are free to turn our backs on yesterday's failures and concentrate on today and tomorrow's successes as God works all things for our good and His glory.

Father, thank you so much for Your assurance that You are there to comfort and restore even in my failures. Amen.

Lord, You Are _____

Forgive Me For _____

Thank You For _____

Needs of Others _____

Personal Needs _____

Answered Prayers _____

Adjusting Our "Wanters"

"Don't copy the behavior and customs of this world, but let God transform you into a new person by changing the way you think. Then you will know what God wants you to do, and you will know how good and pleasing and perfect His will really is." Romans 12:2 NLT

The holy transformation that takes place in the new birth we experience when we receive Jesus Christ as Savior and Lord should be evidenced by a great "wanter" adjustment.

"But they delight in doing everything the LORD wants; day and night they think about His law."
Psalm 1:2 NLT

Many of the things we used to want to do and places we wanted to go lose their appeal as our love of God and desire to please Him gives us better things to do.

Along with the peace that surpasses all understanding, we receive the grace of godly contentment in knowing that God has promised to supply all of our needs and that no good thing will He withhold from those who love Him and abide in Him.

Failure to distinguish between wants and needs has led many into the bondage of credit card debt and slavery to maintaining an unrealistic standard of living, which robs them of true security and true joy.

When obeying God's commandments go to the top of our wants list along with becoming imitators of Christ, it is absolutely amazing how God works to supply so many of the desires of our hearts along with our physical, financial, emotional, relational and spiritual needs.

"And those who are Christ's have crucified the flesh with its passions and desires. If we live in the Spirit, let us also walk in the Spirit."
Galatians 5: 24, 25 NLT

When our prayers reflect our wanting what God wants instead of what we want, we will be amazed at how well and how often God answers our prayers.

When we seek God's moral excellence more than our old self-centered pleasures, we will begin enjoying the abundant life in Christ that will satisfy our every longing. We will experience the sublime truth of Scripture that God is able to do abundantly more than we dare ask or think. This includes His ability to adjust our "wanters."

Father, help me to adjust my wanter so that I want the things that You want for me above all. Amen.

Lord, You Are _____

Forgive Me For _____

Thank You For _____

Needs of Others _____

Personal Needs _____

Answered Prayers _____

Power From on High

"Behold, I send the Promise of My Father upon you; but tarry in the city of Jerusalem until you are endued with power from on high." Luke 24:49

There is a continual power struggle going on in every believer. We have the power from below, the power of our corrupted flesh, and the power of a world system.

"But those who wait on the LORD shall renew their strength; they shall mount up with wings like eagles, they shall run and not be weary, they shall walk and not faint."
Isaiah 40:31

God in His foreknowledge knew all about the control battle raging within us. He promised and delivered the Holy Spirit as our power source from on high.

The same resurrection power that raised Christ from the dead is ours to claim by faith to raise us from being dead in sin to becoming alive in Christ.

With this power from on high, we no longer have to be slaves to sin, but can become slaves to righteousness. We can harness the power of God's goodness and love to light up and overcome the darkness of sin and despair.

Our power from on high is wonder-working power. Just as it transformed a rag tag, motley, defeated group of disciples into bold and effective kingdom builders, it transforms us from sinners to saints and gives us all the power we need for leading victorious lives in Christ.

The height of pride and conceit is to believe that our own strength and power rather than God's grace and power are sufficient for all our needs.

"A final word: Be strong with the Lord's mighty power."
Ephesians 6:20

If we were sufficient in our own power and strength, Jesus Christ would never have had to suffer and die to become our Savior.

We should never under estimate the power from on high that is ours to appropriate by faith in Jesus Christ.

Father, thank you for the power for living a life pleasing to You that is ours through the power of the Holy Spirit. Amen.

Lord, You Are _____

Forgive Me For _____

Thank You For _____

Needs of Others _____

Personal Needs _____

Answered Prayers _____

We are Climbing

"Then he dreamed, and behold, a ladder was set up on the earth, and its top reached to heaven; and there the angels of God were ascending and descending on it." Genesis 28:12

God has given us all a stairway to heaven in Jesus Christ. By Christ's mediation on our behalf, He becomes our ladder by means of which we climb from human nature to divine nature as we become righteous in God's sight by faith in Christ.

"Who may climb the mountain of the LORD? Who may stand in His holy place?"
Psalm 24:3 NLT

By the providence of God, Jesus has become the ladder by which all of God's grace and favor comes to us and by which all our sacrifices of praise in the lives we live and good works we produce rise to Him.

Every step of faith we take takes us higher and higher as we grow into the fullness of Christ as we submit to His yoke of obedience by which we become imitators of Him in every area of our lives.

As we climb higher by growing stronger through abiding in His Word, we see more and more of the glory of God all around us. We become conduits of His glory as we accomplish the tasks that He ordained for us before we were even born.

When we climb by faith through growing in the knowledge of Christ, we are promised Jesus' friendship, His joy, increased awareness of the love of God and of others, and answered prayers.

As we climb the ladder by faith, the awareness of Christ living in us truly becomes our hope of glory and our transformed life becomes obvious to everyone around us as they see Christ in us.

"But grow in the special favor and knowledge of our Lord and Savior Jesus Christ."
2 Peter 3:18 NLT

When we climb Jacob's ladder, we will find the strength and the power to climb the mountains of distress and doubt with which the world, our old flesh, and the devil seem to be continually trying to block our way.

Father, help me to climb every mountain as I climb the ladder You provide to all who call upon the name of Your Son Jesus Christ. Amen.

Lord, You Are _____
Forgive Me For _____
Thank You For _____
Needs of Others _____
Personal Needs _____
Answered Prayers _____

Pray it Up!

"If you abide in Me, and My words abide in you, you will ask what you desire, and it shall be done for you." John 15:7

God answers prayers! We need to harness the power of prayer in every area of our life. Lifting our prayers up to God's throne of grace helps our spirits to be lifted up above the ordinary and into the extraordinary grace, peace, and joy of the Lord.

> **"In my distress I prayed to the LORD, and the LORD answered me and rescued me."**
> **Psalm 118:5 NLT**

God promises that when we pray up our sorrows and disappointments He will send down comfort, healing, and peace to our souls.

Prayer should be our channel for strength in times of conflict. When we pray the problem up before we bring it up, we are able to diffuse our anger and address the problem in a more conciliatory manner.

When we are faced with the often unpleasant task of speaking the truth in love, it is absolutely essential that we "pray it up" before we talk it up.

When we "pray it up" by praying unselfish prayers and submitting them to the good and gracious will of God, we will find His grace coming down in abundance in answer to our prayers.

> **"Be anxious for nothing, but in everything by prayer and supplication, with thanksgiving, let your requests be made known to God; and the peace of God, which surpasses all understanding, will guard your hearts and minds through Christ Jesus."**
> **Philippians 4:6, 7**

When David prayed it up, he received not only the protection and strength he requested but also the cleansing and restoration for which he hungered.

When Paul and Silas were imprisoned, they prayed it up in rejoicing and thanksgiving, and an angel of the Lord came down to set them free.

Scripture tells us that Jesus "prayed it up" through and during the triumphs and trials of His ministry.

When we are praying up, we are standing tall in the eyes of God.

Father, help me to experience the joy of answered prayers more and more as I abide in You and grow in knowledge of You and Your will. Amen.

Lord, You Are _____
Forgive Me For _____
Thank You For _____
Needs of Others _____
Personal Needs _____
Answered Prayers _____

Live It to Give It!

"Therefore by Him let us continually offer the sacrifice of praise to God, that is, the fruit of our lips, giving thanks to His name. But do not forget to do good and to share, for with such sacrifices God is well pleased." Hebrews 13:15 NLT

It's not only a privilege but also a commandment to give thanks to God. God inhabits the praises of His people. He ordained thanksgiving offerings and giving Him the first fruits of all that He has given us.

"I take joy in doing Your will, my God, for Your law is written on my heart." Psalm 40:6 NLT

As pleasing as songs of thanksgiving and praise may be to God and as generous as our material offerings might be, God is most pleased when we make our lives a celebration of praise to Him for the great things He has done and continues to do for us.

When we live the love He has shown to us by giving it to others unconditionally as He has given it to us, we will put a smile on God's face.

When we live on the sunny side of life with the peace that surpasses all understanding and the true joy that is ours in Christ, we will be giving this peace and joy to others.

As we live and imitate Christ more and more, we are going to find more and more for which to give God thanks and glory.

When we start living the life of a servant and displaying the moral excellence and obedience of Christ, we are going to be giving the faith, hope and love that we have received to others.

Giving lip service to thanks without the gratitude that is expressed in living out our thanks in lives fully pleasing to God makes us become "sounding brass and tinkling symbols."

"Though I speak with the tongues of men and of angels, but have not love, I have become sounding brass or a clanging cymbal." 1 Corinthians 13:1 NLT

How many times we can put our names in the place of the word love in 1 Corinthians 13:4-7 should be a reminder to us all of how much living is involved in real thanksgiving.

Father help me to live out my thankfulness in every area of my life. Amen.

Lord, You Are _____

Forgive Me For _____

Thank You For _____

Needs of Others _____

Personal Needs _____

Answered Prayers _____

Virtue Has Its Rewards

"Finally, brethren, whatever things are true, whatever things are noble, whatever things are just, whatever things are pure, whatever things are lovely, whatever things are of good report, if there is any virtue and if there is anything praiseworthy—meditate on these things." Philippians 4:8

We are all called to be imitators of Christ. The Holy Spirit comes to live within us to make this task that is impossible for us to do in

"The LORD knows the days of the upright, and their inheritance shall be forever," Psalm 37:18

our own strength to become doable in the resurrection power and strength the Spirit provides.

The theological virtues of faith, hope, and love and the cardinal virtues of prudence, justice, temperance, and fortitude should define the character and moral excellence of every believer.

Our hope of glory is in having Christ in us and living through us as we grow in these virtues and live them out in our every day lives.

When we survey the wondrous cross and the totality of God's love for us in Christ that it represents, we cannot help but respond in love to God with a desire to get to know Him better, to love Him, and to serve Him more.

As we accomplish this by abiding in Him and His Word, we receive the rewards promised to those who seek Him.

We will not only experience the satisfaction of being fruitful in the good works for which God created us, but we will experience Jesus' joy, His friendship, the awareness of His love and the love of others, and more answered prayers than we ever thought possible as we begin praying with the mindset of Christ.

"But also for this very reason, giving all diligence, add to your faith virtue, to virtue knowledge, to knowledge self-control, to self-control perseverance, to perseverance godliness," 1 Peter 1:5, 6

When we let eternal life begin on this earth by dying to sin and becoming alive in Christ, His ways, His truths, and His life, we will know the godly peace and contentment of living life to the fullest.

Father, help me to appropriate moral excellence in every area of my life. Amen.

Lord, You Are _____

Forgive Me For _____

Thank You For _____

Needs of Others _____

Personal Needs _____

Answered Prayers _____

The Other Graces

"And I am sure that God, who began the good work within you, will continue His work until it is finally finished on that day when Christ Jesus comes back again." Philippians 1:6 NLT

We all know about grace in terms of the unmerited love and favor of God poured out on the cross for us for our salvation. We seem to often forget about growing in the graces of moral excellence as imitators of Christ.

"Cause me to hear Your loving kindness in the morning, for in You do I trust; cause me to know the way in which I should walk, for I lift up my soul to You."
Psalm 143:8

Our new life in Christ comes with a new heart that the Holy Spirit will help us to grow in the graces that define our Christian character and virtue.

Christ modeled and defined most of these graces in the Sermon on the Mount. Other passages of Scripture list the fruit of the Spirit and other graces of holiness, without which we will not see the Lord and others will not see Him through us.

We should continually check our godly character development by examining how well we have incorporated these graces into our lives.

Developing godly character involves excelling in the graces of generosity, courage, and gentleness. We need to thrive on hope, kindness, and knowledge. Our diligence, longsuffering, love, meekness, and patience should be reflected in every area of our lives.

The grace of our peace should abound in our perseverance, purity, steadfastness, temperance, and wisdom.

"You must crave pure spiritual milk so that you can grow into the fullness of your salvation. Cry out for this nourishment as a baby cries for milk,"
1 Peter 2:2 NLT

Our Christ-bought freedom from domination by sin and the ressurrection power of the Holy Spirit allow us to be willing participants in God's character-development program.

We are all different works in progress. Some develop and mature more quickly than others. We need to avoid the pitfalls of sin and indifference that stunt our growth.

Father, give me a full measure of the graces that confirm who I am in Christ. Amen.

Lord, You Are _____

Forgive Me For _____

Thank You For _____

Needs of Others _____

Personal Needs _____

Answered Prayers _____

You've Been Redeemed!
"Let the redeemed of the LORD say so," Psalm 107:2a NLT

In terms of monetary value, the elements of a human body are worth a few dollars. Down through the ages of slavery, slaves were sometimes sold and traded for less than horses or cattle. Many became slaves because of the inability to pay their debts and were indentured until the debt was paid.

> **"I will go in the strength of the Lord GOD; I will make mention of Your righteousness, of Yours only."**
> **Psalm 71:16**

In God's eyes, we slaves to sin were worth His coming to earth as Jesus Christ and suffering a horrendous death on the cross to redeem us by paying our sin debt in full.

When we have been redeemed by the blood of Jesus through receiving Him as our Savior by faith, we have not only had the price paid for the forgiveness of every sin, but we have been redeemed and set free from the bondage of being held captive to and dominated by our sinful human nature.

As the redeemed brothers and sisters of Christ and children of the Living God, we have had our fellowship and right standing with God restored. We are free to live as "redeemed of the Lord."

Although this wonderful new life is a free gift, we should be ever mindful and ever grateful for the great price that Jesus paid to redeem us and live accordingly.

We should never pass up the opportunity to share the means and blessing of our redemption with others when the opportunity presents itself. We should always remember that we have been redeemed "that you may walk worthy of the Lord, fully pleasing Him, being fruitful in every good work and increasing in the knowledge of God" (Colossians 1:10).

In addition to saying we are redeemed, we should give evidence of the reality of our redemption by living like redeemed sons and daughters of the living God.

> **"Yet now He has brought you back as his friends. He has done this through His death on the cross in His own human body. As a result, He has brought you into the very presence of God, and you are holy and blameless as you stand before Him without a single fault."**
> **Colossians 3:22 NLT**

Father, keep me ever mindful of the price that was paid for my redemption and let me live like I really appreciate it. Amen.

Lord, You Are _____

Forgive Me For _____

Thank You For _____

Needs of Others _____

Personal Needs _____

Answered Prayers _____

Special Privileges

"Because of our faith, Christ has brought us into this place of highest privilege where we now stand, and we confidently and joyfully look forward to sharing God's glory." Romans 5:2

There are few privileges to match those enjoyed when we are fortunate enough to be part of a live and loving body of believers in fellowship with God and each other.

**"May He remember all your offerings, and accept your burnt sacrifice."
Psalm 20:3**

We receive double doses of blessings. The love, comfort, and encouragement of other believers are added to the love, comfort, and encouragement of God as we travel the journey of life together.

The privilege of being united in purpose with others in a cause bigger than ourselves and of growing together in our relationship with Christ as we grow in our relationship with others is something we should never take for granted.

The privilege of being part of the family of God with others who multiply our joys by rejoicing in our blessings with us and divide our sorrows by sharing and encouraging us through difficult times is also a great privilege.

When we have the privilege of being part of a body that brings out God's best in us to share with others, we will find the best of God's blessings flowing back to us.

Whether we are talking about giving of our time, talents, or treasures, we need to always be mindful of what a great privilege it is to give back a portion for the glory of the One Who has given them all to us in the first place.

**"They gave offerings of whatever they could—far more than they could afford!—pleading for the privilege of helping out in the relief of poor Christians."
2 Corinthians 8:4 MSG**

No matter in what area we are giving, we need always to remember that God loves and blesses cheerful givers. If we can't give our money, our talents, our time, or our praise cheerfully and not grudgingly, we are better off not giving it at all.

We should always remember that our giving is the only area in which God allows us to test Him. He wants us all to know that we can never out give Him.

Father, keep me ever mindful that giving everything cheerfully is the real celebration of praise and worship. Amen.

Lord, You Are _____

Forgive Me For _____

Thank You For _____

Needs of Others _____

Personal Needs _____

Answered Prayers _____

Are You Being Fertilized?

"Now no chastening seems to be joyful for the present, but painful; nevertheless, afterward it yields the peaceable fruit of righteousness to those who have been trained by it." Hebrews 12:11

We are not only called to salvation and eternal life, but we are also called to bear fruits of righteousness that are worthy of repentance. In other words, we are called to glorify God in the way we live our lives by showing that our repentance is real.

"They shall still bear fruit in old age; they shall be fresh and flourishing," Psalm 92:14

If, as Scripture says, we will be known by our fruits, what fruits do others see in us that indicate we are bearing the fruits of righteousness?

Along with showing our love for God and for others, we should also be excelling in the graces of giving, forgiving, and living as imitators of Christ.

God is long suffering and patient in waiting for us to receive His call, but He is not going to wait forever.

Once we have entered into His kingdom of righteousness by faith, we have the Lord Jesus Christ and the Holy Spirit fertilizing us with sanctifying strength and power to bear the fruits of righteousness in every area of our lives.

God loves us enough to do whatever it takes to instill the discipline of righteousness within us.

If we neglect our great gift of salvation and shut ourselves off from God's grace, strength, and power and no longer bear the fruits of righteousness or allow God to do the things through us that He purposed before we were ever born, we must question whether we are truly saved.

If we are just going through life just taking up space and not paying our rent with the fruits of righteousness, we need to pray for the cleansing blood of Jesus and the fertilizing power of the Holy Spirit to renew, restore, and refresh us and make us faithful to our calling as sons and daughters of God.

"The gardener answered, 'Give it one more chance. Leave it another year, and I'll give it special attention and plenty of fertilizer.'" Luke 13:8

Father, help me to live a live faith fruitful in every good work for which you created me. Amen.

Lord, You Are _____
Forgive Me For _____
Thank You For _____
Needs of Others _____
Personal Needs _____
Answered Prayers _____

Where Shall We Go?

"But Simon Peter answered Him, 'Lord, to whom shall we go? You have the words of eternal life. Also we have come to believe and know that You are the Christ, the Son of the living God.'" John 6:68

The phrase: "Don't go there" has become widely used as a warning or reminder to help us avoid arguments, sins, and other dangers. There are neighborhoods in practically every city where we are told, "Don't go there!"

"There is a way that seems right to a man, But its end is the way of death."
Proverbs 16:2 NLT

Many arguments, sins, and their consequences can be avoided if we just "don't go there" when temptations or provocations arise.

The road to destruction is wide and heavily travelled. When God gave us our free will, He knew that many would go to places they shouldn't go, do things they shouldn't do, and live lives wandering aimlessly lost and separated from God.

The narrow gate and more difficult road that we must travel as disciples of Jesus Christ are well worth the going.

As believers, we are clearly taught, empowered, and encouraged where and to whom to go for help in time of trouble, for forgiveness, for strength, and for grace sufficient for our every need.

We are invited to go to God's throne of grace daily for confession, repentance, and refreshing from the well of living water. We are privileged to go on the road to holiness by going into God's Word and into God's house where we receive the nourishment that only the Bread of Life can provide.

"But the way of getting right with God through faith says, 'You don't need to go to heaven' (to find Christ and bring him down to help you)."
Romans 10:6 NLT

We must sometimes go to the dark Gethsemane of suffering with and for the sake of Christ if we are to share in His glory.

The sooner we learn to obey the green lights of go in obedience to God and to stop going our own disobedient and sinful ways, the sooner we will know what the true peace and joy of the Lord is all about.

Father, help me to go Your way in every area of my life. Amen.

Lord, You Are _____

Forgive Me For _____

Thank You For _____

Needs of Others _____

Personal Needs _____

Answered Prayers _____

Second Thoughts

"Then Jesus told them, "I assure you, if you have faith and don't doubt, you can do things like this and much more. You can even say to this mountain, 'May God lift you up and throw you into the sea,' and it will happen." Matthew 21:21 NLT

Henry Blackaby and Claude King's life-changing Experiencing God – Knowing and Doing the Will of God *calls it a "crisis of belief."*

"Choose to love the LORD your God and to obey Him and commit yourself to Him, for He is your life."
Deuteronomy 30:20a

Whatever you want to call it, Satan can be depended upon to throw darts of doubt anytime we go on mission for or with God.

The key issue is overcoming the fear of trusting God. The children of Israel's fear in trusting God resulted in a whole generation never seeing the Promised Land that He had promised. God had parted the sea, destroyed the pursuing Egyptian army, and they still did not trust Him to give them the land flowing with milk and honey. As a result, they spent 40 years wandering aimlessly lost in the desert.

When we start having second thoughts about doing something God has laid upon our hearts to do, we need to remember to "walk by faith and not by sight" and "believe that God exists and is a rewarder of those who seek Him." We need to let go and let God go through us.

It is absolutely amazing at how second thoughts vanish and renewed strength and resolve take over when we turn our fears over to God in total trust and dependency.

Sometimes the Holy Spirit gives us second thoughts to deter pursuing ill conceived agendas that are not really God driven. We need to diligently pursue spiritual wisdom and discernment in order to be sure that our leadings are from God.

"So, you see, it is impossible to please God without faith. Anyone who wants to come to Him must believe that there is a God and that He rewards those who sincerely seek Him."
Hebrews 11:6 NLT

We only have one life to live on this earth, and we dare not let second thoughts keep us from living it in the fullness of Christ.

Father, give me the courage to obey Your leadings. Amen.

Lord, You Are _____

Forgive Me For _____

Thank You For _____

Needs of Others _____

Personal Needs _____

Answered Prayers _____

Read 1 John 2, Exodus 20:6-17

What Part of Not?

"Don't you realize that whatever you choose to obey becomes your master? You can choose sin, which leads to death, or you can choose to obey God and receive His approval." Romans 6:16 NLT

It's amazing that so many of us at times seem to not understand this simple, three-letter word. Maybe we inherited our apparent misunderstanding from Eve, who did not obey it.

"But I lavish My love on those who love me and obey My commands, even for a thousand generations." Exodus 20:6 NLT

Most children are born with a rebellious streak that will make them want to do whatever is forbidden just to test the boundaries their parents set for them.

Sin seems to have an insidious way of starting with something small and then mushrooming into major rebellion as we find ourselves seeming to get by with our disobedience without any obvious, dire consequences. Satan seems to still be working overtime to cause us to doubt if God really said "don't" or thou "shalt not."

We seem to have many churches that seem to have rewritten the Bible and have taken out all the prohibitions and made our freedom in Christ a license to do whatever we want in the name of love.

God is love, and He has set us free not to live in bondage to sin but to live above it in the power of the Holy Spirit living within us if we believe in Jesus.

Because God is love, He wants the very best for all of us and gives us guidelines for bringing out our very best. Failure to realize this often leads to falling for the deceits of the world, the flesh, and the devil and doing the very things God has commanded us not to do. We don't do the things He has commanded and came to earth to model for us as Jesus Christ.

"If someone says, 'I belong to God,' but doesn't obey God's commandments, that person is a liar and does not live in the truth." 1 John 2:4 NLT

Whether our disobedience is in the area of putting gods of pride, possessions, applause, or pleasure in front of God; not honoring our parents; or lying, stealing, or committing adultery, our failure to understand and obey God's "shalt nots" will make it impossible for us to experience life in the fullness of Christ.

Father, keep me ever mindful of the guide posts You have set for my good and Your glory. Amen.

Lord, You Are _____

Forgive Me For _____

Thank You For _____

Needs of Others _____

Personal Needs _____

Answered Prayers _____

A Sell Out!

"Demas has deserted me because he loves the things of this life and has gone to Thessalonica. Crescens has gone to Galatia, and Titus has gone to Dalmatia." 2 Timothy 4:10 NLT

Every merchant, sports team, theatrical producer, or manufacturer likes nothing better than a "sell out."

"Then Jacob gave Esau some bread and lentil stew. Esau ate and drank and went on about his business, indifferent to the fact that he had given up his birthright."
Genesis 25:34 NLT

As believers, we are called to become sold out to Christ. When we by faith buy into the wonderful new life in Christ by receiving Jesus Christ as our Savior, we are called into a personal relationship where we sell out our old sinful nature and replace it with a new heart filled with the love, joy, peace, and resurrection power of the Holy Spirit who comes to live within us.

There is nothing God likes better than a heart sold out to Him in total adoration, obedience, and commitment. Unfortunately, there is a dark side to a sell out that is probably the worst thing that can happen to anyone.

When we sell out our birth right as sons and daughters of the living God for the pottage of sin and the trivial pursuits of power, possessions, and pleasure, we begin sliding down a slippery slope towards destruction and misery where there is no lasting joy and no bright hope for tomorrow.

God knows our hearts even better than we know them. When our minds' attention and hearts' affection are not anchored in His love and His Word, we are fair game for the attacks of the devil who is out to destroy us.

God does not give us guidelines to rob us of our happiness and joy. Rather, He gives us guidelines that will give us happiness and joy to the fullest because He loves us and wants us to experience the fullness of joy that can only come through a right relationship with Him through His Son.

"Watch out for the Esau syndrome: trading away God's lifelong gift in order to satisfy a short-term appetite."
Hebrews 12:16 MSG

Before we completely sell out we need to take broken spirits and contrite hearts to God's throne of grace restoration of the joy of our salvation.

Father, let me be sold on You and Your will for my life in Christ. Amen.

Lord, You Are _____

Forgive Me For _____

Thank You For _____

Needs of Others _____

Personal Needs _____

Answered Prayers _____

Our Daily Bread

"But Jesus answered him, saying, "It is written, 'Man shall not live by bread alone,but by every word of God.'"Luke 4:4

Our Lord knows and provides for our physical needs for nourishment. He always has and always will provide.

"All this happened so they would follow His principles and obey His laws. Praise theLORD!" Psalm 105:40

As we pray daily for physical bread, we need to always remember that we need our spiritual daily "Bread of Life" even more.

For most of us, spiritual starvation is a much bigger problem than physical starvation.

When we neglect feeding on Jesus, the Bread of Life, we create a vacuum that the world, the flesh, and the devil are more than willing to fill.

The world has become Satan's playground, and evil has taken over a vast majority of what used to be good things God gave us to enjoy and to glorify Him. All we have to do is watch TV on any given evening or even watch with horror what is happening in the name of free speech, freedom to choose, and the promotion of alternative life styles. We will find the mammon of death and decay.

While our flesh may flourish on physical bread alone, when we let our flesh get the upper hand by starving our spirit, we are heading down the wide road to destruction and despair.

Satan is the master of deceit and manipulation. He knows the art of finding and exploiting our every weakness. Without the daily Bread of Life, we are fair game and sitting targets for the darts the evil one throws at us daily.

Our all-knowing, ever-loving God also knows our every weakness, and in His love and mercy, He has provided His grace to overcome them in His strength.

"Jesus replied, 'I am the bread of life. No one who comes to Me will ever be hungry again. Those who believe in Me will never thirst.'" John 6:35

God's marvellous provision is His full armor that He provides as we dine at His sumptuous table of grace when we feed on the daily Bread of Life through reading His Word, prayer, and the fellowship of other believers.

Father, may I never neglect feeding on the daily bread of my spiritual life in Christ. Amen.

Lord, You Are _____
Forgive Me For _____
Thank You For _____
Needs of Others _____
Personal Needs _____
Answered Prayers _____

Who's Minding the Store?

"And He said to them, 'Why did you seek Me? Did you not know that I must be about My Father's business?'" Luke 2:49

Franchising has become the most successful means yet devised for expanding business. Once you get a good restaurant, cleaning method, or prosperous store, you can sell franchises, teach others your methods, and give them a franchise to conduct the business in another location.

> **"All goes well for those who are generous, who lend freely and conduct their business fairly." Psalm 112:5 NLT**

When you think about it, this is the way that God has chosen to expand His business throughout the world. He works through the Word and the Holy Spirit to franchise and train people to fulfill the Great Commission.

Denominations are constantly expanding the kingdom of God by franchising and planting new churches.

On a personal basis, we all need to be ever mindful that we have been "franchised" by God to do business on His behalf until Christ returns. God's business is all about the Great Commandment and Great Commission, and this must be our business if we are to live lives pleasing to Him and fruitful in the good works that He has planned for us.

God's franchise gives each franchisee special gifting for ministry. Some are called to proclaim truth, others to teach it. Some are gifted to help and serve others. Others are given a passion for giving or leadership. You may be gifted to be an encourager or merciful.

If you have been saved, you have been gifted, and you need to recognize your gift and use it to expand God's business by using it to build up the Kingdom of God. You will see and be encouraged by the blessing of seeing your gift used by God to build up the body.

> **"You did not choose me, but I chose you and appointed you to go and bear fruit— fruit that will last. Then the Father will give you whatever you ask in My name." John 15:16**

We all need to be ever mindful of how well we manage the store God has given us in this life will determine how much we will be privileged to manage in the next. We must make God's business our business.

Father, help me to manage well the business of the life You have given me. Amen.

Lord, You Are _____

Forgive Me For _____

Thank You For _____

Needs of Others _____

Personal Needs _____

Answered Prayers _____

First Things First

"Your heavenly Father already knows all your needs, and He will give you all you need from day to day if you live for Him and make the Kingdom of God your primary concern." Matthew 6:32b, 33 NLT

Noah was all about putting first things first. He put his faith in God and obedience to Him ahead of all the ridicule of the world and labored with perserverance for 120 years in building the ark.

"And the LORD was pleased with the sacrifice and said to Himself, 'I will never again curse the earth, destroying all living things, even though people's thoughts and actions are bent toward evil from childhood.'" Genesis 8:21 NLT

It is good to remember that the first thing He did after leaving the ark was to build an altar and make a burnt offering to God. Noah knew Who to put first in all things.

Because of Noah's faithfulness in putting first things first, we have the rainbow as a sign of God's promise that He will not destory the earth with a flood and the promise that there will always "be springtime and harvest, cold and heat, winter and summer, day and night" (Genesis 8:22b).

Abraham's putting obedience to God above the life of his own son and many other examples of the heroes of the faith putting first things first and the blessings they received for this should keep us ever focused on putting God and His righteousness first in our lives.

When we put the possessions, the pleasures, and the approvals of this world first, we are going to miss out on many of the great plans God has made to bless us. God hates idolatry of any kind and will certainly not settle for being less than first in our heart's affection.

When our faith leads us to obey God cheerfully and faithfully in every area of our lives, the channels of God's blessings are opened, and God's overflowing cup of blessings will be poured out upon us all the days of our lives forever.

"Then He said to the crowd, 'If any of you wants to be My follower, you must put aside your selfish ambition, shoulder your cross daily, and follow Me.'" Luke 9:23 NLT

Father, may I always make You my first consideration in all things. Amen.

Lord, You Are _____

Forgive Me For _____

Thank You For _____

Needs of Others _____

Personal Needs _____

Answered Prayers _____

Stunting Our Growth

"From the ends of the earth I call to you, I call as my heart grows faint; lead me to the rock that is higher than I." Psalm 61:1-3 NIV

I remember being told as a child that smoking cigarettes would stunt my growth. Today, malnutrition is widely recognized as the leading cause of stunted growth.

> **"They are like stunted shrubs in the desert, with no hope for the future. They will live in the barren wilderness, on the salty flats where no one lives."**
>
> **Jeremiah 17:6 NLT**

When it comes to stunting our spiritual growth, our flesh, the world, and Satan are all doing their best to make us spiritual dwarfs unworthy of claiming, and actually shaming, the name of Christ.

We are being fed lie after lie by TV programs, commercials, humanism in the schools that stunt our spiritual growth before we realize it..

When we buy into the world's definitions of success and pleasure, we are selling out God's plans and purposes.

When we put a steady diet of garbage into our minds, it is going to pollute our hearts, and we are never going to be or do all that God wants us to be or accomplish, which He planned for us even before we were born.

Our ever-loving and all-knowing Heavenly Father is never taken by surprise. He knew we needed a Savior and also a comforter and enabler to overcome the forces of evil conspiring against us.

God provides His own vitamins to assure our spiritual growth into the fullness of Christ. The helmet of salvation, breastplate of righeousness, sandals of peace, sword of the spirit, shield of faith, and belt of truth will allow us to grow strong and withstand all of the darts that come our way.

> **"You must crave pure spiritual milk so that you can grow into the fullness of your salvation. Cry out for this nourishment as a baby cries for milk."**
> **1 Peter 2:2 NLT**

Along with God's vitamin supplements, Christ has come to set us free from bondage to the besetting sins that stunt our growth. What joy there is in knowing that "greater is He that is in you than he who is in the world."

Father, help me to grow strong and mature by the power of Your Spirit and the armor You provide. Amen.

Lord, You Are _____

Forgive Me For _____

Thank You For _____

Needs of Others _____

Personal Needs _____

Answered Prayers _____

The Return Trip

"But if you warn them and they repent, they will live, and you will have saved your own life, too." Ezekial 3:21 NLT

Before going down the primrose path of sin, it is good to think of the return trip.

"Repent, and turn from all your transgressions, so that iniquity will not be your ruin." Ezekial 18:30b NLT

Is the fleeting pleasure in satisfying our lust, our anger, or our egoes really worth the guilt or other consequences that we will have to carry back?

Are the consequences that others will have to pay for our misconduct something we want to live with, often, for the rest of our lives?

When we willfully sin against God with unrepented sins, we are burning the bridge of reconciliation that Jesus built for us on the cross of calvary. When we willfully and deliberately offend others without the slightest trace of remorse or sorrow, we are burning bridges that may never be rebuilt.

We need to burn the bridges of our past sins and failures against God and others with true godly sorrow, confession, and repentance at the cross.

We must always strive to build bridges of forgiveness towards others if we ever hope to receive the forgiveness we are going to need.

The old saying that what goes around comes around is especially true in the area of reaping what we sew in the area of our sins.

The only way we can ever hope to break this circle is to repent or turn away from our sins and return to the sheltering wings of God's grace where we will find the outstretched arms of God ready to forgive and forget.

"So he returned home to his father. And while he was still a long distance away, his father saw him coming. Filled with love and compassion, he ran to his son, embraced him, and kissed him." Luke 15: 20 NLT

God will not only give the grace of forgiveness but also the power to break the chains of sin that have bound us and to return to living lives fully pleasing to Him.

Father, keep me ever mindful that there is never a point of no return for those Who truly return to You with a broken spirit and contrite heart. Amen.

Lord, You Are _____

Forgive Me For _____

Thank You For _____

Needs of Others _____

Personal Needs _____

Answered Prayers _____

Just Like You?

"For the Christian wife brings holiness to her marriage, and the Christian husband brings holiness to his marriage. Otherwise, your children would not have a godly influence, but now they are set apart for Him."
1 Corinthians 7:14 NLT

It should be a very sobering and challenging reminder to think that your children will most likely grow up to be "just like you."

"Then they will not be like their ancestors stubborn, rebellious, and unfaithful, refusing to give their hearts to God."
Psalm 78:8 NLT

In this day and age, the question of who your children are going to grow up to be like takes on new importance as we entrust so much of our children's lives to daycare centers, schools, and the worst baby center ever invented – TV.

Do you really want your children to grow up being like their day school caregiver, their teachers of various orientations and persuasions, or the so called "beautiful people" on TV who seem to enjoy alternative life styles and hedonism to the max?

Do you want your children to be "just like you" always nagging and complaining, angry, treating your spouse like dirt, or breaking promises and commitments as if they were never made?

Do you want your children to be "just like you" when you ignore God and religion as irrelevant and make yourselves the center of the universe instead of God?

When you monitor and restrict the garbage intake from TV, give careful consideration as to whom you will entrust your children's care, education, and friendships. You can make a difference in whom your child will grow up to be when you model the love of Christ and love of others in your life.

"And now a word to you fathers. Don't make your children angry by the way you treat them. Rather, bring them up with the discipline and instruction approved by the Lord."
Ephesians 6:4 NLT

Father, help me to take seriously the modelling of Christ to my children. Amen.

Lord, You Are _____

Forgive Me For _____

Thank You For _____

Needs of Others _____

Personal Needs _____

Answered Prayers _____

Changing "Haves" to "Wants"

"For this is the love of God, that we keep His commandments. And His commandments are not burdensome." 1 John 5:3 NLT

God does not honor giving, serving, or obeying grudgingly. Just as He loves a cheerful giver, He loves the faithful believer who worships, serves, and obeys willingly and joyfully.

"A wise person is hungry for truth, while the fool feeds on trash."
Proverbs 15:14

Obedience is the channel of God's blessing when we obey out of love and respect for God and what He has done for us through Jesus.

When we are truly born again, we are given freedom not only from bondage to sin but freedom to love God with all of our mind, heart, and soul.

We are given the freedom and power to bear the fruit of the Spirit – to live lives filled with love, joy, peace, longsuffering, kindness, goodness, faithfulness, gentleness, and self-control.

God's desire that we live lives fully pleasing to Him and fruitful in every good work becomes the desire of our hearts as we submit ourselves to obedience to Christ by the power of the Holy Spirit.

When our relationship with Christ is right, we will find that it is not a matter of having to do anything but of wanting to do everything that pleases Him.

"And all of us have had that veil removed so that we can be mirrors that brightly reflect the glory of the Lord. And as the Spirit of the Lord works within us, we become more and more like Him and reflect His glory even more."
2 Corinthians 3:18

As we grow into the fullness of Christ, the old sins that used to control us no longer have that control. The old ideas of what it takes to be happy are replaced by the discovery of the true happiness and real joy we find in a love relationship with Jesus.

Just as Jesus found joy in doing the will of the Father Who sent Him, we will find joy in wanting to do the will of the Father Who loved us enough to send Jesus to die that we might live forever.

Father by the power of Your Spirit, help me to find the real joy of cheerful obedience in every area of my life. Amen.

Lord, You Are _____

Forgive Me For _____

Thank You For _____

Needs of Others _____

Personal Needs _____

Answered Prayers _____

A Matter of Urgency

"I will come upon you as a thief, and you will not know what hour I will come upon you." Revelation 3:3

To settle the issue of where we are going to spend eternity once and for all

"Therefore, let all the godly confess their rebellion to you while there is time that they may not drown in the floodwaters of judgment."
Psalm 32:6 NLT

buries the weight of our guilt at the cross and lifts us into the arms of God's grace where we move forward in the newness of life.

As soon as we have this issue settled in our own lives, we need to direct our attention to helping others to settle the issue in their lives.

We all have friends, relatives, and loved ones who are going to be left behind if they do not hear and respond to Jesus' knock at the doors of their hearts.

The influence of family and friends is the number one influence in spreading the Gospel and building up the Kingdom of God.

We need to harness the power of prayer that God will prepare the hearts of our lost loved ones that they might hear and receive God's call.

We need to invite them to "come see" Jesus at church on Sunday and model the love of Christ to them every day of our lives that they might see what a difference this love has made in our lives.

Our Christianity should be like the most contagious virus known to man, spreading like wildfire to bring revival and restoration to our families, our communities, our countries, and the world.

We need to understand that faith is not only taught but caught when people see our faith in action.

"But of that day and hour no one knows, not even the angels of heaven, but My Father only."
Matthew 24:36

When it comes to determining whether one of our loved ones has a saving relationship with God through faith in Jesus Christ, it is sometimes easy to find out by simply asking: "Am I going to see you in heaven?"

It is also helpful to constantly ask ourselves who we are going to see in heaven as a result of our faithfulness to the Great Commission.

Father, keep me ever mindful of the urgency of helping others find Christ before it is too late. Amen.

Lord, You Are _____
Forgive Me For _____
Thank You For _____
Needs of Others _____
Personal Needs _____
Answered Prayers _____

Token Faith
"But since you are like lukewarm water, I will spit you out of my mouth!"
Revelation 3:16 NLT

It appears that we have too many token Christians in the household of faith. A lot of people seem to think that they can hedge their risks by a token faith just in case "all of this stuff" about God is really true.

"But the love of the LORD remains forever with those who fear Him."
Psalm 103:17 NLT

"What have you got to lose?" is often used as an inducement to receive Jesus Christ as Savior, without mentioning the cost of discipleship in submitting to Jesus Christ as Lord.

Jesus tells us that we must be born again. We must lose our life of bondage to our sin nature in order to find our new life and identity in Christ.

To think that we can somehow "con" God and come to Him on our terms instead of His is a travesty. The story of the rich young ruler bears out this truth very clearly.

Anyone who tries to come to God or tries to get anyone to come to God without realizing that no one can really call Jesus Lord except by the power of the Holy Spirit is promoting carnal Christianity that is an insult to God and the true faith that He demands.

Saving faith is not a salad bar where we pick and choose what we will and will not obey, what areas of our lives we will give to God, and what areas we will reserve for our flesh.

God does not want bits and pieces of us; He wants the whole essence of our being. He wants us to die to sin and become alive in Christ. There must be some evidence of a changed life when we are truly born again and submit to the control of God in our lives through the power of the Holy Spirit living within us.

"If you refuse to take up your cross and follow Me, you are not worthy of being Mine."
Matthew 10:38

Real faith is a live, growing faith where the reality of Christ in us is a growing reality as we grow into the fullness of Christ. We must never settle for anything less.

Father, let me never be lukewarm in my relationship with You. Amen.

Lord, You Are _____

Forgive Me For _____

Thank You For _____

Needs of Others _____

Personal Needs _____

Answered Prayers _____

Read Hebrews 11, Psalm 119:6-13 May 4

Don't Die Without It

"I assure you, anyone who doesn't have their kind of faith will never get into the Kingdom of God." Mark 10:15 NLT

From the very beginning, God has made it very clear that we must have the key element of faith if we are to enjoy His fellowship and His blessings. The difference between Cain and Abel's sacrifices was the key element of faith.

"The LORD protects those of childlike faith; I was facing death, and then He saved me." Psalm 119:6 NLT

Everyone has faith in something or someone, if only themselves. Ninety percent of everyone, including even the devil, believes in God.

The problem is in what kind of faith we have. Anything short of saving faith in God through believing in Jesus Christ will not satisfy the longing for God that He has placed in the heart of every child born of woman.

To say we have saving faith without showing any evidence of the sanctifying faith that comes with it is pure rubbish. Unless our faith results in a changed heart evidenced by changed conduct and changed perspectives, we are still dead and have not been truly born again. (As James said, "Faith without works is dead.")

The reality of physical death is something that we all have to realize. When the time comes for us leave this world, all of the worldly possessions along with all of faith we had in ourselves and other people is not going to amount to anything. We came into the world naked and are going to leave naked.

The great gift of salvation and the wonderful robe of righteousness that it provides is not something we should wear on Sundays and put in the closet the rest of the week.

It is something that we should keep clean by the daily cleansing of confession and repentance.

"So, you see, it is impossible to please God without faith. Anyone who wants to come to Him must believe that there is a God and that He rewards those who sincerely seek Him." Hebrews 11:6

We dare not be caught without it when the time comes for us to leave this temporary home.

Father, let me never leave behind or lay aside my shield of faith for any one or any thing. Amen.

Lord, You Are _____
Forgive Me For _____
Thank You For _____
Needs of Others _____
Personal Needs _____
Answered Prayers _____

Substitutes

"Those who worship false gods turn their backs on all God's mercies."
Jonah 2:8 NLT

We live in the age of substitutes. Today, substitutes for eggs, sugar, bacon, and many other foods are common place.

"God looks down from heaven on the entire human race; He looks to see if there is even one with real understanding,"
Psalm 53:2

The world is promoting secular humanism as a substitute for God and relative truth as a substitute for the absolute truths of God.

Every believer must be on guard for the false teachings and doctrines being substituted for the real thing. The "golden calves" of idolatry and substitute false gods are all around us.

To teach that God wants us all to be rich and healthy and that if we're not it's because of our lack of faith is a terrible substitute for the truth that God's strength is made perfect in our weaknesses. God has not promised a rose garden but rather His sustaining and all-sufficient grace to see us through troubles common to everyone living in this sin-sick world.

To substitute man-made programs for receiving eternal life instead of depending on receiving the grace of God for salvation by the power of the Holy Spirit and through a personal faith relationship with Jesus Christ is another substitution that is widespread among many churches.

On an individual basis many are all too often looking for substitutes for finding happiness, which does not exist apart from a living and growing relationship with Jesus Christ.

"That the genuineness of your faith, being much more precious than gold that perishes, though it is tested by fire, may be found to praise, honor, and glory at the revelation of Jesus Christ."
1 Peter 1:7

The only substitution we need to consider is that Jesus Christ bore our sins as our substitute on the cross of Calvary. There can be no eternal life or real happiness without believing this.

Father, let me never settle for any substitutes for You and Your death on the cross as a substitute for me. Amen.

Lord, You Are _____
Forgive Me For _____
Thank You For _____
Needs of Others _____
Personal Needs _____
Answered Prayers _____

God's Equipping

"Yet who knows whether you have come to the kingdom for such a time as this?" Esther 4:14b

God surely does work in a mysterious way to accomplish His purposes sometimes. Who except God could have taken a rag tag bunch of fisherman and losers and changed the world for Christ?

"You have said, 'What's the use of serving God? What have we gained by obeying his commands or by trying to show the LORD Almighty that we are sorry for our sins?'"
Malachi 3:14

Who but God could have ordained that Joseph would be sold into slavery by His brothers, been jailed, and then restored to favor to become the most respected man in Egypt?

Only God could have equipped a shepherd lad with a sling shot to slay the giant that was paralyzing the whole Israelite army with fear.

When troubles come, as they are sure to do, instead of getting angry at and abandoning God or throwing a pity party and going into deep depression, we need to ask ourselves if this might be part of God's equippping process for using us to fulfill that for which He created us.

Jesus was certainly equipped through a lot of suffering, and Scripture tells us that if we are to share His glory, we must share His suffering.

Rick Warren reminds us that "God never wastes a hurt." We need to accept by faith that "God works all things for the good of those who love Him and who are called according to His purposes" *(Romans 8:28).*

"And now, may the God of peace, who brought again from the dead our Lord Jesus, equip you with all you need for doing His will."
Hebrews 13:20 NLT

Sometimes it is only through receiving God's comfort in times of illness, grieving, failure, or other trouble that we can comfort others.

Other times God equips us through education, talents, or other circumstances.

When the time comes that we experience the great joy of knowing that God has equipped us to glorify Him for a particular time or reason, we can be thankful that we didn't give up and miss out on His using us for His purposes.

Father, by the power of the Holy Spirit, keep me every mindful of Your equipping me for Your purposes and Your glory. Amen.

Lord, You Are _____

Forgive Me For _____

Thank You For _____

Needs of Others _____

Personal Needs _____

Answered Prayers _____

Out of Control

"With promises like this to pull us on, dear friends, let's make a clean break with everything that defiles or distracts us, both within and without. Let's make our entire lives fit and holy temples for the worship of God."
2 Corinthians 7:1 MSG

The gift of the fruit of the Spirit of self control is God's gift to every believer. Although it is a fruit and not a spiritual gift, we need

"Stop your anger! Turn from your rage! Do not envy others— it only leads to harm." Psalm 37:8 NLT

to always remember that we have it to appropriate by faith during times of extreme stress and conflict.

It is all too easy to lose control of our emotions, say things we shouldn't say, do things we shouldn't do, and needlessly suffer so much grief, pain, and worry that only make matters worse.

When we lose control of our anger and let it become rage, we have become the devil's foot stool. When we let fear or worry paralyze us, we become the walking wounded instead of soldiers of the cross.

The natural reaction of the flesh and the sin nature that continues to dwell in us is to react in the pride, anger, lust, and harmful emotions of the flesh instead of through bearing the love, joy, peace, longsuffering, kindness, goodness, faithfulness, gentleness, and self control fruit of the Spirit.

There are many circumstances over which we have absolutely no control. The problem is that we often forget about the security we have in letting God be in control and proceed to weave a web of needless frustration and disappointment by letting our emotions control us and take us out of control.

"But you are not controlled by your sinful nature. You are controlled by the Spirit if you have the Spirit of God living in you." Romans 8:9 NLT

When we exercise our God-given gift of self control, we can choose to respond in the power of the Spirit rather than in the weakness of our flesh, and God promises that we will receive that "peace that surpasses all understanding" through the troubles of life.

Father, by the power of Your Spirit living within me and the armor You have provided, help me to stay in control of my emotions in every situation. Amen.

Lord, You Are _____
Forgive Me For _____
Thank You For _____
Needs of Others _____
Personal Needs _____
Answered Prayers _____

Wasted Trips

"For what profit is it to a man if he gains the whole world, and loses his own soul?" Matthew 16:26a

We have all probably experienced the frustration and disappointments of wasted trips. Sometimes we go to visit and no one's at home. We may have gone out to eat and found the restaurant closed.

"Do not tremble; do not be afraid. Have I not proclaimed from ages past what my purposes are for you? You are my witnesses—is there any other God? No! There is no other Rock—not one!" Isaiah 44:8 NLT

The wasted trips of life are the biggest wastes of all. We travel roads of anger that waste energy and get our joy hijacked. We travel roads of pride that lead to falls. We waste our time on any number of wasted trips.

The worst wasted trip of all is the life travelled without God.

We can make all the money in the world, climb the highest of mountains, and enjoy phenomenal success in athletics or any other endeavors, but accomplishments without God are wasted trips down a deadend road.

Our journey on this earth is barely a blip in terms of eternity. For those who travel it without God, no accomplishments are going to take away the sting and finality of death.

For those who travel through life with God, death is not the end of anything but the beginning of everything good that will last forever and ever, and we don't have to die physically to begin living it.

When we receive Jesus Christ as our Lord and Savior, we become dead to sin and experience a new birth in Christ. We are immediately made righteous in God's sight, and we are empowered to live free from bondage to sin and free to become imitators of Christ.

"Then I heard a voice from heaven saying to me, "Write: 'Blessed are the dead who die in the Lord from now on.'" Revelation 14:13a

We dare not make Jesus Christ's trip to the cross for us a wasted trip by unbelief and by travelling through this life without Him.

Father, let Your accomplishment on the cross be the driving force for any success that I might enjoy through my new birth in You. Amen.

Lord, You Are _____

Forgive Me For _____

Thank You For _____

Needs of Others _____

Personal Needs _____

Answered Prayers _____

May 9   *Read Matthew 24:43-50, Psalm 100*

Principles of Accounting

"So then each of us shall give account of himself to God." Romans 14:12

In business, government, or any endeavor, accountants essentially call the shots. Big businesses use high speed data bases and internet connections to do a daily accounting of business done at all locations.

"Serve the LORD with gladness; come before His presence with singing." Psalm 100:2

On a personal level, most people do accounting when they balance their checkbooks and keep track of their credit card purchases.

Accounting is a great principle to apply to our daily lives, especially in the area of what business we have done for the Lord on any given day with the time, talents, and treasures He has given us.

Daily confession and repentance does wonders for maintaining damage control for our sins. When we confess and turn away from them, they do not get a chance to build up and overwhelm us or let our consciences become hardened. While we can know that our sins will be forgiven, we need to know that we will be without excuse when we are called to give account of our lives at the resurrection of the just.

The parable of the minah and the parable of the talents make it abundantly clear that God cares about how well we manage our lives.

Holding ourselves accountable for the stewardship of our lives on a daily basis will assure that we will not be ashamed when we stand before God and see what remains after all the wood, hay, and stubble is burnt away.

"Who is a faithful, sensible servant, to whom the master can give the responsibility of managing His household and feeding His family?" Matthew 24:43

We should open each day as though opening for business for the Lord and by asking who we can bless, who we can love, and how we can glorify God today.

When we do this and then close our days by recounting who we did love, bless, and how we did glorify God this day, we will begin to see God use this principle of accounting to do great things for us and through us.

Father help me to manage the life You have give me well. Amen.

Lord, You Are _____
Forgive Me For _____
Thank You For _____
Needs of Others _____
Personal Needs _____
Answered Prayers _____

Threshholds

"And you yourselves be like men who wait for their master, when he will return from the wedding, that when he comes and knocks they may open to him immediately." Luke 12:36

We all have different thresholds or points of entry in our spiritual lives.

"Open to me the gates of righteousness; I will go through them, and I will praise the LORD," Psalm 118:19

God brings some to the threshold of salvation at a very early age, others very late in life. Sadly some never reach the point of entry into that wonderful, life- changing gift that keeps on giving forever and ever.

Once we arrive at the entry point of our salvation, we also arrive at the threshold of what effect our receiving Jesus Christ as Savior will have upon our lives. The evidence of being born again will be indicated by its effect on our conduct.

When we are truly born again, we are rescued from bondage to our old sinful natures and freed to become imitators of Christ.

Sometimes the effects are immediately visible for all to see. At other times, it is a life-long process of being transformed by the power of the Holy Spirit by the renewing of our minds.

When we cross the threshold of salvation, we immediately enter the threshold of God's other graces, which we appropriate by faith as we grow in spiritual maturity.

We grow in spiritual maturity as we grow in our personal relationship with Jesus by getting to know Him through His Word, through personal and corporate worship, and through the prayers of the Holy Spirit and Jesus for us as well as our prayers for ourselves.

"Behold, I stand at the door and knock. If anyone hears My voice and opens the door, I will come in to him and dine with him, and he with Me. Revelation 3:20

We can never grow into the fullness of Christ without imitating His love, His humility, and His servanthood.

What thresholds of God's graces have you entered and claimed by faith?

Father, keep me ever mindful that I will always be a work in progress as I seek You ever more diligently. Amen.

Lord, You Are _____

Forgive Me For _____

Thank You For _____

Needs of Others _____

Personal Needs _____

Answered Prayers _____

Crumbs Beget Crumbs

"It is possible to give freely and become more wealthy, but those who are stingy will lose everything" Proverbs 11:24 NLT

The principle of reaping what you sew is taught throughout Scripture.

Scripture teaches that what you sew not only affects the

"Happy are those who fear the LORD. Yes, happy are those who delight in doing what He commands." Psalm 112:1b NLT

When we apply this principle in terms of our relationship with God, we can clearly see that God not only demands, but He rewards our giving the best of our times, talents, and treasures.

When we give God the crumbs or leftovers of our time, we are assuring that not much is going to be left after the wood, hay, and stubble of our wasted time is burned away at the resurrection of the just.

God has given each of us talents to equip us to do the things for which He created us. We dare not let these talents go to waste when they can be used to build up the Kingdom of God.

The crumbs of worshipping only on Christmas and Easter and of living weakly instead of strongly in a daily sacrifice of praise and communion with God through prayer and growing in His Word will keep us from entering into God's promise of the abundant life on earth.

Why in the world would anyone choose to partake of the crumbs of God's grace when He wants to give us so much more?

"Remember this—a farmer who plants only a few seeds will get a small crop. But the one who plants generously will get a generous crop." 2 Corinthians 6 NLT

Growing into the fullness of Christ and becoming imitators of Him should be the number one priority of every believer. When God gave us His only begotten Son, He was not sewing a crumb to harvest crumbs. He was giving us His best so that we could be and do our best for fulfilling His purposes through us.

Are you leading a crumby life? It's never too late to go back to first fruit giving, loving, and living.

Father, keep me ever mindful of the joy set before me through daily abiding in Jesus and His teachings. Amen.

Lord, You Are _____
Forgive Me For _____
Thank You For _____
Needs of Others _____
Personal Needs _____
Answered Prayers _____

Read 2 Peter 3:11-18, Psalm 84

May 12

Are You Fully "Graced"?

"Let your roots grow down into him and draw up nourishment from him, so you will grow in faith, strong and vigorous in the truth you were taught. Let your lives overflow with thanksgiving for all he has done."

Colossians 2:7 NLT

Grace is defined as "unmerited divine assistance given humans for their

> **For the LORD God is a sun and shield; the LORD will give grace and glory; no good thing will He withhold from those who walk uprightly."**
> **Psalm 84:11**

regeneration or sanctification; a virtue coming from God; a state of sanctification enjoyed through divine grace; <u>mercy</u>; <u>pardon;</u> a special favor; privilege; courtesy; a temporary exemption."

Everyone, whether they are saved or unsaved, are "graced" to some degree. We are all given life, breath, and the necessities of life.

The just and the unjust are graced by and enjoy advances in medical science, technology, and knowledge and by the beauty of God's creation.

Moving beyond the basics of God's unmerited favor upon all, we need to understand the workings of God's grace in the lives of believers.

We are "graced" for salvation, transformation, good works, security, and significance.

No one can call Jesus Lord and be saved except by the grace of God. The transforming power to die to sin and become alive in Christ through the new birth can only be received by the grace of God.

We cannot be fruitful in every good work for which God created us if we are not "graced" by God   We get "graced" by being in relationship with Jesus, as we get to know Him and seek to imitate Him by learning what He means when He says He is "the Way, the Truth, and the Life."

> **"But grow in the special favor and knowledge of our Lord and Savior Jesus Christ."**
> **2 Peter 3:18 NLT**

We are never going to be fully "graced" until we achieve the perfection of Christ in heaven, but there is more grace than we can ever absorb in this life available to all who submit to the lordship of Christ and maturie through abiding in His Word.

Father, help me to becomefully "graced" in every area of my life. Amen.

Lord, You Are ___
Forgive Me For ___
Thank You For ___
Needs of Others ___
Personal Needs ___
Answered Prayers ___

One of God's Greatest Honors

"Since you have been raised to new life with Christ, set your sights on the realities of heaven," Colossians 3:1 NLT

Of the countless blessings that God bestows on all of His children, perhaps one of the greatest, but least appreciated, is the honor of not seeing us as we are but as what we will become.

"Restore us, O God; cause Your face to shine, and we shall be saved!" Psalm 80:3

God did not come to us because we were righteous, but "while we were yet sinners...." (Romans 5:8). In His forbearance and love, God has come in the humanity of Jesus to save sinners like us.

We need to understand that if God says we are free from the penalty and bondage of sin we are free indeed and need to start living like it.

If God says we must be born again, we need to show the evidence of our new birth by wearing our new robe of righteouness and taking care to keep it clean by the daily washing of confession and repentance.

From God's perspective, there was nothing free or cheap about grace. It cost Him the life of His only begotten son. God must have thought we were worth saving, or He would never have saved us.

All of this begs the question that if God thought we were worth dying for, why is it so hard to understand that God is worth living for? Why is it so hard to submit every area of our lives to the lordship of Jesus Christ?

"He died for everyone so that those who receive His new life will no longer live to please themselves. Instead, they will live to please Christ, who died and was raised for them." 2 Corinthians 5:15 NLT

God's command is that we love Him with all our hearts, souls, minds, and bodies. He held nothing back from us, and we should hold nothing back from Him.

When we exchange what we were for what God would have us become, God sends the streams of living water to flow in us and through us. He gives us the power and strength to be all that He created us to be and to do all that He created us to do even before we were ever born.

Do we really want to take a chance on short changing God?

Father, help me to grow into the fullness of Christ by Your grace and by the indwelling strength and power of the Holy Spirit. Amen.

Lord, You Are _____

Forgive Me For _____

Thank You For _____

Needs of Others _____

Personal Needs _____

Answered Prayers _____

Portals of Prayer

"While Jesus was here on earth, he offered prayers and pleadings, with a loud cry and tears, to the one who could deliver him out of death. And God heard his prayers because of his reverence for God." Hebrews 5:7 NLT

There is something special about prayer. It is the portal or entrance to the throne of grace where God reigns and dispenses grace and mercy to all who call upon His name in faith.

**"You faithfully answer our prayers with awesome deeds, O God our Savior. You are the hope of everyone on earth,"
Psalm 65:5a NLT**

Jesus understood the importance of and necessity for prayer. He never failed to give thanks to the Father or express the longings of His heart through prayer to the Father.

Prayer is the portal to wisdom, healing, joy, peace, power, and strength. Just as exercise strengthens our muscles, praying exercises and builds spiritual muscle.

Jesus gave us a lot of good instruction on using the portals of prayer. We should pray to God privately and corporately. We should not let our prayers be hindered by any unresolved anger or unforgiveness towards anyone. We should not pray selfish prayers but God-honoring and God-glorifying prayers that acknowledge the glory, majesty, soveriegnty and divine wisdom of God.

We can learn a lot about prayer by learning and appropriating the model of the Lord's Prayer. A) We acknowledge and adore God's holiness by hallowing His name. B) We pray for God's good and gracious will. C) We pray for physical and spiritual needs for ourselves and others. D) We acknowledge and praise the sovereignty of God.

One of the greatest blessings of abiding in Christ through His Word is that as we get to know Him and abide in Him more and more, we begin praying from His perspective. As a result, we experience the joy of more and more prayers being answered affirmatively.

**"But if you stay joined to Me and My words remain in you, you may ask any request you like, and it will be granted!"
John 15:7 NLT**

We shoiuld learn to keep the portals of prayer open throughout the day by practicing the presence of Christ in us and carrying on an ongoing dialogue with Him.

The portals of prayer are always open. We can go in 24/7/365!

Father, thank you for keeping Your throne of grace open for me. Amen.

Lord, You Are _____

Forgive Me For _____

Thank You For _____

Needs of Others _____

Personal Needs _____

Answered Prayers _____

Beware of Casual

"Expose all who drift away from your sayings; their casual idolatry is lethal. You reject earth's wicked as so much rubbish; therefore I lovingly embrace everything you say." Psalm 119:118 MSG

We too often develop a casual attitude toward sin. Satan started it in the Garden of Eden when he told Eve that she surely would not die if she disobeyed God.

"O God, You take no pleasure in wickedness; You cannot tolerate the slightest sin." Psalm 5:4 NLT

Today, we do not believe sin to be as big a deal as Scripture clearly says it is. When we forget that God hates sin, we tend to tolerate, co-exist, harden our hearts, and develop a casual attitude toward it.

We deny, rationalize, and perceive the Ten Commandments to be the ten suggestions and allow the relative truth of the world to over ride the relevant truth of God's Word in many areas of life.

Sexual conduct has now been trivialized and reduced to the biological instead of the theological. The impact of millions of men, women, and children feeding daily on pornography has not been fully felt, but it is bad and going to get worse.

As we buy into the humanistic theology of being all that we can be in ourselves, that we are the masters of our fate, and that we don't need God's help, we become carnal Christians in love with ourselves instead of in love with Jesus.

There is nothing casual about sin and its consequences. God hates it, and so must we.

Our sin cost God's Son His life on the cross. We should never trivialize the magnitude of what Jesus did for us by allowing our casual attitude towards sin to mislead us into a casual relationship with a false god of our own making, which is idolatry at its worst.

"But exhort one another daily, while it is called 'Today,' lest any of you be hardened through the deceitfulness of sin," Hebrews 3:13

Father, let me never become casual about sin. Amen.

Lord, You Are _____

Forgive Me For _____

Thank You For _____

Needs of Others _____

Personal Needs _____

Answered Prayers _____

Stop the Mo

"Temptation comes from the lure of our own evil desires. These evil desires lead to evil actions, and evil actions lead to death. So don't be misled, my dear brothers and sisters." James 1:14-16 NLT

The momentum of sin is like an avalanche picking up speed as it rolls down a mountain. The sooner we can "stop the mo," the less likely we are to succumb to the temptations all around us.

"Blessed is the man to whom the LORD does not impute iniquity, and in whose spirit there is no deceit."
Psalm 32:2

Eve made the mistake of opening the door to the devil by engaging in conversation with him. He takes advantage of this opening by creating doubt as to the truthfulness of God and the consequences of disobeying Him and selling the idea of how great knowing as much as God would be.

David would never have sinned with Bathsheba if he had just stayed off the roof.

The best way to stop the mo, is just don't go. When we are tempted, we need to fight or flee, but we never have to give in.

When Jesus died on the cross for our sins, He set us free from bondage to sin, which can have no more dominion over us, unless we let it. We can stop the momentum because we just don't have to go down the slippery slope that turns temptation into sin.

We begin by guarding our hearts, which we do by obeying God's command that: "You must love the Lord your God with all your heart, all your soul, and all your mind" (Matthew 22:37).

When we pollute our minds by allowing garbage in, it is going to pollute our hearts and souls, and it will give sin a toehold from which to operate.

When we love ourselves or others more than we love God, we are fair game for the wiles of the devil.

"And then He added, 'It is the thought-life that defiles you.'"
Mark 7:20 NLT

A horse can never run away from the barn if the door is kept shut.

Father, by the power of your Spirit, enable me to say "no." Amen.

Lord, You Are _____

Forgive Me For _____

Thank You For _____

Needs of Others _____

Personal Needs _____

Answered Prayers _____

Discontentment

"Work at getting along with each other and with God. Otherwise you'll never get so much as a glimpse of God. Make sure no one gets left out of God's generosity. Keep a sharp eye out for weeds of bitter discontent." **Hebrews 12:14 MSG**

There are two kinds of discontentments, and it behooves us all to understand and recognize the difference, as we are going to encounter both on our journey of life.

"As for me, I will see Your face in righteousness; I shall be satisfied when I awake in Your likeness." Psalm 17:15

Satan is a master at sewing seeds of unholy discontentment. He created it in Eve in the garden and tempted her to sin. He sews in us in every area of life.

He sews discontent in our marriages, our jobs, our churches, and about every arena of life. If he can get enough grumbling and complaining going, he can sew enough discord to make everyone around miserable.

He loves to get us comparing our haves to the haves of others and becoming envious and discontent.

We need to be ever mindful that these kinds of discontent do not come from God and refuse to let them take root in our hearts.

There is a holy discontentment that comes from God by the power of the Holy Spirit, and this is good. Holy discontentment makes us dissatisfied with our lives of sin and leads us to receive Jesus as our Savior.

Holy discontentment continually convicts us of our shortcomings, and it works repentance and the desire to do better.

Holy discontentment helps us respond to the pain and suffering of those around us and makes us want to help them.

"Yet true religion with contentment is great wealth," 1 Timothy 6:6

Holy discontentment with the garbage of our world leads us to seek the fullness of Christ and to grow into a deeper relationship with Him.

When the apostle Paul says that he has learned to be content in all things, he is saying that he has overcome unholy discontent.

Father, help me to discern and deal with both kinds of discontent. Amen.

Lord, You Are_____
Forgive Me For _____
Thank You For _____
Needs of Others _____
Personal Needs _____
Answered Prayers _____

Read Hebrews 13, Psalm 16 **May 18**

Getting Carried Away

"He personally carried away our sins in His own body on the cross so we can be dead to sin and live for what is right. You have been healed by his wounds!" 1 Peter 2:24 NLT

It's easy to get carried away at times. Eve got carried away by the temptations of the serpent. We often get carried away by our trivial pursuits that afford no lasting satisfaction or value.

"Those who chase after other gods will be filled with sorrow,"
Psalm 16:4a

Politicians often get carried away by their own egos and the corruption of power. Churches often get carried away by building programs and other internal affairs, which have nothing to do with building up the body of believers.

We let ourselves get carried away for all the wrong reasons. When we let anything carry us away or distract us from being all we were made to be in Christ, we will miss out on the real blessings of life.

God came to earth as Jesus Christ to carry away our sins and give us a new abundant and everlasting life through faith in what He did on the cross to pay for our passover from death to life.

When we let the love of God carry us away from our old selfish, sinful nature and into a new life filled with the goodness of God, we are not only going to be carried away to heaven one of these days, but we are going to find ourselves being carried away in a love affair with Jesus that will literally bless our socks off.

This love affair that begins with the gift of salvation will grow into a personal relationship that will carry over into every area of our lives. We will want what He wants and to do the things that He wants us to do, and He will supply His grace and power to accomplish this and more.

There are personal "border bullies" trying to keep us from getting carried away with Jesus and into the abundant and fulfilling life that this affords even in the here and now. We must never be discouraged or deterred from fulfilling our destiny in and through Christ.

"Do not be carried away by all kinds of strange teachings."
Hebrews 13:9a NIV

Father, may I never get carried away from the security of your love and eternal life. Amen.

Lord, You Are _____
Forgive Me For _____
Thank You For _____
Needs of Others _____
Personal Needs _____
Answered Prayers _____

May 19   *Read Hebrews 6:11-13, Deuteronomy 8*
The Key to Fulfillment

"Observe the requirements of the LORD your God and follow all His ways. Keep each of the laws, commands, regulations, and stipulations written in the Law of Moses so that you will be successful in all you do and wherever you go." 2 Kings 2:3 NLT

We know that faith is required for salvation. We must believe that Jesus died on the cross for our sins in order to be saved.

"Be careful to obey all my commands so that all will go well with you and your children, because you will be doing what pleases the LORD your God." Deuteronomy 8:1 NLT

We often have a tendency to gloss over the fact that God also requires obedience. He gave us the commandments in His Word and has written them in our hearts so that we might obey.

Our freedom of choice is over once we choose to receive God's wonderful gift of salvation. When we choose to receive Christ, we choose to die to sin and be born again as new creatures in Christ.

Our lives are no longer ours; they now belong to Christ who lives in us through the Holy Spirit. Our love for God for what He has done for us through Jesus Christ not only leaves us no choice but to obey, but it also gives us His resurrection power to obey.

The blessings of obedience are made abundantly clear throughout Scripture. We will never know all of the great plans God has to bless us and fulfill our every longing unless we obey.

As God reveals Himself to us through Scripture, He will clearly lay out the path of obedience that we are to follow, and we will know the peace and joy that only living lives of obedience can afford.

"Then you will not become spiritually dull and indifferent. Instead, you will follow the example of those who are going to inherit God's promises because of their faith and patience." Hebrews 11:12 NLT

Father, let all my needs be fulfilled in You by Your all-sufficient grace. Amen.

Lord, You are_____
Forgive Me For _____
Thank You For _____
Needs of Others _____
Personal Needs _____
Answered Prayers _____

The Healing Touch

"For she thought to herself, 'If I can just touch His clothing, I will be healed.'" Mark 5:28 NLT

An issue of blood was not something someone went around talking about. It was deemed uncleanliness in Levitical circles. The lady who was healed did not want to talk about her problem openly; she just knew by faith that Jesus could heal her.

"He forgives all my sins and heals all my diseases." Psalm 103:3 NLT

The same healing power that went out of Jesus the moment this woman touched the hem of His garment is the power that is available to all who call upon the name of the Lord in faith. When Jesus told the woman: "your faith has made you well" (Mark 5:32) He was telling her and us that it was her faith, not her physical touch that healed her.

Jesus is alive and through the Holy Spirit is pouring out the power of His love on all who come to Him in faith. His saving power is poured out to all who respond to the knock at the door of their hearts. His sustaining power is poured out to all who call upon His name. His comforting touch reaches out to all who love Him in times of mourning and suffering.

There are two types of healing. One is physical and has to do with the healing of physical diseases or injuries. The other is spiritual, which has to do with the healing of the sin diseases of the heart and soul.

Jesus is the Great Physician of the mind, body, and spirit. All who come to Him in true faith will be healed according to God's will and God's perfect plan and timing. Jesus' prayer in the Garden of Gethsemane asked that above all not His will but God's will be done.

"How God anointed Jesus of Nazareth with the Holy Spirit and with power, Who went about doing good and healing all who were oppressed by the devil, for God was with Him." Acts 10:38 NLT

Whether God's healing touch comes instantly, over a period of time, or through the ultimate healing of death itself, we can be sure that our faith will make us well.

Father, thank you for Your healing touch that is mine to appropriate by faith. Amen.

Lord, You Are _____

Forgive Me For _____

Thank You For _____

Needs of Others _____

Personal Needs _____

Answered Prayers _____

Did They Get it All?

"The night is almost gone; the day of salvation will soon be here. So don't live in darkness. Get rid of your evil deeds. Shed them like dirty clothes. Clothe yourselves with the armor of right living, as those who live in the light." Romans 13:12 NLT

The first question everyone asks after any kind of cancer surgery is

"Get rid of your sins and leave all iniquity behind you." Job 14:11

"Did they get it all?" Surgeons diligently seek to "get it all" because any remaining cancer cells will usually start growing, multiplying, and spreading to other parts of the body.

When we find ourselves dealing with our sin problems, we need to diligently seek to "get rid of it all" when it comes to confession, repentance, and forgiveness because any sin not fully confessed and repented of will usually come back to haunt us.

In the area of forgiveness, we often hear, "I'll forgive but I will never forget." This indicates that the poison of an unforgiving spirit lingers on, and it is an insult to God Who says that He not only forgives but remembers our sins no more.

When Jesus Christ comes to set us free, we become free indeed.

In His longsuffering and patience, God gives us time and does whatever it takes to get rid of all traces of our sin nature as He molds, melds, and conforms us into the image of Christ.

We can take great comfort in Philippians 1:6 which tells us, "Being confident of this very thing, that He who has begun a good work in you will complete it until the day of Jesus Christ."

"But now is the time to get rid of anger, rage, malicious behavior, slander, and dirty language." Colossians 3:8 NLT

When God finally "gets it all," we experience the fullness of joy and all- surpassing peace that come only when we surrender not only our spirit but also our hearts, minds, bodies, and all that we possess to the lordship of Jesus Christ.

Father, help me to experience the new birth to the fullest by getting rid of all my sins through the indwelling power and presence of the Holy Spirit. Amen.

Lord, You Are _____

Forgive Me For _____

Thank You For _____

Needs of Others _____

Personal Needs _____

Answered Prayers _____

Wholeness

"When you obey me, you remain in my love, just as I obey My Father and remain in His love. I have told you this so that you will be filled with My joy. Yes, your joy will overflow!" John 15:10, 11

"You will show me the path of life; in Your presence is fullness of joy; at Your right hand are pleasures forevermore."
Psalm 16:11

Spiritual wholeness is God's desire for every one of His children. Our faith should never become dead and stagnant, dull and dreary, or only partially appropriated.

As a living, growing confidence our faith should grow through the trials and temptations of life fed by the all-sustaining grace of God received by growing in the daily disciplines of prayer and abiding in God's Word.

We will never achieve perfection in this life, but we can achieve a perfect peace and godly contentment through being transformed and renewed daily by putting off our sins and putting on the righteousness of Christ through daily confession and repentance.

We begin our quest for wholeness by receiving Jesus Christ as our Savior and forgiver. As our relationship with Him grows through practicing the spiritual disciplines of life, we begin submitting every area of our lives and learn to lean on Him to take supply our financial, physical, and relational needs.

There is no key to succeeding like success, and as we begin walking the walk of faith and experience the amazing grace of God along the way, we cannot help but grow into the fullness of Christ and find the true treasures of life that are the birth right of every believer who is truly born again in Christ.

"And I pray that Christ will be more and more at home in your hearts as you trust in Him. May your roots go down deep into the soil of God's marvelous love."
Ephesians 3:17 NLT

Wholeness promises friendship with Jesus, experiencing Jesus' joy, and prayers prayed and answered because they are God honoring and glorifying prayers. We will experience the awareness of God's love and the love of others.

Wholeness will give us that total security that nothing else can afford.

Father, by the power of Your Spirit living within me, help me to grow into the fullness of Christ. Amen.

Lord, You Are _____
Forgive Me For _____
Thank You For _____
Needs of Others _____
Personal Needs _____
Answered Prayers _____

Suicide Watch

"For you were buried with Christ when you were baptized. And with Him you were raised to a new life because you trusted the mighty power of God, Who raised Christ from the dead." Colossians 2:12 NLT

Almost every jail and prison has a suicide watch list for prisoners deemed potential suicide risks. They are monitored closely in an attempt to prevent them from taking their lives.

"The pains of death surrounded me, and the pangs of Sheol laid hold of me; I found trouble and sorrow. Then I called upon the name of the LORD: 'O LORD, I implore You, deliver my soul!'"
Psalm 116:3, 4 NLT

God is waiting for us to die to sin so that we can become alive in Christ.

The old Adam in us all is impossible to kill completely and has so many lives it often takes a lifetime to kill just a part of them.

If we have really been born again, we have become temples of the Holy Spirit where He has come to reside, to guide us into all truth, and to give us the grace and strength to put to death the old thoughts, words, and deeds that used to define our identity in the flesh.

As we take off the old garments of pride, anger, envy, lust, greed, unbelief, unforgiveness, etc., we make room for putting on the new righteousness and holiness we have received from being born again.

When we learn to "commit suicide" daily by dying to sins and burying them at the cross through daily confession and repentance, God will make a way, by the power of the Holy Spirit, to enable us to live lives fully pleasing to Him and fruitful in every good work.

"So you should consider yourselves dead to sin and able to live for the glory of God through Christ Jesus."
Romans 6:11 NLT

We won't have to give up anything, but because of our new identity as born again believers, we will want to give up everything that does not reflect who we are in Christ.

It is only when we die to self, that we can become truly alive as born again believers who have been "transformed by the renewing of our minds."

Father, help me to kill off the remaining vestiges of my old sin nature so that I can make room for the fullness of joy that only comes from Your empowering grace. Amen.

Lord, You Are _____

Forgive Me For _____

Thank You For _____

Needs of Others _____

Personal Needs _____

Answered Prayers _____

Are You Out of Order?

"God's grace and order wins; godlessness loses." Psalm 10:16 MSG

Among the many wonderful attributes of God, one is all too often not given the prominence it deserves.

"Who put the world in His care? Who has set the whole world in place? Job 34:13 NLT

We hear a lot about the omnipotence, omniscience, and everlasting qualities of God and a lot about His love and holiness. We often overlook the fact that God is a God of order.

God created the earth and all that is in it in a very precise and orderly manner. He created it specifically as an abode for man who was the reason for all other creation.

Until the fall of man, there was perfect order in creation all testifying to the glory and majesty of the Creator, and the ordaining of darkness and light, plants and animals, and perfect harmony in the paradise created.

The divine order of God is still in effect, although we have become so disorderly, it is sometimes hard to remember and even harder to find.

Orderliness begins with putting our priorities in order. God's plan is 1) God First 2) Others Second 3) Self Third.

When we put God first, He promises that all things will be added to us. He promises not only to provide the necessities but even the desires of our heart spiritually, physically, and emotionally when we abide in a right relationship with Him through faith in a continually growing relationship with Jesus.

"For though I am absent in the flesh, yet I am with you in spirit, rejoicing to see your good order and the steadfastness of your faith in Christ." Colossians 2:5 NLT

When we value others as God values us, we become imitators of Jesus and receive the blessings that only obedience to the Great Commandment and Great Commission can bring.

When we submit to the yoke of loving and serving God and others, we find more joy and real pleasure than we will ever know through getting priorities out of order and trying to move up from 3 to 1.

Father, help me to keep my priorities in order. Amen.

Lord, You Are _____

Forgive Me For _____

Thank You For _____

Needs of Others _____

Personal Needs _____

Answered Prayers _____

The Ultimate Metal Detector

"Nothing in all creation can hide from Him. Everything is naked and exposed before His eyes. This is the God to whom we must explain all that we have done." Hebrews 4:13

September 11, 2001, has triggered a frenetic drive to develop the most sensitive and accurate metal, weapon, and explosive detecting devices possible to increase airport and airplane security throughout the world. Test after test has shown that these devices can fail.

"Surely there is a mine for silver, and a place where gold is refined."
Job 28:1

All of this is a means of pointing out the fact that we are all going to have to undergo God's fool-proof, fail-proof, and 100-perfect effective metal detection process at the resurrection of the just.

This is where everything we have done with the time, talents, and treasures we have been given will be thrown into the refiner's fire to detect what, if any, gold remains after all the wood, hay, and stubble of trivial pursuits and selfish, self-centered lives remains.

It will be too late for denials, rationalizations, and comparing ourselves to other people.

For those whose works survive the refininer's fire, our Lord's "well done, thou good and faithful servant," will be the sweetest words we have ever heard, and we will have the great pleasure of serving God to the fullest in heaven.

For those who have trusted in Jesus for their salvation, they will be ushered into heaven by the skin of their teeth with nothing on deposit in their heavenly bank account.

"But if the work is burned up, the builder will suffer great loss. The builders themselves will be saved, but like someone escaping through a wall of flames."
1 Corinthians 3:15

The worst of heaven is going to surpass anything that we could ever imagine. The best of heaven awaits those who lead fruitful lives that glorify God and fulfill His purposes on this earth. We should all be getting ready for this ultimate metal detection.

Father, by Your grace, help me to store up treasures that will survive the refiner's fire. Amen.

Lord, You Are _____

Forgive Me For _____

Thank You For _____

Needs of Others _____

Personal Needs _____

Answered Prayers _____

Read Hebrews 3:7-19, Proverbs 8:13-36   May 26
Weekly, Not Weakly
"And daily in the temple, and in every house, they did not cease teaching and preaching Jesus as the Christ." Acts 5:42

"Happy are those who listen to me, watching for me daily at my gates, waiting for me outside my home," Proverbs 8:34 NLT

As much as we need to obey the commandment to remember the Sabbath and keep it holy, we must never forget that we need God daily and not try to get by with just feeding on Him weekly.

Satan, the world, and our flesh are working 24 hours a day, 7 days a week, 365 days out of the year trying to distract us and cause us to fail in our mission to grow into the fullness of Christ by abiding in the Word.

The idea that we can store up enough manna in one day to keep us spiritually nourished throughout the week is a bad idea.

When we bathe daily in the waters of confession and repentance, we keep the road dirt of life from building up and overloading our capacity for righteousness.

When we receive Jesus Christ as our Savior, we need also to receive Him into our hearts as our Lord and grow in our relationship with Him daily. We do this by getting into His Word daily, not weekly— and certainly not weakly.

Being clothed in the righteousness of Christ is not clothing to be worn to church on Sundays. We must wear the righteousness of Christ and the full armor of God daily in order that we might stand against the temptations and evil that come our way daily.

"But exhort one another daily, while it is called 'Today,' lest any of you be hardened through the deceitfulness of sin." Hebrews 3:13 NLT

If we don't know our target, we will miss it every time. Our purpose in life is to become more like Christ day by day and year by year, so the reality of His living in us and the blessings of abiding in Him will be ours to enjoy in this life as well as the next.

We certainly don't want to stunt this process by growing in Him weakly instead of weekly.

Father, do not let a day go by without my spending time in relationship with You through Your Word. Amen.

Lord, You Are _____
Forgive Me For _____
Thank You For _____
Needs of Others _____
Personal Needs _____
Answered Prayers _____

May 27   Read Romans 8:18-39, Psalm 119:71-77
Why are You Being Squeezed?
"My Father! If it is possible, let this cup of suffering be taken away from Me. Yet I want Your will, not Mine." Matthew 26:39 NLT

When our comfort zone gets squeezed, our natural response is to cry out "Why me, oh Lord?!"

"The suffering You sent was good for me, for it taught me to pay attention to Your principles." Psalm 119:71 NLT

In God's overall plan to work all things for our good and His glory by conforming us into the image of Christ, we need to understand that He is going to do whatever it takes to accomplish His purpose.

In His perfect knowledge of us, our past, present, and future, He is uniquely qualified to prescribe whatever help we need to become like the Christ Who is in us. His ways are so much higher than our ways, we will never fully understand everything, but He has certainly given us insight and knowledge about a lot of things and how He works our worst into His best.

Job and Joseph's lives are examples of how God can turn evil into good and pain and suffering into joy and victory. The squeezing Jesus endured as the price of our salvation and the declaration that we must share in His sufferings should remind us that there is relief and joy ahead.

When we are getting squeezed, we need to seriously judge ourselves to see if we are suffering the consequences of some sin that we need to confess and from which repent.

If the Holy Spirit does not convict us of any sinful conduct, we can assume that God is squeezing us to see how ripe we are for being fully conformed into the image of Christ.

Scripture after scripture makes it abundantly clear that we are to respond to suffering by "counting it all joy," rejoicing, and praising God. We are promised that when we do this, no matter what the suffering, we will receive that "peace that surpasses all understanding."

"Yet what we suffer now is nothing compared to the glory He will give us later." Romans 8:18 NLT

We can't always control our squeezings, but we can always control the way we choose to respond.

Father, help me to find the peace and comfort of Your grace by rejoicing in my sufferings. Amen.

Lord, You Are ___
Forgive Me For ___
Thank You For ___
Needs of Others ___
Personal Needs ___
Answered Prayers ___

"Doin' Business"

"So he called ten of his servants, delivered to them ten minas, and said to them, 'Do business till I come.'" Luke 19:13

It's a fact of life that we are all "doin' business" every day of our lives.

We are going about the business of making a living, learning, leaning, and loving.

"The LORD demands fairness in every business deal; He sets the standard." Proverbs 16:11

For many of us, there is too much "monkey business" going on in our lives where we have sold out to sin and the temporary pleasures of this world without even considering the consequences that are sure to follow eventually.

Some of us may be into the applause business where we daily go about coveting and seeking the approval of others without realizing how short lived it is, and that's all we are going to get out of it.

God has made it abundantly clear through Scripture that He has put us on earth to do business on His behalf until He returns.

God has equipped us with an inventory of gifts and talents to make us successful in the kingdom-building business, if we don't waste them on living a life controlled by the flesh instead of the Spirit.

The time God allots each one of us is exactly the amount of time it takes to accomplish the purposes for which God created us before we were ever born. We can't afford to waste it by worry, wordliness, or on trivial pursuits that will be burned in the refiner's fire.

"Look here, you people who say, 'Today or tomorrow we are going to a certain town and will stay there a year. We will do business there and make a profit.'" James 4:13

The financial treasures that God trusts us with are sometimes the hardest gifts to manage. We all too often squander them on trinkets and have none left to spare for the important purposes God had in trusting us with them.

We were created for God's pleasure and for His glory. When seeking His pleasure and glory become the holy ambition of our lives, we will find great joy in doin' business for God.

Father, help me to be a good steward of the life You have given me. Amen.

Lord, You Are _____

Forgive Me For _____

Thank You For _____

Needs of Others _____

Personal Needs _____

Answered Prayers _____

"Playing it Safe" with God

"For God has not given us a spirit of fear and timidity, but of power, love, and self-discipline." 2 Timothy 1:7

Fears of failure and rejection are two of the greatest fears we have to overcome before we can ever become all that God wants us to be.

"The LORD is my light and my salvation; whom shall I fear? The LORD is the strength of my life; of whom shall I be afraid?"
Psalm 27:1 NLT

These "border bullies" can be very intimidating, and unless we appropriate God's promised power and strength, they are going to keep us from doing what God has created us to do – make disciples.

The parable of the unfruitful steward is a sobering reminder that God is going to hold us accountable for the good stewardship of the life that He has given us. There is no "playing it safe" with God.

God's reminder that our fear and timidity do not come from Him should make us realiaze that they come from the evil one who is out to destroy us if he can and from the pride of our flesh, which does not allow us to handle failure or rejection very well.

The disciples "played it safe" by tucking tail and running when Jesus was arrested. Peter "played it safe" by denying Christ. When the Holy Spirit came, He brought the power, love, and self discipline the disciples needed to carry out their mission.

The Holy Spirit comes today to give us the power, love, and self discipline we need to overcome our fears and failures and to live lives fully pleasing to God and fruitful in every good work. We may often fail, and we will most likely suffer rejection for the cause of Christ.

The good news is that failure is never final with God, and we will never suffer rejection with the One who counts the most.

He has promised never to leave us or forsake us and to comfort us with His love and strengthen us with His power when we do business for Him until He comes.

"I was afraid I would lose your money, so I hid it in the earth and here it is."
Matthew 25:25

Father, remove my fears and replace them with Your strength and power that I might quit "playing it safe" with You. Amen.

Lord, You Are _____
Forgive Me For _____
Thank You For _____
Needs of Others _____
Personal Needs _____
Answered Prayers _____

Honesty is the Best Policy

"But you desire honesty from the heart, so you can teach me to be wise in my inmost being." Psalm 51:6 NLT

In today's world, saying that someone is honest seems to imply some special and rare quality. What once was taken for granted is now deemed a special quality in this age of relative truth.

"Yes, what joy for those whose record the LORD has cleared of sin, whose lives are lived in complete honesty!" Psalm 32:2 NLT

The spin masters try to turn black into white. Misinterpreters of the Bible try to turn sin into virtue and Jesus into a mere man.

Ananias and Sapphira have gone down in history as examples of what happens when people are dishonest with God. The severity of their instant punishment of death for lying should be a sober reminder to us all that God does not take dishonesty lightly.

Being honest with ourselves is probably the hardest habit we can ever acquire. When Adam and Eve lost their innocence, they could not handle standing before God naked and ashamed, and they tried to cover themselves.

We don't like to admit that we were wrong or made a mistake. We like to excuse our actions by blaming circumstances or other people. People will spend years in bondage to some addiction or other sin and go to their graves denying that they have a problem.

When we understand and know that our God is an ever present, all-knowing God, we will understand the futility of trying to con or deceive Him. He knows our motives and knows our hearts.

"We can say with confidence and a clear conscience that we have been honest and sincere in all our dealings. We have depended on God's grace, not on our own earthly wisdom. That is how we have acted toward everyone, and especially toward you." 2 Corinthians 1:12 NLT

How much better to own up to our sins, be sorry for them, and repent, than to deceive ourselves and try to deceive God, Who will not be mocked or never deceived.

Honesty is not only the best policy; it should be the only policy for anyone who claims the name of Christ.

Father, help never have to bear the consequences of dishonesty. Amen.

Lord, You Are _____

Forgive Me For _____

Thank You For _____

Needs of Others _____

Personal Needs _____

Answered Prayers _____

What Do You Treasure?

"But this precious treasure—this light and power that now shine within us—is held in perishable containers, that is, in our weak bodies. So everyone can see that our glorious power is from God and is not our own."
2 Corinthians 4:7 NLT

When we think of treasure, most naturally start counting their money and their material possessions. There is no place to list our biggest asset on any financial statement.

> **"I rejoice in Your word like one who finds a great treasure."**
> **Psalm 119:162 NLT**

We usually take precautions to safeguard our treasures. We put them in banks, take out insurance policies, or hide them under a mattress.

When we receive the free gift of eternal life through faith in Jesus Christ, we receive the greatest treasure anyone could ever have.

This "pearl of great price" transforms us from the poverty and misery of being in bondage to sin and makes us instant winners in the lottery of life. We are freed from bondage to our debt of sin.

Although we receive this treasure as a free gift, we must never forget that it is the most expensive gift we will ever receive. It cost God the life of His own Son, and down through the ages, it has cost the lives of many Saints who have died to preserve it for us.

There is no room for a casual attitude or taking the priceless gift of salvation for granted. We were not given this treasure to squander like the prodigal son squandered his inheritance. We were given this treasure that we might glorify the One who gave it.

> **"By doing this they will be storing up their treasure as a good foundation for the future so that they may take hold of real life."**
> **1 Timothy 6:19 NLT**

We house this treasure in the earthen vessel of our flesh, which is transformed into a temple, where this treasure can be polished and cleaned so that it brightly reflects the love and character of the One who gave it to us and wants to pass it on to others through us.

We all need to treasure this treasure by constantly seeking to use it for the purposes for which God gave it to us.

Father, help me to take my treasure out of hiding and share it generously with others. Amen.

Lord, You Are _____
Forgive Me For _____
Thank You For _____
Needs of Others _____
Personal Needs _____
Answered Prayers _____

God's Limit of Generosity

"I, the LORD your God, am a jealous God who will not share your affection with any other god!" Deuteronomy 5:9b NLT

Our God is a very generous God. He lavishes every good and perfect gift upon us to share and enjoy with Him and with others.

"I am the LORD your God, who rescued you from slavery in Egypt. Do not worship any other gods besides Me. Exodus 22:2, 3 NLT

He even shares His character with us so that we can be longsuffering, patient, compassionate, kind, slow to anger, and full of love for Him and for others.

God's purpose in creating us was so that we could glorify Him in all things by reflecting His character as we live out our lives being conformed into the image of Christ.

In the beginning, God gave Adam and Eve everything limited only by the tree of life, and they could not handle it.

Today, God gives us everything limited only by not sharing His glory with any other God; we all too often cannot handle it.

We sell out our wonderful birth right in Christ and buy into the kingdoms of pleasure, power, possessions, pride, or other kingdoms of darkness which crowd the kingdom of God out or put it below the preeminent place God deserves and demands.

"Yes, a person is a fool to store up earthly wealth but not have a rich relationship with God." Luke 12:21 NLT

When we let any thing or any body crowd God out of first place in our heart's affection, we set ourselves up for disaster in this world and the next.

Everything that God gives, He can also take away in a heart beat, and only a fool will jeopardize who they are and what they have in Christ by placing their trust and allegiance in any other god.

Father, keep me safe and secure in Your sheepfold, and never let me wander into the pastures of other gods. Amen.

Lord, You Are _____

Forgive Me For _____

Thank You For _____

Needs of Others _____

Personal Needs _____

Answered Prayers _____

Defining Better

"Train up a child in the way he should go, and when he is old he will not depart from it." Proverbs 22:6

One of the biggest mistakes most of us make as parents is in wanting our children to have it better than we did and defining better in material terms.

> "He commanded our ancestors to teach them to their children, so the next generation might know them," Psalm 78:5b, 6 NLT

Lavishing all of the material things that we didn't have is not letting our children have it better.

There is nothing wrong with wanting our children to be happy and to give them good gifts, as long as we define happiness.

Allowing our children to grow up as spoiled brats is not the way to assure their happiness. It is a recipe for disaster.

Allowing our children to grow up as the center of attention will help them grow up as self-centered egocentrics who think life is all about them.

To a large degree, our children will become what we model. If we model worldliness, our children will be worldly. If we model anger, our children will grow up angry. If we reflect God's love, our children will more likely do the same.

If we really want our children to have it better, we will want them to have it better in terms of their relationship with Jesus Christ, apart from which no true happiness can be found.

We must have a singlemindedness of purpose of raising them in the nurture and admonition of the Lord, so when the time comes that they are no longer under our influence of control, they will have transferred control to the lordship of Jesus Christ.

> "You, therefore, who teach another, do you not teach yourself?" Romans 2:21

The more armor we can help them to put on and use, the better equipped they will be to go out into the often cold, often cruel, and always sinful world and to do life God's way, which will assure their having it better.

Father, help me to understand how to help my children have it better through You. Amen.

Lord, You Are _____

Forgive Me For _____

Thank You For _____

Needs of Others _____

Personal Needs _____

Answered Prayers _____

Man-Made Gods

"Little children, guard yourself from idols," 1 John 5:21

Those who don't know any better have worshipped the sun, the moon, and all sorts of false gods because God has put it in the heart of all to know Him, and many only know him through what they see in nature and the forces of nature. In His time, God will deal with all of this.

"Those who chase after other gods will be filled with sorrow. I will not take part in their sacrifices or even speak the names of their gods."
Psalm 16:4 NLT

The really sad commentary is that many people who know better and who would never think of worshipping a golden calf or the sun worship a god created by them and for them without even realizing what they are doing.

When we equate God with our own casualness about sin and somehow think that He didn't really mean what He said, we have created our own god who kind of overlooks our participation in or condonement of things that He specifically warns against and calls abominations.

When we get God confused with Santa Claus and think that He is going to make us healthy, wealthy, and wise, we are completely losing sight of the pain and suffering of all those Saints who have gone before.

When we get God confused with an insurance policy that assures we will go to heaven when we die if we just say the magic words, we are not worshipping the God who says we must be born again and transformed by the renewing of our minds.

"For they themselves keep talking about the wonderful welcome you gave us and how you turned away from idols to serve the true and living God."
1 Thessalonians 1:9 NLT

Any time we put God in a box all tied up by our own definitions and opinions, we are worse than the dumbest of savages who worship animals and nature because they don't know any better.

We must never forget that God is the God who created us and will not tolerate our trying to create Him into something that does not come close.

Father, help me to know, trust, and obey You as You have revealed Yourself in Scripture. Amen.

Lord, You Are _____
Forgive Me For _____
Thank You For _____
Needs of Others _____
Personal Needs _____
Answered Prayers _____

Some Things Never Seem to Change

"What happened was this: People knew God perfectly well, but when they didn't treat Him like God, refusing to worship Him, they trivialized themselves into silliness and confusion so that there was neither sense nor direction left in their lives." Romans 1:22 MSG

The history of God's people is an ongoing saga of their falling into idolatry.

"I have known from my earliest days that Your decrees never change." Psalm 119:52 NLT

God made covenant after covenant with His chosen people, none of which were kept by succeeding adulterous generations who prostituted God's glory by turning to false gods and graven images for seeking what only a right relationship with God can afford.

Today, the false god of secular humanism and the worship of popularity, possessions, and pleasure may be on the throne in more people's lives than ever before, and we see the results all around us.

The same Deliverer, who parted the Red Sea and delivered His people from destruction down through the ages, has come in the person of Jesus Christ to deliver all who will call upon His name and be saved.

Our deliverance is a two-fold process. The hour we first believed we are made holy and righteous in the sight of God forever, and we also begin being made holy through the ongoing process of being transformed.

Our biggest obstacle in growing into the fullness of Christ is the same as it has been forever. We trivialize God and refuse to worship and obey Him.

We put our self centeredness ahead of God centeredness and lose our way.

We praise God for His unconditional love that continues in spite of our sins and for His sustaining grace that will deliver us when we fall into sin. Then we confess and repent.

"For God has reserved a priceless inheritance for His children. It is kept in heaven for you, pure and undefiled, beyond the reach of change and decay." 1 Peter 4:7 NLT

This is the change that God came into the world in the person of Jesus Christ to effect for all who will call upon His name to be saved.

Father, let me be an example of the changed life in Christ. Amen.

Lord, You Are _____

Forgive Me For _____

Thank You For _____

Needs of Others _____

Personal Needs _____

Answered Prayers _____

"It Was Very Good"

"Then God saw everything that He had made, and indeed it was very good." Genesis 1:31a

When we read about God's stage by stage creation of the world and everything in it in Genesis 1, we should notice that God saw to it that each stage was good as well as proclaiming that all that He had created was "very good."

> "O God, You have cast us off; You have broken us down; You have been displeased;
> Oh, restore us again!"
> Psalm 50:1

When Adam and Eve disobeyed God and brought sin into this good and perfect world, the "apples of His eye" brought tears to His countenance; God's good and perfect creation was no longer good and perfect.

We, like the children of all previous generations, have come into the world not with the God-breathed perfection with which Adam and Eve were created but rather with the sin-laden guilt with which they left this world and passed on to us.

The original sin of disobedience has given root to the sins of pride, anger, envy, lust, idolatry, unforgiveness, unbelief, hatred, perversion, hypocrisy, and all of the other evils we now see all about us.

Paradise has been lost by man's disobedience. God's justice tempered by His love for His children has provided that paradise will be restored by the perfect obedience of a man called Jesus Christ.

Just as we inherited a sin nature from Adam and Eve, we inherit perfect righteousness in God's sight by becoming co-heirs with Christ when we receive Him as our Lord and Savior.

As we travel through this imperfect world as and with imperfect people, isn't it good to know that as brothers and sisters of Christ we enjoy the peace, security, and joy of the Lord that enables us to enjoy the goodness that still remains in this world and the perfection that is

> "Everyone who is victorious will eat from the tree of life in the paradise of God."
> Revelation 2:7b NLT

to come in our forever home in heaven? It will once again be "very good"!

Father, help me to enjoy the joy of knowing who I am in You. Amen.

Lord, You Are _____

Forgive Me For _____

Thank You For _____

Needs of Others _____

Personal Needs _____

Answered Prayers _____

One of Our Biggest Mistakes

"You are mistaken, not knowing the Scriptures nor the power of God."
Matthew 22:29

The Sadduces were not the only ones with this problem. Millions of professing Christians are content with just knowing enough Scripture to get to heaven and miss out on the incredible power of God that is ours to appropriate by faith from Scripture

"And I'm an olive tree, growing green in God's house. I trusted in the generous mercy of God then and now."
Psalm 52:8 MSG

Knowing Scripture is to know God through Christ, who is God the Word made Flesh. We are all given a hard drive where the Holy Spirit stores up the Word of God in our hearts and recalls it to our remembrance just when we need it the most.

He uses the Word to inspect, correct, protect, and perfect us with the resurrection power that raises us from the deadness of our old life in the flesh to the new transformed life in the Spirit.

We can not be imitators of Christ without knowing Him personally and intimately as He reveals Himself in Scripture.

The better we get to know Christ by abiding in His Word, the more like Him we will become. He will move from our heads to our hearts and become our best friend, our refuge, and our strength.

The more we abide in Christ, the more answered prayers we will experience because we will be praying unselfish, God-glorifying prayers that God always answers.

"So make every effort to apply the benefits of these promises to your life. Then your faith will produce a life of moral excellence. A life of moral excellence leads to knowing God better."
2 Peter 1:3 NLT

We will become more and more aware of the love of others as they respond to the power of love transmitted through us.

Perhaps best of all, Jesus promises to fill us with His joy when we abide in Him through knowing Scripture.

Is there any reason why we should not know the power of God that is to be found in knowing Scripture?

Father, let knowing You through knowing Your Son be the number-one priority of my life. Amen.

Lord, You Are _____
Forgive Me For _____
Thank You For _____
Needs of Others _____
Personal Needs _____
Answered Prayers _____

Is it None of Your Business?

"And He said to them, 'Why did you seek Me? Did you not know that I must be about My Father's business?'" Luke 2:49

The responsibility of taking care of God's business is serious business that we are often not very good at as a body of believers and as individual Christians.

"All goes well for those who are generous, who lend freely and conduct their business fairly." Psalm 112:5 NLT

Personal agendas, egoes, distractions, discouragements, and the ongoing battle between the world, the devil, and our flesh are continually interfering with doing business God's way and doing the good works for which we were created.

We most usually think of stewardship in terms of giving money, but God makes it clear that stewardship is about much more than money. Stewardship is about being about our Father's business and leading lives fully pleasing to Him and fruitful in every good work.

We begin by seeking first the kingdom of God and His righteousness. We continue by obeying the Great Commandment to love God and others and the Great Commission to baptize and make disciples of all nations.

We all too often seek first our own pleasures, possessions, and agendas. Churches often get so involved in building programs or engrossed in culture wars that they forget to keep the main thing the main thing.

It is a scary thought for pastors and teachers to realize that they will be subject to a stricter judgment for the way they kept about the Father's business and that an accounting will be required.

"When he returned, the king called in the servants to whom he had given the money. He wanted to find out what they had done with the money and what their profits were." Luke 19:15

Whether our business is raising godly children, winning souls for Christ, helping those in need, healing, or protecting others, our business must always be conducted "as unto the Lord."

We must manage well in every area of our lives until our Lord returns.

Father, by the power of your Spirit, help me to take care of Your business first. Amen.

Lord, You Are ___
Forgive Me For ___
Thank You For ___
Needs of Others ___
Personal Needs ___
Answered Prayers ___

God Has His Secrets

"There are secret things that belong to the LORD our God, but the revealed things belong to us and our descendants forever, so that we may obey these words of the law." Deuteronomy 29:29

God has revealed more than enough about Himself in nature and in Scripture. We are "without excuse" for not knowing God.

"And I will give you treasures hidden in the darkness—secret riches. I will do this so you may know that I am the LORD, the God of Israel, the One Who calls you by name." Isaiah 45:3 NLT

God reveals Himself as creator, all powerful, ever present, and all knowing. He reveals that He is loving and kind, just, holy, faithful, and full of wisdom.

He reveals that He will send a Savior in the Old Testament Who comes in the flesh in the New Testament to be who He promised and to do what He promised to do.

No matter how hard we try, we are never going to know all of God's secrets. We can take comfort that all things will be revealed in heaven.

In the meantime, our number one goal in life should be to get to know God as well as we possibly can by knowing His Son through a close and personal relationship by abiding in Him through His Word, prayer, and obedience.

When we sometimes feel that God doesn't make sense, we should remember that everything God does makes sense to Him. God has clearly told us that His ways are higher than our ways, and His thoughts are higher than our thoughts.

"For since the creation of the world His invisible attributes are clearly seen, being understood by the things that are made, even His eternal power and Godhead, so that they are without excuse," Romans 1:20

We will be a lot happier and lead much more fruitful and God-pleasing lives if we spend our energies getting to know Him by studying what He has revealed rather than getting caught up in conjecture about what He has not clearly revealed.

God has His secrets but has not kept anything we really need to know from us.

Father, thank you for not keeping Your wonderful plan of salvation a secret from anyone. Amen.

Lord, You Are _____
Forgive Me For _____
Thank You For _____
Needs of Others _____
Personal Needs _____
Answered Prayers _____

Practice Makes Imperfect

"He replied, 'But even more blessed are all who hear the Word of God and put it into practice.'" Matthew 27:30 NLT

Practicing sin has a big downside. The more we sin, the better we get at it, as our consciences become duller and duller.

"Give me understanding and I will obey your law; I will put it into practice with all my heart."
Psalm 119:34 NLT

We have a natural tendency to test our boundaries. We start out testing the limits of our parents' patience and boundaries as children, and if there is no parental discipline, we can grow up as wild seeds.

So many seem to lose their fear of God because they don't see the wrath of His judgment coming to bear as it did in Old Testament stories.

Many seem to continue to test the limits of God's boundaries, and when they don't suffer any consequences or divine retribution immediately, they become emboldened to sin more and more.

If we practice at sinning real hard, we can get really good at it. We can actually begin believing our own lies and even that the righteous ones are the bad people who dare speak out against the things that God calls abominations and sin.

If we continue practicing sin real hard, we can earn a one way ticket to the destination of the doomed, who die in their unrepented sins.

Worthwhile learning and character-development disciplines usually require a lot more practice than sinning because sinning comes naturally. Godly righteousness and obedience can only come naturally after we have been born again through receiving God's call to salvation through faith and repentance.

"Keep putting into practice all you learned from me and heard from me and saw me doing, and the God of peace will be with you."
Philippians 4:9

Practiice in hearing and obeying God's Word will never make us perfect in this life, but it will keep us perfect in God's eyes until we become the perfect, sinless, brothers and sisters of Christ in heaven. This is the kind of practice we should all get good at.

Father, help me to practice Your godly disciplines until they become as natural as practicing sin. Amen.

Lord, You Are _____

Forgive Me For _____

Thank You For _____

Needs of Others _____

Personal Needs _____

Answered Prayers _____

June 10 *Read 1 Peter 4:7-11, Psalm 65*

Dead Sea Christianity

"He who believes in Me, as the Scripture has said, out of his heart will flow rivers of living water." John 7:38

They don't call the Dead Sea dead for nothing. Because there is no out flow, the water becomes stagnant, salty, and of little use.

"You take care of the earth and water it, making it rich and fertile. The rivers of God will not run dry; they provide a bountiful harvest of grain, for you have ordered it so." Psalm 65:9 NLT

Dead Sea Christians take in all of God's blessings and hoard them for themselves, and there is no outflow.

The Great Commandment and Great Commission fall by the way side as churches and individuals get distracted by personal agendas, which major in minors.

We must never forget that the river of living water we have been given is not to be hoarded or stored. It must flow through until it becomes an ocean of love.

When we build dams of prejudice, discrimination, or doubt, we become stagnant. When we selfishly hold back the flow of God's generosity, His grace, or His love, we are bound to choke off the supply as we live self-centered lives in pursuit of love, happiness, and security in all the wrong places.

Churches and individual Christians are not to be stagnant. As living organisms, we cannot help but grow unless we become stunted and stagnant because we don't allow God's grace flow through us.

We need to excel in the grace of giving so that God's generosity of money can flow through us and meet the needs of God's kingdom and its people.

"God has given gifts to each of you from His great variety of spiritual gifts. Manage them well so that God's generosity can flow through you." 1 Peter 4:10 NLT

We must let God's love flow through us by becoming salt and light to those around us.

Whatever God has trusted us with must be managed well. He hasn't gifted us for our own edification but for the edification of His body and the upbuilding of His kingdom.

Where would we be if God cut of the flow of His generosity, love, and mercy to us?

Father, let Your blessings flow through me and into others. Amen.

Lord, You Are _____
Forgive Me For _____
Thank You For _____
Needs of Others _____
Personal Needs _____
Answered Prayers _____

Read Colossians 2, Isaiah 62:10-24   **June 11**
Cut Out the Junk Food
"Then Jesus explained: 'My nourishment comes from doing the will of God, who sent Me, and from finishing His work.'" John 4:34

We all have two natures fighting for control of our lives. Although the ultimate victory has been won for us by Jesus's death on the cross, we have to fend off attacks daily by our old sin nature trying to regain control of our lives.

"That you may feed and be satisfied with the consolation of her bosom," Isaiah 62:11

We are all too often guilty of feeding the wrong nature. When we spend hours feeding on junk food like TV trash, internet porn, and pursuing ego-pleasing approval, possessions, and power, we are creating a monster that will keep us from knowing the real joy of the Lord and ultimately lead us to eternal torment.

If we were to keep a diary of time spent in trivial or evil pursuits versus time spent in growing in an intimate relationship with God, which nature would we find ourselves feeding the most?

Now that Jesus Christ, the Light of the World, has come into the world to set us free from the control of our sin nature, we are without excuse for persevering in sin.

We no longer have to feed the old nature. In Christ, we are new creatures who have been set free to pursue holiness by feeding upon the love of God that is revealed in the life, death, and resurrection of Jesus Christ.

As we feed on the Word and appropriate it into our lives by imitating Christ and abiding in Him, we will experience all of the promised blessings of abiding.

"Let your roots grow down into Him and draw up nourishment from Him, so you will grow in faith, strong and vigorous in the truth you were taught." Colossians 2:7 NLT

Friendship with Jesus, Jesus' joy, the awareness of God's love and the love of others, answered prayers, and lives spent glorifying God by doing the things for which He created us are just a few of the benefits of feeding our souls on the good food that God has provided in His Word.

Father, help me to feast on the nourishment of Your Word. Amen.

Lord, You Are_____
Forgive Me For _____
Thank You For _____
Needs of Others _____
Personal Needs _____
Answered Prayers _____

Living Carelessly

"Watch out! Don't let me find you living in careless ease and drunkenness, and filled with the worries of this life." Luke 21:34 NLT

One of the greatest dangers confronting us in our new life in Christ is falling into the habit of living carelessly. We must be on the look out and avoid carelessness in any area of our lives.

"Don't let me so much as dream of evil or thoughtlessly fall into bad company." Psalm 141:4 MSG

Careless words that hurt our witness and the feelings of others are sometimes too easy to speak out but so hard to take back.

A careless and indifferent attitude towards sin makes us the kind of lukewarm Christians that God mentions in Revelation 3.

When we get careless with our priorities, we start putting other things ahead of God and commit spiritual adultery by giving the pursuit of pleasure, possessions, or the approval of others precedence over growing into the fullness of Christ, which should be the number-one priority of every believier.

When we get careless with our finances, we fall into bondage to debt and are not able to let God's generosity flow through us or give God any reason to trust us with more material blessings.

Carelessness in choosing our friends and our past times can also have disastrous consequences.

Using our freedom from condemnation for sin carelessly will kill.

"I know all the things you do, that you are neither hot nor cold. I wish you were one or the other! But since you are like lukewarm water, I will spit you out of my mouth!" Revelation 3:15, 16 NLT

We have not been set free to sin but free to live free from the power of sin and in the power of the Spirit.

We should always remember that God's grace is free, but it was not cheap. Jesus had to die to earn it for us.

We must never let anything tear us down or deter us from living lives fully pleasing to God and fruitful in every good work.

Father, may I never be guilty of getting careless in the way I live the life You have given me. Amen.

Lord, You Are _____

Forgive Me For _____

Thank You For _____

Needs of Others _____

Personal Needs _____

Answered Prayers _____

God's Asbestos

"When you walk through the fire of oppression, you will not be burned up; the flames will not consume you." Isaiah 43:2b

Fire can be one of the greatest or one of the most dangerous energies.

"He was amazed to see that no one intervened to help the oppressed. So He Himself stepped in to save them with His mighty power and justice"
Isaiah 59:16 NLT

We are fueled physically and spiritually by the fires of emotion. The secret of a happy and secure life is in whether we control these fires or let them control us.

We are born with built in furnaces of anger, pride, lust, fear, worry, etc. that are subject to burning out of control at any time. This is why we need God's asbestos, a.k.a. the Holy Spirit.

God sometimes fights fire with fire. He sometimes allows raging fires of anger, addiction, lust, or other sins to burn out before He lights the fire of our passion for Him. This is kind of like the controlled burn used by forest rangers to clean up an overcrowded forest.

We often speak of Spirit-filled Christians as being *"on fire for the Lord."* Since we are all filled with the Holy Spirit the hour we first believed in Jesus Christ as our Savior, we all should show some signs of burning with passion for the passion of Christ.

When God extinguishes the fires of our old sin natures and replaces them with the grace to be like Jesus and live for Him, holy transformation begins, and we will begin living lives burned out to sin and fueled by the fire of the Spirit.

"And God will provide rest for you who are being persecuted and also for us when the Lord Jesus appears from heaven. He will come with His mighty angels, in flaming fire, bringing judgment on those who don't know God and on those who refuse to obey the Good News of our Lord Jesus."
2 Thessalonians 1:8 NLT

The Spirit even equips us with fire proof armor to help keep us from getting burned by the tempests of sin raging within and without. We should never try to fight any fire of sin without this asbestos that God provides.

Father, keep the fires of sin extinguished by the power of Your Spirit. Amen.

Lord, You Are _____

Forgive Me For _____

Thank You For _____

Needs of Others _____

Personal Needs _____

Answered Prayers _____

Go to Your Room!

"Then Joseph made a hasty exit because he was overcome with emotion for his brother and wanted to cry. Going into his private room, he wept there." Genesis 43:30 NLT

Sending misbehaving children to their rooms seems to be the punishment of choice used by many parents.

"Be a guest room where I can retreat; You said Your door was always open! You're my salvation—my vast, granite fortress." Psalm 71:3 MSG

When you think about it, this is what God tells us to do when we misbehave. We need to go to our room so that we can confess, repent, and receive the forgiveness we need.

We can go to a room, closet, or just to the closet of our hearts. The main thing is to go where we can focus our minds' attention and hearts' affection on the everlasting, all-sufficient grace of God which forgives us of all our sins and restores our damaged relationship with Him.

Going to our room in the great house of God is the privilege and not the punishment of every believer.

We can go to our room for strength in time of weaknes and for thanksgiving in times of prosperity. We can go to our room for supplication and intercession for other and for healing and help in times of trouble. We can go to our room to seek the favor of God upon our lives and all our endeavors.

When we really get comfortable in this room by abiding in it often as we grow in the knowledge of God through His Word, we begin to understand what Jesus meant when He said that we would have His joy, His friendship, His love, and His blessing in our lives.

"But you, when you pray, go into your room, and when you have shut your door, pray to your Father Who is in the secret place; and your Father Who sees in secret will reward you openly." Matthew 6:6

As believers, we can look forward with longing and joy to going to our room in the mansion Christ has gone to prepare for us where we will dwell with Him and our loved ones in sinless perfection and bliss forever.

May we all learn to go to our room on a regular basis.

Father, thank you for giving me Your room of love to which I may go. Amen.

Lord, You Are _____

Forgive Me For _____

Thank You For _____

Needs of Others _____

Personal Needs _____

Answered Prayers _____

Living Graciously

"The unfailing love of the LORD never ends! By His mercies we have been kept from complete destruction. Great is His faithfulness; His mercies begin afresh each day." Lamentations 3:22, 23 NLT

The unmerited favor of God is the power that not only saves but that also allows us to be conduits of God's unfailing love, faithfulness, and grace to others.

"The LORD spread out a cloud above them as a covering and gave them a great fire to light the darkness." Psalm 105:39 NLT

Just like the physical manna that God used to feed His children in the wilderness, God sends renewed mercy and grace to each of us every day. We can't hoard it or save it for tomorrow. We must spend it daily by living graciously through imparting grace to others.

When we are truly born again we are transformed into a newness of life in a personal relationship with Christ that transcends our own personal imperfections and begins a process where we become more like Christ every day in every way.

The Holy Spirit moves into our unholy temples and begins cleaning them up and making them fit for God to live in and through us. The more we learn to receive the daily bread of God's grace and live in its sanctifying power, the more graciously we will live.

God's grace is the grace that transforms us from sinners into saints and the grace that grows us into the image of Christ.

Living graciously is living the abundant life to its fullest. When faith in Christ meets all our needs for security and significance, we begin living in the fullness of His joy and the assurance of His promises.

"We find ourselves standing where we always hoped we might stand—out in the wide open spaces of God's grace and glory, standing tall and shouting our praise." Romans 5:2 MSG

As we become imitators of His obedience, humility, compassion, and graciousness, we leave our old self-centered agendas and priorities behind us. We start living Christ-centered lives of obedience and servant hood that glorify and radiate His love, grace, and mercy to others.

Father, help me to live graciously. Amen.

Lord, You Are _____
Forgive Me For _____
Thank You For _____
Needs of Others _____
Personal Needs _____
Answered Prayers _____

God's Forgetfulness

"No more shall every man teach his neighbor, and every man his brother, saying, 'Know the LORD,' for they all shall know Me, from the least of them to the greatest of them, says the LORD. For I will forgive their iniquity, and their sin I will remember no more." Jeremiah 31-34

We often get confused by what we perceive to be God's forgetfulness.

"As far as the east is from the west, so far has He removed our transgressions from us."
Psalm 103:12 NLT

When our prayers aren't answered as quickly as we want, we wonder if God has forgotten us.

When we are suffering through deep waters of grief, pain, failure, or other problems such as are common to man, the devil sews seeds of doubt that can lead to doubt and despair.

When things don't seem to be working for good, we wonder if God has forgotten us.

It is through the tough times that we need to understand the truth about God's forgetfulness. The truth is that God is immutable. He or His promises do not change. They are the same today, yesterday, and forever. He still knows the number of hairs on our head and how He is going to use us for His glory.

There is only one exception to God's omniscience. He is forgetful of our sins when we confess and repent. God buries our sins in His sea of forgetfulness and remembers them no more.

This is a big part of what justification is all about. Because of our faith in Jesus Christ, God's justice has been rendered by the blood of Jesus, and He sees us just as if we had never sinned when we confess and repent.

"Let us go right into the presence of God, with true hearts fully trusting Him. For our evil consciences have been sprinkled with Christ's blood to make us clean, and our bodies have been washed with pure water."
Hebrews 10:22 NLT

What joy there is in knowing that when we stand before God there will be no confessed sins recorded in our book of life.

What fear awaits the unbelievers who choose to reject God's forgiveness and will have all sins recorded in the book of life used to convict and condemn them to eternal torment.

Father, thank you for Your forgetfulness. Amen.

Lord, You Are _____
Forgive Me For _____
Thank You For _____
Needs of Others _____
Personal Needs _____
Answered Prayers _____

When He's All You Have

"I sink in deep mire, where there is no standing; I have come into deep waters, where the floods overflow me. I am weary with my crying; my throat is dry; my eyes fail while I wait for my God." Psalm 69:2, 3

Millions of people are stunned with the realization that God is all they have.

"When you go through deep waters and great trouble, I will be with you. When you go through rivers of difficulty, you will not drown!" Isaiah 43:2 NLT

Everything else except life and, hopefully, family has been lost to the ravages of Hurricane Katrina, the biggest disaster in the history of our country.

Homes, cars, personal belongings, jobs, and security have disappeared. Millions of people have been stripped of everything. They are stunned, angry, confused, and overcome with grief and suffering.

Through all this the only hope is the assurance of God's Word and God's grace that He really is all they need.

Our faith is a lot like an insurance policy. You don't know how good it is until you have to use it.

God is not unkind. He does not delight in causing hurt and harm to His children whom He dearly loves.

For whatever reason He has in allowing this disaster to happen, we all must have enough faith to believe that He has allowed it for His glory and our ultimate good.

God does not waste hurts. He uses them to draw us closer to Him and to realize our total dependency upon Him. No one can be sure why God allowed Katrina to happen, but as believers, "we know that God causes everything to work together for the good of those who love God and are called according to His purpose for them" (Romans 8:28 NLT).

"And He said to me, 'My grace is sufficient for you, for My strength is made perfect in weakness.'" 2 Corinthians 12:9

Throughout all the heartbreak, suffering, doubts, and disillusionments, the realization that God's all-sustaining grace is sufficient for our every need should give help to the helpless and hope in times of hopelessness to all believers.

Father, I pray for the comfort of Your love, the strength of Your Spirit, and Your sustaining grace for all hurricane victims. Amen.

Lord, You Are _____
Forgive Me For _____
Thank You For _____
Needs of Others _____
Personal Needs _____
Answered Prayers _____

June 18 **Read 2 Timothy 2:1, Deuteronomy 7:6-17**

We are Special

"You have been set apart as holy to the LORD your God, and He has chosen you to be his own special treasure from all the nations of the earth." Deuteronomy 14:2 NLT

We don't deserve it, we often don't feel like it, and we too often don't act like it, but we believers are all a special treasure to God.

"For you are a holy people, who belong to the LORD your God. Of all the people on earth, the LORD your God has chosen you to be His own special treasure." Deuteronomy 7:6 NLT

How special are we that God knows and calls us by name? How special are we that God would love us enough to send His only begotten Son to die for us? This fact, above all, offers proof positive of how special we are to God.

That God not only knows us by name, but has "plans for good and not for disaster, to give you a future and a hope" (Jeremiah 29:11b) *is something of which we must never lose sight.*

The reality that God is not always that special to us should not only fill us with godly sorrow, but it should be a catalyst for change in the way we live our lives and choose to honor and appreciate who we are in Christ.

That God declares us righteous in His sight long before we show any signs of righteousness should inspire us to be imitators of Christ.

In our priority list of special things and special people God does not deserve and will not tolerate being on our "left over" list.

We are not told to seek first our own agendas, the pleasures of this world, or the approval of men but rather to seek first the kingdom of God and His righteousness. We need to let God provide the riches of His grace and wonders of His love to us and through us.

"Timothy, my dear son, be strong with the special favor God gives you in Christ Jesus," 2 Timothy 2:1 NLT

When we respond to being special to God by making Him special to us, we are going to start living life to the fullest as we get to know Him better through His Word and become more like Jesus day by day.

Father, help me to treasure what I have in being a treasure to You. Amen.

Lord, You Are _____

Forgive Me For _____

Thank You For _____

Needs of Others _____

Personal Needs _____

Answered Prayers _____

The Selfishness of Despair

"Why am I discouraged? Why so sad? I will put my hope in God! I will praise Him again—my Savior and my God!" Psalm 43:5 NLT

As hard as it may seem to understand, the truth is that an awful lot of our despair and all of our depression is the result of our own self-centered idea that the world revolves around us. We focus on our problems instead upon the problem solver.

"He lifted me out of the pit of despair, out of the mud and the mire.
He set my feet on solid ground and steadied me as I walked along."
Psalm 40:2 NLT

Scripture after scripture prescribes rejoicing and thanksgiving as the antidote for despair. The Bible promises that when we rejoice and "count it all joy" our depression and despair will be replaced by all-sustaining grace and all-surpassing peace.

God is often at His best when we are at our worst. He can only make His strength perfect in our weakness. We often don't feel the need for a Savior or a comforter when we are experiencing the highs of life.

When our self-centered pride kicks in, we have a tendency to kick God out of first place in our hearts' attention and minds' affection.

In addition to rejoicing and counting it all joy, we can overcome despair and depression by remembering God's grace and presence through previous difficulties and also by focusing on managing what we can manage instead of worrying about things over which we cannot manage or control.

When we deposit God's Word into our spiritual bank account, the Holy Spirit will remind us that "God is our refuge and strength, our very present help in time of trouble," "God works all things for the good of those who love Him and are called according to His purposes," God gives us "a future and a hope and has plans to bless us and not to harm us," etc.

"Rejoice in the Lord always. Again I will say, rejoice!" Philippians 4:4 NLT

The next time depression and despair come knocking, send them packing by claiming the power of God's grace through prayer and obedience.

Father, keep me ever mindful of my need to focus on You instead of my problems. Amen.

Lord, You Are _____
Forgive Me For _____
Thank You For _____
Needs of Others _____
Personal Needs _____
Answered Prayers _____

June 20 Read Matthew 17:14-21, Psalm 38

The Scars of Life

"From now on, don't let anyone trouble me with these things. For I bear on my body the scars that show I belong to Jesus." Galatians 6:17 NLT

Plastic surgery is a wonderful healing art. It is absolutely amazing what it can do to remove many of the marks left by accidents and injuries.

"My guilt overwhelms me—it is a burden too heavy to bear." Psalm 38:4 NLT

The inner scars that we carry as results of our than plastic surgery. They need the healing touch of our Lord and Savior Jesus Christ that is ours to receive by fervent prayers of faith.

The failure of Peter in denying Christ three times even after bragging about how He would never do such a thing gave him a godly sorrow that he carried all the days of his life. Nevertheless, Peter confessed, repented, and received not only forgiveness but the power to preach and live courageously secure in the love and forgiveness of God.

When Jesus cried out "It is finished," He was crying out that His work of paying for every sin that we have ever committed was finished. The scars are the marks of healing to remind us that we have been forgiven.

Many people say that they know that they have received forgiveness from God, but that they cannot forgive themselves. This is a mistaken idea.

Forgiveness has nothing to do with forgiving ourselves but everything about having enough faith to believe not only that God will and has forgiven us, but God also forgets our sins.

We need to accept by faith the reality of God's forgiveness when we come to Him, confess with a broken spirit and contrite heart, and move on in true repentance, turning our backs on yesterday's failures. It is then that we can experience that wonderful renewal and restoration of our relationship with God that we have in Christ.

"'You didn't have enough faith,' Jesus told them. 'I assure you, even if you had faith as small as a mustard seed you could say to this mountain, 'Move from here to there,' and it would move. Nothing would be impossible.'" Matthew 17:20

Father, let my scars of lost battles with sin be a constant reminder of Your grace, mercy, and forgiveness. Amen.

Lord, You Are _____

Forgive Me For _____

Thank You For _____

Needs of Others _____

Personal Needs _____

Answered Prayers _____

Flow River Flow

"He who believes in Me, as the Scripture has said, out of his heart will flow rivers of living water." John 7:38

The love of God manifests itself through the lives of His Saints. As His love floods into our hearts and our souls, it cannot help but gush out and turn into streams of living water to fill others.

"For my people have done two evil things: They have forsaken me—the fountain of living water. And they have dug for themselves cracked cisterns that can hold no water at all!" Jeremiah 2:13 NLT

Like the daily manna from heaven, we can't hoard it; we can't build a dam to contain it. We can only pass it on to make room for the ongoing and unceasing outpouring of God's grace to us and through us.

Everything we have is on loan from God. There is nothing good that we have not been given by God and nothing that we have that cannot be taken away by God at any time.

We are commanded to manage every area of our lives well so that God's purposes may be accomplished through us.

If we pursue self-centered rather than Christ-centered goals and agendas, we are not managing our time, talents, and treasures well. We are wasting the love that God has provided and restricting its flow through us.

Our new life in Christ is all about responding to God's love by by showing love to others in the way we walk, talk, and daily live our lives to the glory of God.

"God has given gifts to each of you from His great variety of spiritual gifts. Manage them well so that God's generosity can flow through you." 1 Peter 4:10 NLT

We dare not build dams of indifference, unforgiveness, or unbelief. Selfishness and pride have got to give way to the humility and generosity of Jesus that we are commanded to imitate.

When we let the river of God's love in Christ flow through us unimpeded by our sins, we are going to discover that it is more than ample for us to be generous with all the gifts, time, and resources we have been given.

Father let your river of love flow freely through me. Amen.

Lord, You Are _____
Forgive Me For _____
Thank You For _____
Needs of Others _____
Personal Needs _____
Answered Prayers _____

You've Been Redeemed!

***"Let the redeemed of the LORD say so,"* Psalm 107:2a NLT**

In terms of monetary value, the elements of a human body are worth a few

"I will go in the strength of the Lord GOD; I will make mention of Your righteousness, of Yours only." Psalm 71:16

dollars. Down through the ages of slavery, slaves were sometimes sold and traded for less than horses or cattle. Many became slaves because of the inability to pay debts and were slaves until the debt was paid.

In God's eyes, we slaves to sin were worth His coming to earth as Jesus Christ and suffering a horrible death on the cross in order to redeem us by paying our sin debt in full.

When we have been redeemed by the blood of Jesus through receiving Him as our Savior by faith, we have not only had the price paid for the forgiveness of sin, but we have been redeemed and set free from the bondage of being held captive to and dominated by our sinful human nature.

As the redeemed brothers and sisters of Christ and children of the Living God, we are free to live as "redeemed of the Lord."

Although this wonderful new life is a free gift and cost us nothing, we should be ever mindful and ever grateful for the great price that Jesus paid to redeem us and live lives of thanksliving that show our appreciation to God.

We should never pass up the opportunity to share the means and blessing of our redemption with others when the opportunity arises. We should always remember that we have been redeemed so: "that you may walk worthy of the Lord, fully pleasing Him, being fruitful in every good work and increasing in the knowledge of God" *(Colossians 1:10).*

"Yet now He has brought you back as His friends. He has done this through His death on the cross in His own human body. As a result, He has brought you into the very presence of God, and you are holy and blameless as you stand before Him without a single fault." Colossians 3:22 NLT

In addition to saying we are redeemed, we should give evidence of the reality of our redemption by living like sons and daughters of the living God.

Father, keep me ever mindful of the price that was paid for my redemption and let me live like I really appreciate it. Amen.

Lord, You Are _____

Forgive Me For _____

Thank You For _____

Needs of Others _____

Personal Needs _____

Answered Prayers _____

Can God Trust You?

"The eyes of the LORD search the whole earth in order to strengthen those whose hearts are fully committed to Him." 2 Chronicles 16:9

We hear a lot about "in God we trust" and trusting God but not enough about God trusting us. "Are we trustworthy?" is a question we

"The trustworthy will get a rich reward. But the person who wants to get rich quick will only get into trouble."
Proverbs 28:20 NLT

should ponder daily and a character quality we should seek to grow in, especially in our love relationship with God.

When we receive Jesus Christ as our Savior, we get reborn into a new life in and from Christ. This new life involves total trust on our part and the desire to have God trust us in every area of our lives.

Obedience to God is the evidence of the new birth we have received in Christ. God already knows how much He can trust us, but He is continually testing our obedience to show us how much He can trust us.

We usually find out quickly how little God can really trust us, and this sends us running to the throne of grace for forgiveness and strength.

The stewardship of life is all about God trusting us to live a life fully pleasing to Him and fruitful in the good works He created us and gifted us to do. God trusts us with a certain amount of time on this earth to complete the tasks He ordained for us. God trusts us with certain talents and gifts in order to equip us to do what He has planned for us.

"'Well done!' the king exclaimed. 'You are a trustworthy servant. You have been faithful with the little I entrusted to you, so you will be governor of ten cities as your reward.'"
Luke 19:17

God trusts us with material blessings so that He can reveal His generosity through us as we support His kingdom work and help others in need. If we are trustworthy in little things, God will trust us with bigger and better things in every area of our lives.

Whether it involves our time, talents, or treasures, God hates waste. He holds everyone of us accountable for the stewardship of our lives. Can He trust you to be a good steward?

Father, help me to be more trustworthy. Amen.

Lord, You Are _____
Forgive Me For _____
Thank You For _____
Needs of Others _____
Personal Needs _____
Answered Prayers _____

Our Equal Opportunity Employer

"The great God who formed everything gives the fool his hire and the transgressor his wages." Proverbs 26:10

Whether we like to admit it or not, we are all "moonlighting" for an equal opportunity employer. He has full or part-time jobs available for everyone and pays generous wages.

"And when all the workers of iniquity flourish, it is that they may be destroyed forever." Psalm 92:7

He recruits and hires worldwide and has employees in every home, neighborhood, city, state, or country.

This job doesn't require a lot of experience, everyone seems to have a natural talent for the job, and your employer provides excellent on the job training.

The devil, although mortally wounded, is still going around hiring everyone he can to become a practicing sinner.

This severe taskmaster makes the job so easy and makes it appear so attractive it is sometimes hard to resist his offer.

Satan promises fulfillment, gratification, pleasure, and solutions to problems. However, he fails to mention the horrible side effects of consequences and guilt or that his wages are death and eternal torment.

Thank God that by His grace we don't have to work for the devil either full or part time. God gives us a job that delivers the fulfillment, gratification, pleasure, significance, and solutions to problems that we desire. He sends His own personal trainer and body guard to come live with us and assure that we will succeed and enjoy the greatest benefit package ever offered.

When we sign up with God through faith in Jesus Christ, we get a lifetime, non-cancellable contract that promises an abundant life that will never end.

When we sign up to work for God and His glory, we get a special inoculation against our old employer's attempts to hire us back into bondage.

"Take My yoke upon you and learn from Me, for I am gentle and lowly in heart, and you will find rest for your souls." Matthew 11:29

We all have to decide for whom we are going to work. Our future and our hope depend on our making the right choice.

Father, thank you for giving me the opportunity to make a wise career choice. Amen.

Lord, You Are _____

Forgive Me For _____

Thank You For _____

Needs of Others _____

Personal Needs _____

Answered Prayers _____

Integrity for Sale

"In all things showing yourself to be a pattern of good works; in doctrine showing integrity, reverence, incorruptibility," Titus 2:7

The old hymn "What Would You Give in Exchange for Your Soul" asks a vital question when we see personal integrity and even belief in God's integrity put on sale cheap in the market places of the world.

> **"Declare me innocent, O LORD, for I have acted with integrity; I have trusted in the LORD without wavering."**
> **Psalm 26:1 NLT**

Corporate scandals continually reveal the dishonesty and greed of high-ranking, successful officers of large corporations.

Recruiting violations continue to plague and impugn the integrity of the athletic programs at major universities. Politicians at every level continue to get caught in scandals and every unseemly conduct imaginable.

Worst of all, millions of believers put belief in God's integrity on sale as they sell out to pride, power, sex, drugs, or other temptations that are common to man.

The shocking scandals that have come to light in the largest of church bodies, the fall of some of the country's greatest religious leaders, and the all too frequent falls of local pastors and church leaders fuel the doubts and derisions of unbelievers who use such examples to validate their beliefs that the church is full of hypocrites.

The truth is that there is nothing new under the sun. All of the problems listed above have gone on almost forever and will continue to occur. We can find hope and comfort in God's Word where we discover how God has and will continue to turn evil into good, that He has founded His church on the rock of Jesus Christ, and that the gates of hell will never prevail against it.

> **"Woe to the world because of offenses! For offenses must come, but woe to that man by whom the offense comes!"**
> **Matthew 18:7**

We persevere in our faith not because of the hypocrisy and lack of integrity within the church and world but in spite of it. We have read the end of the story and can be sure that the war over sin and death has been won.

Father, may I never give anyone cause to question Your integrity. Amen.

Lord, You Are _____
Forgive Me For _____
Thank You For _____
Needs of Others _____
Personal Needs _____
Answered Prayers _____

June 26

Read Romans 5:1-11, Psalm 111

Let's Get Intimate!

"Everyone who confesses that Jesus is God's Son participates continuously in an intimate relationship with God." 1 John 4:12 MSG

God knows us better than we know ourselves. He knew us before we were born and knows everything we have ever done or will ever do. The secret to a complete and fulfilling life is to get to know God. We do this by getting to know Jesus.

"He paid the ransom for His people, He ordered His Covenant kept forever. He's so personal and holy, worthy of our respect." Psalm 111:9 MSG

Our call to salvation is a call into a close and personal new birth in Christ. Jesus not only wants us to know Him as our forgiver and brother but also as that friend that sticks closer than a brother.

He wants us to know the goodness, sovereignty, holiness, wisdom, love and faithfulness of God as God has revealed it through Jesus, Who is God Incarnate—the Living Word.

When we fall in love with someone, we can't spend too much time with them. We want to know everything about them.

When we fall in love with Jesus, we will want to enjoy His presence through the Holy Spirit in every aspect of our daily life. We will want to know everything about Him.

It is only when we know what Jesus did that we can begin to know what Jesus would do if He were in our shoes in any given situation.

"So now we can rejoice in our wonderful new relationship with God—all because of what our Lord Jesus Christ has done for us in making us friends of God." Romans 5:11 NLT

Our intimate relationship with Jesus grows as we grow in His Word through hearing it preached and Bible study.

It also grows through our prayers and the encouragement of and fellowship with other believers as we grow together in spiritual maturity.

The more intimate we get with Jesus through a close and personal relationship with Him, the more like Him we will become. This is what being conformed into the image of Christ is all about.

Father, help me to grow in my relationship with You by spending more and more time with You. Amen.

Lord, You Are _____
Forgive Me For _____
Thank You For _____
Needs of Others _____
Personal Needs _____
Answered Prayers _____

Go With the Flow

"He who believes in Me, as the Scripture has said, out of his heart will flow rivers of living water." John 7:38

It's much easier to go with the flow than to paddle upstream.

"A river brings joy to the city of our God, the sacred home of the Most High."

Psalm 46:4

When this principle is applied to following the crowd, it should warn us that we have been sanctified and set apart by God, and we should not go with the flow of relative truth, peer pressure, or anything that is against the commandments of God.

In terms of going down the river of life powered with the presence of the Holy Spirit and kept afloat by God's incredible grace, this is the flow with which we should go all the days of our lives.

The teaching ministry of the Holy Spirit will enlighten us unto all truth and fill us with spiritual wisdom and discernment when we cooperate by reading and hearing the Word.

Our spiritual hard drive memory will be filled with the truth of God's Word and called to our remembrance whenever we need the guidance, comfort, strength, or power from on high.

When we go with the flow of God's love, it flows through us and irrigates every area of our lives as we become viaducts of this love into the lives of others.

When we go with the flow of God's will for our lives, we begin living lives fully pleasing to Him and fruitful in every good work. God is able to use us to accomplish the good works for which we were created. We will get to know and experience God at work in us.

"God has given gifts to each of you from His great variety of spiritual gifts. Manage them well so that God's generosity can flow through you."
1 Peter 4:10 NLT

The older we get, the more we realize how much more rewarding our lives have been when we have gone with the flow instead of stubbornly trying to swim upstream in the rebellion and disobedience of the flesh.

Father, help me to float on the waves of Your love all the days of my life. Amen.

Lord, You Are _____

Forgive Me For _____

Thank You For _____

Needs of Others _____

Personal Needs _____

Answered Prayers _____

Looking Out for #1

"Most people around here are looking out for themselves, with little concern for the things of Jesus," Philippians 2:19 MSG

From the title of a best-selling book of years ago to the underlying premise of secular humanism to the basic problem caused by our sin nature, "Looking out for #1" is a hot topic.

"The rivers of God will not run dry; they provide a bountiful harvest of grain,"
Psalm 65:9b NLT

Most people immediately think of themselves when they hear this phrase. After all, if you don't look out for yourself, who will?

We often give glory and adulation to another person instead of God. Sometimes we get so intent on pursuing pleasure, wealth, power, or the approval of others that this becomes the number-one priority in our lives.

Rick Warren has reminded millions of people all over the world that it's not about us.

God says that when we put Him number one in our lives, He will add all things to us. He goes on to tell us that He will work all things for our good, that nothing can ever separate us from His love, and that He will take care of all our needs in Christ Jesus.

God's ways are so much higher in so many ways that they transcend human understanding. It's hard to understand how you can have more by giving away or why we are supposed to rejoice in times of trial and suffering.

The truth is that it is only when we give up our self-centered, inflated opinion of ourselves, die to self, and become alive in Christ that we can experience the true joy of living life to it's fullest under the authority and control of the lover of our soul and the giver of every good and perfect gift.

"And He will give you all you need from day to day if you live for Him and make the Kingdom of God your primary concern."
Matthew 6:33 NLT

One thing is certain. When our relationship with God is right and Christ sits on the throne of our heart, we have Number One looking out for us!

Father, thank you for looking out for me all the days of my life. Amen.

Lord, You Are _____
Forgive Me For _____
Thank You For _____
Needs of Others _____
Personal Needs _____
Answered Prayers _____

Read 1 Corinthians 13, Psalm 1 June 29

Are You Blowing Smoke?
"Everything under the sun is meaningless, like chasing the wind."
Ecclesiastes 1:14

Unless our new birth results in a change in the way we live our lives, we are just "blowing smoke" when we say we love Jesus and have received the gift of eternal life.

"The ungodly are not so, but are like the chaff which the wind drives away." Psalm 1:4 NLT

When we receive Jesus Christ as Savior, we die to sin and become alive in Christ. The old bondages, attitudes, and trivial pursuits have got to go!

When the Holy Spirit moves in, He cleans house and removes the chains that bind us to our old sinful nature. He begins the ongoing and never-ending metamorphosis of change required to conform us into the image of Christ.

God's love is unconditional. He loves us just as we are, but He also loves us enough to do whatever it takes to change us for the better day by day, year by year.

God's target is very clear. He wants the world to see us as He sees us. He wants the world to see Jesus in us just as He sees Jesus in us and accounts it as righteousness in His sight.

All of the "talkin' the talk" in the world is just "blowing smoke" if we are not "walkin' the walk" of becoming one who has been born again, freed from the bondage of sin, and freed to reflect the love of God to others in every area of our lives.

We will never be all that we should be until we achieve total perfection in heaven. However, we should be able to look back to where we've been and see that we have made and are making progress in becoming more like Jesus as we grow in spiritual maturity by the power of the Holy Spirit living and working in us.

"If I could speak in any language in heaven or on earth but didn't love others, I would only be making meaningless noise like a loud gong or a clanging cymbal." 1 Corinthians 13:1 NLT

As works in progress, we should see progress in the way we live that is not clouded by the meaningless vanity of the world.

Father, help me to keep the main thing of becoming more like Jesus the main thing in my life. Amen.

Lord, You Are _____
Forgive Me For _____
Thank You For _____
Needs of Others _____
Personal Needs _____
Answered Prayers _____

An Affair to Remember

"And do not bring sorrow to God's Holy Spirit by the way you live. Remember, He is the one who has identified you as His own, guaranteeing that you will be saved on the day of redemption." Ephesians 4:30 NLT

We all have some occasions to remember. Whether they be events or relationships, the memory continues to linger.

"My heart is breaking as I remember how it used to be," Psalm 42:4 NLT

The most blessed of us are still carrying on an affair to enjoy and remember forever with the spouses who are the loves of our lives.

Many people can remember the exact momemt they began their love affair with God by receiving Jesus Christ as their Lord and Savior.

From God's standpoint, this has begun His love affair with us, and He has even placed the Holy Spirit in our hearts to "seal the deal" and guarantee that we are adopted sons and daughters.

Unfortunately, many of us often get involved in extra idolatrous affairs that denigrate the beauty, purity, and joy of our love affair with Jesus.

When we let our guard down, the forces of evil within and about us rise up to take over and lead us to do things that we would not do, say things we would not say, and put people, pleasures, and pride above the righteousness of God.

Our new life in Christ is not only about believing but also about being in love with Jesus in an intimate relationship that grows sweeter and more meaningful with each passing day as we abide in Him through His Word.

"Don't ever forget those early days when you first learned about Christ. Remember how you remained faithful even though it meant terrible suffering." Hebrews 10:32 NLT

Our "affair to remember" fills us with the joy of our salvation, the reality of God's presence through the Holy Spirit living within us, and the will, desire, and strength to do those things that please and glorify Him.

We need to keep this affair going strong by feeding daily on the Bread of Life, drinking the cup of salvation, and washing our robes in the blood of Christ by daily confession and repentance. This will keep our affair going until we see Jesus face to face.

Father, help me to stay in love with You. Amen.

Lord, You Are _____

Forgive Me For _____

Thank You For _____

Needs of Others _____

Personal Needs _____

Answered Prayers _____

Read James 1:16-25, Isaiah 66:4, 5 July 1

The Disillusionment of Delusions

"The poor, deluded fool feeds on ashes. He is trusting something that can give him no help at all. Yet he cannot bring himself to ask, 'Is this thing, this idol that I'm holding in my hand, a lie?'" Isaiah 44:20 NLT

Delusions are one of Satan's favorite weapons for waging war against us.

"So will I choose their delusions, and bring their fears on them; because, when I called, no one answered, when I spoke they did not hear; but they did evil before My eyes, and chose that in which I do not delight." Isaiah 66:4

Some get delusions of grandeur and think more highly of themselves than they ought.

Some get deluded about what they think will give them pleasure and make them happy.

Others get a wrong concept of God which gives more delusions and prevents us from ever knowing God as He would have us know Him.

Every delusion will sooner or later bring disillusionment because they are based on lies and misconceptions and will never stand up to the truth.

When we maintain the awareness that we have nothing other than what God has given us and that we are totally dependent upon Him alone even for every breath we take, we can avoid delusions of grandeur.

When we receive the wisdom that comes from on high by abiding and growing in God's Word, we will realize that true pleasure and happiness cannot be found apart from living in a right relationship with Him.

When we get to know God as He reveals Himself in the Bible, we will not be deluded into thinking that He is a Santa Claus who promises us a rose garden free from all pain and suffering on this earth.

St. Paul is not deluding us when He says that God "is able to do exceedingly abundantly above all that we ask or think, according to the power that works in us" (Ephesians 3:20). He is ready to heal all of our disillusionments when we come to Him with a broken spirit and contrite heart, and we worship Him in spirit and in truth.

"But be doers of the Word, and not hearers only, deceiving yourselves." James 1:24

Father, protect me from being deluded by the evil one. Amen.

Lord, You Are _____
Forgive Me For _____
Thank You For _____
Needs of Others _____
Personal Needs _____
Answered Prayers _____

Lift High the Cross!

"Behold, My Servant shall deal prudently; He shall be exalted and extolled and be very high." Isaiah 52:13 NLT

"The sky's the limit" is not relevant when it comes to how high the cross of Jesus Christ has lifted us into the heavenly realms that have no limit.

"Lift up your heads, O you gates! And be lifted up, you everlasting doors! And the King of Glory shall come in." Psalm 24:7 NLT

It is unfortunate that so many cannot lift the cross of Jesus above the walls of race and denomination that often divide the body of Christ and destroy the unity wherein all who believe in Jesus Christ as their Lord and Savior are commanded to abide.

When Jesus is not lifted up, His body is torn down by internal quarrels, divisions, conduct, and comments that are anything but edifying.

Many times, we who should be building blocks become stumbling blocks who give offense to others all because we do not lift high the cross by glorifying God in every area of our lives.

We often have a hard time lifting Jesus above our guilt and shame.

We often cannot lift who we are in Christ above who we are in our old nature and often sink back into the bondage to sins for which Christ died to set us free.

We are never asked to lift alone. We have the indwelling presence of the Holy Spirit to strengthen and sustain us as we persevere through trials and temptations by lifting up our praises and prayers to the One we should be exalting above everything and every one.

"And as Moses lifted up the serpent in the wilderness, even so must the Son of Man be lifted up," John 3:14 NLT

Is there anyone or anything you are exalting and holding up above the cross? Do you really want to make Jesus' death on the cross have no effect by the way you live your life?

Father, help me to always lift high the cross. Amen.

Lord, You Are _____

Forgive Me For _____

Thank You For _____

Needs of Others _____

Personal Needs _____

Answered Prayers _____

Who Can You "Love to Heaven"?

"Live in such a way that God's love can bless you as you wait for the eternal life that our Lord Jesus Christ in his mercy is going to give you. Show mercy to those whose faith is wavering." Jude 1:21,22 NLT

Jesus "loved us to heaven" by dying on the cross for us. We are called to "love others to heaven" by making them disciples.

"I will tell everyone about Your righteousness. All day long I will proclaim Your saving power, for I am overwhelmed by how much You have done for me." Psalm 71:15 NLT

The idea is that when we love others, they will be so impressed by our love they will want to know where it came from and how to get it for themselves.

We help love others to heaven when we establish friendships and relationships that will open the doors to faith sharing and witnessing.

We help love others to heaven when we support missionaries and ministries who are dedicated to obeying the Great Commission.

We help love others to heaven when we participate in and support ministries of healing, feeding the hungry, and visiting the prisoners.

Comforting those who mourn, being a peace maker, blessing those who spitefully use us, and praying for the Holy Spirit to give someone ears to hear and hearts to believe are other avenues for "loving someone to heaven."

When we let others "know we are Christians by our love," we are participating in evangelism at its finest.

When we live out our lives bearing the fruit of the Spirit, the holy transformation that has taken place in our lives through our new birth in Christ will make us "sermons in shoes" that will light up our world.

We can all think of friends, neighbors, and relatives who do not know the love of God that offers eternal life through faith in Jesus Christ.

"And this commandment we have from Him: that he who loves God must love his brother also." 1 John 4:21 NLT

We dare not hoard this love for ourselves, but we are commanded to pass it on by being conduits of God's love to others.

Who do you need to help "love to heaven"?

Father, help me to help "love someone to heaven." Amen.

Lord, You Are _____

Forgive Me For _____

Thank You For _____

Needs of Others _____

Personal Needs _____

Answered Prayers _____

July 4
Read 1 Corinthians 1:18-31, Psalm 119:45-52

The Real Declaration of Independence

"So those now who live by faith are blessed along with Abraham, who lived by faith—this is no new doctrine! And that means that anyone who tries to live by his own effort, independent of God, is doomed to failure."
Galatians 3:9 MSG

While July 4th is generally celebrated as the day we declared independence from the tyrannical rule of the British and the birthday of our country, there are many other major declarations of independence.

"I will walk in freedom, for I have devoted myself to Your commandments."
Psalm 119:45 NLT

The day Adam and Eve declared their independence from God by disobedience is the day for which we all are still paying.

Secular Humanism teaches that man is the captain of his fate, that he does not need God, and that he can advance civilization and bring peace to the world in his own strength. This declaration of independence is being taught in our schools and advanced in our courthouses and legislative assemblies.

The greatest declaration of independence in the history of the world was when Jesus Christ died on the cross, and He declared us free from bondage to sin and free to pursue life to the fullest through a new birth as sons and daughters of God.

We can appropriate independence from sin and death by faith as we enter into a personal relationship with Jesus by the power of the Holy Spirit.

"God alone made it possible for you to be in Christ Jesus. For our benefit God made Christ to be wisdom itself. He is the one who made us acceptable to God. He made us pure and holy, and He gave himself to purchase our freedom."
1 Corinthians 1:30 NLT

When we declare our independence from bondage to sin, the Holy Spirit comes to live within us and begins the lifelong process of holy transformation through which we are transformed into the likeness of Christ by the renewing of our minds.

We should be celebrating Independence Day every day as we confess and live in the freedom of God's forgiveness.

Father, thank you for declaring me free to live totally dependent on and in You. Amen.

Lord, You Are _____

Forgive Me For _____

Thank You For _____

Needs of Others _____

Personal Needs _____

Answered Prayers _____

Beware of Common Sense

"There is a way that seems right to a man, but its end is the way of death."
Proverbs 14:2

We all have a tendency to admire the quality of common sense without realizing it is often a characteristic of our human nature that often misleads and causes us great harm.

"Train me in good common sense; I'm thoroughly committed to living Your way."
Psalm 119:66 MSG

Human common sense told Eve that it would be good to know everything that God knew. Human common sense fuels our self-centered motives and makes it hard to understand and follow God's higher thoughts and directives.

Failure to acquire spiritual common sense along with wisdom and spiritual understanding will cause us to reject and fail to understand God's higher ways.

What is common sense telling you about living together apart from marriage…the foolishness of giving…the effects of fooling around with drugs and alcohol…the foolishness of turning over control of every area of your life to God?

How does human common sense allow us to believe the teachings of the Sermon on the Mount which stand in sharp contrast to worldly wisdom and common sense?

Worldly common sense has its place in life but should never be confused with wisdom or spiritual discernment that accompanies spiritual common sense. Human common sense will never allow us to comprehend the oracles of God that are spiritually discerned.

"But the law code itself is God's good and common sense, each command sane and holy counsel."
Romans 7:9 MSG

Spiritual discernment and wisdom are the supernatural gifts of the Spirit to those who put Jesus on the throne. We must never allow common sense that is based on our own human understanding to undermine our faith or our knowledge of who we are in Christ.

Father, by the power of Your Spirit, endow me with godly common sense. Amen.

Lord, You Are _____

Forgive Me For _____

Thank You For _____

Needs of Others _____

Personal Needs _____

Answered Prayers _____

Unemployment

"He said to His disciples, 'The harvest is so great, but the workers are so few. So pray to the Lord who is in charge of the harvest; ask Him to send out more workers for His fields.'" Matthew 9:37

Unemployment figures are a major prosperity index for our economy. Elections have been won and lost by these numbers.

"I said to the LORD, 'You are my Master! All the good things I have are from You.'" Psalm 16:2 NLT

Sometimes it seems that we do not have as much of an employment problem as we do an employable problem. The numbers of homeless, street people and dysfunctional welfare recipients who can't seem to get or hold any job distort the unemployment figures.

As staggering as our country's unemployment figures might seem sometimes, they cannot begin to compare with God's ranks of the unemployed.

The harvest of souls lies rotting in the fields because there are not enough workers to harvest them. God often has to work through others because His own have quit their jobs or refused to work.

Many of God's unemployables cannot be used because they have let bitterness, doubt, or despair take root. Others are leading such wretched lives of blatant sin that they can no longer be used as candles to light up the darkness.

"And a servant of the Lord must not quarrel but be gentle to all, able to teach, patient," 2 Timothy 2:24 NLT

God is the greatest employer anyone could ever have. He never fires, and His employee benefits are the best ever offered.

Although many may seem to take some extended vacations and leaves of absence, and others moonlight in other occupations, God's patience is exceeded only by His love. He is patiently waiting for us to come back to work and "be about our Father's business."

Father, may I never file an unemployment claim against You. Amen.

Lord, You Are _____

Forgive Me For _____

Thank You For _____

Needs of Others _____

Personal Needs _____

Answered Prayers _____

How's Your Prosperity Index?

One of the biggest problems confronting God's chosen ones down throughout all generations has been their inability to handle prosperity.

> "Behind closed doors, you have set up your idols and worship them instead of Me. This is adultery, for you are loving these idols instead of loving Me. You have climbed right into bed with these detestable gods."
> Isaiah 57:9

From God's remarkable deliverance by the parting of the Red Sea to receiving the gift of eternal life through faith in Jesus Christ, God's very own have a track record of falling into idolatry when they start enjoying the blessings of prosperity from God.

The pursuit of pleasure, possessions, and power all too often take over and take God out of first place in our lives when we are blessed with an abundance of time, talent, and treasure.

Who needs God when we are living the abundant life according to the world's standards? Who needs the Good Shepherd when we are doing very well feeding on the green pastures of pride?

God's discipline can be very hard at times, but it can usually be avoided by keeping our eyes on Jesus, the Author and Perfecter of our faith. When we realize that God is the source of all our blessings and that we are totally dependent upon Him for every breath we take, we will do a better job of enjoying prosperity without letting it destroy us.

We cannot serve two masters. We can't sell out to the world without selling out Jesus.

God hates spiritual adultery as much or even more than He hates sexual adultery.

We must constantly guard against letting the pursuit of fame and fortune take over seeking the Kingdom of God and His righteousness.

> "Prosperity is as short-lived as a wildflower, so don't ever count on it. You know that as soon as the sun rises, pouring down its scorching heat, the flower withers. Its petals wilt and, before you know it, that beautiful face is a barren stem. Well, that's a picture of the 'prosperous life.'"
> James 1:10-11 MSG

Father, in counting my blessings daily, let me never forget their source or let them come between me and my relationship with You. Amen.

Lord, You Are _____
Forgive Me For _____
Thank You For _____
Needs of Others _____
Personal Needs _____
Answered Prayers _____

July 8 **Read 2 Corinthians 12:1-10, Job 1**

Does God Trust Us Too Much?

"But he said to her, 'You speak as one of the foolish women speaks. Shall we indeed accept good from God, and shall we not accept adversity?' In all this Job did not sin with his lips." Job 2:10

There is great comfort in knowing that God will not give us more trials and temptations than we can bear and that He will provide a means of escape.

"Satan replied to the LORD, 'Yes, Job fears God, but not without good reason! You have always protected him and his home and his property from harm. You have made him prosperous in everything he does. Look how rich he is! He has, and he will surely curse You to Your face!'"

Job 1:9, 10 NLT

When we see the trials and tribulations of some of the saints we know, we are absolutely amazed at how much God has put in their cups of sorrow and suffering.

We can't even imagine how we could go through some of the problems others are encountering.

If ever God seemed to trust someone too much, it would have to be Job. When Satan said that Job was good only because he had been so blessed, God allowed Satan to throw any misfortune imaginable Job's way (except death).

Job's refusal to curse God and die or to give up on God sets the standard for all believers. We, like Job, should always remember that our Redeemer lives and that He will work all things for our good and His glory.

Jesus tells us to rejoice when we are persecuted. Paul tells us to count it all joy when we suffer and to give thanks for it.

"And He said to me, 'My grace is sufficient for you, for My strength is made perfect in weakness.'"

2 Corinthians 12:9

We also need to be mindful of the trust God puts in us when He doles out an abundance of talents and treasures.

Sometimes the biggest failures of all come from betraying the trust God has put in us to be good stewards of our lives.

Father, thank you for not trusting me with more than I can handle with the strength You provide. Amen.

Lord, You Are _____
Forgive Me For _____
Thank You For _____
Needs of Others _____
Personal Needs _____
Answered Prayers _____

In Spite of and Through

"But God demonstrates His own love toward us, in that while we were still sinners, Christ died for us." Romans 5:8

This is a phrase worth remembering, applying, and inwardly digesting.

"As far as the east is from the west, so far has He removed our transgressions from us."
Psalm 103:12

God hates sin but loves us "in spite of and through" it. Even when we are at our worst, God is at His best through His all-sustaining grace and the power of the Holy Spirit in completing that good work that was begun in us the hour we first believed.

A good marriage requires many of the fruit of God's spirit working "in spite of and through" times of disappointment, disagreement, and frustration often encountered in living life together.

We are called to rejoice and praise God "in spite of and through" circumstances that are anything but pleasant. We are promised to be filled with that peace that surpasses all understanding when we do this.

As disciples of Jesus Christ, we are commanded to love others "in spite of and through" being despitefully used and disappointed.

As saints of God, we are commanded to persevere "in spite of and through" the deep waters of doubt, distress, pain, and suffering that are common in a life lived in a sin-sick world in a corruptible body that is our temporary home on this earth.

"There's no particular virtue in accepting punishment that you well deserve. But if you're treated badly for good behavior and continue in spite of it to be a good servant, that is what counts with God."
2 Peter 2:18 MSG

Jesus Christ manifested His love for us "in spite of and through" our sinfulness when he died on the cross and ransomed us through His blood so that God would love us and accept us as sons and daughters.

What comfort there is in knowing that in spite of our sins, through His grace, God renews His mercies to us every day of our lives.

Father, by the power of Your Spirit, help me be fruitful and faithful in spite of and through all of the oppression of my flesh, the world, and Satan. Amen.

Lord, You Are _____

Forgive Me For _____

Thank You For _____

Needs of Others _____

Personal Needs _____

Answered Prayers _____

Issues of Control

"But let the Lord Jesus Christ take control of you, and don't think of ways to indulge your evil desires." Romans 13:14 NLT

Every day, thousands of pilots turn the control of their airplanes over to flight controllers to guide them to a safe landing.

"Keep me from deliberate sins! Don't let them control me. Then I will be free of guilt and innocent of great sin." Psalm 19:13 NLT

We have control freaks demanding the TV remote in order to be in control.

There is drive, instinct, or ambition in many people to be in control of others. The old adage that "power corrupts" is evidenced in about every area of life. We see it in politics, businesses, churches, and about every other organization.

It is generally believed that a large majority of people who reject Christ's wonderful gift of salvation do so because they are not willing to submit control of their lives and conduct to a higher power.

Overly controlling parents have caused great harm to their children. Overly controlling spouses have been the cause of many divorces.

When we insist on self control and self centeredness instead of God control and Christ centeredness in any area of our life, we are "cruising for a bruising."

When we bear the fruit of self control, which is a gift of God's grace to believers, we can stand firm in God's power when temptations come.

"If your sinful nature controls your mind, there is death. But if the Holy Spirit controls your mind, there is life and peace." Romans 8:6 NLT

It's a no brainer to even consider being controlled by anyone or anything other than the great, all-powerful, all-knowing, ever-present, and ever-loving Lord and Creator of the Universe and Lover of our souls.

We cannot control a lot of things in this life. We can't always control our circumstances, our finances, or our health, but we can always control what kind of an attitude we will have when it comes to responding to these things we cannot control.

Father, help me to submit to Your will and the guidance of Your Spirit that will see me home to a safe landing in Heaven. Amen.

Lord, You Are _____

Forgive Me For _____

Thank You For _____

Needs of Others _____

Personal Needs _____

Answered Prayers _____

Turning Our Backs on Yesterdays

"Finally, brethren, whatever things are true, whatever things are noble, whatever things are just, whatever things are pure, whatever things are lovely, whatever things are of good report, if there is any virtue and if there is anything praiseworthy—meditate on these things." Philippians 4:8

Dwelling on offenses and bad experiences of the past seems to haunt many people. While we naturally seem to and should remember the good and forget the bad, many prefer to blame their problems on emotional scars of the past.

"Blessed is the man whose strength is in You, whose heart is set on pilgrimage." Psalm 84:4

We hear a lot of talk about the "good old days," which were not that good at all. Sin and the effects of sin have always been around and will continue to be around until Christ returns, and we have sinless paradise restored.

Others seem to dwell on the "bad old days" and ignore the love of God and others, which has also always been around. This allows roots of bitterness to take root and rob us and those around us of peace and joy.

The greatest gift that God gives us besides eternal life itself is the gift of not only forgiving but of not even remembering our confessed and repented sins. This is a gift we should give to ourselves and to others.

Just as we tend to rationalize our sins and mistakes by blaming our sinful nature and the wiles of the devil, we often blame our past hurts for present failures, which causes difficulties in getting on with our new lives in Christ and what real faith is all about.

God did not give us a free will to choose bondage but to choose freedom and completeness in Christ by the power of the Holy Spirit.

"To know the love of Christ, which passes knowledge, that you may be filled with all the fullness of God," Ephesians 3:19 NLT

We were not called to dwell on the past and any of its pains and problems but rather to dwell on the virtues of moral excellence which are ours by the power of the Holy Spirit living in us.

We need to imitate Christ and move upward in our journey of growing into His fullness and enjoying the abundant life God promises and wants for all believers.

Father, forgive me for dwelling on the hurts of the past and help me to enjoy Your present of the present and future. Amen.

Lord, You Are _____

Forgive Me For _____

Thank You For _____

Needs of Others _____

Personal Needs _____

Answered Prayers _____

Chooser or Choosee?

"You did not choose Me, but I chose you ..." John 15:16

We hear often about making decisions for Christ or deciding to follow Jesus.

> "Happy are those who hear the joyful call to worship, for they will walk in the light of your presence, LORD."
> Psalm 89:15 NLT

Somewhere along the way, we tend to lose sight of the fact that "no one can say that Jesus is Lord, except by the Holy Spirit" *(1 Corinthians 12:3b).*

We cannot accept an invitation we have not received, and we cannot take credit for something God did by the power of the Holy Spirit.

We are called to make disciples by proclaiming the Good News through which the Holy Spirit gives people the power to open the door when Jesus calls.

When God chooses us, He also gives us a new birth. A transformed life is the real evidence that we are "choosees" instead of "choosers." When someone says that they were saved years ago but there is absolutely no evidence of holy transformation in the way they live their lives, it should give cause to wonder about the state of their souls and the reality of their salvation.

The fact that "many are called, but few are chosen" *(Matthew 22:14)* is easy to understand with regard to those who outwardly reject God's call to salvation. It also speaks to the fact that many who call Jesus Lord by the call of man are not really saved at all.

> "Not all people who sound religious are really godly. They may refer to me as 'Lord,' but they still won't enter the Kingdom of Heaven. The decisive issue is whether they obey My Father in heaven."
> Matthew 7:21 NLT

Scripture says "by their fruits you shall know them" *(Matthew 7:16). We all need to* constantly examine ourselves by our fruitfulness in making manifest the fruit of the Spirit in our everyday lives.

While only God knows our hearts and judges us accordingly, we need to "Therefore, brethren, be even more diligent to make your call and election sure, for if you do these things you will never stumble" *(2 Peter 1:10).*

Father, thank you for choosing me by the power of Your Spirit. Amen.

Lord, You Are _____

Forgive Me For _____

Thank You For _____

Needs of Others _____

Personal Needs _____

Answered Prayers _____

Getting The Rug Pulled Out From Under Us

"So the Word became human and lived here on earth among us. He was full of unfailing love and faithfulness. And we have seen His glory, the glory of the only Son of the Father." John 1:12 NL

We have all experienced and will continue to experience "getting the rug pulled out from under us."

"O LORD God Almighty! Where is there anyone as mighty as You, LORD? Faithfulness is Your very character."
Psalm 89:8 NLT

At work or at play, at home or away, we are going to experience troubles in this life that will test and inspect our faith.

Just as we never know how good our insurance company is until we file a claim, we will never know how strong our faith is until it has been tested.

Pruning and disciplining are all part of God's character-development program for us as He conforms us into the image of Christ.

When we put our hope in people, popularity, possessions, or anything other than God, we are going to get the rug pulled out from under us.

People are human, and in their humanity, they make mistakes that will often disappoint and even shock us.

Popularity is a fleeting, fragile, and very risky attribute on which to pin much hope.

Possessions can often possess us, and when we put our hope for the future in them, we are hoping on sinking sand.

There is only one person Who will never fail us. He is the One Who loves us with an everlasting love, Whose character will never allow Him to lie or to break a promise.

When our hope is built on nothing less than Jesus' blood and righteousness, we will stumble and fall, suffer and endure, but through it all, we will experience the love and faithfulness of God.

"We can rejoice, too, when we run into problems and trials, for we know that they are good for us—they help us learn to endure."
Romans 5:3 NLT

How could we ever think of putting our hope in anyone else?

Father, let Your faithfulness be my anchor and my hope through all of the disappointments of life. Amen.

Lord, You Are _____

Forgive Me For _____

Thank You For _____

Needs of Others _____

Personal Needs _____

Answered Prayers _____

Making Life Work

"'For I know the plans I have for you,' says the LORD. 'They are plans for good and not for disaster, to give you a future and a hope.'" Jeremiah 29:11 NLT

"I did it my way," "I am the captain of my fate," and "go for the gusto" are a few examples of some perspectives on how to make life work.

"When wisdom enters your heart and knowledge is pleasant to your soul, discretion will preserve you; understanding will keep you," Proverbs 2:10,11

Everyday, millions of people wander aimlessly lost seeking love and significance in all the wrong places without a clue as to how to make life work.

We need always to remember Jesus' reminder that "apart from me, you can do nothing" (John 15:5). When we try to make life work without the resurrection power of God at work in us through the Holy Spirit, we can be sure that we will never be able to make life work the way God intended.

Many ignore their need for God when enjoying all of the pleasures and blessings of life without any of the heartbreak or problems about which we are warned will come time and time again in Scripture.

Making life work in our marriages, parenting, relationships, finances, and work places often requires more longsuffering, patience, self control, and love than we can supply in our own strength.

"He is especially hard on those who follow their own evil, lustful desires and who despise authority. These people are proud and arrogant, daring even to scoff at the glorious ones without so much as trembling." 2 Peter 2:10 NLT

Jesus tells us that He is the Way, the Truth and the Life. When we seek to be our own way, truth, and life, we are headed for trouble.

Trying to make life work without the miracle worker is a futile pursuit. Jesus not only promises but has the power to keep His promises to work all things for the good of those who love Him.

Father help me to make life work through faith in and obedience to You. Amen.

Lord, You Are _____

Forgive Me For _____

Thank You For _____

Needs of Others _____

Personal Needs _____

Answered Prayers _____

Issues

"And don't sin by letting anger gain control over you. Don't let the sun go down while you are still angry, for anger gives a mighty foothold to the Devil." Ephesians 4:26 NLT

We often find ourselves carrying many unresolved matters in our agendas of life.

"It's best to stay in touch with both sides of an issue. A person who fears God deals responsibly with all of reality, not just a piece of it."
Ecclesiastes 7:18

Issues concerning morality, mortality, and accountability and regarding relational problems, education, marriages, stewardship of time, and treasures often go unresolved and keep us from ever growing into the fullness of Christ.

The resolving of any issues we have regarding our relationship with God through faith in Jesus Christ should not be ignored. Any lingering guilt or unforgiveness should be laid at the Cross immediately, if not sooner.

Any doubts about God's love and acceptance of us by virtue of our faith and trust in Jesus Christ should be resolved by really getting into God's Word and receiving the grace, strength, and assurance it provides in dealing with doubt.

Any besetting sins that we are allowing to hold us in bondage need to be resolved by confession, repentance, and prayer for the Holy Spirit to overcome our weaknesses with God's strength.

Unresolved anger and bitterness that take root in our hearts suck up a lot of joy and waste a lot of energy that could be better spent in building up rather than tearing down.

"Let us strip off every weight that slows us down, especially the sin that so easily hinders our progress. And let us run with endurance the race that God has set before us."
Hebrews 12:1b NLT

We have the greatest issue resolver ever given. Faith in the blood of Jesus not only resolves the issue of our mortality, but it gives a new birth which empowers us to walk free from the dominion and power of sin and gives us the power to resolve any issues of morality.

Father, grant me the resurrection power of Your Spirit to resolve any issues that are stunting my growth into Your fullness. Amen.

Lord, You Are _____

Forgive Me For _____

Thank You For _____

Needs of Others _____

Personal Needs _____

Answered Prayers _____

God's Justice Will Not Be Denied

"The Lord is slow to anger and rich in unfailing love, forgiving every kind of sin and rebellion. Even so He does not leave sin unpunished, but He punishes the children for the sins of their parents to the third and fourth generations." Numbers 14:18 NLT

Justice, like beauty, is often in the eye of the beholder. We often think that life is not fair when we see the bad people prosper and good people having a hard time.

"For I envied the proud when I saw them prosper despite their wickedness." Psalm 73:3 NLT

We have a tendency within us to rejoice when bad things happen to bad people and get angry and question God when good things happen to bad people

The world's standard for retribution is "don't get mad—get even." What should our standard be as disciples of Jesus?

There is often cause for anger and righteous indignation, which is not sin unless we let it take control of us and cause us to sin.

God's justice is basically in seeing that we reap what we sew. He is the one who demands the right of meting out vengeance, and He does not need our help. We may not live to see it, but we can be sure from God's Word that unrepented sin will not go unpunished.

Jesus' suffering the consequence of our sins by dying on the cross for them so that we would not have to die for them does not mean that we are going to escape the divine retribution and consequences that God's justice demands.

Just as it is more blessed to give than receive, it may well be even more blessed to forgive than let anger and bitterness take root and cause us to sin by seeking to be avengers.

"But no, you won't listen. So you are storing up terrible punishment for yourself because of your stubbornness in refusing to turn from your sin," Romans 2:5 NLT

We need to filter our response to wrongdoing and sins through the fountain of God's grace and remember what Jesus Himself said about being merciful, being a peace maker, and turning the other cheek. God will take care of the wrong doer.

Father, don't let me fret about the good fortune of bad people. Amen.

Lord, You Are _____

Forgive Me For _____

Thank You For _____

Needs of Others _____

Personal Needs _____

Answered Prayers _____

Being Image Conscious

"For whom He foreknew, He also predestined to be conformed to the image of His Son, that He might be the firstborn among many brethren."
Romans 8:29 NLT

The world and its people seem to be obsessed with image. Companies, movie stars, and politicians often hire professional public relations people to project and protect their images.

"We justify our actions by appearances; GOD examines our motives."
Proverbs 21:2 MSG

It doesn't take very long for any school child to become aware of peer pressure and the importance of having a good image among their classmates.

People spend billions of dollars each year on trying to improve their physical image by working out, dieting, getting nose jobs, buying the best cosmetics, or being seen in the right places.

Many people are image conscious about the cars they drive, the homes they have, the churches they attend, and the clothes they wear.

Psychologists stress the importance of a good self image. When we do not measure up to what we would like to be or think we ought to be in any area of our life, this often translates into a poor self image, which leads to inferiority complexes and insecurity.

The realization that we are to be conformed into the image of Christ is often overlooked by many believers and nonbelievers alike as they are so self centered and self focused they miss the importance or being conscious of our image in the sight of God and man.

"And all of us have had that veil removed so that we can be mirrors that brightly reflect the glory of the Lord. And as the Spirit of the Lord works within us, we become more and more like Him and reflect His glory even more."
1 Corinthians 3:18 NLT

When we grow in the likeness of Christ to where others see us as God sees us, we become living proof of the transforming power of the Holy Spirit as evidenced by one who has been truly born again in Christ.

Shouldn't we all be more image conscious in projecting the love of God and character of Christ in our every day life?

Father, by the power of Your Spirit, help me to become more conscious of my image as one of Your redeemed. Amen.

Lord, You Are _____
Forgive Me For _____
Thank You For _____
Needs of Others _____
Personal Needs _____
Answered Prayers _____

Think of Getting Back Before You Go!

"The LORD your God will delight in you if you obey his voice and keep the commands and laws written in this Book of the Law, and if you turn to the LORD your God with all your heart and soul." Exodus 30:10

"Oh, give me back my joy again; you have broken me— now let me rejoice." Psalm 51:8 NLT

We purchase round trip tickets for about every trip. We begin our journeys with great energy and expectations. Then, we often get worn out and exhausted thinking about the trip home.

The return trip for the sinner is always the hardest trip of all, and sometimes we can never fully return back into the good graces of those we have sinned against and will bear painful consequences of our sins far beyond any temporary pleasure received.

When we rebel against God and jump out of the sheep fold of His goodness, mercy, and saving grace in a frenzy of passion or unholy lust for sexual gratification, possessions, power, or prestige, we often become so overcome with guilt that we can never fully forgive ourselves.

Counting the cost of our sin to others and ourselves can be an effective means of escaping temptation.

The cost of the hurt our sins cause to others should be more than enough to nip any unholy thoughts, words, or actions before they happen.

When we look around, we can see too many examples of the brokenness caused by the effects of sin on not only the sinner but on those the sinner loves.

Counting the cost of the return trip from sin will make us realize that it is just not worth it, and it will help keep us from going where we should not go and doing what we should not even think of doing.

"A few days later this younger son packed all his belongings and took a trip to a distant land, and there he wasted all his money on wild living." Luke 15:13 NLT

If it's too late and you are experiencing the hard way of a transgressor who has wandered into the ambush of sin, keep in mind that the Father is always standing at the door waiting to receive you back when you return with godly sorrow, a broken spirit, and a contrite heart.

Father, help me to count the cost before I take any detour into any sin that might be tempting me. Amen.

Lord, You Are _____

Forgive Me For _____

Thank You For _____

Needs of Others _____

Personal Needs _____

Answered Prayers _____

Giving Out More Than You Take In

In business or money, if you spend more than you take in, you will either end

"For the Lord does not abandon anyone forever. Though He brings grief, He also shows compassion according to the greatness of His unfailing love. For He does not enjoy hurting people or causing them sorrow."
Lamentations 3:31

up in bondage to credit cards or go bankrupt, or sometimes both.

The same principle applies to emotional strength and stability in the lives of many people.

Pastors especially are called upon so often to supply comfort, guidance, and emotional strength and stability that they become drained and weakened, falling prey to temptations and satanic oppression.

God's grace is sufficient for all our needs, and His strength can overcome any weakness. Sometimes we lose sight of the absolute necessity of receiving God's grace daily through abiding in His Word, prayer, and the encouragement, fellowship, and accountability of other believers.

It is interesting to note that some studies of fallen pastors show that a large majority were lone rangers who did not draw strength from the fellowship and encouragement of other believers.

Satan often siezes the opportunity to oppress or tempt us when the emotional or relational demands of others weaken and drain us.

We have the well of living water that will never run dry, but we have to drink of it. We have the Bread of Life, but we have to partake of it. We have the full armor of God, but we have to put it on daily.

"May you experience the love of Christ, though it is so great you will never fully understand it. Then you will be filled with the fullness of life and power that comes from God."
Ephesians 3:19 NLT

We need to give of ourselves and our treasures from an overflowing cup that we fill daily through confession, repentance, drawing strength from other believers, and abiding in Christ through prayer and the Word.

Father, through Your grace and by the power of Your Spirit, help me to keep my cup filled. Amen.

Lord, You Are _____

Forgive Me For _____

Thank You For _____

Needs of Others _____

Personal Needs _____

Answered Prayers _____

Satan's Notches

"Keep alert and pray. Otherwise temptation will overpower you. For though the spirit is willing enough, the body is weak!" Matthew 26:41

The old-time custom of carving a notch on a gun for every kill probably started with the devil. This master of deceit also known as the roaring lion, seeking who he may devour, holds the all-time record for kills and continues to carve his notches every minute of every day.

"The LORD is close to all who call on Him, yes, to all who call on Him sincerely." Psalm 145:118 NLT

The siren's song of temptation to lust and to satisfy that lust has brought down some of the best Christian pastors and other believers through the ages.

If David, "the man after God's own heart," was not immune, no one should think that they are. Whether the lust is sexual, material, or egocentric pride, we should never underestimate the power of temptation.

"It can never happen to me" are words that come back to haunt. Just as Peter said that he would never deny Christ and failed miserably, others who thought they could play with fire and not get burned are a sad testimony to the reality and consequences of succumbing to temptation.

The wake of broken homes, shattered dreams, pain, and suffering for not only the sinner but often for those they love most engulfs churches, families and organizations when the wave of temptation succeeds in breaking down the barriers.

The saddest thing of all is that none of these falls have to happen among believers. God has promised to provide a means of escape from every temptation. Christ has set us free from bondage to and domination by sin. We cannot succumb unless we allow seeds of unrighteousness to take root in our hearts, refuse to use the full armor of God that He has provided, or do not flee via the escape route He provides. As long as we think we can handle

"Don't let anyone under pressure to give in to evil say, 'God is trying to trip me up.' God is impervious to evil, and puts evil in no one's way. The temptation to give in to evil comes from us and only us." James 1:13 MSG

temptation on our own, we will be fair game for the devil's target practice.

Father, deliver me from evil and bind Satan that he not notch me as another one of his kills. Amen.

Lord, You Are _____

Forgive Me For _____

Thank You For _____

Needs of Others _____

Personal Needs _____

Answered Prayers _____

The Kingdom Principle

"But seek first the kingdom of God and His righteousness, and all these things shall be added to you." Matthew 6:23 NLT

We need to be ever mindful of the millions of kingdoms that we visit throughout our lives. Starting with the kingdom of our homes, which are castles of our kingdom, we rule as or are ruled by the head of this kingdom. We are given certain inalienable rights of privacy, freedom, and security in this kingdom.

"For the kingdom is the LORD's, And He rules over the nations."
Psalm 22:28 NLT

In every church, prison, workplace, school, political party, organization, or business, there are kingdoms with rulers in place, and we need to be aware of and sensitive to this.

Many people try to establish a relationship with a head waiter or athletic director in order to get special favors from the heads of these kingdoms.

We should never underestimate the power and influence of these kingdoms and always be sensitive to the reality of their existence when we are in any of the many kingdom territories.

Of all the kingdoms, the two most important are the kingdom of light and the kingdom of darkness. Whichever of the rulers of these we choose to follow and pledge our allegiance will determine the quality of our life now and forever.

"Therefore, since we are receiving a kingdom which cannot be shaken, let us have grace, by which we may serve God acceptably with reverence and godly fear."
Hebrews 12: 28

When we choose to obey the desires of our flesh and live in the kingdom of darkness, we will have misery upon misery, guilt upon guilt, and consequence upon consequence to suffer through before suffering the consequence of everlasting doom and destruction.

When we seek and receive the kingdom of God, good things will be added to us beyond anything that we can even imagine, and the gift of living in the perfect bliss of heaven is imputed to us by faith.

Whose kingdom rules you?

Father, help me to receive and enjoy all of the blessings of eternal life for now and forever in Your kingdom. Amen.

Lord, You Are _____
Forgive Me For _____
Thank You For _____
Needs of Others _____
Personal Needs _____
Answered Prayers _____

                   Read Colossians 1:18-23, Proverbs 14:12-18

By-product or Condition?

"And I am convinced that nothing can ever separate us from His love. Death can't, and life can't. The angels can't, and the demons can't. Our fears for today, our worries about tomorrow, and even the powers of hell can't keep God's love away." Romans 8:38 NLT

The concept that God's love is unconditional is hard, if not fully impossible for us to understand. That He thought we were worth dying for should shame us all because deep down we know that we were not worth it.

"There is a way that seems right to a man, but its end is the way of death." Proverbs 14:12 NLT

Even those who shout "by faith alone by grace alone" will often say that they are going to go to heaven because of their goodness instead of because of God's unconditional love.

We need to know that any good that we do and any love that we show are not conditions to be met for our salvation, but they are by-products of the love that God has first shown us in Jesus Christ.

God does not love us because of our sins but in spite of them. No matter what we do, He can never love us any more than to die for us or any less than to receive us as beloved sons and daughters as joint heirs with Christ when we receive His wonderful gift of salvation through faith in Jesus Christ.

The transformed life of becoming imitators of Christ and reflecting His love to others through any good that we might do or kindness that we might show is the by-product of God's unconditional love.

"Yet now He has brought you back as His friends. He has done this through His death on the cross in His own human body. As a result, He has brought you into the very presence of God, and you are holy and blameless as you stand before Him without a single fault." Colossians 1:22 NLT

We need to let our light shine and let our good works glorify God to others, but we should never seek to glorify ourselves or think that we can do anything to earn our salvation. How insulting to think that we need to add anything to God's amazing grace.

Father, give me a proper understanding of the completeness and unconditional nature of Your love. Amen.

Lord, You Are _____

Forgive Me For _____

Thank You For _____

Needs of Others _____

Personal Needs _____

Answered Prayers _____

Worshipping Our Religion

"These people honor me with their lips, but their hearts are far away. Their worship is a farce, for they replace God's commands with their own man-made teachings." Mark 7:7 NLT

There is a real danger in becoming over zealous about our particular denomination and its doctrines. While it is good to

> **"How can a young person stay pure? By obeying Your word and following its rules."**
> **Psalm 119:9 NLT**

know what your church believes and for which it stands, it is even better to know Jesus and make Him the ruler of your heart. Sometimes you have to stop being religious to do this.

The differences between building up the kingdom of God and building up the kingdom of a certain individual church or denomination are often ignored and overlooked. Defending the faith often seems more important than saving the lost.

Many denominations and pastors miss out on the blessings of great Christ-edifying and kingdom-building resources because they believe that no good thing can come from anyone outside of their denomination and refuse to use these wonderful resources.

We are not talking about watering down or compromising the inerrancy of Scripture or the truth of God's Word. The centrality of the gospel is that faith in Jesus Christ is the only means of salvation.

Martin Luther adapted the bar songs of the day to spread the gospel before Bibles and literacy were widely available.

> **"Don't let anyone lead you astray with empty philosophy and high-sounding nonsense that come from human thinking and from the evil powers of this world, and not from Christ."**
> **Colossians 2:8 NLT**

Billy Graham has probably led more people to Christ than any other person in the twentieth century and has never changed the message but has changed the music and packaging to reach today's culture.

We should never fall into the trap of worshipping a denomination or tradition above God.

Father, help me to focus my mind's attention and heart's affection on Jesus. Amen.

Lord, You Are _____

Forgive Me For _____

Thank You For _____

Needs of Others _____

Personal Needs _____

Answered Prayers _____

Call of the Wild

"Put on the whole armor of God that you may be able to stand against the wiles of the devil." Ephesians 6:11

There are some calls we are better off not answering. When the evil one starts calling us back to the wild side of life, we had best hang up the phone.

"Don't let me lust for evil things; don't let me participate in acts of wickedness." Psalm 141:4a NLT

We need to be ever mindful that although Satan has been defeated on the cross of Calvary and the war has been won, He is still a very dangerous wounded animal that is on the prowl seeking to destroy.

Although we have been set free from the dominion of sin and condemnation from sin spiritually, we need to be ever mindful that there is an ongoing battle within our flesh between the good we would do and the evil that we would not do, and we are not going to win every battle.

Although we have died to sin and become alive in Christ spiritually, we still have pockets of pride, envy, anger, lust, and greed left over that we do not always give up so easily.

This is why we are all works in progress and have been given the Holy Spirit and His power to overcome the powers of evil when they come.

We are all works in progress being molded and melded into the likeness of Christ through a lifetime of tests and temptations of every description. How well we manage to endure and overcome these daily battles against the "call of the wild" is proportional to how well and how often we put on the full armor of God.

When we keep the sword of the Spirit sitting unopened in our homes and the shield of faith, helmet of salvation, breastplate of righteousness, and sandals of peace relegated to the closet, we are going to lose the battle when evil comes calling.

"When I want to do good, I don't. And when I try not to do wrong, I do it anyway." Romans 7:19 NLT

When we flee temptation or stand firm clothed with the full armor of God, we can be sure that God will provide a means of escape and that we will not be overcome.

Father, help me to hang up when my old sinful nature calls. Amen.

Lord, You Are _____
Forgive Me For _____
Thank You For _____
Needs of Others _____
Personal Needs _____
Answered Prayers _____

Read 2 Corinthians 7:8-12, Isaiah 1:19-20   July 25

Keep Shoveling!

"Be brave. Be strong. Don't give up. Expect GOD to get here soon."
Psalm 31:24 MSG

There is a lesson to be learned from one of my favorite old stories about the little boy shoveling away in a stall sure that with all that manure there had to be a pony in there somewhere.

"If you will only obey me and let me help you, then you will have plenty to eat." Isaiah 1:19 NLT

When we keep shoveling through the manure of life, we will eventually find the pony of God's blessing upon us.

We need to cling to God's promises and the fact that He has never broken one no matter what.

When God's Word says that He works all things for our good and His glory, we need to believe it.

When God's Word goes on to say that nothing can separate us from the love of God which is ours through Christ Jesus, we need to believe it.

God never promised any of us a rose garden in this stage of our forever life.

Sin abounds, and because of sin, we are going to experience the sadness and suffering of the pain and sorrow it brings. The important thing to remember is that where sin abounds, God's grace abounds even more, and God specializes in turning what was meant for evil into good.

Usually a large part of our wounds are self inflicted by our own lapses into sin and other bad choices that we make. We shovel away at these by examining ourselves and confessing and repenting where necessary.

"Now I rejoice, not that you were made sorry, but that your sorrow led to repentance. For you were made sorry in a godly manner, that you might suffer loss from us in nothing." 2 Corinthians 7:9

We need to view our other wounds as part of God's character-development program designed to chip away at our pride, selfishness, idolatry, etc., that stunt our growth in Christ.

We are actually talking about the perseverance of the saints for which God promises the crown of everlasting life.

Father, keep me in that perfect peace that comes when my mind is stayed on You. Amen.

Lord, You Are _____
Forgive Me For _____
Thank You For _____
Needs of Others _____
Personal Needs _____
Answered Prayers _____

Decently and in Order
"Let all things be done decently and in order." 1 Corinthians 14:40

God has so many wonderful character attributes and qualities; it is easy to

"For all the earth is the LORD'S, and He has set the world in order."
1 Samuel 2:8 NLT

overlook one of the most prominent. We tend to lose sight of the fact that God is a God of order.
From the orderliness of creation to the laws of the universe, God's marvelous provision for everything to work in harmony and in order is a wonder to behold.

We need to be ever mindful of the fact that God created heaven and earth as the center of His love. He created them as the perfect dwelling place for the man He created in His image for fellowship and love.

The fall of man in the garden disrupted God's plan for a perfect paradise on earth, and God's justice demanded that Adam, Eve, and all their descendents bear the penalty for their sin of disobedience.

The disorderliness that sin brought into the world is very visible today. The peace and harmony with which all of those created in God's image should be living and getting along together has all but disappeared from the face of the earth.

God tried to install order through covenants, which promised blessings for obedience and death for disobedience, to no avail. In His love, He came to earth as Jesus Christ to restore order through a covenant of grace that sets all who believe free from the eternal death penalty of sin and gives us a new life that will allow us to live forever.

God's perfect order will be restored in heaven where there will be no more sorrow, sadness, or suffering, because there will be no more sin.

"For wherever there is jealousy and selfish ambition, there you will find disorder and every kind of evil."
James 3:16 NLT

As believers live each day in this world, we are called to live lives of holiness and obedience to the Lord, fruitful in every good work.

We are not only called to live lives of orderliness according to God's commands, but we are empowered to do so by the power of the Holy Spirit who lives in us to provide the strength to live victoriously in Jesus.

The lives of every believer should be lives lived "decently and in order."

Father, give me the strength to live a life fully pleasing to You. Amen.

Lord, You Are _____
Forgive Me For _____
Thank You For _____
Needs of Others _____
Personal Needs _____
Answered Prayers _____

Read 1 Peter 3:8-12, Psalm 86   **July 27**

"A Happy Life and Good Days"

"Every good gift and every perfect gift is from above, and comes down from the Father of lights, with whom there is no variation or shadow of turning." James 1:17

No one willfully chooses a miserable life and bad days, but we can often bring them about by the consequences of our bad choices made in the flesh and apart from any godly guidance or influence.

"Give me happiness, O Lord, for my life depends on You."
Psalm 86:4

There is a great misconception in what pleasures bring happiness.

We too often raise our children wanting them to be happy without being holy, which is impossible. We pursue the pleasure of the flesh and the world apart from God, apart from whom there can be no real happiness.

God certainly did not create us to have a miserable life and bad days. He created us with a free will that allows this to happen if we choose not to receive His free gift of reconciliation and eternal life by receiving Jesus by faith when He stands and knocks at the door of our hearts.

A happy life and good days are gifts to be found only in the all-surpassing peace and joy of knowing God the Father through the Son that He has sent.

When we have the all-surpassing peace and joy of the Lord, we have the happy life and good days not because of our external circumstances but sometimes often in and through the worst of them.

Jesus Himself said, "I have told you all this so that you may have peace in me. Here on earth you will have many trials and sorrows. But take heart, because I have overcome the world" *(John 16:33 NLT).*

"For the Scriptures say, if you want a happy life and good days, keep your tongue from speaking evil, and keep your lips from telling lies."
1 Peter 3:10 NLT

When we have the joy of the Lord in our hearts, we are going to experience the real pleasures of life that can only be found when we live life God's way.

Father, help me to find the lasting happiness and real pleasure that can only be found in a close personal relationship with Jesus. Amen.

Lord, You Are _____
Forgive Me For _____
Thank You For _____
Needs of Others _____
Personal Needs _____
Answered Prayers _____

Due Diligence

"But without faith it is impossible to please Him, for he who comes to God must believe that He is, and that He is a rewarder of those who diligently seek Him." Hebrews 11:6

Our salvation is a free gift of God's grace. We did nothing to earn or deserve it. Jesus did it all by dying on the cross to pay our sin debt in full.

"I call to remembrance my song in the night; I meditate within my heart, and my spirit makes diligent search." Psalm 77:6

Once we receive this wonderful gift by faith and are born again, we will want to exercise reasonable care or due diligence in allowing the grace of God to manifest Jesus in our hearts and lives so that we can be faithful to the great commandment and Great Commission God has given every believer.

Before we can make disciples, we need to become disciples by being diligent in developing the godly character of Jesus in our hearts and lives that is the evidence of the new birth experienced by every true believer.

The discipline of discipleship is a day by day, year by year, never-ending process through which we become more like Christ in every area of our lives.

As we grow in our knowledge of God through growing in His Word, we receive the grace to develop self control, perseverance, godliness, kindness, and love.

The more diligent we are in seeking God, the more of Him we will find and the more like Christ we will become.

"But also for this very reason, giving all diligence, add to your faith virtue, to virtue knowledge," 2 Peter 1:5

The rewards of answered prayers, friendship with Jesus, Jesus' joy, and the awareness of God's love and the love of others are promised to all who abide in Christ through the grace of Spirit-powered Christian discipline.

Father, help me to maintain due diligence in maintaining and growing in my personal relationship with Jesus. Amen.

Lord, You Are _____

Forgive Me For _____

Thank You For _____

Needs of Others _____

Personal Needs _____

Answered Prayers _____

Faithful and True

"Then I saw heaven opened, and a white horse was standing there. And the one sitting on the horse was named Faithful and True. For He judges fairly and then goes to war." Revelation 19:11 NLT

Scripture records many names for God derived from combining "El," which means God, with nouns or adjectives to express a particular attribute or characteristic of God. For example God was called El Shaddai to describe Him as God Almighty.

"The LORD leads with unfailing love and faithfulness all those who keep His covenant and obey His decrees." Psalm 25:10 NLT

The English translation of Yahweh as Jehovah is also combined with other words to express a particular aspect of God. Jehovah-Jireh is often used to describe the God who will provide, although it is actually a name given by Abraham to denote where God provided the sacrifice to spare Isaac.

God simply called Himself "I AM" when Moses asked His name, and He called Himself "Faithful and True" to John in Revelation 19:11.

There is great comfort for all believers who live out their lives secure in their faith that God is indeed faithful and true.

Knowing that God is faithful and true empowers us to claim the promises of God with great joy and assurance.

Because God is faithful and true, we can know for sure that He is Who He says He is. He has done and will do what He has said He has done and will do.

Because God is faithful and true, we can be sure that He will never leave us or forsake us and that He will work all things for our good and His Glory.

"So the Word became human and lived here on earth among us. He was full of unfailing love and faithfulness." John 1:14 NLT

In His faithfulness, God has given us the Holy Spirit to guarantee that all who call upon His name have a future and a hope for now and forever.

Father, thank you for helping me believe and know that You are faithful and true. Amen.

Lord, You Are _____

Forgive Me For _____

Thank You For _____

Needs of Others _____

Personal Needs _____

Answered Prayers _____

What More?

"What more could have been done to My vineyard that I have not done in it? Why then, when I expected it to bring forth good grapes, did it bring forth wild grapes?" Isaiah 5:4

"Where did I go wrong?" or "What more could I have done?" are oft asked questions anguished parents ask themselves when their children go astray.

"Woe to those who call evil good, and good evil; who put darkness for light, and light for darkness; who put bitter for sweet, and sweet for bitter!" Isaiah 5:20

These are the questions God asked when the apples of His eye (upon whom He lavished every good and perfect gift and blessing) rejected God and committed the spiritual adultery of idolatry.

Even after God came on earth to live and die as the ultimate sacrifice and perfect atonement for sin, the problem of the free will of willfulness keeps many in bondage to sin instead of giving the freedom from it that Jesus Christ died to earn for all.

When we take the time to prayerfully and honestly ask these questions regarding our own sins, we usually will not have to think very long before we realize that our own willfulness and disobedience is the answer.

God has done everything He could possibly do by dying on the cross to save us and by coming as the Holy Spirit to live within us with the strength and power to live fruitful lives fully pleasing to Him.

Instead of bringing a smile to God's face, we bring tears to His eyes because we choose to live in the darkness and bondage of the flesh instead of becoming alive in the peace and joy of God through a new birth through faith in Jesus.

"Therefore take up the whole armor of God that you may be able to withstand in the evil day, and having done all, to stand." Ephesians 6:13

God has done it all in Jesus Christ. When we believe in Him and put on His armor daily, we can be sure we will stand.

Father create a clean heart and renew a right spirit within me daily, Oh Lord, that You will not have cause to shed tears over me. Amen.

Lord, You Are _____
Forgive Me For _____
Thank You For _____
Needs of Others _____
Personal Needs _____
Answered Prayers _____

Spiritual Thermo Dynamics

"As long as the earth remains, there will be springtime and harvest, cold and heat, winter and summer, day and night." Genesis 8:22 NLT

Whether we are talking about engines, furnaces, or air conditioners, temperature is a big issue. This begs the question I once read as to whether we, as believers, are thermometers or thermostats.

"My thoughts grew hot within me and began to burn, igniting a fire of words," Psalm 39:3 NLT

Does our life reflect the temperature of the world around us? Do we "go with the flow" and let the company we keep and the places we go determine our conduct?

We are all called to be thermostats. We should be setting the spiritual temperature around us by reflecting the warmth of God's love, and we should be fueled by the fire of the Holy Spirit living within us.

As thermostats, we will become difference makers within our families, our schools and work places, our neighborhoods, and our churches by letting the warmth of God's love cool anger, envy, and strife as we bear the fruit of the Spirit in our everyday lives.

When we think about it, God has given us the Holy Spirit to serve as our own personal thermostat. When we are "plugged in," the Holy Spirit will sear our consciences when necessary and cool our anger and unholy passions.

He will set us on fire with desire to please God and keep us from becoming lukewarm and indifferent to God's will for our lives.

In order to keep our thermostat working properly, we need to clean our sin filters daily through sincere confession and repentance, plug into God's Word as our power source, and pray with Spirit-filled passion and confidence.

"I know all the things you do, that you are neither hot nor cold. I wish you were one or the other." Revelation 3:15 NLT

Father, help me to be a thermostat by the power of the Holy Spirit. Amen.

Lord, You Are ___
Forgive Me For ___
Thank You For ___
Needs of Others ___
Personal Needs ___
Answered Prayers ___

Appeasing Worship
"And what God wants is for us to be made holy by the sacrifice of the body of Jesus Christ once for all time." Hebrews 10:8 NLT

Worship of some kind of god has been recorded in every study of primitive cultures. God has put in the heart of everyone a desire to know Him.

"You take no delight in sacrifices or offerings. Now that You have made me listen, I finally understand—You don't require burnt offerings or sin offerings." Psalm 40:6 NLT

Unfortunately, many cultures have never had the benefit of God's clear revelation in Scripture and as a result, have become children of a lesser god.

There have been sun or moon worshippers, tree worshippers, gold or brass idol worshippers, and worshippers of false teachings of false gods since time began.

The common element of worship except Christianity is the worship of appeasement. The belief is that one can earn a god's favor and escape his wrath by doing something or sacrificing something.

Even human sacrifices to the gods have been prevalent in many cultures of ages past.

Worshipping God is not about what we must do but is all about what God has done. This is the truth that separates Christianity from all other religions.

"And I know it is important to love Him with all my heart and all my understanding and all my strength, and to love my neighbors as myself. This is more important than to offer all of the burnt offerings and sacrifices required in the law." Mark 12:33 NLT

We worship God by loving Him because He first loved us. He loved us so much that He sent His only Son to die so that we would never have to die.

Our worship should never be to appease but to please God out of love for the wonderful gift He has given us through faith in Jesus Christ.

Father, let me never confuse earning by what I do with receiving freely because of what Jesus has done for me. Amen.

Lord, You Are _____

Forgive Me For _____

Thank You For _____

Needs of Others _____

Personal Needs _____

Answered Prayers _____

"Stubbornitis" of the Soul

"It wasn't so long ago that we ourselves were stupid and stubborn, dupes of sin, ordered every which way by our glands, going around with a chip on our shoulder, hated and hating back." Titus 3:3 MSG

God's gift of a free will for all His children is a slippery slope for many.

"Then they will not be like their ancestors— stubborn, rebellious, and unfaithful, refusing to give their hearts to God."
Psalm 78:8 NLT

Our freedom to choose also grants the freedom to stubbornly resist God's desire that all would be saved.

As long as we obstinately refuse to yield to God's call on our life or receive His wonderful gift of salvation through faith in Jesus Christ, we will continue to wander aimlessly lost in the poverty of the soul and will never enjoy the riches of God's grace.

Yielding to God is voluntarily dying to self will and submitting to the yoke of Christ as Lord and manager of our life.

Why anyone would choose to live as a pauper when they could live as joint heir with Christ for now and forever is one of the great mysteries of life for those who have seen and embraced the light of God's love and found a new life in Christ.

Jesus Christ came that we might have a life of abundance.

He promises us the power of His presence through the Holy Spirit living within us. He is our very present help in time of trouble. He not only answers our prayers but prays and intercedes for us constantly before the throne of God.

When we choose to live life apart from God, we are choosing to live a life without the all-surpassing peace and joy that only a right relationship with God through faith in Jesus can provide.

"You stubborn people! You are heathen at heart and deaf to the truth. Must you forever resist the Holy Spirit? But your ancestors did, and so do you!"
Acts 7:51 NLT

Choosing to do life in the stubbornness of "my way" instead of "The Way" is choosing to live in bondage to sin and death and all of the consequences for now and forever.

Father, let not my stubbornness rob me of the peace and joy that can only be found in You. Amen.

Lord, You Are _____
Forgive Me For _____
Thank You For _____
Needs of Others _____
Personal Needs _____
Answered Prayers _____

Our Deep Pocket God

"And this same God who takes care of me will supply all your needs from His glorious riches, which have been given to us in Christ Jesus."
Philippians 4:19 NLT

Although He has never appeared on Forbes magazine's "richest men in the world" rankings, God has deeper pockets than the combined pockets of everyone on the list.

"For all the animals of the forest are mine, and I own the cattle on a thousand hills." Psalm 50:10 NLT

Not only are God's pockets deep, but His arms are long. He can dig down and reach out to anyone and everyone at the same time.

God not only owns the cattle on a thousand hills; He has also cornered and stockpiled all of the world's treasures of grace and mercy.

God's pockets are so deep; He has supplied every person on this earth with every dollar they own. No one has anything even life itself that they have not been given by the providence of or permissive will of God.

The lofty aim of liberal, socialistic, or communistic government is to redistribute wealth by taking from the rich and giving to the poor.

God makes people rich and gives them more and more, so they can be more and more generous to the poor.

Our deep-pocket God is the God of abundance. When He gives us an overflow of treasures, it's so that we can be generous to others on all occasions.

When God gives us an abundance of talents, it's so that we can be generous in using these talents to glorify Him and serve others.

The abundance of God's power and strength is legendary. He covers our weaknesses, enables the blind to see, the lame to walk, and raises all who call upon His name from death into life everlasting.

"Yet true religion with contentment is great wealth." 1 Timothy 6:6 NLT

God's arms are never too short for us, and ours should never be too short in reaching out to Him.

Our deep-pocket God has promised to supply all of our needs out of the richness of His grace.

Father, thank you for letting me live richly drawing on the deep pockets of Your love, grace, and mercy. Amen.

Lord, You Are _____

Forgive Me For _____

Thank You For _____

Needs of Others _____

Personal Needs _____

Answered Prayers _____

Read John 6:22-59, Isaiah 59:4-21

Energy Conservation

"Oh! May the God of green hope fill you up with joy, fill you up with peace, so that your believing lives, filled with the life-giving energy of the Holy Spirit, will brim over with hope!" Romans 15:7b MSG

We often hear of something "taking a lot out of" someone. "My illness took a lot out of me." "Complaining took a lot of enthusiasm out of me." "That failure took my ambition right out of me."

"They spend their time and energy spinning evil plans that end up in deadly actions," Isaiah 59:4 NLT

Jesus was acutely aware of the woman who touched his garment taking power out of Him.

We are all given a certain amount of energy that is renewed continually as we breathe oxygen into our bloodstream that provides energy for living and converts our physical nourishment into energy for physical strength and growth.

We are also given a certain amount of spiritual power that is renewed continually as we feed on the Bread of Life and convert this nourishment into energy for living the abundant life in Christ.

The question of how to use our energy is one that we should ask ourselves often, as it can make a big difference in the quality of our life.

We can choose to waste our physical energy by living unhealthy lives and burning the candle at both ends.

We can choose to waste our energy by worrying, sweating the small things, being angry, carrying grudges, or going through life carrying an energy-draining chip on our shoulder.

When we realize that we were given the energy of life to glorify the Creator of all life and to accomplish the purposes for which He created us before we were even born, we will become more conscious of conserving our energy for these purposes rather than wasting it on trivial pursuits or counter-productive attitudes.

"But you shouldn't be so concerned about perishable things like food. Spend your energy seeking the eternal life that I, the Son of Man, can give you. For God the Father has sent me for that very purpose." John 6:27 NLT

Father, keep me from wasting my energy on wood, hay, and stubble. Amen.

Lord, You Are _____
Forgive Me For _____
Thank You For _____
Needs of Others _____
Personal Needs _____
Answered Prayers _____

The Big Picture
"'For I know the plans I have for you,' says the LORD. 'They are plans for good and not for disaster, to give you a future and a hope.'" Jeremiah 29:11 NLT

Sometimes it seems that our comfort zones get squeezed so badly that we can't seem to focus on the big picture.

"You will show me the way of life, granting me the joy of Your presence and the pleasures of living with You forever." Psalm 16:11 NLT

The crisis of the moment takes over and panic begins. We can't see anything except the present danger, pain, or suffering we are experiencing.

The big picture that we need to keep in our minds is that all is not lost as long as we have Jesus in our hearts.

We can lose our fortunes, friends, our spouses, or our health, but all is not lost as long as we have Jesus.

When we stay focused on our Problem Solver instead of our problems, God's amazing grace and the power of the Holy Spirit living within us provides the means to escape, strength to endure, wisdom and spiritual discernment, or sometimes divine intervention to resolve our problems.

The big picture shows us that no pain or suffering lasts forever, that grace and mercy are available, and that God's sovereignty is supreme and His promises are sure.

When God assures us that He works all things for our good and His glory, we need to look at the big picture of eternity.

The lives we are given on this earth are not even a blip on God's time line that has no beginning or no end.

It is the big picture that allows God to do extraordinary things through ordinary people whose mind is stayed on Him.

The big picture is the only thing that makes it possible to rejoice and give thanks in all circumstances and to receive that peace that surpasses all understanding.

"Now we see things imperfectly as in a poor mirror, but then we will see everything with perfect clarity." 1 Corinthians 13:12 NLT

Father, may You always be the big picture in my life. Amen.

Lord, You Are _____

Forgive Me For _____

Thank You For _____

Needs of Others _____

Personal Needs _____

Answered Prayers _____

Are You Broad Minded?

"Enter through the narrow gate. For wide is the gate and broad is the road that leads to destruction, and many enter through it." Matthew 7:13 NIV

In these days of relative truth and political correctness, it's all about being "broad minded." Tolerance is the virtue of the vanity of man and the abomination of our holy and just God.

"O God, You take no pleasure in wickedness; You cannot tolerate the slightest sin." Psalm 5:4 NLT

As sin is flaunted on TV, movies, and the internet and community and morality are at or near an all time low, it is good to consider how broad minded we have become.

The voices in the wilderness calling for repentance are being drowned out by the voices of the world calling for pleasure seekers to be all they can be in living in cesspools of sin in total disregard for the clear commandments and teachings of God.

God is very accommodating in giving us all the choice of being broad minded or narrow minded.

We can choose to lose our lives forever, or we can choose to lose our lives and find life forever through Christ.

When we choose to reject the call of Christ when He comes knocking, we are choosing the broad path to destruction and death.

When we, in the power of the Holy Spirit, receive Jesus Christ into our hearts as our Lord and Savior, we have found the narrow way and the only way that leads to life forever as sons and daughters of the living God.

God is not broad minded about sin. He has decreed that its wages are death and damnation.

All of the broad mindedness in the world will not be enough to save anyone from the death and destruction of hell reserved for those who choose to refuse Jesus Christ.

"Their destruction is their reward for the harm they have done. They love to indulge in evil pleasures in broad daylight. They are a disgrace and a stain among you. They revel in deceitfulness while they feast with you." 2 Peter 2:13 NLT

Father, keep me on the narrow path that leads to the true joy and eternal bliss of heaven. Amen.

Lord, You Are _____
Forgive Me For _____
Thank You For _____
Needs of Others _____
Personal Needs _____
Answered Prayers _____

August 7   Read Ephesians 2, Ezekiel 36:25-32

Guest of Honor

"Don't you realize that all of you together are the temple of God and that the Spirit of God lives in you?" 1 Corinthians 6:19 NLT

Whoever heard of inviting a guest to your home and then treating them badly? As uncivilized as this may seem, we all are, or at some time have been, guilty of doing this very thing.

"And I will put My Spirit in you so you will obey My laws and do whatever I command." Ezekiel 36:27 NIV

When we received Jesus Christ as our Savior, we invited Him to come into our hearts as honored guest. The pleasure of enjoying His company and soaking up His goodness is the means through which we find that peace that surpasses all understanding.

When Jesus comes into our hearts as the Holy Spirit, He does not come as a free loader. He comes to help us clean up our messes and make the houses of our hearts homes fit for habitation by royalty.

When Jesus is the guest of honor in our hearts, we become temples where the Holy Spirit dwells in power and majesty, and we become members of the royal priesthood of believers.

If this is all true as Scripture tells us it is, why, oh, why do we choose to neglect this heaven-sent visitor or put Him in the closet as someone of whom we are ashamed and will only let out for special occasions?

When we utterly neglect and willfully disregard this guest of honor, we are either putting the sincerity and reality of our salvation into question, or the home of our heart is being invaded by forces of darkness that are trying to rob us of the power for living the abundant life in Christ that He has sent the Holy Spirit to provide.

David understood the need to cleanse the temple of our heart through confession and repentance.

"In whom you also are being built together for a dwelling place of God in the Spirit." Ephesians 2:29

God is always ready to restore the joy of our salvation and renew a right spirit within us when we give our guest the love and respect due the One heaven sent to be our honored guest.

Father, help make me a temple fit for Your habitation. Amen.

Lord, You Are _____

Forgive Me For _____

Thank You For _____

Needs of Others _____

Personal Needs _____

Answered Prayers _____

Blaming or Claiming

"Just as He chose us in Him before the foundation of the world, that we should be holy and without blame before Him in love," Ephesians 1:4

The blame game started in the Garden of Eden when Eve blamed the serpent

"Don't hurt your friend, don't blame your neighbor; despise the despicable."
Psalm 15:3.4 MSG

for her disobedience. It has been going on ever since in the lives of practically all of Eve's descendents, including you and me.

We often blame our sins and failures on everything and everyone except our selves.

"I'm only human," "I had an unhappy childhood," "she caused it," "he started it," and "I was mislead" are just a few of the many excuses given for placing blame elsewhere for messes that we most often created by our own stubbornness, stupidity, or weaknesses.

While all of these statements may be true and contributing factors in some instances, we cannot afford the luxury of dodging personal accountability by blaming others.

We need to learn to claim instead of blame. We cannot relive the past. We need to learn from it, repent of it, and move on.

Life is too short to waste its energy on blaming. How much better to spend our energy claiming all of the wonderful promises of God that are ours through faith in Jesus Christ!

Forgiveness and mercy are ours for the claiming, not only to receive but to give to others. Cleansing and restoration are available on demand when we claim them before God with a broken spirit and contrite heart.

'I have sinned," "I am sorry," "please forgive me," and "I forgive you" are words of healing and comfort that can give us victory over the often debilitating effects of trying to assess blame and let it fester into a root of bitterness in our souls.

"Who will also confirm you to the end, that you may be blameless in the day of our Lord Jesus Christ."
1 Corinthians 1:8

Father, help me to avoid playing the blame game in any area of my life. Amen.

Lord, You Are _____
Forgive Me For _____
Thank You For _____
Needs of Others _____
Personal Needs _____
Answered Prayers _____

The No Shame Game

"'And I will establish My covenant with you. Then you shall know that I am the LORD, that you may remember and be ashamed, and never open your mouth anymore because of your shame, when I provide you an atonement for all you have done,' says the Lord GOD." Ezekiel 16:62, 63

In this age of relative truth and reality TV shows, it often seems that there is no longer such a thing as shame.

"How long, O you sons of men, will you turn my glory to shame? How long will you love worthlessness and seek falsehood?" Psalm 4:2

The guilty conscience that once convicted us of our sinfulness and need for a Savior has been deadened to where it is barely a whisper in today's world.

Improprieties that used to shock us with shame are now so commonplace that we barely even notice the grossest of sins.

God's abominations have become much of the world's acceptable lifestyles and standards of conduct.

Many seem to think that we can eliminate sin by eliminating shame and guilt through changing freedom of religion to freedom from religion.

If man can somehow get God and His authority out of the picture, man can become his own god and do or believe whatever he wants with no moral restraints whatsoever. It's as if we eliminate shame, then we can eliminate guilt.

Those who dare question questionable attitudes and conduct are subjected to the shame of ridicule and being called self righteous, prudish, or some sort of religious nuts.

"For many walk, of whom I have told you often, and now tell you even weeping, that they are the enemies of the cross of Christ: whose end is destruction, whose god is their belly, and whose glory is in their shame—who set their mind on earthly things." Philippians 3:19, 20

When we become tempted to play the no shame game, we need to remember that God is not mocked and there is hell to pay for all who dull their consciences and wallow in the idolatry of self glorification and living life the world's way.

Father help me to acknowledge my shame and guilt and live a life of true repentance fully pleasing to You. Amen.

Lord, You Are _____

Forgive Me For _____

Thank You For _____

Needs of Others _____

Personal Needs _____

Answered Prayers _____

Read 1 Peter 2:1-7, Psalm 119:103,104

Whitman's Sampler

"Oh, taste and see that the LORD is good; blessed is the man who trusts in Him!" Psalm 34:7

I always enjoyed being able to find out what each piece was made of in a box of Whitman's Sampler chocolates with the handy printed diagram. I well remember my brothers and sisters squeezing some other pieces of chocolate and leaving the squeezed crèmes while they took all the nuts and chewy ones.

"How sweet are Your words to my taste, sweeter than honey to my mouth!" Psalm 119:103

Forrest Gump's momma made a profound impression on him by saying that "life is like a box of chocolates – you never know what you're gonna get."

The mysteries of life that unfold often leave us wondering what's in store next as we travel through the highs and lows of our lives on this earth.

When God's Word becomes our box of life, we are going to taste words of love, peace, and joy; words of exhortation and encouragement; and words of judgment and displeasure.

The important thing is not what's in the box but WHO is in the box! When we have the presence of God the Holy Spirit in our box of life, we can get our crèmes squeezed and our nuts and chewy ones stolen, but we can patiently endure the disappointments and failures of ourselves and others.

We can know by faith that God will put nothing in our box without wrapping it in sustaining grace to escape or overcome it through the power of the Holy Spirit.

"You must crave pure spiritual milk so that you can grow into the fullness of your salvation. Cry out for this nourishment as a baby cries for milk, now that you have had a taste of the Lord's kindness." 2 Peter 2:2, 3

May we sample all of the sacred delights of the great plans and blessings God has for those who love Him and are called according to His purposes that He has placed in our box of life.

Father, thank you for the wonderful samples of the foretastes of glory I will experience and enjoy forever in heaven. Amen.

Lord, You Are _____

Forgive Me For _____

Thank You For _____

Needs of Others _____

Personal Needs _____

Answered Prayers _____

You've Been Gift Wrapped!
"A spiritual gift is given to each of us as a means of helping the entire church." 1 Corinthians 12:7 NLT

The hour we first believed we became wrapped with spiritual gifts for ministry and the power of the Holy Spirit to edify the body of Christ and to build up His Kingdom.

**"In those days, I will pour out my Spirit even on servants, men and women alike."
Joel 2:29 NLT**

Our gifts are discovered and developed best by involvement in the body of Christ with other believers.

These gifts can and will fill our lives with meaning and purpose. We will experience the joy and satisfaction that only comes from glorifying God by using our gifts to accomplish His purposes through us.

Although many are multi-gifted, each one of us can be sure that we have at least one primary spiritual gift. When we concentrate on discovering what turns us on and harness this passion and ability to minister within and through our body of believers, we will see the Lord blessing our gifting by using it to bless others.

Talents are natural gifts; giftings are supernatural gifts that God gives all believers for the common good of His Church, which is our body of believers. Aaron had no talent for speaking but was supernaturally gifted. The apostles had no special talents but were supernaturally gifted with power from on high to spread the Gospel throughout the world.

We need to be very careful in discerning between giftings and commands. We need to pray for wisdom and spiritual discernment in how to best use our gifts for obeying God's commands to make disciples.

Instead of saying that we are not gifted to evangelize by teaching or prophecy, we need to develop our gift to evangelize by giving, helping, encouraging, or showing mercy to others.

**"God has given each of us the ability to do certain things well."
Romans 12:6a NLT**

Discovering and using our spiritual gifts is not an option but a command. We will all give an account of what we did with the gifts we have been given.

Father, help me find and develop that "sweet spot" for which You have gifted me for Your purposes. Amen.

Lord, You Are _____
Forgive Me For _____
Thank You For _____
Needs of Others _____
Personal Needs _____
Answered Prayers _____

Walking the Walk

"But take careful heed to do the commandment and the law which Moses the servant of the LORD commanded you, to love the LORD your God, to walk in all His ways, to keep His commandments, to hold fast to Him, and to serve Him with all your heart and with all your soul." Joshua 2:25

The way to the cross was a way of suffering, humiliation, and sorrow for Jesus. Scripture warns us that our walk with God will often be a similar walk and that we should not be expecting to share in Christ's glory without sharing in His suffering.

"You shall walk in all the ways which the LORD your God has commanded you, that you may live and that it may be well with you, and that you may prolong your days in the land which you shall possess."
Deuteronomy 5:33

The Good News is that because of Jesus' suffering and death on the cross for our sins, we can walk in the joy of our salvation and in right standing with God.

As imitators of Christ, we are commanded to walk in love as Christ has loved us and to walk worthy of the Lord and fruitful in every good work.

"Walking the walk" is all about walking by faith and not by sight. It's about walking controlled by the Spirit and not by our flesh.

We are exhorted to "walk in the light," to walk properly, and for everything we say and do, to be pleasing in God's sight.

Even though we have been set free from bondage to sin through faith in Jesus Christ, the crippling effects of sin still linger in the bodies we share with our flesh.

God knew this and sent the Holy Spirit to come live within us and be our crutch to help us walk through the troubles of life with grace and strength to sustain us and see us through.

"There is therefore now no condemnation to those who are in Christ Jesus, who do not walk according to the flesh, but according to the Spirit."
Romans 8:1

How good it is to know that when we "walk the walk" in Christ, we will never have to walk alone!

Father, by the indwelling power of the Holy Spirit, help me to "walk the walk" of faith. Amen.

Lord, You Are _____

Forgive Me For _____

Thank You For _____

Needs of Others _____

Personal Needs _____

Answered Prayers _____

August 13   **Read 1 Thessalonians 2:4, Psalm 17**

Agendas

"The heart is deceitful above all things, and desperately wicked; who can know it?" Jeremiah 17:9

God's agenda for each believer is that we be conformed into the image of Christ and do the good works for which He created us.

"Hear a just cause, O LORD, attend to my cry; give ear to my prayer which is not from deceitful lips." Psalm 17:1

When thinking of agendas as underlying plans or motives, we need to be aware of our own often ulterior motives as well as those of others.

We can rationalize and justify almost anything. We can fool others and even ourselves. The important thing to know is that we cannot fool God.

God often gets projects advanced in His name when the underlying motive has nothing to do with glorifying or advancing the kingdom of God.

Only God knows and can judge hearts, but we should continually pray for wisdom and spiritual discernment in examining our own agendas as well as those of others to determine that they are above board and as they are represented to be.

Powerful political interests have agendas that do not reflect the best interests of all. Upheaval in congregations and denominations are often fueled by personal agendas that cause division and conflict rather than promote the spirit of unity and bond of peace among brothers and sisters in Christ.

The conflicts of interest that are often present in any agenda need to be recognized and evaluated before acting on any proposal.

"For we speak as messengers who have been approved by God to be entrusted with the Good News. Our purpose is to please God, not people. He is the one who examines the motives of our hearts." 1 Thessalonians 2:4

Above all, we need to continually examine our motives at God's throne of grace so that we will not unknowingly become willing accomplices in promoting self instead of the kingdom of God and His righteousness.

Father, help me to recognize and discard my ulterior motives. Amen.

Lord, You Are _____
Forgive Me For _____
Thank You For _____
Needs of Others _____
Personal Needs _____
Answered Prayers _____

The Waiting Game

"But those who wait on the LORD shall renew their strength; they shall mount up with wings like eagles; they shall run and not be weary; they shall walk and not faint." Isaiah 40:31

Waiting is a fact of life. We are waiting to be born, to grow up, to die, and to go to heaven. We are always waiting for something or someone.

"Wait on the LORD; be of good courage, and He shall strengthen your heart; wait, I say, on the LORD!" Psalm 27:14

When we get impatient with God and decide to do life in our own flesh instead of waiting upon Him, we will most often make bad choices and have to suffer consequences and pains we were never meant to bear.

The key to blessings and success in waiting is not for what we are waiting but in Whom we are waiting.

When we are abiding in Christ and His indwelling presence, we are promised that our waiting upon Him will be blessed and that our prayers will be heard.

When we are waiting in Christ, we will know the joy of our salvation and experience the goodness of God. We shall be continually renewed and strengthened.

The peace and security that comes with faith in knowing that God will come through in all the glorious ways He has promised fill our waiting with great anticipation and joy.

No matter what good thing for which we are waiting, when we wait under the shelter of God's wings of grace, we will not be disappointed.

How great it is to know by faith that God's wonderful gift of salvation and the eternal bliss of heaven are well worth the wait!

"But as it is written: 'Eye has not seen, nor ear heard, nor have entered into the heart of man the things which God has prepared for those who love Him.'" 1 Corinthians 2:9

Father, give me the long suffering and patience to wait on You as I live in You through my relationship with Jesus. Amen.

Lord, You Are _____

Forgive Me For _____

Thank You For _____

Needs of Others _____

Personal Needs _____

Answered Prayers _____

Who's Got You Covered?

"Blessed is he whose transgression is forgiven whose sin is covered."
Psalm 32:1

We have been told for years that we are "in good hands with All State."

"You have forgiven the guilt of Your people— yes, You have covered all their sins." Psalm 85:2 NLT

As good as the best policy they have ever written might be, their coverage will mean nothing when we stand before the judgment throne of God.

As well pleased as God is when we live fruitful lives fully pleasing to Him, all of the good works we do mean nothing as coverage to get us into heaven.

God's free gift of salvation by grace through faith in what Jesus Christ did for us is our ticket.

The love that covers a multitude of sins is not our human love. It is the love of God that manifests itself in His sending His only begotten and beloved Son Jesus Christ to endure the sin of the world without sinning and to die as the perfect sacrifice for our sins.

The blood of Jesus Christ covers in full the death penalty for every sin we have ever committed or will ever commit.

When we have our sins washed away by faith in the blood of Jesus on the cross of Calvary, we are also covered with a white robe of Christ's righteousness in God's sight. This is the wedding garment our faith supplies with which we can boldly come before God's throne of grace.

How sweet it is to know that because of the righteousness of Christ, which we receive by grace through faith in Him, we are covered against all of the attempts of the world, the flesh, and the devil to separate us eternally from God's love that covers our multitude of sins

"So he said to him, 'Friend, how did you come in here without a wedding garment?' And he was speechless." Matthew 22:12

Because the blood of Jesus has covered all our sins, we can look forward to living forever as the children of God and heirs to all of His wonderful promises.

Father, thank you for covering me with the umbrella of Christ's love. Amen.

Lord, You Are _____
Forgive Me For _____
Thank You For _____
Needs of Others _____
Personal Needs _____
Answered Prayers _____

A Sure Thing

"I write these things to you who believe in the name of the Son of God so that you may know that you have eternal life." 1 John 5:13 NIV

Sometimes, it seems that the only sure thing is that nothing is a sure thing. A horse thought sure to win breaks a leg. A heavily favored team loses. The hottest of hot stocks goes down instead of up.

"In that day He will be your sure foundation, providing a rich store of salvation, wisdom, and knowledge. The fear of the LORD is the key to this treasure."

Isaiah 33:6 NLT

"Sure thing" marriages fail. People we trust the most often fail us the worst. The security we seek in possessions, power, or other efforts often fails to deliver.

How good it is to know that God's love for us is a sure thing! How sweet to know that He is in control of the world and everything in it, and He works things for our good if we truly love Him and receive Jesus as His gift of life forever for all who believe on His name.

People often wonder how in the world anyone can be sure that Jesus is the sure thing.

In addition to the divine revelation of Scripture and the many miracles that Jesus did while alive, we have the historical fact of over 500 people seeing Jesus alive after He had been crucified. The apostles were witnesses to His ascension.

Best of all, we have the assurance of the Holy Spirit living within us continually supplying the faith within us to know that Our Redeemer lives, and because He lives, we also shall live forever.

"This hope we have as an anchor of the soul, both sure and steadfast, and which enters the presence behind the veil,"

Hebrews 9:19

How blessed we are to know what we know is what we know by faith in spite of the troubled times when we cannot stand the sight of what we see in this life.

Father, I believe that Jesus is a sure thing. Take away any doubts or unbelief by the power of the Holy Spirit. Amen.

Lord, You Are _____

Forgive Me For _____

Thank You For _____

Needs of Others _____

Personal Needs _____

Answered Prayers _____

August 17   **Read Ephesians 4:26-39, Psalm 19:7-14**
Hostile Takeovers
"Be sober, be vigilant; because your adversary the devil walks about like a roaring lion, seeking whom he may devour." 1 Peter 5:8

In the financial world, hostile takeovers are the means by which corporations or individuals acquire enough stock to take over control of another corporation in spite of the objections and resistance of those in control.

"Keep me from deliberate sins! Don't let them control me. Then I will be free of guilt and innocent of great sin."
Psalm 19:13 NLT

Throughout the world, governments are being taken down by hostile takeovers through revolutions or voting out parties in power.

Many churches have lingering scars from successful and unsuccessful hostile takeover attempts by unsatisfied members who want to oust a pastor or take control of the congregation.

As believers, we need to know that we are targets for a hostile takeover by the deceiver of our souls who is hell bent on trying to reclaim us for the kingdom of darkness.

Not only is Satan a liar and a thief, he is a cunning adversary with considerable satanic power at his disposal.

Unfortunately, he knows our every weakness and will exploit it at every opportunity to get us to bow down to Baal or to curse God and die in our sin.

We have a hard time empathizing with those who succumb to weaknesses that we don't have. If booze or sexual lust is not a problem for us, it is hard to identify with those who succumb to these temptations.

Our weaknesses may well be in the area of pride or anger, greed or envy, or some other sin.

"And don't sin by letting anger gain control over you. Don't let the sun go down while you are still angry."
Ephesians 4:26 NLT

The one thing we can be sure of is that the roaring lion is going to constantly attack us in the areas of our weakness, and it is only by putting on the full armor of God and appropriating His strength that we can escape.

How good it is to know that the Holy Spirit will provide the strength to overcome our weaknesses and provide a means of escape from these hostile takeover attempts.

Father, give me your grace and strength to stand firm. Amen.

Lord, You Are _____
Forgive Me For _____
Thank You For _____
Needs of Others _____
Personal Needs _____
Answered Prayers _____

Speed Bumps

"Ignorant zeal is worthless; haste makes waste." Proverbs 19:2 MSG

When everything else fails to curb speeding in congested areas or neighborhoods speed bumps control speed 24 hours a day, 7 days a week, better than traffic cops or traffic lights.

"Careful planning puts you ahead in the long run; hurry and scurry puts you further behind." Proverbs 21:5 MSG

Failure to slow down results in severe jolts to driver and passengers and can cause damage to the car's suspension system. Motorists usually learn to slow down very quickly.

Some of God's chastening and consequences serve the same purposes of speed bumps. They slow us down when we get in too big a hurry while driving through life.

We have physical speed bumps of crippling injuries or illnesses which force us to slow down for physical therapy and healing.

Emotional burn outs and depression often slow us down when the pace of life gets too fast. When we can't keep up with the constant turmoil and stress, we sometimes rush to anger, judgment, lust, or to take matters into our own hands instead of waiting upon the Lord. We need to learn when to slow down and back off when emotions threaten to get out of control.

"So then, my beloved brethren, let every man be swift to hear, slow to speak, slow to wrath," James 1:19

Financial problems mount as we start spending money faster than we are earning it. Maxed out credit cards and bad credit reputations are certainly speed bumps to slow down spending.

Speed bumps of failure await those who get in too big a hurry about anything. The godly virtues of patience and holiness will usually eliminate the need to hit the speed bumps of life.

Father, give me the wisdom and discernment to slow down and steer clear of the speed bumps of life. Amen.

Lord, You Are _____
Forgive Me For _____
Thank You For _____
Needs of Others _____
Personal Needs _____
Answered Prayers _____

August 19   **Read 1 Timothy 4:7-14, Psalm 2**
Waste Management Systems
"'Yes,' says the Spirit, 'and blessed rest from their hard, hard work. None of what they've done is wasted; God blesses them for it all in the end.'"
Revelation 14:13 MSG

Garbage disposal is a multi-billion dollar business and an increasing problem all over the world. We have already polluted too many rivers, too many aquifers, and the pile ups continue.

"Why do the nations rage? Why do the people waste their time with futile plans?"
Psalm 2:1 NLT

As believers, we are called to be waste management specialists if we are to be faithful in doing what God has created us.

Our Lord himself commanded the disciples to pick up the leftovers so that "nothing was wasted."

We waste enough time majoring in minors within the church to fuel a major revival if our time was put to better use for the Lord.

We waste so much time consuming the garbage produced on TV that we have little left to spend with God and grow in His goodness.

We waste our talents pursuing ego-driven agendas that do nothing to glorify God or build up His kingdom.

We waste enough food to feed the starving all over the world.

We waste enough money on toys and self indulgence to support a missionary in the field abundantly well.

Good stewardship is all about being faithful and giving to God from the top. It is also about managing all of the resources with which He blesses us so that none of them are wasted on trivial pursuits with no redeeming value.

"Do not waste time arguing over godless ideas and old wives' tales. Spend your time and energy in training yourself for spiritual fitness."
1 Timothy 4:7 NLT

A life lived apart from God is a wasted life. We are called to live it richly and not wastefully by managing well until the Lord comes, and we will be called to give an account of what we have done with what we have been given.

Father help me to do better in waste management. Amen.

Lord, You Are _____

Forgive Me For _____

Thank You For _____

Needs of Others _____

Personal Needs _____

Answered Prayers _____

Memory Upgrade

*"Sing praise to the L*ORD*, you saints of His, and give thanks at the remembrance of His holy name." Psalm 30:4*

It is amazing what a memory upgrade can do for your computer.

"My heart is breaking as I remember how it used to be" Psalm 42:4a

The old seemingly slow processes and common lockups often disappear as soon as we put a tiny little extra R.A.M. memory chip into the slot.

We all need a regular memory upgrade for the computer of our souls as the road dirt of life seems to sneak into the crevices and dull our recollections.

We too easily forget the greatness and goodness of God. The wonder of His love and the majesty of His power and presence sometimes seem to lose their luster as we get distracted by the trials and tribulations of life in the jungle it has become.

God's holiness seems forgotten in our age of relative truth and increased tolerance and acceptance of what God calls abominations as alternative lifestyles.

The memory of confirmation vows and profession of faith vows made to God often seem to have vanished from our consciousness as though they were never made or mean nothing.

Worst of all, we too often forget who we are and Whose we are in Christ and the wonderful promises He gives to all who receive Him.

In His foreknowledge, love, and grace, God has provided us all with a memory upgrade. He installs the Holy Spirit Who comes to live within us to convict us, strengthen us, and guide us into all truth.

"But the Helper, the Holy Spirit, whom the Father will send in My name, He will teach you all things, and bring to your remembrance all things that I said to you." John 14:25

Best of all, the Holy Spirit will help us to recall God's Word as we study it and commit it to this memory bank of our souls. We can upgrade it daily through abiding in Christ through His Word.

Father, refresh my memory of You daily through Your Word and by the power of the Holy Spirit living within me. Amen.

Lord, You Are _____

Forgive Me For _____

Thank You For _____

Needs of Others _____

Personal Needs _____

Answered Prayers _____

Wisdom

"This is what the LORD says: 'Let not the wise man gloat in his wisdom, or the mighty man in his might, or the rich man in his riches. Let them boast in this alone: that they truly know Me and understand that I am the LORD Who is just and righteous, Whose love is unfailing, and that I delight in these things. I, the LORD, have spoken!'" Jeremiah 9:23, 24 NLT

The world is filled with worldly wisdom. Courses are taught, books are written, and life is lived in worldly wisdom. We can become extremely wise in the ways of the world but bankrupt in true wisdom.

"You felt secure in all your wickedness. 'No one sees me,' you said. Your 'wisdom' and 'knowledge' have caused you to turn away from Me and claim, 'I am self-sufficient and not accountable to anyone!'"
Isaiah 47:10 NLT

Solomon, the wisest man who ever lived, wandered away from the wisdom of God into seeking wisdom in the ways of the world. His pursuit of pleasure, wealth, and power was relentless. It was also futile.

Scripture tells us: "There is a way that seems right to a man, but its end is the way of death" *(Proverbs 14:12).* "'For My thoughts are not your thoughts, nor are your ways My ways,' says the LORD" *(Isaiah 55:8).*

Job 28:12b tells us, "The fear of the LORD is true wisdom; to forsake evil is real understanding."

True wisdom comes only from God. It is promised to all who earnestly seek and ask for it. The wisdom to discern truth as God reveals it and to respond to it in God's way instead of the world's way should be the desire and goal of every believer.

"But the wisdom that is from above is first pure, then peaceable, gentle, willing to yield, full of mercy and good fruits, without partiality and without hypocrisy."
James 3:17

True wisdom will lead us to no other conclusion than there is no real happiness apart from peace with God through faith in Jesus Christ.

Father, make me wise with the spiritual wisdom of Your truth. Amen.

Lord, You Are _____

Forgive Me For _____

Thank You For _____

Needs of Others _____

Personal Needs _____

Answered Prayers _____

Graduations

"These hard times are small potatoes compared to the coming good times, the lavish celebration prepared for us." 2 Corinthians 4:17 MSG

Life seems to be a series of graduations that mark our passage from childhood to maturity.

"For the LORD is our judge, our lawgiver, and our king. He will care for us and save us."
Isaiah 33:13:22 NLT

The greatest graduation of all is the one all believers have to look forward to when they graduate from the school of life into the fullness of forever life with Christ.

The minute we receive Jesus Christ as our Savior we enter the finishing school for eternal life. This is the school of godly character-development where we are being conformed into the image of Christ day by day, week by week, year by year, through the seasons of life on this earth in preparation for the life of sinless perfection and eternal bliss in heaven.

The tuition and taxes that have been paid to make our earthly graduations possible are mere "chump change" when compared to the tuition Jesus Christ paid to assure our graduation from temporal life to eternal life. He gave His life so that we would never have to lose ours.

The commencement ceremonies we have experienced on this earth cannot compare with our glorious graduation into heaven.

"For people can't come to Me unless the Father Who sent Me draws them to Me, and at the last day I will raise them from the dead."
John 6:44 NLT

The mortar boards and tassels will be replaced by our crowns of righteousness. We will probably be singing "Amazing Grace" instead of the Alma Mater with a choir of angels the likes of which this world has never seen.

The robe we will wear will be the robe of righteousness that will glow with the radiance of Christ's joy as He presents us to the Father as one of his beloved brothers or sisters.

All of our tests and trials will be over. Every tear will be wiped away. There will be no more darkness as we dwell in the light of that great City of God forever!

Father, thank you for paying my tuition through this college of life. Amen.

Lord, You Are _____

Forgive Me For _____

Thank You For _____

Needs of Others _____

Personal Needs _____

Answered Prayers _____

Getting in the Way

"Don't you realize that this is not the way to live? Unjust people who don't care about God will not be joining in His kingdom. Those who use and abuse each other, use and abuse sex, use and abuse the earth and everything in it, don't qualify as citizens in God's kingdom." 1 Corinthians 6:9 MSG

As believers, "We know that God causes everything to work together for the good of those who love God and are called according to His purpose for them" *(Romans 8:28).*

"But as for me, I will walk in my integrity; redeem me and be merciful to me."
Psalm 26:11

When things seem at their worst, we will most often find God at His best and live to see how God has worked things for our good and His glory. What we often perceive as bad turns out to be exceedingly and abundantly good when God is on the throne in the temple of our hearts.

We need to be ever mindful that the consequences of willful and deliberate sins often get in the way and nullify God's good and perfect will for our lives.

When we are undergoing reverses in life, the first thing we need to ask is whether these are consequences of our own bad choices and actions or the loving chastening of God as He molds us into the image of Christ.

When we judge ourselves and take the corrective action of confession and true repentance, we can still not always evade some of the severe consequences of our sins, but we can find forgiveness and strength to endure and find restoration in God's grace.

"Examine yourselves as to whether you are in the faith. Test yourselves. Do you not know yourselves, that Jesus Christ is in you?— unless indeed you are disqualified."
2 Corinthians 13:5 NLT

How much better to live with blessings instead of consequences by seeking the blessings of obedience as we live out our lives in the circle of God's will.

Father, deliver me from willful and deliberate sins by the resurrection power of the Holy Spirit living within me. Amen.

Lord, You Are _____

Forgive Me For _____

Thank You For _____

Needs of Others _____

Personal Needs _____

Answered Prayers _____

Conflicts of Interest

"Then He said to the crowd, 'If any of you wants to be my follower, you must put aside your selfish ambition, shoulder your cross daily, and follow Me.'" Luke 9:23

We live in a world of conflicts of interest. Public interest is often thwarted by powerful private interests who have their own agendas to promote.

"Who are those who fear the LORD? He will show them the path they should choose."
Psalm 25:12 NLT

Some churches seem to have been built as legacies to a leader instead of to the glory of The Leader.

The old saying, "everyone wants to go to heaven, but no one wants to die" is often true in the lives of many people.

Our freedom to choose is often the freedom to lose. The rich young ruler chose his riches over eternal life. Judas chose 30 pieces of silver over Jesus. Annanias and Sapphira chose to lie. The Scribes and Pharisees chose to reject the Messiah.

We will all have conflicts of interest to deal with all our lives. Even after we resolve our biggest conflict by dying to self and becoming alive in Christ by grace through faith in His death on the cross, we will often run into conflicts between our will, the will of others, and God's will.

The key to growing into the fullness of Christ is to submit our own personal interests and agendas to God's agenda and plans that He made for us before we were born.

Whether it is in the area of time, talent, or treasures, who we worship will become abundantly clear by the way we use these resources in our everyday life.

"If we are living now by the Holy Spirit, let us follow the Holy Spirit's leading in every part of our lives."
Galatians 5:25 NLT

How we choose to resolve the conflicts between growing in God's Word and watching our favorite TV show, serving our own interests instead of God's, or robbing God by spending His share on ourselves should give us all cause to pause and reprioritize our lives.

Father, help me to resolve my conflicts of interest by the power of the Holy Spirit living within me. Amen.

Lord, You Are _____

Forgive Me For _____

Thank You For _____

Needs of Others _____

Personal Needs _____

Answered Prayers _____

Mystery of Life

"For to me, to live is Christ and to die is gain." Philippians 2:21

The idea that we have to die to live and then live to die is one of God's mysteries of life.

"For you will not leave my soul among the dead or allow your godly one to rot in the grave." Psalm 16:10

From our own human perspective, it makes no sense that we can gain by losing, unless we are talking about weight or bad habits.

When Jesus Christ becomes the Lord of our life and the Holy Spirit comes to live within us, we become dead to sin and alive to Christ in the resurrection power that the Holy Spirit brings.

Through faith in Jesus Christ, we have become righteous and holy in the eyes of God. Sin and death have no more dominion over us as we die to sin and are born again into newness of life in Christ.

We need all the power of the Holy Spirit as we live to become in actuality what we have become by grace in the eyes of God.

Even though we are saved spiritually, we still coexist with our sinful flesh and our lives become a battle ground. The goodness of God and His righteousness, which we earnestly seek and desire, will become more and more evident in our lives as we become transformed into the image of Christ.

Our longing to be like Christ will be fulfilled completely when we die to live with Him in heaven with no more sin, no more sorrow, and no more sadness.

"Of course not! Since we have died to sin, how can we continue to live in it?" Romans 6:2 NLT

To understand the truth of what it means to die in order to live and to really live forever is to have the blessed assurance of what we have through faith in Jesus Christ.

Father, help me to know the joy of being dead to sin and alive in Christ for now and forever. Amen.

Lord, You Are _____
Forgive Me For _____
Thank You For _____
Needs of Others _____
Personal Needs _____
Answered Prayers _____

Read John 14:23-30, Psalm 34   **August 26**
Spiritual Heartburn
"Into the hovels of the poor, into the dark streets where the homeless groan, God speaks: 'I've had enough; I'm on my way to heal the ache in the heart of the wretched.'" Psalm 12:5 MSG

The heartburn of an upset stomach is nothing compared to the heartburn of a vexed spirit.

"The LORD is close to the brokenhearted; He rescues those who are crushed in spirit." Psalm 34:18 NLT

When our consciences are seared by guilt and shame, we feel our hearts will break until we find relief at the cross. There is nothing like a good dose of godly confession, sorrow, and repentance to sooth the lining of our hearts.

Sometimes we suffer an attack of spiritual heartburn through circumstances over which we have absolutely no control. Trusting in the sovereignty of God and His promise to work all things for the good is the only way we can find peace amidst turmoil.

The heart break of divorce often triggers a spiritual heartburn that will sometimes last forever to some degree. We need to know that God specializes in healing broken hearts and that He has promised to supply His all-sufficient grace to give healing and comfort to our hearts.

Getting angry at God can cause some of the worst attacks of spiritual heartburn imaginable.

An unforgiving spirit triggers a heartburn that if left unhealed can lead to physical problems and spiritual poverty.

The good news for believers is that God is at His best when our spiritual heartburn is at its worst. Jesus came to heal the broken hearted and replace sorrow with joy, anxiety with peace, and to change heartburn to hearts burning for Him and His love.

"I am leaving you with a gift—peace of mind and heart. And the peace I give isn't like the peace the world gives. So don't be troubled or afraid." John 14:27 NLT

Relief is often just a prayer or Scripture verse away.

Father, help me to avoid spiritual heartburn by bathing daily in the cleansing waters of confession and repentance and by trusting in You and Your promises. Amen.

Lord, You Are _____
Forgive Me For _____
Thank You For _____
Needs of Others _____
Personal Needs _____
Answered Prayers _____

August 27   **Read 2 Corinthians 7:8-12, Psalm 103**
Valley of the Giants

"I, even I, am He who blots out your transgressions for My own sake; and I will not remember your sins." Isaiah 43:25

We have all probably experienced low ebbs in life. When we look back, we will often recognize mistakes made and be filled with godly sorrow for times when we have fallen short of the glory of God.

"He has removed our rebellious acts as far away from us as the east is from the west." Psalm 103:12 NLT

Many times it is too late for restitution or apologies. Although God's forgiveness is final and complete, we often have to live a lifetime with sorrow over the consequences of wronging others.

Satan will often bring remembrance of past sins to mind as a means of discouraging or undermining our faith and our confidence we have in our right standing with God through faith in Jesus Christ.

The Holy Spirit will sometimes call past sins to our remembrance as a means of teaching us not to repeat them and as a means of keeping us humble and not so self righteous.

It's a good thing to have godly sorrow, but we should never let ghosts of the past come back to haunt us or rob us of the joy of our forgiveness and salvation in Christ.

Instead of being overcome with grief, guilt, and shame over past confessed and repented sins, we should concentrate on rejoicing in how great God's love and mercy has been in forgiving us. When we have the faith to base our security on what Jesus Christ has done, instead of what we may have done or left undone, even our godly sorrow will become an instrument of joy.

"Now I rejoice, not that you were made sorry, but that your sorrow led to repentance. For you were made sorry in a godly manner, that you might suffer loss from us in nothing." 2 Corinthians 7:9

It will help us realize the width and depth of God's love and our total dependency upon His grace and mercy. This is what having peace that surpasses all understanding is all about.

Father let my sins of the past never come back to haunt but to help me appreciate the width and depth of Your love and the security I have in You. Amen.

Lord, You Are _____

Forgive Me For _____

Thank You For _____

Needs of Others _____

Personal Needs _____

Answered Prayers _____

Working it Out

"I have been crucified with Christ; it is no longer I who live, but Christ lives in me; and the life which I now live in the flesh I live by faith in the Son of God, who loved me and gave Himself for me." Galatians 6:20

What do we do with the wonderful new life we have in Christ? How do we work out our salvation that we have so graciously been given by the grace of God? What do we do with the faith that God has placed in our hearts?

> **"Commit your works to the LORD, and your thoughts will be established." Proverbs 16:3**

Scripture makes it very clear that being a new creature involves a lot of doing as we surrender control of our will from the bondage of self and sin to the control of the Holy Spirit now living within us.

Working out the faith that God has worked in us is all about living out our faith as evidenced by the way we live our lives in Christ.

The evidence that we are living out our faith is evidenced by the "love, joy, peace, longsuffering, kindness, goodness, faithfulness, gentleness, self-control" (Galatians 5:22) that we exhibit in our relationships with others.

Working it out means working on getting rid of the character defects that ruin our witness and keep us from truly reflecting the love and lordship of Jesus Christ in our lives. It involves allowing what God has worked in our hearts to carry over into our lives.

We are no longer under the domination of sin. As new creatures in Christ, we are now free to choose how we will respond not only to the joy of our salvation but to the trials and tribulations of living life in a sin-sick world.

We should all be single minded in working out ways to become more like Christ in every area of our lives.

> **"Therefore, my beloved, as you have always obeyed, not as in my presence only, but now much more in my absence, work out your own salvation with fear and trembling," Philippians 2:12**

Father, let me always be a work in progress growing in Your fullness until I see You face to face. Amen.

Lord, You Are _____

Forgive Me For _____

Thank You For _____

Needs of Others _____

Personal Needs _____

Answered Prayers _____

How Grateful Should We Be?

"But giving thanks is a sacrifice that truly honors me. If you keep to my path, I will reveal to you the salvation of God." Psalm 50:23

Among all of the Christian virtues an attitude of gratitude is the one that most pleases God.

"But let all those rejoice who put their trust in You; let them ever shout for joy, because You defend them; let those also who love Your name be joyful in You." Psalm 5:11

When we ponder the joy of our salvation, we are awed by the great thing God has done for us in Christ. If honest, we know that we can never be worthy of God's unmerited favor, but we need to know that we can always be grateful.

When we are truly grateful, obedience to God is not a painful, joyless exercise of having to do all sorts of things we don't want to do and not being allowed to do things we long to do.

An attitude of gratitude makes us want to do the things that please Him and that show our appreciation to Him for all He has done and is doing for us in Christ.

God inhabits the praises of His people. As we live our lives as sacrifices of praise to Him, we can be sure of God's presence and power in our lives. We find that all-surpassing peace and joy that only a right relationship with God through faith in Jesus Christ can afford.

We should be grateful enough that we can be blessable by God.

We should be grateful enough to know that God loves a cheerful giver and has promised to make us rich so that we can be generous on all occasions.

We need to be grateful enough that our generosity of spirit lets us see the love of Christ in us as we generously love and serve others.

"Rejoice in the Lord always. Again I will say, rejoice!" Philippians 4:4-20

Perhaps most important of all, we need to be thankful during our times of pain and suffering, so we can rejoice in seeing God's strength being made perfect in our weakness.

Father, help me to live my life as a celebration of thanksgiving and praise to You. Amen.

Lord, You Are _____

Forgive Me For _____

Thank You For _____

Needs of Others _____

Personal Needs _____

Answered Prayers _____

The 5 "W's"

"By this time you ought to be teachers yourselves, yet here I find you need someone to sit down with you and go over the basics on God again, starting from square one." Hebrews 5:11 MSG

We read many newspaper articles which seem to ignore the "5 W's" of good journalism – who, what, where, why, and when.

> **"Put your ear to the earth—learn the basics."**
> **Job 12:8 MSG**

As believers, we need to know the "5 W's" of our faith. We need to know who Jesus was and is! He was and is God in the Flesh, Savior, Redeemer, and the Son of God, who died and rose again from the dead. Jesus is Love!

What Jesus did should be etched in our hearts. He lived the perfect life, became the perfect sacrifice for our sins, died on the cross of Calvary over 2,000 years ago, and rose again to live forever.

Because He loves us, He had to live the perfect life and die as the perfect sacrifice to fulfill God's requirements for perfection under the law so that we could be forgiven of our sins and be reconciled to God.

When the fullness of God's time comes, Jesus will come again in glory to raise both the living and the dead, and all who have died in Him through faith in Jesus Christ will be raised from the dead and live forever with Him through all eternity.

There is so much more about the who's, what's, why's, and when's of Christ and our life in Him that we will never know them all even after a lifetime of abiding in His Word and earnestly seeking Him.

But we know that God will continue to reveal Himself to those who earnestly seek Him and that He also blesses those who do.

The 5 W's provide a handy checklist and point of reference for learning all that God would have us know about Him.

These also provide an outline for constantly reminding us of who we are in Him, what He has done for us, that He did it because He loves us, and that He lives in our hearts, and we will see Him face to face when we stand before Him in eternity.

> **"All who proclaim that Jesus is the Son of God have God living in them, and they live in God."**
> **1 John 4:15 NLT**

Father, keep me ever mindful of the 5 W's of my salvation. Amen.

Lord, You Are _____

Forgive Me For _____

Thank You For _____

Needs of Others _____

Personal Needs _____

Answered Prayers _____

August 31   Read Ephesians 3:8-21, Isaiah 55
Doing It My Way
"There is a way that seems right to a man, but its end is the way of death."
Proverbs 14:12

It is a great inspiration to see people who are able to rise above circumstances and handicaps to succeed in sports, business, or other arenas of life.

"'My thoughts are completely different from yours,' says the LORD. 'And my ways are far beyond anything you could imagine.'"
Isaiah 55:8

Unfortunately, as Will Rogers liked to say, "Whenever I see a self-made man, I usually see what a bad job he's done."

Scripture is full of people who insisted on doing it their way. Rebekah and Jacob plotted to steal Esau's birthright instead of waiting for God to do it.

The children of Israel drew back instead of going into the Promised Land God had promised, and a whole generation never got there.

God has given us all freewill, and He will allow us to live life our way if we are dumb enough or stubborn enough to do it.

We all probably try doing it our way instead of God's from time to time only to find out that it doesn't work. The pride that usually accompanies the determination to live in our own strength instead God's has been the downfall of many.

We need to understand that God's ways are so much higher than our ways that we often cannot begin to comprehend what He is doing.

God does not help those who help themselves because as long as we insist on doing it our way we will never seek or receive God's help.

It is only when we come to realize our total dependency upon God, and we die to self and become alive in Christ that we can ever live life in all of its abundance and fullness.

"To know the love of Christ which passes knowledge that you may be filled with all the fullness of God."
Ephesians 3:19

That anyone would even think of doing life their way instead of God's way not only speaks volumes about the poverty of one's soul but also raises serious questions about whether their brain is fully loaded.

Father, help me to accept by faith that doing it my way never works instead of having to find it out the hard way. Amen.

Lord, You Are _____
Forgive Me For _____
Thank You For _____
Needs of Others _____
Personal Needs _____
Answered Prayers _____

You Gotta Give It to Keep It

"This is what the LORD has commanded: A man who makes a vow to the LORD or makes a pledge under oath must never break it. He must do exactly what he said he would do." Numbers 30:1a, 2 NLT

I don't know who said this, but it certainly bears repeating: "Your word is the only thing you have to give to keep."

"The LORD hates those who don't keep their word, but He delights in those who do." Proverbs 12:22 NLT

Long gone are the days when a simple handshake sealed a deal, and "my word is my bond" was a character quality of most people.

In today's world, we have millions of lawyers making a good living because too many people don't keep their word.

Divorce courts are overflowing with people who did not keep their word.

The rudeness of keeping others waiting because some cannot keep their word to be anywhere on time, collection agencies working overtime because some do not pay as promised, undone repairs, and unfinished construction projects are just a few symptoms of the disease of people not keeping their word.

Our Lord tells us that our word should be good enough that we should not have to swear an oath to make it binding and that we should be suspicious of such validations.

We all have probably given our word or made promises that we have not kept for one reason or another to our children, spouses, or others.

We have made and broken promises to God by repenting and then repeating our repented sins.

We need to know that God takes the sin of broken promises seriously, and we should also.

A reputation for keeping our word should be one of the top priorities of our lives as we seek to become imitators of Christ, who is our ultimate keeper of His Word.

"Just say a simple, 'Yes, I will,' or 'No, I won't.' Your word is enough. To strengthen your promise with a vow shows that something is wrong." Matthew 5:37 NLT

Father, help me to make no promise I do not intend to keep and to keep the promises I make by the power of your Spirit. Amen.

Lord, You Are _____
Forgive Me For _____
Thank You For _____
Needs of Others _____
Personal Needs _____
Answered Prayers _____

Are You Coasting?

"You enlarged my path under me, so my feet did not slip." Psalm 18:36

Whether in churches, business, relationships, or faith, coasting is not the way to grow. You can only coast downhill.

"Therefore evil shall come upon you; you shall not know from where it arises. And trouble shall fall upon you; you will not be able to put it off. And desolation shall come upon you suddenly, which you shall not know."
Isaiah 47:10

Churches and businesses are either going to go forward or fall behind. Our relationship with others and our relationship with Jesus are either growing or getting ready to coast downhill due to neglect or indifference.

Our eternal life is meant to be a growing life. We are to continually grow into the likeness and fullness of Christ day by day by climbing our ladders of faith fueled by the power of the Holy Spirit living in us.

We have the enemy of our souls working 24 hours a day, 7 days a week, trying to get us to coast down to where we cut ourselves off from the power and strength of the armor God has provided for us.

Churches that are content to coast along in a maintenance mode without any real passion for seeking and saving the lost or adapting styles of worship to keep and attract young people are closing everyday throughout this country.

Many leading businesses of the past are nonexistent because they coasted or failed to grow (Woolworth, A & P, and Plymouth Automobiles to name a few).

We need nourishment if we are to grow.   A once a week meal at the Lord's buffet of grace is alright. Many people try to coast through life on this diet, but few will ever grow in spiritual maturity this way.

"But since you are like lukewarm water, I will spit you out of my mouth!"
Revelation 3:16 NLT

The world around us and our flesh nourish our baser instincts daily instead of weekly. We need to take our spiritual nourishment daily in order to keep from coasting back down into the valleys of sin and despair.

Father, don't let me coast back down to the pits of sin. Amen.

Lord, You Are _____

Forgive Me For _____

Thank You For _____

Needs of Others _____

Personal Needs _____

Answered Prayers _____

Trustees of Truth

"Hold fast the pattern of sound words which you have heard from me, in faith and love which are in Christ Jesus." 2 Timothy 1:13

When we hear or think of stewardship, it is usually within the context of money and tithing. While it is true that the stewardship of life is managing well the time, talents, and financial resources God gives, the most important aspect of stewardship is probably the most overlooked.

"Lead me in Your truth and teach me, For You are the God of my salvation; on You I wait all the day." Psalm 25:5

As believers, we are all stewards of the truth God has given us by the power of the Holy Spirit.

The truth of the Good News for our salvation and the truth God teaches through His Word for our sanctification and edification and for His glory is something we must manage well.

We have all been given the awesome responsibility to be witnesses by proclaiming God's truth to others.

We are all given the high privilege of learning and knowing truth by knowing and growing in a close and personal friendship with Jesus, Who is "the Way, the Truth, and the Life."

As parents, we are commanded to teach the truth to our children so that they will not depart from it.

As members of the royal priesthood of believers, we must perpetuate and maintain God's truth, and we must protect it from all those who would try to change or distort it.

This is no easy task. It gets more difficult all the time as the world and even sincere but misguided individuals try to water down or supplant God's truth and wisdom with the counterfeit truth of man.

"For the law was given through Moses, but grace and truth came through Jesus Christ." John 1:17

We manage and are good stewards of God's truth when we learn it as God teaches it to us through His Word and when we appropriate it by faith and apply it to our lives of obedience to it as we go about managing until He comes.

Father, help me to be a good steward of Your truth. Amen.

Lord, You Are _____

Forgive Me For _____

Thank You For _____

Needs of Others _____

Personal Needs _____

Answered Prayers _____

September 4   Read Jude 1:21-25, Psalm 119:56-68
                          Having it My Way
"There is a way that seems right to a man, but its end is the way of death."
Proverbs 14:12

We all like to have things go our way. Having it our way in the self-centered pursuit of pleasure and control is the worst possible way to live.

"This is my happy way of life: obeying Your commandments." Psalm 119:56 NLT

Having it our way at the expense of others will often bring the painful consequences of others having it their way at our expense. The Golden Rule is a two-way street.

In order not to force anyone to love Him, God gave us all a free will. When Adam and Eve chose to disobey God, the painful consequence of their bondage to sin became the legacy of all who would follow up to this present age.

God, in His mercy, decided to provide a means of freeing us from bondage to sin and the death penalty it carries by sending His own Son Jesus to pay the penalty for our sin at the cross and by sending the Holy Spirit into our hearts to enable us to receive this wonderful gift of salvation.

When we, by faith, choose to have it God's way, dead to sin and alive in Christ, we find the peace and joy of having it the only way in which "God causes everything to work together for the good of those who love God and are called according to his purpose for them" *(Romans 8:28 NIT).*

The best way to do life God's way is to focus our hearts' affection and minds' attention on God and His will. We are even promised that whatever we ask in Jesus name will be given when we ask unselfishly in accordance with His will.

"Live in such a way that God's love can bless you as you wait for the eternal life that our Lord Jesus Christ in His mercy is going to give you." Jude 1:21 NLT

Although the way of the cross may often be a way of suffering and sorrow, "having it our way" no longer means having it my way, but it now means that we have the presence and power of the Holy Spirit living within us to make having it "our way" mean having it God's way.

Father, let the reality of Your presence in my life change my ways to our ways as I seek to live a fruitful life pleasing to You. Amen.

Lord, You Are _____
Forgive Me For _____
Thank You For _____
Needs of Others _____
Personal Needs _____
Answered Prayers _____

As Little As Possible

"The thief's purpose is to steal and kill and destroy. My purpose is to give life in all its fullness." John 10:10 NLT

Whether it is in giving, serving, or growing, "as little as possible" is an all too prevalent and insidious mindset. It is a terrible way to live life in Christ, because in many ways it is an invitation for God to do as little as possible for us.

"The LORD is gracious and full of compassion, slow to anger and great in mercy."
Psalm 145:8

The basic scriptural principle of reaping what you sew is a strong reminder that whatever you sew sparingly you will reap sparingly, whether it is time, treasures, talents, love, or forgiveness.

If God decided to do as little as possible for us, we would all be in big trouble.

When we try to do life in our own strength with as little help as possible from God, we are doomed to fail. It is only when the reality of God and our total dependence upon His sovereignty and providence sinks in that we can break out into the fullness of our abundant life in Christ.

Instead of trying to figure out how to give as little of our treasures as possible, we should be trying to figure out how to be good stewards of our finances so that we can give more and be generous on all occasions.

When we go through life doing as little as possible in being fruitful in every good work and live instead for the wood, hay, and stubble of the trivial pursuits of self-centered pleasure and worldliness, we are setting ourselves up for a big disappointment when we are called to give an account of the stewardship of our lives.

The only area of life that we should concentrate on doing as little as possible is in the area of sinning. We should all make this a top priority as we seek to do life God's way in the fullness of peace and joy.

"To know the love of Christ which passes knowledge, that you may be filled with all the fullness of God,"
Colossians 3:9

Father, help me to concentrate on doing and being as much as possible to glorify You in every area of my life. Amen.

Lord, You Are _____
Forgive Me For _____
Thank You For _____
Needs of Others _____
Personal Needs _____
Answered Prayers _____

Live Him Up!

"...Because God made humans in His image reflecting God's very nature. You're here to bear fruit, reproduce, lavish life on the Earth, live bountifully!" **Genesis 9:6b, 7 MSG**

We all have a lot to live up to. Whether it's living up to our own expectations or the expectations of parents, spouses, children, or employers, living life well has a lot to do with living it up.

"Glory in His holy name; let the hearts of those rejoice who seek the LORD!" Psalm 105:3

The downside to living it up is when we think that it is all about pursuing pleasure and self gratification.

The key to finding true happiness is learning to live it up in the fullness of joy that only a close and personal relationship with Jesus Christ can give.

When we live it up by lifting Him up as our living Lord Who has come that we may have life forever in His fullness, we will have found the key for unlocking the door to our hearts and letting the Son come in.

When we lift Jesus up and make Him the focus of our lives, the high expectations of His promises become realities in our lives to be experienced and enjoyed.

We receive the supernatural strength and power of the Holy Spirit to be lifted up above our burdens of sin and to be transformed by the renewing of our minds and conformed into the very likeness of Christ.

The more we live it up in Christ, the more like Him we will be come. His thoughts will become our thoughts, His prayers will become our prayers, and His love will fill us to overflowing so that it pours out into the lives of others through us.

"Therefore gird up the loins of your mind, be sober, and rest your hope fully upon the grace that is to be brought to you at the revelation of Jesus Christ;" 1 Peter 1:13

Living it up should add new meaning to our high calling in Christ.

Father, help me to live life up in You. Amen.

Lord, You Are _____
Forgive Me For _____
Thank You For _____
Needs of Others _____
Personal Needs _____
Answered Prayers _____

Devaluing the Dollar

"Jesus refused, 'First things first. Your business is life, not death. Follow me. Pursue life.'" Matthew 8:22 MSG

The value of various currencies fluctuates almost daily. All anyone has to do is price groceries, houses, cars, or gasoline to experience the devalued dollar in this country.

**"They defiled themselves by their evil deeds, and their love of idols was adultery in the LORD'S sight."
Psalm 106:39 NLT**

There is a much more serious devaluation happening. We seem to be living in an age of devalued faith.

God has too often become mistaken with Santa Claus. The prosperity gospel would have us believe that God wants us all to be healthy, wealthy, and wise with no financial problems, health problems, pain, or suffering, and if this is not our experience, it's because of our lack of faith.

The inherent evil of this world has pulled out all the stops on moral restraint. Holiness, without which no one will see God, has taken a back seat to worldliness in our everyday lives.

The spiritual adultery of the children of Israel pales by comparison to the spiritual adultery of today where the gods of money and pleasure and the worship of self have taken God off the throne and devalued Him to the back seat or thrown Him out of millions of lives.

The evidence of our devalued faith is all around us. Christians are divorcing as often, if not more than, nonbelievers. Too many of us are feeding on the garbage of the world via TV, movies, and internet instead of the Bread of Life.

Service to God has too often become lip service with absolutely no fruits of righteousness evidenced in the lives of many believers.

God will not be devalued or mocked. He is the same yesterday, today, and forever. He came to earth as Jesus to show us the way, the truth and the life. We dare not lose our way.

**"Then He said to the crowd, 'If any of you wants to be my follower, you must put aside your selfish ambition, shoulder your cross daily, and follow me.'"
Luke 9:23 NLT**

Father, let me add value to my life and my love for You daily by getting to know You and become more and more like Jesus. Amen.

Lord, You Are _____
Forgive Me For _____
Thank You For _____
Needs of Others _____
Personal Needs _____
Answered Prayers _____

Wrong Focus

"But without faith it is impossible to please Him, for he who comes to God must believe that He is, and that He is a rewarder of those who diligently seek Him." Hebrews 11:6

We need to be very careful about the motivation behind our relationship with Jesus. We can be seeking His love and friendship for all

"Delight yourself also in the LORD, and He shall give you the desires of your heart." Psalm 37:4

the wrong reasons.

We need to be ever mindful that we are to seek first the kingdom of God and His righteousness and that everything else is incidental to this.

God is the Giver of every good and perfect gift, and He loves to give good gifts to His children. He is our provider, but He is not Santa Claus. He is the "Author and Perfector of our faith," and we need to focus on getting to know Him, rather than on what He can give us.

When our focus is on growing into the fullness of Christ and becoming more like Him everyday in every way by getting to know Him better through His Word, His incidental blessings will be so great we will not have to ask for anything for ourselves because we will learn that He knows and supplies our needs even before we ask.

As we grow into the fullness of our relationship with Christ we will experience the joy of more answered prayers as we begin praying unselfish prayers with the mindset of Christ instead of self-centered prayers based on our own agendas and wants.

As we focus on abiding in Christ and getting to know Him better and better as He reveals himself to us through His Word, all of the blessings of abiding will become manifest in our lives.

"When you obey me, you remain in My love, just as I obey My Father and remain in His love." John 15:10 NLT

The blessings of friendship with Jesus, His fullness of joy, answered prayers, and the awareness of God's love and the love of others are all ours when our focus is right.

Father, help me to always keep my focus on You and Your righteousness. Amen.

Lord, You Are _____
Forgive Me For _____
Thank You For _____
Needs of Others _____
Personal Needs _____
Answered Prayers _____

What Shall We Sacrifice?

"The sacrifice you want is a broken spirit. A broken and repentant heart, O God, you will not despise." Psalm 51:17 NLT

Since Cain and Abel offered sacrifices to God at harvest time as an act of worship, the principle of sacrifices to God as offerings of thanksgiving, praise, atonement, and commemoration have been well documented throughout Scripture.

"What can I offer the LORD for all He has done for me?" Psalm 116:12 NLT

Pagan cultures thrived on even human sacrifices to appease and worship their gods.

God not only gave Moses the Ten Commandments but also specific commandments for governing and worshiping through sacrificial offerings of every kind for every occasion. "These are the laws, regulations, and instructions that the LORD gave to the Israelites through Moses on Mount Sinai" (Leviticus 26:46 NLT).

The principle of sacrifice for sin reached fulfillment and completion when God gave His only begotten Son as the one-time, perfect sacrifice for our sins.

Jesus made atonement for all of the requirements of the law for us. Through Jesus, God made a new covenant of grace whereby we would be saved by grace through faith instead of through the law.

All of this brings up the question of what should we sacrifice in response to God's great sacrifice for us.

We can still offer sacrifices of praise and thanksgiving. The blessings of the sacrifice of the tithe are still available to us.

Just as Jesus' perfect sacrifice did what the blood of goats or other animals could not do, living our lives as living sacrifices of obedience and praise to God will become the sweet fragrance that will please God more than all of the ceremonial laws and rituals could ever do.

"And so, dear brothers and sisters, I plead with you to give your bodies to God. Let them be a living and holy sacrifice— the kind he will accept. When you think of what He has done for you, is this too much to ask?" Romans 12:1 NLT

Father, help me to be a living sacrifice to You in every area of my life. Amen.

Lord, You Are _____

Forgive Me For _____

Thank You For _____

Needs of Others _____

Personal Needs _____

Answered Prayers _____

How Perfect is Your Love?

"For the commandments against adultery and murder and stealing and coveting—and any other commandment—are all summed up in this one commandment: 'Love your neighbor as yourself.' Love does no wrong to anyone, so love satisfies all of God's requirements." Romans 13:9, 10 NLT

Perfect love not only casts out all fear; it is the fulfillment of the law. As works in progress, we need to frequently check our life of love and seek to improve in areas where we are less than perfect.

"For you bless the godly, O LORD, surrounding them with Your shield of love."
Psalm 5:12

One of the best ways to check your love life is to just put your name in the blanks before the statements that are true of you:

____suffers long and is kind; ____does not envy; ____does not parade itself, is not puffed up; ——does not behave rudely, ____does not seek his/her own, ____is not provoked, thinks no evil; ____does not rejoice in iniquity, but rejoices in the truth; ____bears all things, ____believes all things, ____ hopes all things, ____ endures all things.

The qualities that we cannot put our name to are qualities that we need to develop if we are to become all that we can be in Christ.

In His mercy, God has sent the Holy Spirit to live within us to provide the power to do what we cannot do in our own strength.

The ongoing process of receiving literally the righteousness of Christ that we already have received by faith theologically is called sanctification or being set apart for God.

"If I could speak in any language in heaven or on earth but didn't love others, I would only be making meaningless noise like a loud gong or a clanging cymbal."
1 Corinthians 13:1 NLT

The power of God unto salvation is also the power of God unto sanctification. When we submit our will to the sovereignty of God, we receive this power to live in the freedom of our new birth in Christ, which is the freedom to express perfect love in every aspect of our lives.

Father, help me to reflect Your love in every area of my life. Amen.

Lord, You Are _____
Forgive Me For _____
Thank You For _____
Needs of Others _____
Personal Needs _____
Answered Prayers _____

Our Two Resurrections

"If then you were raised with Christ, seek those things which are above, where Christ is, sitting at the right hand of God." Colossians 3:1 NLT

We often lose sight of the fact that there are two resurrections. We need to be ever mindful that we cannot look forward to our resurrection from physical death without receiving the spiritual resurrection of being born again.

"Why not help us make a fresh start—a resurrection life? Then Your people will laugh and sing! Show us how much You love us, GOD! Give us the salvation we need!" Psalm 85:6 MSG

Our first resurrection happens when, by the undeserved favor of God, we die to sin and become alive in Christ by the miraculous cleansing from all sin and unrighteousness through regeneration by the Holy Spirit into a new life as sons and daughters of God. We are clothed in the righteousness of Christ through faith in Christ's death on the cross for the atonement of our sin.

Along with this miracle of a new birth, we receive the sanctifying power of the Holy Spirit to live free from bondage to sin and death, and we are free to grow in the incredible peace and joy of the Lord which is the birth right of every born again believer.

When we receive Jesus Christ as our Savior through faith by the power of the Holy Spirit, our salvation has been both accomplished and begun.

The perfection of Christ we received in God's sight the hour we first believed will become a growing reality as we become more Christ like and grow into His fullness day by day, year by year, until we enjoy our total perfection in heaven.

"These things I have told you are all true. I want you to insist on them so that everyone who trusts in God will be careful to do good deeds all the time." Titus 3:8 NLT

Saving faith is an operative working faith which will bring forth the fruits of righteousness and validate the new birth in the life of every true believer. The good works for which God created us before we were born will be manifest in our lives as we seek to live lives "fully pleasing to Him and fruitful in every good work."

Father, help me to live in the knowledge of and faith in both resurrections. Amen.

Lord, You Are _____

Forgive Me For _____

Thank You For _____

Needs of Others _____

Personal Needs _____

Answered Prayers _____

September 12   Read 1 Corinthians 3:8-21, Isaiah 65:21-24
Is it Worth Doing Well?
"Whatever your hand finds to do, do it with your might …"
Ecclesiastes 9:10

"My chosen ones will long enjoy the works of their hands."
Isaiah 65:22b NIV

There's a little bit of the worker and shirker in all of us. It is sometimes hard to get enthused about the task that lies before us, and we often just want to get it done and not worry about doing it well.

The discipline of pursuing excellence in all that we do in every area of our lives is probably the most important quality of character we can ever develop. This is probably the most common trait among truly outstanding people in every walk of life.

Many can pursue excellence in developing a particular pursuit for which they have a passion but often lack the self discipline to work at developing relational skills or work habits in other areas.

We often see outstanding professionals who are lousy parents, spouses, and miserable human beings because they do not pursue excellence in every area of their lives.

Neatness is a trait that needs to be encouraged and developed early so that it becomes a habit and trademark for everything we do.

When we think of our spiritual life, we need to be ever mindful of the importance of doing life well.

When we allow the Holy Spirit to guide us along the paths of moral excellence and righteousness in every area of our lives, we are going to find the peace, joy, and fulfillment that only abiding in Christ can afford.

When we stand before the judgment seat of Christ to give an accounting of how we have used the time, talents, and resources we have been given, our Lord's *"well done thou good and faithful servant,"* is going to give us all-surpassing joy in knowing that life was worth doing well.

"For we are God's fellow workers; you are God's field, you are God's building,"
1 Corinthians 3:9

Father, give me the self discipline, passion, and power to live a life worth living in and through You. Amen.

Lord, You Are _____
Forgive Me For _____
Thank You For _____
Needs of Others _____
Personal Needs _____
Answered Prayers _____

God's Royal Command

"Now the purpose of the commandment is love from a pure heart, from a good conscience, and from sincere faith." 1 Timothy 1:5

The apostle James reminds us all that you can't have one without the other.

"Your royal decrees cannot be changed. The nature of your reign, O LORD, is holiness forever." Psalm 93:5 NLT

It's easy to obey the royal command in words. It's quite another story to obey it in action by the way we respond to others.

It's a lot easier to say we believe in God than to validate our faith by the way we live our lives in obedience to Him.

James's reminder that even demons believe in God and tremble should give us all cause to ponder that faith without any evidence of good works is dead and useless.

We need to be ever mindful of some of the strongholds of sin that keep us from obeying God's royal command.

When we harbor any prejudices against others because of their color or their economic status, we are failing to obey.

Love is nowhere to be found when we seek to make ourselves look good by comparing our sins with the sins of others.

It is only when we respond to God's love by loving and serving others as He has loved and served us that we can put our faith into action and live lives fully pleasing to Him and fruitful in every good work.

God never forces us to do anything. He gives us a free will to receive or reject His calling to salvation through faith in Jesus Christ. His love sets us free that we not only can but want to obey Him.

"Yes indeed, it is good when you truly obey our Lord's royal command found in the Scriptures: 'Love your neighbor as yourself.'" James 2:8 NLT

When we love others enough to witness to them and try to make disciples of them for Christ, we are going to begin living out the royal commandment and great commission in the way God intended.

Father, help me to live an active faith of obedience in loving others. Amen.

Lord, You Are _____
Forgive Me For _____
Thank You For _____
Needs of Others _____
Personal Needs _____
Answered Prayers _____

September 14   **Read 1 John 4:17-21, Psalm 16**

Our Choice Possession

"In His goodness He chose to make us His own children by giving us His true word. And we, out of all creation, became His choice possession." James 1:18 NLT

"My choice is you, GOD, first and only. And now I find I'm Your choice!" Psalm 16:5 MSG

We all hold some things dear. It may be something material like a house, car, or money. It may be friends. Often it is the things that we let define our self image like appearance, pride, or status.

Amidst all of the distractions that if held too dearly can take our eye off our real prize we need to know Who holds us dearly.

Of all creation, we are God's choice possession. He created us for His pleasure. He delights in us and sings over us.

We cannot buy anything that comes close to the price that reveals what choice possessions we are to God.

That He would send His one and only Son to offer His life as a sacrifice for the sin that corrupted us validates just how dear we are to Him.

In light of what choice possessions we are to God, it is good to ask ourselves how choice a possession is God to us.

Is God number one in our minds and hearts, or do we make Him play second fiddle or put Him lower on our list of what we hold dearly?

Dare we compare the time we spend in close communion with God in His Word or prayer with the time we spend on other activities? Are we ready to stand before God and give an accounting? Do our lives reflect that He is our choice possession?

"And as we live in God, our love grows more perfect. So we will not be afraid on the day of judgment, but we can face Him with confidence because we are like Christ here in this world." 1 John 4:17 NLT

We need to be ever mindful that although God loves us dearly and unconditionally, He is a jealous God and will not share His glory with an idol of any description that we treasure and value above Him.

Father, let me hold You as my choicest possession and let every area of my life reflect this. Amen.

Lord, You Are _____
Forgive Me For _____
Thank You For _____
Needs of Others _____
Personal Needs _____
Answered Prayers _____

Read Luke 18:18-29, Psalm 37

Are You Choking?

"Now the ones that fell among thorns are those who, when they have heard, go out and are choked with cares, riches, and pleasures of life, and bring no fruit to maturity." Luke 8:14

Many people choke to death every year. In spite of the widespread knowledge and use of the Heimlich maneuver to dislodge particles of food stuck in the throat that shut off breathing, many die from choking.

"For evildoers shall be cut off; those who wait on the LORD, they shall inherit the earth." Psalm 37:9

Scripture makes it very clear that spiritual choking is a very real and present danger in the lives of believers and nonbelievers alike.

Some ignore the call to salvation because they are choking on the desire to sew some wild oats before they settle down or accomplish some other top worldly priority.

Others receive the Good News with great joy and good intentions, but soon let self-centered worries and ambitions cough out their joy and spit out their good intentions without ever realizing the true peace and joy of their salvation.

When we let the love of God get stuck in our heads without making it to our hearts, there can be no real conversion or holy transformation.

Jesus Christ came to set us free from the blockage of sin that was choking us to death and suffocating us with eternal damnation.

He not only came to set us free, but He has given the Holy Spirit to breathe new life into us that we can live dead to sin and alive in Christ.

No matter what sin may be sticking in our craw and threatening to destroy us, we can find strength and comfort in God's promises that He has provided the power to overcome them through the cleansing of confession and true repentance.

"But when the man heard this, he became sad because he was very rich." Luke 18:23 NLT

The power that is in us through faith in Jesus Christ is greater than the power of the world, the flesh, and the devil put together.

Father, help me breathe free from the obstructions of sin in my new life in You, by the power of the Holy Spirit. Amen.

Lord, You Are _____

Forgive Me For _____

Thank You For _____

Needs of Others _____

Personal Needs _____

Answered Prayers _____

September 16   Read 2 Timothy 3, Psalm 119:73-77

Watching Out for the Revisionists

"I will say it again: If anyone preaches any other gospel than the one you welcomed, let God's curse fall upon that person." Galatians 1:9 NLT

There seems always to be a movement in place to revise history and put a different spin on about everything that ever happened.

"Your hands have made me and fashioned me; give me understanding, that I may learn Your commandments."
Psalm 119:73

Many scholars of the Constitution would have us believe that the writers wanted freedom from religion instead of freedom of religion. Others have demanded revisions in history relating to slavery, the conquest of the West, and even the horror of the Holocaust.

The Christian faith based on the truth and inerrancy of Scripture has been the target of revisionists since the beginning of time. Satan began revising God's Word by trying to get Eve to doubt that God really said what He said.

Many professing Christians have allowed revisionist teaching to undermine Scripture and its authority. The virgin birth and the deity of Christ have been called into question. God's abominations have become politically, socially, and legally correct standards of conduct for many.

The intellectual pride of man continues to try to undermine the truth of God and the authority of Scripture. Itching ears are scratched with what we want to hear instead of what God wants us to hear.

If we can just undermine the authority of Scripture, we are free to believe what man would have us believe or to just pick and choose for ourselves what we will believe and how we will live our lives.

"All Scripture is inspired by God and is useful to teach us what is true and to make us realize what is wrong in our lives. It straightens us out and teaches us to do what is right."
2 Timothy 3:16 NLT

We must never forget that the wisdom of man is foolishness to God. We need to remember and look out for those "wolves in sheep's clothing" who God said would come to try to undermine our faith.

Father, protect me from the revisionist teachings that would undermine my faith and belief in Your Word. Amen.

Lord, You Are _____

Forgive Me For _____

Thank You For _____

Needs of Others _____

Personal Needs _____

Answered Prayers _____

Read James 1:19-27, Isaiah 29:15-21 **September 17**
Are You Careful Where You Sit?

"Blessed is the man who walks not in the counsel of the ungodly, Nor stands in the path of sinners, nor sits in the seat of the scornful," Psalm 1:1

What are the seats of the scornful? My Bible Study Fellowship leader believes that movie theaters and TV's are good examples.

"For the terrible one is brought to nothing, the scornful one is consumed, and all who watch for iniquity are cut off—" Isaiah 29:20

The preponderance of sex, violence, and evil flaunted in a vast majority of movies is scornful to God and His righteousness and does nothing to bless or edify the soul.

That favorite couch or chair can easily become a seat of the scornful when the garbage of most TV is allowed to come in and mock God and everything holy.

The saying "you are what you eat" is used to encourage good nutrition and diet for our physical health. It also has great spiritual relevance.

If we feed on garbage as we sit in the seats of the scornful, it is going to sooner or later deaden our consciences, harden our hearts, and stunt our growth in Christ or affect us in some other way. Sin is contagious, and no one is immune.

How much better to sit at the feet of the one who loves us with an everlasting love and who came to show us how to live a life of prosperity that goes far beyond material wealth.

Today's Psalm goes on to promise that whoever "sits at the feet" of the Master and delights in and meditates on Him and His law will prosper in whatever he or she does.

"Pure and lasting religion in the sight of God our Father means that we must care for orphans and widows in their troubles and refuse to let the world corrupt us." James 1:27 NLT

God has made plans for us that give us a future and a hope, plans that bless and prosper us, not harm us. We dare not short circuit these plans by wasting our minds' attention and hearts' affection sitting in the seats of the scornful.

Father help me to sit at Your feet and enjoy the blessings that abiding in You promise. Amen.

Lord, You Are ___
Forgive Me For ___
Thank You For ___
Needs of Others ___
Personal Needs ___
Answered Prayers ___

September 18   Read John 15:5-17, Psalm 16
Is Your Cup Overflowing?
"My heart is overflowing with a good theme; I recite my composition concerning the King; my tongue is the pen of a ready writer." Psalm 45:1

Scripture speaks of the cup of God's wrath, anger, and judgment. It refers to the cup of God's poison, fury, terror, and deep sorrow. We should all be ever mindful that God takes sin seriously, hates it with a passion, and that we should seek to avoid the pain of drinking from any of these cups by sinning.

"LORD, You alone are my inheritance, my cup of blessing. You guard all that is mine. The land You have given me is a pleasant land. What a wonderful inheritance!" Psalm 16:5, 6 NLT

On a more positive note, Scripture also mentions the cup of blessings, salvation, and joy. We should all diligently seek to have these cups filled and overflowing into rivers of life for us and those around us.

We are called to be channels of God's love, grace, forgiveness, and generosity. This can only happen when we get so full of these virtues that they overflow into the lives of others. This is what makes the Great Commandment and Great Commission come to life.

When we drink at the well of God's grace, we become filled with the living water that overflows into the lives of others as we spread it.

God's love is not something that we can hoard. It is something that we must share. If everything comes in and nothing goes out, we become stagnant or like salt that has lost its flavor.

Our supply of living water is unlimited. We are drinking from a well that will never run dry.

When we share our overflowing cups of salvation, blessings, and joy with others, we can be sure that we are living the fruitful lives fully pleasing to God for which we were created. This makes our cups overflow even more.

"I have told you this so that you will be filled with My joy. Yes, your joy will overflow!" John 15:11 NLT

Father, let me be a conduit of your love through sharing my overflowing cup of blessings. Amen.

Lord, You Are _____

Forgive Me For _____

Thank You For _____

Needs of Others _____

Personal Needs _____

Answered Prayers _____

Why Live Among the Dead?

"And as the women were terrified and bowed their faces to the ground, the men said to them, 'Why do you seek the living One among the dead?'" Luke 24:5 NIV

Not too many people would enjoy living in a graveyard, yet many live out their lives among the dead without even realizing it.

"You will make known to me the path of life; in Your presence is fullness of joy; in Your right hand there are pleasures forever." Psalm 16:2 NIV

The world is filled with two kinds of people. There are those living dead in sin controlled by their own flesh, the world, and the devil, and there are those living dead to sin and alive in Christ.

The darkness of sin darkens our hearts and puts our will in bondage to all of the selfishness and sin that blind us and keep us dead in trespasses and sin.

When Jesus Christ stands and knocks at the door of our hearts by the power of the Holy Spirit, He comes inviting us to come out of the darkness and into the light by dying to sin and becoming alive in Him by this transforming power of the Holy Spirit.

When we see the light of God's love and receive Jesus and His death on the cross for the payment of our sins with true repentance, our bondage to domination by sin and the condemnation it brings in God's sight is ended. Sin has no more dominion over us, and we are free to live as born again sons and daughters of God and heirs to all of His wonderful promises.

"May it never be! How shall we who died to sin still live in it?" Romans 6:2 NIV

When we are born again through faith in Jesus Christ, we are endued with the sanctifying power from on high to be transformed into the very likeness of Christ as we seek to learn, know, and do what He did in every circumstance of life.

We will no longer be living among the dead. We will become alive in the forever forgiveness and abundance of peace and joy that is our birthright in Christ.

Father, help me to live in the fullness of joy that is mine in my new life in You. Amen.

Lord, You Are _____

Forgive Me For _____

Thank You For _____

Needs of Others _____

Personal Needs _____

Answered Prayers _____

Bad Saturday

"So he went and preached to the spirits in prison…" 1 Peter 3:19 NLT

The day after the crucifixion and before the resurrection had to be one of the worst days in the history of the Christian faith. Even though it was a holy day in the Old Testament tradition and is still commonly referred to as Holy Saturday, it was doomsday for many.

"For troubles surround me—too many to count! They pile up so high I can't see my way out. They are more numerous than the hairs on my head. I have lost all my courage."
Psalm 40:12 NLT

Many had begun the week praising the triumphal entry of the Messiah into Jerusalem to bring deliverance and restoration. They were finishing a week of horrors abandoned, were fearful for their lives, and totally confused.

The Scribes and Pharisees were gloating in self righteous glory over getting rid of a rebellious upstart who had claimed to be God and who had dared question their righteousness.

If ever there was a time of total darkness before the dawn, this bad Saturday was it. Jesus even went into the darkness of hell to proclaim His victory over sin and death to the souls languishing there.

We sometimes find ourselves in great fear or distress in overwhelming circumstances over which we have no control and in which we find no hope.

People will let us down. Our health will fail. We have financial reverses. Any number of tragedies may strike. The darkness of despair threatens to consume us.

"So don't get tired of doing what is good. Don't get discouraged and give up, for we will reap a harvest of blessing at the appropriate time."
Galatians 6:9 NLT

Jesus lives! Because He lives, we can face the darkness with the comfort of His love and the all-surpassing peace in knowing that He has promised to work all things for our good.

Father, help me find strength in bad Saturday to see me through the bad days of my life. Amen.

Lord, You Are _____

Forgive Me For _____

Thank You For _____

Needs of Others _____

Personal Needs _____

Answered Prayers _____

Read 1 Corinthians 15, Job 19:23-27   September 21

Holy Confirmation

"If then you were raised with Christ, seek those things which are above, where Christ is, sitting at the right hand of God." Colossians 3:1

Holy confirmation is generally understood by many Christians to be the rite of passage wherein children confirm the baptismal vows made for them by their parents or sponsors when they were initiated into the family of God as infants, and they confirm their faith by confessing it publicly.

"For I know that my Redeemer lives, and He shall stand at last on the earth." Job 19:25

Easter is perhaps best understood as the holy confirmation of the Good News of eternal life through faith in the life, death, and resurrection of Jesus Christ.

The historical fact of the resurrection of Jesus Christ turns the blessed hope of our salvation and eternal life into the blessed assurance that we too shall be raised from the dead to live forever with Christ.

We must never overlook the significance of the fact that the veil of the temple was split in two at the instant of Jesus' death confirming that we can now go directly into God's presence.

We have Easter as confirmation that because Jesus lives we too shall live forever through faith in Him. We have the Holy Spirit living within us as further confirmation that we have received the power of God from on high as the guarantor of our salvation and guardian of our souls.

These holy confirmations should fuel our lives with great peace, strength, and joy as the resurrection power from on high comes down to empower us to live lives fully pleasing to God and fruitful in every good work.

"Everyone dies because all of us are related to Adam, the first man. But all who are related to Christ, the other man, will be given new life." 1 Corinthians 15:22

When we let these holy confirmations work holy conformation into the image of Christ within us, we will celebrate Easter in our hearts every day of our lives as we grow into the fullness of Christ by becoming more like Christ in every area of our lives on this earth.

Father, thank you for giving me holy confirmation. Amen.

Lord, You Are _____
Forgive Me For _____
Thank You For _____
Needs of Others _____
Personal Needs _____
Answered Prayers _____

Growing Up or Down

"You don't need a telescope, a microscope, or a horoscope to realize the fullness of Christ, and the emptiness of the universe without Him."
Colossians 2:8 MSG

Growth is a fact of all life. Business runs on the principle that you either grow or die. We are all growing older and, hopefully, wiser. Only death stops growth.

"But the godly will flourish like palm trees and grow strong like the cedars of Lebanon." Psalm 92:12 NLT

The question for all believers should be whether we are growing up into the fullness of Christ and His righteousness, or are we bogged down in idolatry, self centeredness, or sins that are stunting our growth.

Just as water follows the path of least resistance and flows down, we sometimes fall into the trap of evil companions that will grow us down as they infect us with their sinfulness. We need to always be mindful of the danger of playing with fire.

God knows our every weakness and our constant need for strength and encouragement.

God gives us the Holy Spirit to come live within us as our comforter, counselor, and strength. He gives us His Word to feed and nourish us, so we can grow strong in Him as we grow strong in the Word.

Jesus Christ is our Word incarnate, our Word in the flesh, Who came to teach us everything and to become our role model for growth.

Jesus has given us His body – a family of believers called a church – to strengthen and encourage us to grow up instead of down. Here is where the Bread of Life comes to life in community with other saints, and the building up of the body, both individually and globally, best takes place as we feed on Christ and His love together.

"Until we come to such unity in our faith and knowledge of God's Son that we will be mature and full grown in the Lord, measuring up to the full stature of Christ," Ephesians 4:13 NLT

We all need to be aware that if "we aren't going, we aren't growing."

Father, help me to grow up into the fullness of Jesus. Amen.

Lord, You Are _____
Forgive Me For _____
Thank You For _____
Needs of Others _____
Personal Needs _____
Answered Prayers _____

Sin Epidemic

"For men will be lovers of themselves, lovers of money, boasters, proud, blasphemers, disobedient to parents, unthankful, unholy, unloving, unforgiving, slanderers, without self-control, brutal, despisers of good, traitors, headstrong, haughty, lovers of pleasure rather than lovers of God."
2 Timothy 3:2-4

If the Center for Disease Control in Atlanta would track this, there would be contagious disease warnings posted throughout the land. There is a sin epidemic running rampant around the world.

"Turn us again to Yourself, O God. Make Your face shine down upon us. Only then will we be saved." Psalm 80:3 NLT

By any measure, the sin index is at an all-time high. The divorce rate, crime rate, abortion rate, and other abominations to God continue to increase and abound.

The worship of rock stars, sports heroes, ourselves and our pleasure, possessions, and worldly security makes the spiritual adultery of the children of Israel pale in comparison.

We sound the alarm about influenza, bird flu, AIDS, and a host of other infectious diseases, but those who dare mention the deadliest disease of all are ignored, ridiculed, or mocked by a media and culture that has gotten out of God's control and in control of the forces of evil in this world.

This disease is so contagious that even those who have been inoculated by the Holy Spirit can get infected in the workplace, schools, and even in the home by the bad influences of TV and the internet.

History and the Word of God confirm that God will not allow sin to go unpunished. He will not be mocked.

A revival of faith and repentance is the only hope for stopping the spread of the deadly virus of sin. It must start in our hearts and spread throughout our neighborhoods, city, state, country, and the entire world by the power of the Holy Spirit working in and through all believers to reach the infected before it is too late.

"First, I want to remind you that in the last days there will be scoffers who will laugh at the truth and do every evil thing they desire." 2 Peter 3:3 NLT

Father, let there be a revival of righteousness in the world, and let it begin with me. Amen.

Lord, You Are _____

Forgive Me For _____

Thank You For _____

Needs of Others _____

Personal Needs _____

Answered Prayers _____

Avoiding Pitfalls

"The wise watch their steps and avoid evil; fools are headstrong and reckless." Proverbs 14:16 MSG

There are many hidden dangers and hard-to-recognize snares in life. It takes a lot of grace, wisdom, and spiritual discernment to avoid falling into these pitfalls.

"Do not do as the wicked do or follow the path of evildoers. Avoid their haunts. Turn away and go somewhere else."
Proverbs 4:14, 15

We can often fall into the pitfall of pride and let our egos get us out of God's control and into sin control.

We can fall into the pitfall of greed where worship of money and possessions preempt our worship of God.

Pitfalls of lust, anger, envy, and sins of every kind can trap us in prisons with a life sentence of consequences we can never escape.

Satan camouflages his pitfalls so cleverly we often stumble into them without a moment's hesitation.

God's Word is loaded with advice on avoiding pitfalls. We are told to avoid evil and immoral people, to flee temptation, and to not let the sun set on our anger.

When we let the love of God reign in our hearts, we will receive the proactive power of the Holy Spirit to avoid the dark pitfalls of evil by walking in the light.

When we walk in the light, the pitfalls can no longer be hid in darkness. We will recognize our sins, confess, and turn away from them in godly sorrow and true repentance.

"But those who desire to be rich fall into temptation and a snare, and into many foolish and harmful lusts which drown men in destruction and perdition."
1 Timothy 6:9

The shield of faith and sword of the Spirit are the best defense we can have for avoiding the pitfalls of sin.

Father, let Your Word be the lamp unto my feet that will help me avoid the sinkholes of sin all around me. Amen.

Lord, You Are _____
Forgive Me For _____
Thank You For _____
Needs of Others _____
Personal Needs _____
Answered Prayers _____

Crucified with Christ?

"I have been crucified with Christ; it is no longer I who live, but Christ lives in me; and the life which I now live in the flesh I live by faith in the Son of God, who loved me and gave Himself for me." Galatians 2:20

Becoming dead to sin and alive in Christ is the birth rite of every believer through their new birth in Christ.

"When you send Your Spirit, new life is born to replenish all the living of the earth." Psalm 104:30 NLT

The hour we first believe is the hour that we are covered with the righteousness of Christ in God's sight and no longer live in the deadness and dead end of sin.

The holy transformation that takes place as God conforms us into the image of Christ is not as instantaneous but more often an ongoing process that will continue as long as we draw breath on this earth.

We should never let a Maundy Thursday pass without a special remembrance of our being crucified with Christ and the penalty of our sins dying at the cross with Him.

When we are crucified with Christ, we are set free from the condemnation of, bondage to, and penalty of death for our sins. We are set free to live lives fruitful in every good work and fully pleasing to God by the power of the Holy Spirit living within us.

We must never let this freedom become license to abuse the grace of God that has been poured out upon us because of the crucifixion of Jesus on the cross.

"Our old sinful selves were crucified with Christ so that sin might lose its power in our lives. We are no longer slaves to sin." Romans 6:6 NLT

We must rather claim by faith the power and live in the desire to live in the fullness of Christ and His love by letting Him love others through us.

Father, let me know the comfort of mourning over my sins and living in the freedom of righteousness in Jesus. Amen.

Lord, You Are ___
Forgive Me For ___
Thank You For ___
Needs of Others ___
Personal Needs ___
Answered Prayers ___

Read Mark 10:28-41, Job 20:4-29

Leaving Nothing on the Table

"People who live only for wealth come to the end of their lives as naked and empty-handed as on the day they were born." Ecclesiastes 5:15 NLT

**"Nothing is left after he finishes gorging himself; therefore, his prosperity will not endure."
Job 20:21 NLT**

In contract negotiations of any kind, there are often valuable considerations left on the table. These are the things that could have been gotten if the other party had pressed for them harder.

In sports, we often hear of teams leaving their best games on the floor and sparing no effort.

It is satisfying when we get a deal for less than we expected or were willing to pay or when we get more than we had hoped. The difference is what someone has left on the table.

The table of contents of our lives begins with the plans God made for us before we were even born and how well we accomplish them during our lifetimes.

When we are born again in Christ, we are called to die to sin in every area of our lives and to leave nothing on the table to feed our old flesh and evil desires.

God gives us all a free will to leave all of His saving grace on the table by refusing to open the door of faith when Jesus comes knocking. He allows us to squander treasures we should be storing in heaven for toys and treasures of this life that we can never take with us.

When we are called to give an accounting of the time, talents, and treasures we were given, we should all strive to make sure that there will be something left on the table after all the wood, hay, and stubble of our trivial pursuits and wasted efforts have been burned away.

**"Then Peter began to mention all that he and the other disciples had left behind. 'We've given up everything to follow you,' he said."
Mark 10:28 NLT**

When God calls us, He is calling all of us and there should be no turning back, holding back, or leaving any of our old flesh on the table.

Father, let me concentrate on giving You my best instead of my least. May I leave none of Your purposes for me on the table. Amen.

Lord, You Are ___
Forgive Me For ___
Thank You For ___
Needs of Others ___
Personal Needs ___
Answered Prayers ___

Light at the End of the Tunnel

"I am the light of the world. He who follows Me shall not walk in darkness, but have the light of life." John 8:12

We often enter tunnels of darkness on the roadway of life. There is darkness of doubt, disappointment, defeat, despair, disease, and disobedience.

"You, O LORD, keep my lamp burning; my God turns my darkness into light." Psalm 18:28 NIV

We enter darkness confused and disoriented. We often feel helpless and hopeless. It is through times like these that we need the Word of God "as a lamp unto our feet and light unto our path" and Jesus as our light through and at the end of the tunnel.

The Word of God is not called the "sword of the Spirit" without good cause. It is sharper than any two-edge sword when we not only learn it but learn to use it in times of darkness.

When we learn to walk through the darkness in the light of God's Word, we will learn to respond to sorrow with joy, despair with hope, and doubt with faith. When we are filled with the love of God that is ours in Jesus Christ, we receive the all-sufficient grace that heals, renews, and restores. God really is our refuge and strength in times of trouble and darkness.

The old saying that it is "always the darkest before the dawn" should remind us that God is always ready to light up our lives with the resurrection power of the Holy Spirit and that we will never have to walk through the darkness alone.

"For it is the God who commanded light to shine out of darkness, who has shone in our hearts to give the light of the knowledge of the glory of God in the face of Jesus Christ." 2 Corinthians 4:6

Just as the darkness of Good Friday was the darkest moment in the history of mankind, resurrection Sunday was the dawn of the New Covenant of Grace whereby we can be sure that there is light at the end of every tunnel when we keep our eyes on Jesus, the Author and Perfector of our faith.

Father, by the power of the Holy Spirit, help me to walk in the light of Your love that overcomes all darkness and despair. Amen.

Lord, You Are _____

Forgive Me For _____

Thank You For _____

Needs of Others _____

Personal Needs _____

Answered Prayers _____

Liberal vs. Conservative

"There is a way that seems right to a man, but its end is the way of death."
Proverbs 14:12

The philosophical wars rage. Politically, liberals are charged with wanting to "tax and spend," and conservatives are charged with being selfish and uncaring.

"For I give you good doctrine: Do not forsake my law." Proverbs 4:2

Schools at every level try to influence students towards one extreme or the other, or a moderate posture.

Homes and churches go from almost "anything goes" permissiveness to strict conformity and traces of legalism.

A proper perspective and understanding of Scripture should divide us so that we become both liberal and conservative.

We need to be conservative in doctrine and firm belief that "All Scripture is given by inspiration of God, and is profitable for doctrine, for reproof, for correction, for instruction in righteousness, that the man of God may be complete, thoroughly equipped for every good work" (2 Timothy 3:16,17).

Being conservative does not mean that we try to put others in a straight jacket of conformity to our views but realize that there are some things neither condoned nor forbidden by Scripture in which all have the right to exercise Christian liberty in beliefs and practices in some areas.

We need to be liberal in love. "For the commandments…are all summed up in this saying, namely, 'You shall love your neighbor as yourself.' Love does no harm to a neighbor; therefore love is the fulfillment of the law" (Romans 13:9-10 partial).

Being liberal does not mean that we tolerate sin or evil but that we love and pray for sinners just as Jesus loves and prays for us.

In God's election, it's not about being conservative or liberal but about voting to receive God's wonderful salvation by grace alone, through faith alone, based on Scripture alone.

"Though I speak with the tongues of men and of angels, but have not love, I have become sounding brass or a clanging cymbal." 1 Corinthians 13:1

Father, may I always be conservative in doctrine and liberal in love. Amen.

Lord, You Are _____

Forgive Me For _____

Thank You For _____

Needs of Others _____

Personal Needs _____

Answered Prayers _____

A Great Vaccine

"Your greedy luxuries are a cancer in your gut, destroying your life from within. You thought you were piling up wealth. What you've piled up is judgment." James 5:1b MSG

Vaccines to prevent the crippling effects of polio and other diseases have saved millions of people's lives and health for over a century.

"Such God-denying people are never content with what they have or who they are; their greed drives them relentlessly."
Job 20:20 MSG

The Great Physician has been prescribing the vaccine for greed for over two millennia. It's called generosity, and it must be administered liberally and often to be effective.

Jesus not only modeled generosity in every area of His life, but He taught the principles in many parables.

Love is the greatest of all expressions of generosity, because love is all about giving. "God so loved the world that He gave His only Son, so that everyone who believes in Him will not perish but have eternal life" *(John 3:16)*.

Jesus' generosity in lowering Himself to live in the humanity of man so that we might be lifted up into everlasting glory was the greatest act of giving in the history of civilization.

God is the giver of every good and perfect gift. Everything that we have comes from the generosity of God.

When our hearts are filled with the generosity of God's love, we will never have to worry about greed taking root and selfishness taking over us.

The amazing thing about generosity is that it produces more wealth than greed. When we concentrate on how much we can give, do, and be for God instead of how much we can give, do, and be for ourselves, the seeds of generosity sown will produce a harvest of blessings that cannot be fully contained in this life so that they will flow over into eternity.

"I tell you, use your worldly resources to benefit others and make friends. In this way, your generosity stores up a reward for you in heaven."
Luke 16:9 NLT

Father, keep me inoculated against greed, by Your wonderful vaccine of generosity. Amen.

Lord, You Are ___
Forgive Me For ___
Thank You For ___
Needs of Others ___
Personal Needs ___
Answered Prayers ___

Principles for a Great Marriage

"God gave Solomon great wisdom and understanding and knowledge too vast to be measured." 1 Kings 4:29

King Solomon was not only "beloved by God" from birth; he was filled with such wisdom that even rulers from surrounding kingdoms came to listen to his wisdom.

"It's better to have a partner than go it alone. Share the work; share the wealth. And if one falls down, the other helps, but if there's no one to help, tough!"
Ecclesiastes 4:9, 10 MSG

Of the over 3,000 Proverbs and 1,000 songs written by Solomon, we are blessed to have most of the best recorded for our learning in the Old Testament Books of Proverbs, Ecclesiastes, and Song of Solomon.

Although not generally applied as a teaching on marriage, Solomon's teachings on the value of companionship can well be considered as practical praises of marriage.

The meaningless and futility of life diminishes when we are blessed with a faithful spouse and family who add meaning and purpose to our lives.

"Two people can accomplish more than twice as much as one" is most certainly true regarding marriage. "If one person falls, the other can reach out and help" is an ongoing blessing in a good marriage.

"On a cold night, two under the same blanket can gain warmth from each other," and "A person standing alone can be attacked and defeated, but two can stand back to back and conquer" are also advantages to be realized in a good marriage.

The most important principle of all in any marriage is the strength added by the third person. When Jesus Christ becomes the third strand that binds in the cord of holy matrimony, every marriage will be strengthened by a cord of real love that can not easily be broken.

"And he said, 'This explains why a man leaves his father and mother and is joined to his wife, and the two are united into one.'"
Matthew 19:5 NLT

Father, help me to understand, appreciate, and practice these blessings of marriage. Amen.

Lord, You Are _____

Forgive Me For _____

Thank You For _____

Needs of Others _____

Personal Needs _____

Answered Prayers _____

A Big Mistake

"And who could ever give Him so much that He would have to pay it back? For everything comes from Him; everything exists by His power and is intended for His glory. To Him be glory evermore. Amen." Romans 11:35, 36 NLT

"Will a man rob God? Yet you have robbed Me! But you say, 'In what way have we robbed You?' In tithes and offerings." Malachi 3:8

One of the biggest, yet very common, mistakes made by many of us is the mistake of shortchanging God. We should never forget that it is impossible to shortchange God without shortchanging ourselves even more.

God expects and deserves our best. Anything less is shortchanging God and makes us open for the consequences that are sure to follow in this life or the next.

God has never been satisfied with leftovers.

Scripture not only declares that all have sinned and fall short of the glory of God. It also says that we shortchange and rob God in the area of giving tithes. Instead of trying to figure out how much more we could give or do for the one who has given us everything, we all too often settle for how little.

Our abundant life in Christ that He promises and delights in for all His children is all about fullness. We can never grow into the fullness of Christ without first fruit giving of our times, talents, treasures and faith.

When we give less than our best in any area, we are shortchanging God by not being all that He has created us to be or doing all that He has created us to do. We are cheating ourselves out of knowing the fullness of God's joy and pleasure.

"And do not bring sorrow to God's Holy Spirit by the way you live. Remember, He is the one who has identified you as His own, guaranteeing that you will be saved on the day of redemption." Ephesians 4:30

If Jesus had shortchanged God by taking the devil up on his offer or by failing to live up to the standard of perfection which God's justice demanded, we would all be wandering aimlessly lost without a future and a hope.

Father, may I always give You a full measure of my love and devotion and never shortchange You by giving less than the best You have given me. Amen.

Lord, You Are _____

Forgive Me For _____

Thank You For _____

Needs of Others _____

Personal Needs _____

Answered Prayers _____

October 2   Read 2 Corinthians 7:8-13, Psalm 130
A Blast from the Past
"I, even I, am He who blots out your transgressions for My own sake; And I will not remember your sins." Isaiah 43:25

We all have sins and mistakes of the past which sometime come back to haunt us. The remorse is often overwhelming. We are filled with godly sorrow and lingering embarrassment.

"Lord, if you kept a record of our sins, who, O Lord, could ever survive? But you offer forgiveness, that we might learn to fear you," Psalm 130:3.4 NLT

How could we ever have been so stupid? How could we ever have done such a thing? What will others say? How painful the consequences!

The good news is that although we may vividly remember our past sins, God's memory is short.

He remembers our sins only until we come to Him with godly sorrow to confess and repent of them, and then He remembers them no more.

The fact that we still remember and have godly sorrow for sins of the past is proof in itself that the Holy Spirit is at work in us and conforming us into the image of Christ.

God often brings sorrow and rebuke over our past in order that we will learn from and avoid them in the present and future.

Other times, we may be burdened by a sin of unforgiveness that we can only deal with by forgiving someone after we have confessed and repented.

"For God can use sorrow in our lives to help us turn away from sin and seek salvation. We will never regret that kind of sorrow. But sorrow without repentance is the kind that results in death." 2 Corinthians 7:10 NLT

Most often, God will allow these "blasts from our pasts" to come to mind as a lessons to learn and grow from in the future. We should never be afraid when this happens.

Father, when the "blasts from the past" come, let me always find comfort in knowing that Jesus paid the price for them on the cross and be thankful that nothing that can separate me from Your love in Christ. Amen.

Lord, You Are _____
Forgive Me For _____
Thank You For _____
Needs of Others _____
Personal Needs _____
Answered Prayers _____

When Are You Ready to Stop Receiving?

"Let each one [give] as he has made up his own mind and purposed in his heart, not reluctantly or sorrowfully or under compulsion, for God loves (He takes pleasure in, prizes above other things, and is unwilling to abandon or to do without) a cheerful (joyous, "prompt to do it") giver [whose heart is in his giving]." 2 Corinthians 9:7 (Amplified Bible)

It is utterly amazing that often the biggest takers are the biggest complainers when it comes to being asked to give to the Lord.

"But me--who am I, and who are these, my people, that we should presume to be giving something to You? Everything comes from You; all we're doing is giving back what we've been given from Your generous hand." 1 Chronicles 29:14 MSG

We are glad to receive the good gifts that God chooses to give us. Oh that we would be as glad to give Him the first fruits of what He has given us!

It is a good thing to continually to ask God for material, physical, and relational blessings. He hears and answers our prayers and is able to do abundantly more than we ask or think.

It is an even better thing to give God material, physical, and relational blessings, which we only have because He has given them to us.

Scripture after scripture points out that it is more blessed to give than to receive. It is impossible to out give God! We should all be looking for ways to give as much as possible instead of as little.

God takes no pleasure in people who complain about the church always asking for money, time, and talents.

He loves and takes pleasure in the cheerful givers who find great joy and experience God's pleasure in giving from a heart filled with love and gratitude for what God has given them.

"You will be made rich in every way so that you can be generous on every occasion, and through us your generosity will result in thanksgiving to God." 2 Corinthians 9:11 NIV

When we spend time seeking ways through which God's generosity can flow through us, we will be well on our way towards becoming imitators of Christ Who gave His all for us, so He could live in, through, and with us forever.

Father, may I experience the true riches that come from giving. Amen.

Lord, You Are _____

Forgive Me For _____

Thank You For _____

Needs of Others _____

Personal Needs _____

Answered Prayers _____

October 4 — Read 1 Corinthians 1:18-31, Psalm 19

How Great is Our God!

"I will proclaim the name of the Lord. Oh, praise the greatness of our God!"
Deuteronomy 32:3 NIV

No one has ever been able to measure or comprehend the greatness of God. We see the wonders of His power and glory in the heavens and on earth.

"The heavens declare the glory of God; the skies proclaim the work of His hands."
Psalm 19:1 NIV

The wonders of His love surround us. In His love, He loves the unlovable, forgives the unforgivable, heals the unhealable, comforts the comfortless, and brings the dead back to life through the transforming power of the cross.

God gives hope to the hopeless, strength to the weak, grace, and mercy to all who call upon His name.

God has revealed glimpses of His greatness through the flood, the parting of the sea, and many other miracles that only God could do.

In His love, God came to earth in the humanity of a man called Jesus to not only live the perfect life and die as the perfect sacrifice for the sins of the world but also to reveal Himself as the way, the truth, and the life that we should emulate and appropriate by faith.

The fact that Jesus came back to life after death confirms the bright future all who call upon the name of the Lord to be saved have in Christ for now and forever.

The better we get to know Jesus as He reveals Himself through the Word, the better we will get to know God and His love that is deeper than the ocean and wider than the sea.

God gives all just a glimpse of His glory so that all will have no excuse for wandering aimlessly lost and choosing to reject and rebel against the greatness of God and His calling to eternal life through faith in Jesus Christ.

"It is because of him that you are in Christ Jesus, who has become for us wisdom from God—that is, our righteousness, holiness, and redemption."
1 Corinthians 1:30 NIV

Father, thank you for the foretaste of glory You have given me through the life, death, and resurrection of Your Son and my Savior, Jesus Christ. Amen.

Lord, You Are _____
Forgive Me For _____
Thank You For _____
Needs of Others _____
Personal Needs _____
Answered Prayers _____

God Will Restore

"The LORD says, 'I will give you back what you lost to the stripping locusts, the cutting locusts, the swarming locusts, and the hopping locusts.'" Joel 2:25

There are many locusts of sin swarming around and upon us. The minute we drop our guard they are ready to pounce upon us and literally eat us alive.

"Restore to me the joy of Your salvation, and uphold me by Your generous Spirit."
Psalm 51:12 NLT

Whether it is the locust of pride, anger, envy, lust, possessions, power or approval of others, we are fair game whenever the evil one sends them to attack unless we are safe and secure under the sheltering wings of God and bearing the full armor of God.

The plague of sin started with the disobedience of Adam and Eve in the garden. Abraham, Isaac, and Jacob suffered their share of sin attacks. Moses, David, and other individuals, as well as the entire nation of Israel, were plagued by besetting sins from time to time.

Although Job was godly, he was attacked by swarm after swarm of locusts of sin eating away his family, fortune, health, and about every other reason for living.

The same locusts that attacked and brought low the heroes of the faith are still swarming, seeking whom they may devour.

Through all these attacks, the faithfulness, forgiveness, and mercy of God were made manifest in the lives of all these heroes of the faith.

"In his kindness God called you to his eternal glory by means of Jesus Christ. After you have suffered a little while, He will restore, support, and strengthen you, and He will place you on a firm foundation."
1 Peter 5:10 NLT

God not only restored but increased the fortune and family of Job. He created the clean heart and right Spirit within David and called him the man after His own heart.

Although the consequences of sin often linger and must be endured, God's promise to not only forgive but forget our sins of the past when we confess and repent assures total restoration of our right standing with God through faith in Jesus Christ. He will renew and restore!

Father, restore unto me daily the joy of my salvation as I come to you with godly sorrow, confession, and true repentance. Amen.

Lord, You Are _____

Forgive Me For _____

Thank You For _____

Needs of Others _____

Personal Needs _____

Answered Prayers _____

Breaking God's Heart

"Now the LORD observed the extent of the people's wickedness, and He saw that all their thoughts were consistently and totally evil. So the LORD was sorry He had ever made them. It broke His heart." Genesis 6:5, 6 NLT

The reality of sin is not a popular concept in the world these days. Just as truth is being redefined as relative truth, sin is being glossed over and mocked in many quarters. Even in many churches, people don't want to be reminded of their sinfulness.

"Their pagan orgies provoked God's anger, their obscene idolatries broke His heart."
Psalm 73:58 MSG

Because God takes sin seriously, we must take sin seriously. God did not make us in His image that we should become depraved, corrupted, and defiled by sin.

When we come into the family of God through faith in Jesus Christ, we become sons and daughters of God. Just as a wayward son or daughter breaks the heart of a parent, we break God's heart when we willfully disobey and sin in thought, word, or deed.

In addition to breaking God's heart, our unconfessed and unrepented sins separate us from God. Our just and Holy God has zero tolerance for sin.

Sin not only separates, it corrupts and defiles the temple of the Holy Spirit God has made us to be in Christ. If allowed to go unconfessed and unrepented it becomes the sin against the Holy Spirit that leads to death.

"Try to live in peace with everyone and seek to live a clean and holy life, for those who are not holy will not see the Lord."
Hebrews 12:14 NLT

God took sin seriously enough to send His Son to overcome it by suffering and dying on the cross, so we can die to our sins and become alive in Christ by faith.

When Jesus sets us free from dominion by sin, we are free indeed and have absolutely no excuse for breaking God's heart.

Father, may I never break Your heart by harboring unconfessed and unrepented sins in mine. Amen.

Lord, You Are _____

Forgive Me For _____

Thank You For _____

Needs of Others _____

Personal Needs _____

Answered Prayers _____

Read Matthew 13:33-37, Psalm 65   October 7

A Principle to Bank On

"The harvesters are paid good wages, and the fruit they harvest is people brought to eternal life. What joy awaits both the planter and the harvester alike!" John 4:36 NLT

The principle of reaping what we sow is one of the primary principles of life. Scripture after scripture confirms it and uses it to teach us this basic law of life.

"You take care of the earth and water, making it rich and fertile. The rivers of God will not run dry; they provide a bountiful harvest of grain, for You have ordered it so." Psalm 65:8 NLT

Whatever we sow, we will reap. If we sow wheat seeds we will reap wheat; if corn, corn; if cotton, cotton; etc. Whatever fruit tree we plant, it will produce its own kind.

In the garden of life, we can fully expect to reap what we sow. If we sow seeds of bitterness, anger, or other sins, we can expect to harvest the same. It is sometimes amazing that we seem so surprised when we reap the consequences of our sins.

It is good to know that we reap kindness, love, and mercy when we sow these seeds. We are promised that our harvest of righteousness will be great if we don't quit.

We should always keep in mind that just as a farmer plants seed expecting a harvest, we can expect to reap a harvest when we use our financial resources as seed money for building the kingdom of God.

When Jesus shed His blood on the cross, He was sowing the seed of faith that bears a harvest of righteousness in the good soil of the faith of all in whom it is planted and takes root.

We are all called to be sowers of this Good News to others that they might be found growing in the goodness of God's grace when the wheat is separated from the chaff and the final harvest is gathered in by the angels of God.

"'All right,' He said. 'I, the Son of Man, am the farmer who plants the good seed.'" Matthew 13:37 NLT

What joy there will be when we see the souls God has used us to help come to know and grow in Him through our faith and obedience to the Great Commandment and Great Commission!

Father, let me sow Your love. Amen.

Lord, You Are _____
Forgive Me For _____
Thank You For _____
Needs of Others _____
Personal Needs _____
Answered Prayers _____

Steady Goodness

"So, my dear brothers and sisters, be strong and steady, always enthusiastic about the Lord's work, for you know that nothing you do for the Lord is ever useless." 1 Corinthians 15:58

We live in an unsteady world. Turmoil and upheaval are all around us. Sin abounds everywhere. Only God's all-sufficient grace, which we receive by steady faith, can sustain us.

"He will not be afraid of evil tidings; His heart is steadfast, trusting in the LORD." Psalm 112:7

God pours out His undeserved favor and love on every area of our lives. We receive the grace of salvation to save us and the grace of sanctification to transform us into the image of Christ.

We enjoy the grace of God so that we can bestow grace upon others. Others need the grace of our love, kindness, forgiveness, and generosity that God has so freely bestowed upon us.

When we let the double mindedness of doubt discourage and distract us, we will take our eye off of who we are in Christ and all that He has called us to be. We will waver and waffle through life, missing the fullness and joy that God wants for all of us.

God never promised us a rose garden, but He has promised to be with us through any trial or temptation and to provide a means of escape. He has promised never to give us anything that we can't handle with the help He has promised to provide.

The key to steadiness is in growing in our personal relationship with Jesus Christ wherein we find the love and joy of our salvation, friendship with God, answered prayers, and God's good pleasure.

May we always be found faithful and steadfast to our calling as sons and daughters of the living Lord.

"If you are wise and understand God's ways, live a life of steady goodness so that only good deeds will pour forth." James 3:18 NLT

Father, help me to live a life of strong and steady faith. Amen.

Lord, You Are _____

Forgive Me For _____

Thank You For _____

Needs of Others _____

Personal Needs _____

Answered Prayers _____

Read Hebrews 5:11-14, Psalm 84   October 9

Stunting Our Growth

"Let all bitterness, wrath, anger, clamor, and evil speaking be put away from you, with all malice." Ephesians 4:31

Many of us grew up hearing that smoking cigarettes would stunt our growth long before we learned that they would not only stunt our growth but eventually kill us.

"They will continue to grow stronger, and each of them will appear before God in Jerusalem." Psalm 84:7 NLT

While there are still many things that can stunt our physical growth, there are many more things that stunt our spiritual growth and need to be avoided.

We have a living faith in a living Lord who is living within each and every believer as the Holy Spirit for the express purpose of helping us to grow into the fullness of Christ.

We should be growing from babes to mature Christians day by day, month by month, year by year, by growing in our relationship with Christ and our knowledge of God through Christ, the Word Incarnate, who came to show us how we should live and what we should become.

Our growth is dependent on the nourishment we receive from reading and hearing the Word and becoming more and more obedient to it.

God's character-development program for us is all about growing more like Christ and reflecting His love and righteousness by the way we live our lives. Our life in Christ must increase while our life in the self centeredness of the flesh must decrease.

Any person, passion, precept, or possession that we put ahead of God is idolatry that will drain our energies and stunt our growth.

The lusts of the flesh, anger, or pride are the junk food of the soul that will make it impossible for us to grow in Christ.

The roots of unforgiveness and bitterness are big-time growth stunters that will choke our best efforts at spiritual growth.

"You are like babies who drink only milk and cannot eat solid food." Hebrews 5:12b NLT

The more we grow through abiding in Christ and His Word, the greater our joy and the more abundant our life will be on this earth.

Father, give me the strength of the Holy Spirit to get rid of the growth stunters in my life. Amen.

Lord, You Are _____
Forgive Me For _____
Thank You For _____
Needs of Others _____
Personal Needs _____
Answered Prayers _____

Feeling God's Pleasure

"Do not fear, little flock, for it is your Father's good pleasure to give you the kingdom." Luke 12:32

Rick Warren has done a great job of reminding us that we were created for God's pleasure and glory in his wonderful book The Purpose Driven Life.

"For the LORD takes pleasure in His people; He will beautify the humble with salvation." Psalm 149:4

The high calling of our life should be to live for God's pleasure. This is the life Jesus modeled for us. It begins when we receive Jesus Christ as our Lord and Savior, and we receive the new birth that this brings.

Through this new birth, we are transformed from being slaves to our self-centered sin natures and conformed into the image of Christ by the renewing of our minds as slaves in a Christ-centered nature.

This is an ongoing process that the Holy Spirit begins when He takes up residence within us the hour we first believe, and He has promised to continue until the Lord calls us home to live forever with Him.

God has created all things for us to enjoy and has given us the senses and emotions to enjoy them. The key to enjoying life to the fullest is in living and enjoying life through feeling God's pleasure.

God takes pleasure in our worship, faithfulness, and obedience in living for Him and for the pleasure of His glory. We will feel God's pleasure when our minds are stayed on Him through worship and abiding in the Word as we become imitators of Christ in an everyday life of obedience and trust.

"Having made known to us the mystery of His will, according to His good pleasure which He purposed in Himself," Ephesians 1:9

One of the most often overlooked and neglected aspects of feeling God's pleasure is in our giving of tithes and offerings for kingdom-building purposes. Not only does God find great pleasure in helping us to prosper and multiply (Deuteronomy 28:3), but we can also feel His pleasure through cheerful giving from the heart.

Father, help me to feel Your pleasure in me and my life. Amen.

Lord, You Are _____
Forgive Me For _____
Thank You For _____
Needs of Others _____
Personal Needs _____
Answered Prayers _____

Giving to Get

"'Bring all the tithes into the storehouse, that there may be food in My house, and try Me now in this,' says the LORD of hosts, 'If I will not open for you the windows of heaven and pour out for you such blessing that there will not be room enough to receive it.'" Malachi 3:9

There is a widely misunderstood aspect of giving to the Lord that, if properly understood and applied, can make a significant difference in our prosperity.

> "I, the LORD, search the heart, I test the mind, even to give every man according to his ways, according to the fruit of his doings."
> Jeremiah 17:10

People often deride and put down proponents of the prosperity gospel who boldly preach a "give to get" philosophy that seems to promote a selfish motivation for giving to the Lord.

Scripture provides some very interesting perspective for which we all need to pray for wisdom and spiritual discernment to understand.

The foundation for the receiving of all blessings, whether they are financial, physical, spiritual or relational, is a heart firmly anchored in and seeking the kingdom of God through a close and personal growing relationship with Jesus Christ. It is through this that God promises that "all things will be added to you."

Knowing that the "heart is deceitful above all things," we must be on guard constantly to make sure that it is Christ focused instead of self centered, and we must never forget that God knows our hearts even better than we do. If our hearts are right, we can go forward boldly expecting to be blessed through our giving from the heart.

God challenges us to test Him by giving our tithes.

When our hearts are right and we give cheerfully and generously according to what we have been given, we can fully expect to reap the harvest of the overflowing cup of blessings promised.

There is absolutely nothing wrong with doing what God has told us to do and believing that He will do what He says.

> "And God will generously provide all you need. Then you will always have everything you need and plenty left over to share with others."
> 2 Corinthians 9:8 NLT

Father, help me to experience the joy of real prosperity. Amen.

Lord, You Are _____

Forgive Me For _____

Thank You For _____

Needs of Others _____

Personal Needs _____

Answered Prayers _____

Quenching the Spirit

"I baptize with water those who turn from their sins and turn to God. But someone is coming soon who is far greater than I am—so much greater that I am not even worthy to be his slave. He will baptize you with the Holy Spirit and with fire." Matthew 3:11 NLT

It is a wonderful thing to "be set on fire" by and for the Lord! This is the fire that enlightens our understanding of our salvation, enlivens us with the eternal life of our salvation, and purifies and makes us holy in God's sight by the righteousness of Christ.

"He will not crush those who are weak or quench the smallest hope. He will bring full justice to all who have been wronged." Isaiah 42:3 NLT

Scripture warns that we be careful not to quench the fire the Holy Spirit brings when He takes up residence within us. We rather need to stoke it by fueling it on the Word and through prayer and communion with other torch bearers. We dare not let it burn out for lack of fuel.

We need to be very careful not to quench this fire by watering or throwing dirt on it with the ways of the world or by pouring out our old nature.

The fire extinguishers are all around both within and without us. When we allow bitterness, anger, unforgiveness, or turmoil to take over, we are inviting a burn out.

When we allow malice in thought, word, or deed to take root, we are smothering the fire.

Jealousy, lust, and pride are ever present "grace busters" that we need to avoid if we are to not become lukewarm Christians.

When the flame burns low and we sense burn out, we need to go to God's throne of grace in prayer, confess and repent, and ask that God renew the fire of the Spirit within us.

"And do not grieve the Holy Spirit of God, by whom you were sealed for the day of redemption." Ephesians 4:30 NLT

When we stoke the fire of our soul with love, kindness, and forgiveness to one another, we will never have to worry about the fire going out.

Father, may I never quench the Spirit. Amen.

Lord, You Are _____

Forgive Me For _____

Thank You For _____

Needs of Others _____

Personal Needs _____

Answered Prayers _____

What's on Your Plate

"But fortunately God doesn't grade us on our diet. We're neither commended when we clean our plate nor reprimanded when we just can't stomach it." 1 Corinthians 8:10 MSG

We never know for sure what's going to be served on our plate of life from day to day. Sometimes we are dished out pain and suffering. We sometimes get a taste of terror or rejection. Many eat of the poison of pride or lust.

**"He enjoyed the taste of his wickedness, letting it melt under his tongue. He savored it, holding it long in his mouth."
Job 20:12, 13 NLT**

A lot of what goes on our plate depends on where we eat. If we choose to dine in the darkness of sin and feed on the depravity served on many TV shows and movies, we can expect to get severe heart burn or indigestion at some time or another.

Who we eat with has a big bearing on what we eat. Just as evil companions corrupt good morals, they can also cause us to fill our plates with the poison of sin and its often painful and severe consequences.

Jesus Christ came to serve as the Bread of Life to all who would partake of it by faith.

When we dine at the King's table, we "taste and see that the Lord is good." When we feed daily on God's Word, we are going to find our plates filled with peace and joy that coats sorrows and sufferings with comfort and our sins with forgiveness.

Best of all, when we feed on the Bread of Life through a close and personal relationship with Him, we receive the ultimate anti-acid called all-sufficient grace that will sustain us as the bad foods pass through our lives and are replaced by the security of God's unconditional love, forever forgiveness, and total acceptance.

**"Jesus replied, 'I am the Bread of Life. No one who comes to me will ever be hungry again. Those who believe in me will never thirst.'"
John 6:35 NLT**

When we are suffering from indigestion from what has been put on our plate, we need to remember that relief is just a prayer of confession and true repentance away.

Father, let the indigestions of my sins draw me closer to You in true faith and repentance. Amen.

Lord, You Are _____
Forgive Me For _____
Thank You For _____
Needs of Others _____
Personal Needs _____
Answered Prayers _____

October 14   Read Matthew 8:24-27, Psalm 57
Turbulence Ahead
"And you were so glad when the storm died down, and He led you safely back to harbor." Psalm 197:30 MSG

In spite of the best technology available, we sometimes read of an airliner encountering severe turbulence that injures many passengers as the plane plummets suddenly, sometimes thousands of feet.

"Have mercy on me, O God, have mercy! I look to You for protection. I will hide beneath the shadow of Your wings until this violent storm is past." Psalm 57:1 NLT

The pilots are trained to spot the turbulence and then decide whether it's best to climb over it, fly around it, or, as a last resort, fly through it.

As we fly through life at today's break-neck speeds, we are wise to follow the same procedure as we deal with the stress and turbulence of living in a fast-paced, sin-sick world.

Sometimes we get blind sided and find ourselves encountering turbulence from out of the blue with no warning and for no apparent reason.

We should judge ourselves and see if we are being punished or pruned. We should make sincere and complete confession and repentance if we deem our turbulence to be a consequence of our own sin.

When possible we should seek to avoid the impending trouble by fleeing around it or rising above it through bearing the full armor of God and proceeding in the power and the strength of the Holy Spirit living within us.

When there is no other alternative other than going through a storm of life, what comfort and strength there is in knowing the Lover of our souls Who is all powerful and Who has promised to work all things for our good.

"And Jesus answered, 'Why are you afraid? You have so little faith!' Then He stood up and rebuked the wind and waves, and suddenly all was calm." Matthew 7:26 NLT

How good it is to know Jesus well enough that we can receive the strength to rejoice and be glad even through the turbulence of life, which is never going to last forever. We can always know by faith that there is a safe landing ahead.

Father, by the power of your Spirit, guide me around, over, and through the turbulence of life until I see You face to face. Amen.

Lord, You Are _____
Forgive Me For _____
Thank You For _____
Needs of Others _____
Personal Needs _____
Answered Prayers _____

Extreme Makeovers

"Then He who sat on the throne said, 'Behold, I make all things new.' And He said to me, 'Write, for these words are true and faithful.'" Revelation 21:5

God is the Master Remodeler! Scripture is filled with examples of His making over the absolute worst of sinners into saints.

"He fills my life with good things. My youth is renewed like the eagle's." Psalm 103:5 NLT

Moses was a murderer; Paul was a persecutor and killer of Christians. The other apostles denied Christ, tucked tail and ran when the going got rough, and yet came back with power and strength to lead the cause for Christ with strength and courage.

God is at work in every one of us who believe in Jesus. He is making us over into the image of Christ and will do whatever it takes to accomplish His purpose.

God even went to the extreme of sacrificing His only begotten Son on the cross in order to make us conquerors by faith in Jesus Christ.

God has even sent the Holy Spirit to live within us to complete the extreme makeover that starts when we die to sin and become alive in Christ and continues until the very day we stand before Him in heaven.

As God's sanctification process progresses, we will find ourselves being chastened, tested, and purified in every area of our lives as sin moves out and the love of God moves in with the resurrection power of the Holy Spirit poured out upon us to allow us to do and be what we could never do and be on our own.

"And that you put on the new man which was created according to God, in true righteousness and holiness." Ephesians 4:24

As we get to know Christ better and better by growing in His Word and through abiding in a close and personal relationship, the more like Him we will become.

The more like Him we become, the more others will see and be drawn to Him through us as we become living testaments to the power of God.

Father, may I be completely made over into the fullness of Your Son in every area of my life. Amen.

Lord, You Are _____

Forgive Me For _____

Thank You For _____

Needs of Others _____

Personal Needs _____

Answered Prayers _____

You're on Your Own

"Be prepared. You're up against far more than you can handle on your own. Take all the help you can get, every weapon God has issued, so that when it's all over but the shouting you'll still be on your feet."
Ephesians 6:13 MSG

There are often times in life where we find ourselves on our own. That first day in school or kindergarten, when we leave home to go to college or to live on our own, or when we are separated from our spouse by death or divorce are just a few examples of being on our own to some degree or another.

"Trust in the LORD with all your heart, and lean not on your own understanding,"
Proverbs 3:5

No matter how godly the influence of others, we are on our own when it comes to receiving the gift of salvation through faith in Jesus Christ. It doesn't do us a bit of good if we do not appropriate this fact by faith and receive this greatest of all gifts by entering into a personal relationship with Him.

Parents are instructed to bring up their children in the fear of the Lord so that they will not depart from it when they are on their own.

In an ideal situation, children transfer the authority and support of their parents to the authority and support of God when they go out on their own. As wonderful as being on our own may seem, we need to know that the freedom of being owned by Christ is much more wonderful.

When we invite Jesus into our hearts, we will never have to worry about being alone. We have the promise and the power of the Holy Spirit living within us to comfort us, to guide us, to strengthen and sustain us.

"To him the doorkeeper opens, and the sheep hear His voice; and He calls His own sheep by name and leads them out."
John 10:2

When we are on our own in Christ, we experience the peace and joy of having Christ living in and through us as we are conformed into His image and become more like Him.

Father, keep me ever mindful that being on my own need never mean being alone when I have You in my heart. Amen.

Lord, You Are _____

Forgive Me For _____

Thank You For _____

Needs of Others _____

Personal Needs _____

Answered Prayers _____

Simple Arithmetic

"But seek first the kingdom of God and His righteousness, and all these things shall be added to you." Matthew 6:23

Our Christian initiative should be all about adding, subtracting, multiplication, and division.

"Yes, happy are those who have it like this! Happy indeed are those whose God is the LORD." Psalm 144:15 NLT

We should take the initiative in adding the fruit of the Spirit to our plate of virtues as we grow into the fullness of Christ through God's character-development process.

We need to subtract the sins that are holding us back from becoming all that God would have us to be in Christ. We do this by fleeing the temptations that may come our way and by daily cleansing of confession and repentance.

We multiply our joy by sharing the Good News and our joy in the Lord with others so that God's kingdom may be built up.

Sharing our sorrows with other believers will help divide our pain. Dividing the work of the Lord among others will make it easier to carry on successfully.

Our daily prayer should be that we add whatever the Lord sends our way this day to help us grow in our knowledge and understanding of God and His perfect plan for our lives.

We need to be ever mindful of adding more in the way of the fruit of righteousness in our lives so that there will be plenty left after the trivial pursuits of our lives are subtracted when we stand before Christ to give an accounting.

"Add to your faith virtue, to virtue knowledge, to knowledge self-control, to self-control perseverance, to perseverance godliness, to godliness brotherly kindness, and to brotherly kindness love." 2 Peter 1:5b

The trophies of God's grace that we embrace and add to our Christian character will be the evidence of our lives well lived in and for Christ.

Father, help me to master the principles of simple arithmetic in my everyday life. Amen.

Lord, You Are _____

Forgive Me For _____

Thank You For _____

Needs of Others _____

Personal Needs _____

Answered Prayers _____

The Unforgivable Sin

"Get rid of all bitterness, rage, anger, harsh words, and slander, as well as all types of malicious behavior. Instead, be kind to each other, tenderhearted, forgiving one another, just as God through Christ has forgiven you." Ephesians 4:31, 32 NLT

When we come to saving faith in Jesus Christ in true faith and repentance, we receive the forgiveness for every sin we have ever committed.

"LORD, if you kept a record of our sins, who, O Lord, could ever survive?" Psalm 130:5 NLT

Scripture gives examples of forgiveness of many heinous and personally disgusting sins.

For all who did not sin against the Holy Spirit by maliciously and willfully rejecting His call, there is only one unforgivable sin, and it is more common than we care to admit. Unforgiveness is the unforgivable sin!

We have the parable of the unforgiving servant, and the clear warning of our Lord that if we do not forgive, we will not be forgiven.

We all know professing Christians, many times including ourselves, who pray "forgive us our sins as we forgive those who sin against us," whose hearts are so full of the bitterness of unforgiveness that this prayer becomes an affront and mockery to God.

We do not have to look very far to see the destruction of relationships within marriages, families, and churches fueled by the sin of unforgiveness.

Not only is unforgiveness unforgivable; it is a sin that can even lead to death. When we poison our souls with unforgiveness, the poison often finds it way from our hearts to our bodies and can actually cripple or kill us.

The best way to overcome the sin of unforgiveness is to realize that we can only receive the forgiveness we are always going to need from God by forgiving others as we have been forgiven. None of us can afford the luxury of an unforgiving heart. Forgiveness is not an option; it's a command!

"That's what my heavenly Father will do to you if you refuse to forgive your brothers and sisters in your heart." Matthew 18:35 NLT

Father, remove any roots of bitterness within me caused by an unforgiving spirit as I pray for forgiveness in true sorrow and repentance. Amen.

Lord, You Are _____

Forgive Me For _____

Thank You For _____

Needs of Others _____

Personal Needs _____

Answered Prayers _____

Spiritual Blessings

"Whatever is good and perfect comes to us from God above, who created all heaven's lights. Unlike them, He never changes or casts shifting shadows. In His goodness He chose to make us His own children by giving us His true word. And we, out of all creation, became His choice possession." James 1:17, 18 NLT

We all like to talk about and thank God for all our temporal blessings. He blesses us materially, physically, and relationally, and we should be eternally grateful.

"God is awesome in His sanctuary. The God of Israel gives power and strength to His people. Praise be to God!" Psalm 68:35 NLT

But we will never realize how rich we really are until we appreciate the spiritual blessings that are ours in Christ, who died not only that we might live forever but that we might inherit every spiritual blessing as a legacy of His love.

Eternal life is the greatest of our great spiritual blessings. Through this we receive the blessings of forever forgiveness, righteousness in God's sight, and the security of God's unconditional love.

We need to know and thank God daily for the blessing of His strength. He writes His law in our hearts and gives us the desire to obey Him and the power to do it.

God graces us with the power of His presence and blesses with the strength of His joy. He gives inner peace and healing. He blesses us with spiritual wisdom and discernment. He blesses our children.

God blesses us with answered prayers and gives us the security of knowing that He will not allow us to slip, fall, and lose our inheritance if we are truly His. We need to thank Him for the blessing of His discipline.

"How we praise God, the Father of our Lord Jesus Christ, who has blessed us with every spiritual blessing in the heavenly realms because we belong to Christ." Ephesians 1:3 NLT

God gives us the strength and courage to stand firm in the armor He provides.

The fear of the LORD is the key to this treasure. Faith unlocks the door to all the riches of God's grace.

Father, help me to know and appropriate the richness of Your blessings that are mine in Christ. Amen.

Lord, You Are _____

Forgive Me For _____

Thank You For _____

Needs of Others _____

Personal Needs _____

Answered Prayers _____

God's Time Outs

"Be still, and know that I am God; I will be exalted among the nations, I will be exalted in the earth." Psalm 46:10

Time outs seem to be the choice means of disciplining children for many parents these days.

> "I will both lie down in peace and sleep; for You alone, O LORD, make me dwell in safety."
> Psalm 4:8

Whether for prayer, rest, worship, discipline, healing, renewal, or restoration, God uses time outs to fulfill His purposes in our lives.

God established the Sabbath as a day of rest and time out for and with Him. Society seems to have long since trashed this commandment and turned the Sabbath into a time out for trivial pursuits of pleasure far removed from any holiness.

God used a time out in a pit and in prison as part of Joseph's character-development program. He had Paul take an extended time out before letting him become His apostle to the Gentiles.

God's healing process often requires a time out to allow physical or emotional healing to take place.

Jesus took time out to be alone with God in prayer and meditation. As imitators of Christ, we need to do the same.

There are times in all our lives where we need to relax, take time out, and try to discern what the Lord is trying to teach us through times of trial and disappointments.

It is especially important that we try to discern whether trials and disappointments are being caused by some unconfessed or unrepented sin with which we need to deal.

If we cannot think of any sin that may be the cause of our problems, we need to thank God for the pruning that is going on and learn the lesson He has for us through the problems.

> "Then Jesus brought them to an olive grove called Gethsemane, and He said, 'Sit here while I go on ahead to pray.'"
> Mathew 26:36 NLT

God's instruction to be still and to know that He is God is a call to taking time out to listen to Him.

Father, help me to take time out to enjoy and celebrate Your presence in my life. Amen.

Lord, You Are _____

Forgive Me For _____

Thank You For _____

Needs of Others _____

Personal Needs _____

Answered Prayers _____

God's Penalty Box

"For Christ died to set them free from the penalty of the sins they had committed under that first covenant." Hebrews 9:15b NLT

Hockey is a fast moving, hard fought sport that attracts millions of fans throughout the world. To me, the penalty box is the neatest thing about hockey.

"Redemption does not come so easily, for no one can ever pay enough to live forever and never see the grave" Psalm 49:8, 9 NLT

When you break the hockey rules, you get sent to the penalty box for a time determined by the severity of the infraction. This is a double-edged penalty because it not only penalizes the rule breaker but also his team, who must play short handed.

When children break the rules or are disobedient, they get sent to their rooms for a length determined by the severity of their misbehavior. The detention hall has been the penalty box of choice for disciplining students.

God's penalty box has been in operation for centuries. A whole generation of Israelites had to spend 40 years in the penalty box of the desert and was never allowed to enter the Promised Land.

Jonah's penalty box was in the belly of a big fish. Moses' penalty box for murdering an Egyptian was fleeing into the desert for 40 years. The prodigal son suffered the penalty for his riotous living in a hog trough.

The coffin is the penalty box of death for all who refuse to receive God's wonderful provision for eternal life through faith in Jesus Christ.

As believers, we need to know that God, in His love, is going to do whatever it takes to conform us into the image of His Son.

The highway of "my way" is littered with pot holes of penalty box consequences for those who persist in living in their own strength and apart from the revealed will of God.

When we choose to live life God's way by the power of the Holy Spirit we will seldom have to endure the consequences of the penalty box.

"Because of the sacrifice of the Messiah, His blood poured out on the altar of the Cross, we're a free people—free of penalties and punishments chalked up by all our misdeeds." Ephesians 1:7 MSG

Father, help me to avoid the penalty boxes of life by abiding in You. Amen.

Lord, You Are _____
Forgive Me For _____
Thank You For _____
Needs of Others _____
Personal Needs _____
Answered Prayers _____

October 22

Keep on Keeping On!

"Because you have kept My command to persevere, I also will keep you from the hour of trial which shall come upon the whole world, to test those who dwell on the earth." Revelation 3:10

Holy perseverance is a gift of God's grace to every believer. Having the bold confidence to trust God's love and promises through all of the trials of life is our only hope for avoiding total disaster.

"But Job replied, 'You talk like a godless woman. Should we accept only good things from the hand of God and never anything bad?' So in all this, Job said nothing wrong." Job 2:10

When our comfort zones get squeezed, our threshold of pain and suffering gets tested, or we find ourselves running on empty for any other reason, it's so good to know that we know in whom we believe and in whom we trust.

The fact that we don't have to persevere on blind faith if we are in a close and personal relationship with Jesus should make knowing Jesus the number-one priority of our lives.

When we know Jesus, we will know that He is not only our bridge over troubled waters but also our very present help through them.

To know Christ is not only to share His love, grace, and mercy but also to share the pain of His suffering by firsthand experience.

Just as gold is refined and purified by fire, we can expect to be refined and purified by tests as part of God's character-development process for us.

God did not come into this world as Jesus Christ to punish us but to reconcile and redeem us.

He did not send the Holy Spirit to beat us up but to build us up and endue us with the power from on high to "keep on keeping on" as we go through the process of being conformed into the image of Christ.

"Without wavering, let us hold tightly to the hope we say we have, for God can be trusted to keep His promise." Hebrews 10:23

The victor's crown of life that is awaiting all who persevere in true faith, confidence, and total trust in the Lord is much greater than anything we might have to go through to get there.

Father, give me Your strength to "keep on keeping on." Amen.

Lord, You Are _____

Forgive Me For _____

Thank You For _____

Needs of Others _____

Personal Needs _____

Answered Prayers _____

Works in Progress

"Meditate on these things; give yourself entirely to them, that your progress may be evident to all." 1 Timothy 4:15

We are all living lives as a journey in progress. We progress from infancy, childhood, adolescence, and maturity to senility.

"But the godly will flourish like palm trees and grow strong like the cedars of Lebanon." Psalm 92:12 NLT

The biggest problem in the world today even in the lives of believers is how we progress spiritually.

Many will progress through life in total darkness. They will be dead men walking without even realizing it because they will never receive the light of their salvation.

They are enjoying living for the pleasures of the world totally oblivious to the fact that they have been created in the image of God and given a soul that sets them apart from all creation with which they were created to please and enjoy God.

Many will seemingly find and embrace the joy of their salvation in Christ and then retrogress instead of progress in becoming all that God has created them to be through a new birth in Christ. The parable of the seed and the sewer in Matthew 13:3-30 documents this scenario well.

We were born under the curse of inherited sin but were not created for the purpose of living dead in our sins forever. Jesus came into the world to remove the curse of sin from us when we receive Him as Savior and to give us a new birth whereby we become dead to sin and alive in Him forever.

As born again believers, we become works in progress growing into the fullness of Christ as we are conformed into His image by the power of the Holy Spirit.

Becoming more like Jesus day by day, year by year, until we see Him face to face is the progress we should seek on our journey of life.

"Therefore, since we are surrounded by such a huge crowd of witnesses to the life of faith, let us strip off every weight that slows us down, especially the sin that so easily hinders our progress," Hebrews 12:1 NLT

Father, by the power of the Holy Spirit working and living within me, help me to be a living work in progress for You and Your glory. Amen.

Lord, You Are ___
Forgive Me For ___
Thank You For ___
Needs of Others ___
Personal Needs ___
Answered Prayers ___

Energy Audits

"But you shouldn't be so concerned about perishable things like food. Spend your energy seeking the eternal life that I, the Son of Man, can give you. For God the Father has sent me for that very purpose." John 6:27 NLT

The high price of energy of every kind has governments and companies spending billions of dollars every year studying how to conserve energy.

"He did it so you would never think that it was your own strength and energy that made you wealthy."
Deuteronomy 4:17 NLT

Most utility companies offer free energy audits. The Word of God is the oldest and most successful energy audit system.

Life itself is energy, and we only have so much of it to burn. We are told not to waste it worrying about material things or about the future. We are not to burn it up with anger or lust.

We must never let the cares of this world or sin drain us of the tremendous life-giving source we have in the energy of the Holy Spirit.

The stewardship of life includes the stewardship of our energy. We can use it positively or negatively depending on the choices we are all given the freedom to make.

Self control is all about conserving our energy so that our lives will reflect the positive flow of God's grace to us and through us to others.

When we lose our tempers or control of any of our emotions, we are going to spend energy that could be put to much more productive uses.

"Do not waste time arguing over godless ideas and old wives' tales. Spend your time and energy in training yourself for spiritual fitness."
1 Timothy 4:7 NLT

When our energy is fueled by our flesh, we are going to waste the biggest part of it and never know the peace and joy that only a Spirit- fueled new birth in Christ can generate.

If we will just take the time to audit how much energy we spend on TV, movies, entertainment, and other trivial pursuits in comparison to how much energy we spend on seeking the kingdom of God and His righteousness, we will all find that we can do a much better job of spending our energy.

Father, help me to be a good steward of Your energy. Amen.

Lord, You Are _____

Forgive Me For _____

Thank You For _____

Needs of Others _____

Personal Needs _____

Answered Prayers _____

How Big is Your Spare?

"For the LORD is your security. He will keep your foot from being caught in a trap." Proverbs 3:26 NLT

The innovator that came up with the little spare tire in order to make more trunk room and save the automakers big bucks is not one of my favorite people.

"When they walk through the Valley of Weeping, it will become a place of refreshing springs, where pools of blessing collect after the rains!" Psalm 84:6

When I see those big cars rolling around on those dinky little spares, I don't know whether to laugh or cry.

We can laugh and make fun of these little spare tires, but when we are asked about the size of our spare tire of life, the rubber really meets the road.

The size of your spare makes a big difference when the road hazards of life cause a flat or blow out.

Some people pay more attention to the tires they buy for their cars than to even thinking about how to carry the best spare possible on the road of life. Unlike the tires on a car, we can't just go out and buy a new set of tires for our lives.

The only protection we have against the flats of life is the reserve power and strength of the Holy Spirit.

Sometimes we need more than a dinky little spare that will only get us through a minor problem.

"I know very well how foolish the message of the cross sounds to those who are on the road to destruction. But we who are being saved recognize this message as the very power of God." 1 Corinthians 1:18 NLT

We need a full-size spare built with a full-size faith in a God who cannot fail to keep us on the road for the long haul to heaven.

We dare not follow the world and try to shrink God to where He is no longer the God of our salvation and the Lord of our life. We must always remember that we have the unconditional road hazard guarantee that "God himself has prepared us for this, and as a guarantee He has given us His Holy Spirit" *(2 Corinthians 5:5 NLT)*.

Father, thank you for giving me the big spare of Your grace that will be sufficient for all my hazards of life. Amen.

Lord, You Are _____
Forgive Me For _____
Thank You For _____
Needs of Others _____
Personal Needs _____
Answered Prayers _____

How Do You Spell Success?

"Only then will any one of us get to hear the 'Well done!' of God."
1 Corinthians 4:5 MSG

Success is defined as "attaining wealth, favor, or eminence." The dictionary defines succeed as "to turn out well."

"In this life they consider themselves fortunate, and the world loudly applauds their success."
Psalm 49:18 NLT

These are probably how most people define success and succeed.

The secret of being really successful is to understand that real success has nothing to do with how much money we have, how many "toys" we acquire, or how many awards we win, etc.

Real success is and will be determined by how well we please God! Rick Warren has made millions realize that they were created for God's pleasure and purpose.

It doesn't take a rocket scientist to realize that Scripture makes it very clear that our success will be determined by how well we please God.

If this is Scripture's definition of success, we should take the time to prayerfully consider how we might achieve it.

Scripture tells us that it has pleased God to make us His people, that He is pleased when we seek wisdom, and is pleased when we make sacrifices of righteousness by doing what is just and right.

God is pleased to save us through the preaching of His Word. He is pleased when we share with others. He is pleased when we patiently endure suffering.

"The master was full of praise. 'Well done, my good and faithful servant. You have been faithful in handling this small amount, so now I will give you many more responsibilities. Let's celebrate together!'"
Matthew 25:21 NLT

Most importantly of all, we need to know that God was pleased to live in all His fullness in Christ.

Jesus Christ, God's beloved Son, in whom God was "well pleased," came to model success for us.

The degree to which we become imitators of Christ will determine how truly successful we will be.

Father, let me pursue success by living a life fully pleasing to You and fruitful in every good work. Amen.

Lord, You Are _____

Forgive Me For _____

Thank You For _____

Needs of Others _____

Personal Needs _____

Answered Prayers _____

Fully Equipped

"Put on all of God's armor so that you will be able to stand firm against all strategies and tricks of the Devil." Ephesians 6:11 NLT

We see many automobiles advertised as fully equipped or nicely equipped. Carpenters, mechanics, and other tradesmen need to be fully equipped with tools and experience to do a good job.

"Your people will freely join You, resplendent in holy armor on the great day of Your conquest, join You at the fresh break of day, join You with all the vigor of youth."
Psalm 110:3 MSG

Success in any endeavor involves some sort of equipping process. It may be physical tools, education, experience, practice, or conditioning.

God, in His love and mercy, has made wonderful provisions for equipping us to be members of the royal priesthood of believers and being His ambassadors and ministers in this world.

He has equipped us with the resurrection power of the Holy Spirit to cover our weaknesses and to guide us, keep us, and teach us all truth that we may grow into the fullness of Christ.

Life is not a playground. It's a battleground where only the full armor of God can equip us to not only survive but to thrive.

No soldier would think of going to war without his or her armor. No believer should think of going out into the world without his or her "helmet of salvation, breastplate of righteousness, sandals of peace, belt of truth, shield of faith, and sword of the Spirit."

Sometimes God's equipping involves a lot of specialized training. It often involves much pain and suffering. Sometimes it requires a lot of trial and error.

Through all of God's equipping processes, we can be sure that He will provide the strength to overcome or endure and to know that Christ has won the war for us no matter what battles we may lose.

"It is God's way of preparing us in every way, fully equipped for every good thing God wants us to do."
2 Timothy 3:17

We should all strive to be fully equipped through the discipline of discipleship as we grow in Christ by growing in His Word.

Father, may I be fully equipped that I be able to do the things you planned for me before I was even born. Amen.

Lord, You Are _____

Forgive Me For _____

Thank You For _____

Needs of Others _____

Personal Needs _____

Answered Prayers _____

Read Romans 8:28-39, Proverbs 3:21-26

Where's Your Security?

"Those who trust in the LORD are as secure as Mount Zion; they will not be defeated but will endure forever." Psalm 125:1 NLT

The emotional, physical, financial, and spiritual well being of ourselves and those we love is cause for concern from time to time. To have the confident assurance that all is or will be well with us is cause for great happiness and peace of mind.

"For the LORD is your security. He will keep your foot from being caught in a trap." Proverbs 3:26 NLT

When we are emotionally insecure, we worry about or are defensive about everything, and we make ourselves vulnerable to all sorts of real and imagined problems.

Concerns about our health, weight, appearance, physical strength, or weakness can often make us feel inadequate and insecure.

When the financial means to afford not only the necessities but some of the luxuries to which we may have become accustomed are no longer available, our overall peace of mind takes a big hit.

Our spiritual security is the key to having the confidence that all is or will be well with us no matter what other worries or problems may come.

When we base our security on the fact that God loves us unconditionally, forgives us forever, and accepts us just as we are, we are well on our way to finding that peace that prevails over and through all other real or imagined problems.

When we base our security on Christ's performance instead of ours, we will find the all-sufficient grace that will cover our weaknesses with His strength and allow us to go through life knowing that all is well or will be well.

"Since God did not spare even His own Son but gave Him up for us all, won't God, who gave us Christ, also give us everything else?" Romans 8:32 NLT

Sooner or later, our emotional, physical, or financial security is not going to matter in the least. When we have the eternal security of a right relationship with God through faith in Jesus Christ, we will have the strength and faith to know that God is working all things for our good forever.

Father, thank you for the peace and security I have in You. Amen.

Lord, You Are _____

Forgive Me For _____

Thank You For _____

Needs of Others _____

Personal Needs _____

Answered Prayers _____

How Big is Your God?

"May you experience the love of Christ, though it is so great you will never fully understand it. Then you will be filled with the fullness of life and power that comes from God." Ephesians 3:19 NLT

We all have been given the high privilege of entering into a personal relationship with God through a close and personal relationship with Jesus Christ.

"For the LORD is the great God, and the great King above all gods." Psalm 95:3

Because we are all unique and no two of us are exactly alike, we are all given the freedom of choice to determine how big we will allow God to be in our lives. He will not tarry where He is not welcomed.

We can choose to refuse to let Him be number one in every area of our life. We can choose to put him in a small box in the closet of our hearts and only let Him light up our lives semi-occasionally.

When we choose, by faith and in the power of the Holy Spirit, to celebrate the bigness of God, we open a floodgate of blessings.

Our problems will never be as big as our God when we, by faith, get to know Him as our problem solver.

We can measure how big God is in our lives by measuring how obedient we are to Him. The bigness of God's blessings is often tied to the bigness of our obedience.

God wants to be the biggest and best thing that has ever happened to us. He wants to delight in us and let us be instruments of His delight to others.

The principle of reaping what we sow should be the defining principle of how we celebrate the bigness of God. We need to sow seeds of love and kindness. We need to live big by giving generously in every area of our lives.

"But God, who is rich in mercy, because of His great love with which He loved us," Ephesians 2:4 NLT

God's love is deeper than the ocean and wider than the sea. He is all powerful and ever present. We should let His greatness manifest itself in us and through us by taking Him out of the box and appropriating His greatness in our every area of our life.

Father, let your greatness and fullness reign in me. Amen.

Lord, You Are _____
Forgive Me For _____
Thank You For _____
Needs of Others _____
Personal Needs _____
Answered Prayers _____

October 30   Read Acts 17:24-31, Psalm 145
Sweet Sovereignty
"The Sovereign LORD is my strength! He will make me as surefooted as a deer and bring me safely over the mountains." Habakkuk 3:19 NLT

How sweet it is to know the sovereignty of God! What comfort there is in knowing God is in control when things seem out of control!

"Great is the LORD! He is most worthy of praise! His greatness is beyond discovery!" Psalm 145:3 NLT

As we live through this veil of tears called life, we are going to see and experience the ravages of living in a sin-sick world.

It often seems that Satan is in control. Bad things happen to good people - the evil seem to prosper – idolatry and evil seem to be winning out. There seems to be no end to sin and misery.

When we are empowered by the grace of God to walk by faith and not by sight, we can praise God in every circumstance, because we know that He is in control and that He is working all things for our good and His glory.

When we can read a newspaper or listen to the news knowing that God is in control, we can find the peace to persevere and to sing "Be Still My Soul" in the comfort and assurance of God's sovereignty.

God's sovereignty is reflected in His grace and mercy. Instead of giving fallen mankind the death and destruction our sin deserved, He gave eternal life and victory over sin and death by fulfilling the righteous demands of His law through the perfect life and sacrifice of His Son, our Savior, Jesus Christ.

What peace and joy there is in knowing that we have an all-powerful, ever-loving God who not only makes promises but who has the power to keep them no matter what.

What comfort there is in knowing that the God Who loves us with an everlasting love and created us for His pleasure has plans for us that give us a future and hope. God is on our side!

"He is the God who made the world and everything in it. Since He is Lord of heaven and earth, He doesn't live in man-made temples." Acts 17:24 NLT

What strength there is in knowing that God has promised that nothing can ever separate us from His love that is ours through faith in Jesus Christ.

Father, thank you for Your sweet sovereignty! Amen.

Lord, You Are _____
Forgive Me For _____
Thank You For _____
Needs of Others _____
Personal Needs _____
Answered Prayers _____

What Have We Got to Lose?

"If you try to keep your life for yourself, you will lose it. But if you give up your life for me, you will find true life." Luke 9:24

"For those who believe, no explanation is necessary; for those who do not believe, no explanation is possible." Whoever penned this profound truth cuts to the quick of people's refusal to trust God.

"Wash yourselves and be clean! Let me no longer see your evil deeds. Give up your wicked ways."
Isaiah 1:16 NLT

The privilege of believing in Jesus Christ is a gift of God given by the power of the Holy Spirit. No person can call Jesus "Lord" except through the Holy Spirit working faith in their heart.

For those who continue to reject this gift in the power of their own flesh, we need to pray that the scales of spiritual blindness will be removed from their eyes and that they will come to realize that they have absolutely nothing worthwhile to lose by following Jesus.

The things we lose when we find the new life in Christ is not really that much of a loss at all from God's perspective. Alienation from God, bondage to sin, and the future torments of hell are not bad things to lose.

Guilt, anger, pride and conceit are also not bad things to lose.

When we count up the incredible blessings of our new birth in Christ, we can "count it all joy." When we think about the forgiveness of our sins, reconciliation with God, and the blessings promised for obedience, we rejoice. The all-surpassing peace and joy that only a right relationship with God through faith in Jesus Christ can provide give us even more reason to rejoice.

The bondage to the self-seeking, self-centered desires and pride of the flesh seem hard to give up for many people. That so many would choose eternal death when they are offered eternal life is the real mystery for which there is no valid excuse.

"Let all bitterness, wrath, anger, clamor, and evil speaking be put away from you, with all malice,"
Ephesians 4:31 NLT

Father, by the power of the Holy Spirit, help us all choose to lose what we have in our flesh, for what Your Son died to give us. Amen.

Lord, You Are _____

Forgive Me For _____

Thank You For _____

Needs of Others _____

Personal Needs _____

Answered Prayers _____

The "Good and Acceptable Will of God"

"And do not be conformed to this world, but be transformed by the renewing of your mind, that you may prove what is that good and acceptable and perfect will of God." Romans 12:2

It is sometimes amazing that we talk about knowing the will of God without realizing that He has revealed it to us through His Word.

> **"O God, You are my God; early will I seek You; my soul thirsts for You; my flesh longs for You in a dry and thirsty land where there is no water."**
> **Psalm 63:1**

When we seek the will of God in getting to know Jesus through the Word, we are going to find it.

We too often forget or ignore that we are to "seek first the Kingdom of God and His righteousness" if we hope to know the good and acceptable will of God.

We need to know that we are not going to find the will of God feeding on garbage or in the vanity of our self-centered and self-focused minds.

God is the first one we should think of and feed on when we awaken. He is the last one we should think of and seek before going to sleep.

As we mature in faith by putting God first, an amazing Holy transformation takes place by the power of the Holy Spirit living within us. We receive an attitude adjustment, a thirst for righteousness like we have never known before, and a satisfaction of every longing.

As we practice putting God first in every area of our lives, the practice becomes a habit, and we grow into the fullness of Christ and receive the blessings of abiding in Him.

> **"Not with eye service, as men-pleasers, but as bondservants of Christ, doing the will of God from the heart, with goodwill doing service, as to the Lord, and not to men,"**
> **Ephesians 6, 7**

We will experience the thrill of answered prayers prayed with the mindset of Christ, Jesus' joy and friendship, and increased awareness of God's love and the love of others.

We are without excuse for not knowing the will of God as He has revealed it to us through His Word.

Father, help me to be serious about seeking Your will in every area of my life by seeking You with all of my heart. Amen.

Lord, You Are _____

Forgive Me For _____

Thank You For _____

Needs of Others _____

Personal Needs _____

Answered Prayers _____

God's Manna of Grace

"Yes, He humbled you by letting you go hungry and then feeding you with manna, a food previously unknown to you and your ancestors. He did it to teach you that people need more than bread for their life; real life comes by feeding on every word of the LORD." Deuteronomy 8:3 NLT

God's miraculous provision to provide daily manna for food in the wilderness closely parallels His miraculous daily provision of grace for all our needs.

"He fed you with manna in the wilderness, a food unknown to your ancestors. He did this to humble you and test you for your own good. He did it so you would never think that it was your own strength and energy that made you wealthy." Deuteronomy 8:16, 17 NLT

Manna was good only for the day supplied. You could not save it or store it. You had to use it or lose it.

The key to recovery for most addictions is to find the daily strength to "say no" to the cravings one day at a time. The key to living victoriously in this wilderness of sin is to receive the all-sufficient grace of God on a daily basis.

God's Word is manna for our souls. It is the bread of real life. It is the channel of God's grace for our everyday life and for our forever life.

God's manna of grace is not perishable like the bread that came down from heaven. Although we can store up the nourishment of God's Word by depositing it into our spiritual memory bank, we must keep feeding on it to avoid getting overdrawn during times of peak demand we all seem to encounter.

"Jesus said, 'I assure you, Moses didn't give them bread from heaven. My Father did. And now He offers you the true bread from heaven." John 6:31 NLT

As God's manna of grace supplies our daily minimum requirements, it also provides nourishment for growth into spiritual maturity where we discover the blessings and joy of abiding in Christ.

We must never ever take the manna of grace for granted but always rejoice and be glad in it.

Father, let me savor the sweetness of Your manna of grace every day of my life. Amen.

Lord, You Are _____
Forgive Me For _____
Thank You For _____
Needs of Others _____
Personal Needs _____
Answered Prayers _____

Relational Engineering

"Yes, a person is a fool to store up earthly wealth but not have a rich relationship with God." Luke 12:21 NLT

There is an engineering course you won't find in most colleges, but it should probably be offered as a required course for every grade school, middle school, high school, and college.

"God is educating you; that's why you must never drop out. He's treating you as dear children. This trouble you're in isn't punishment; it's training, the normal experience of children."
Hebrews 12:7 MSG

Those who succeed in this course are assured of a happy and blessed life by the inventor of this course.

Jesus not only taught relational engineering by words, but He also modeled it by living out its principles in His life on this earth.

The character traits taught in the beatitudes are still among the most effective tools known for engineering good relationships.

When we let God's love for us initiate and drive our relationships with Him and with others, we will see the centuries-proven principle of sewing and reaping take root and that the golden rule is really golden.

As we go from being acquaintances, to friends, to brothers and sisters and joint heirs with Christ, we discover a universal community of interest that can be used to bind our hearts together in Christian love and unity of purpose and spirit.

As we bear the fruit of the Spirit in our relationships and become more giver oriented than taker driven, we are going to experience the joy of growing in our relationship with Jesus as we grow in our relationship with others.

"One day as the crowds were gathering, Jesus went up the mountainside with His disciples and sat down to teach them."
Matthew 5:1 NLT

This course teaches us to treasure people and to avoid the pitfalls of indifference, neglect, and unresolved misunderstandings or conflicts.

As we progress in this course, we will learn that in order to have a friend in God or people, you have to be one.

Father, help me to become an expert in relational engineering, especially in my personal relationship with Jesus. Amen.

Lord, You Are _____
Forgive Me For _____
Thank You For _____
Needs of Others _____
Personal Needs _____
Answered Prayers _____

Being Well Remembered

"The memory of the righteous is blessed, but the name of the wicked will rot." Proverbs 10:7

Memories of our lives on this earth will linger. Many people are well remembered in Scripture by virtue of the good things God did through them as He used them for His purposes. Others are remembered less than well as their outrageous conduct has been recorded.

"This is the fate of fools, though they will be remembered as being so wise." Psalm 49:13

People spend billions of dollars annually on "Kodak moments" or building a library of memories with photographs or videos.

Funerals and wakes are often enhanced with eulogies where friends and loved ones celebrate the lives of the dearly departed.

Obituaries often note some identifying accomplishment or other information in remembrance of the deceased.

We would all like to be well remembered by our family and friends and should keep this in mind as we guard our hearts and tongues against doing or saying anything that might taint our memory.

How sad it is to see how some of the brightest and the best slip and slide and have moral failures overshadow otherwise outstanding lives.

When we pursue our own self-gratifying pleasures and ambitions without giving a thought to what others might think or say, that is usually the way we will be remembered.

One of the greatest blessings and joys of peace for believers is to know that we will be remembered well by Jesus when we go to be with Him in heaven. The thief on the cross reminds us that the door to this remembrance is open until closed by death.

"I assure you, wherever the Good News is preached throughout the world, this woman's deed will be talked about in her memory." Matthew 26:13

Hopefully, we have opened this door long before our final day and in time to be well remembered for the good things we have done for God that will earn His "well done" when we stand before Him to give an account of our stewardship of life.

Father, help me to leave precious memories for those I leave behind. Amen.

Lord, You Are _____
Forgive Me For _____
Thank You For _____
Needs of Others _____
Personal Needs _____
Answered Prayers _____

The "ations" of Salvation
"That the name of our Lord Jesus Christ may be glorified in you, and you in Him, according to the grace of our God and the Lord Jesus Christ." 1 Thessalonians 1:12

There are many words that include this Greek word for some sort of going down, out, or emerging. Our salvation involves justification, sanctification, and glorification.

"Therefore if anyone cleanses himself from the latter, he will be a vessel for honor, sanctified and useful for the Master, prepared for every good work."
2 Timothy 2:21

These terms seem to be "all Greek" or misunderstood by many believers, yet they are essential processes in the emergence of our salvation in Jesus Christ.

Justification is our restoration in God's sight the hour we first believe in Jesus.

Our sins are forgiven and forgotten, and our relationship with God is restored just as if we had never sinned. God sees us through the righteousness of Jesus in whom He was well pleased. We move from the position of being lost to being saved.

Sanctification is the process which begins the hour we first believed and continues throughout our life on this earth. We become more and more Christ like in our thoughts, words, and deeds day by day, year by year, all the days of our lives as we grow in our knowledge of and relationship with God through His Word.

This is the Holy Spirit living within us producing the fruit of the Spirit, supplying the strength to overcome our weaknesses, and enabling us to sin less and become more righteous in actuality as we already are in God's sight.

To understand the mystery of "Christ in us is the hope of glory" (Colossians 1:27) is to understand glorification. Justification and sanctification will be completed when we see Jesus face to face. We will dwell with Him in the sinless perfection of our glorified new bodies in heaven.

"Being justified freely by His grace through the redemption that is in Christ Jesus,"
Romans 3:24

We should never cease praising God for His wonderful plan of salvation through justification, sanctification, and glorification.

Father, may growing in the holiness of Christ be my heart's desire on this earth as you make me ready for eternal life in heaven. Amen.

Lord, You Are _____

Forgive Me For _____

Thank You For _____

Needs of Others _____

Personal Needs _____

Answered Prayers _____

Don't Stiff Arm God!

"For this is good and acceptable in the sight of God our Savior, who desires all men to be saved and to come to the knowledge of the truth." 1 Timothy 2:3, 4

God reaches out with open arms to everyone. He would have everyone to be saved, but He wants it to be a free choice and based on real love instead of forced love and compulsion.

"You are my refuge and my shield; your word is my only source of hope." Psalm 119:114 NLY

God will never force salvation on anyone. He will allow anyone to "stiff" their arms out instead of raising them in total surrender. When we reject God when He comes knocking, we are stiff arming Him with the pride of rebellion, and we are deciding that we would rather be our own god or worship something or someone else.

To choose eternal separation from God is to choose to lose the bright hope for today and tomorrow that we have in the promises of a God who cannot lie but can do everything else and has kept every promise He has ever made.

To trade our wonderful inheritance for the fleeting pleasure of sin and self fulfillment is as dumb as Esau trading his birthright forever for the instant gratification of a bowl of soup.

God has put a soul and longing for Him in the heart of every human. This is what separates us from all other creatures. We can try to fill this longing with everything from sex to booze to pride and possessions. If we come to the end of our lives without satisfying this longing that only Jesus can satisfy, we are going to die a miserable, lonely death that will last forever.

"For since the creation of the world His invisible attributes are clearly seen, being understood by the things that are made, even His eternal power and Godhead, so that they are without excuse," Romans 1:20

We can never find true happiness, peace, and joy apart from a close and personal relationship with God through faith in Jesus Christ. All other ground is sinking sand, and we must rise above it by reaching out instead of stiff arming.

Father, keep me in the winners circle of the good life for now and forever through surrender to You and Your Lordship of my life. Amen.

Lord, You Are _____

Forgive Me For _____

Thank You For _____

Needs of Others _____

Personal Needs _____

Answered Prayers _____

Keeping Your Cup Full

"You prepare a feast for me in the presence of my enemies. You welcome me as a guest, anointing my head with oil. My cup overflows with blessings." Psalm 23:5 NLT

We all have a cup of blessings that God wants to keep filled. He wants to bless us in every area of our lives. His grace and His power are unlimited. As we ask, seek, and find, we will experience this wonderful truth that our God is "able to do exceedingly abundantly above all that we ask or think, according to the power that works in us" *(Ephesians 3:20).*

"But I lavish My love on those who love me and obey My commands, even for a thousand generations."
Exodus 20:6 NLT

Even the worst of sinners will receive some of the general blessings God pours out to all. We see many good things happen to many bad people who openly reject God and His commandments.

Once we receive the wonderful gift and blessing of salvation by receiving Jesus Christ as our Lord and Savior, we enter into the wonderful family of God with all the rights and privileges as sons and daughters.

The freedom we received from bondage to sin gives us freedom to obey and receive the many blessings that come only from obedience to God.

Abraham's faith in obeying God brought great blessings. "I will do this because Abraham listened to me and obeyed all my requirements, commands, regulations, and laws" *(Genesis 26:3).*

We need to always remember that obedience opens the flow of God's blessings, and a thankful heart keeps them open. However, disobedience and sin restrict the flow and open the doors of consequences. The more we grow in our relationship with Christ the more prayers we will have answered because we will be asking more unselfishly and in tune with the will of God.

"How we praise God, the Father of our Lord Jesus Christ, who has blessed us with every spiritual blessing in the heavenly realms because we belong to Christ."
Ephesians 1:3 NLT

Jesus came that we could have not only eternal life but "life more abundantly" *(John 10:10b).*

Father, bless me that I might be a blessing to others. Amen.

Lord, You Are _____

Forgive Me For _____

Thank You For _____

Needs of Others _____

Personal Needs _____

Answered Prayers _____

The New Deal

"After supper He took another cup of wine and said, 'This wine is the token of God's new covenant to save you—an agreement sealed with the blood I will pour out for you.'" Luke 22:20

Franklin D. Roosevelt's bold legislative initiatives to reform, revitalize, and restore our economy during the Great Depression dramatically changed the way America operated.

"In those days, I will pour out My Spirit even on servants, men and women alike." Joel 2:29

The perceived role of government as fighting our wars and delivering the mail has given way to the idea that Uncle Sam should be involved in every aspect of our lives from cradle to grave.

Despite its flaws and failures, the New Deal has made a difference and generally improved the standard of living for most Americans.

God's "New Deal" to reform, revive, and restore the souls of all His children changed the way all of us should live our lives. Our peace and right standing with God has been restored for all who will simply receive the grace of God extended.

The requirements of the law have been met and paid in full by the blood of Jesus Christ. God's "New Deal" is a free gift that we cannot earn.

God's "New Deal" puts the law in our hearts to convict us of our sins and need for a Savior, to guide our conduct, and to curb our sin. He moves His presence from the temple of the law to the temple of our hearts where the Holy Spirit takes up residence to comfort, guide, strengthen, and sustain us as we are conformed into the image of Christ.

Under God's "New Deal" we don't _have_ to do anything to earn our salvation, but we _want_ to do everything to show our love and appreciation for the great things He has done.

"And as the Spirit of the Lord works within us, we become more and more like Him and reflect His glory even more." 2 Corinthians 3:18b NLT

God gave us a free will so that we could come to Him freely and out of love instead of being forced to love Him whether we wanted to or not. God's "New Deal" turns obedience from pain to joy.

Father, thank you for the New Covenant that is mine through faith in Jesus Christ. Amen.

Lord, You Are _____

Forgive Me For _____

Thank You For _____

Needs of Others _____

Personal Needs _____

Answered Prayers _____

Wasting God's Time

"For you were bought at a price; therefore glorify God in your body and in your spirit, which are God's." 1 Corinthians 6:20

We live in a time-obsessed world. Whether it's saving time with a high speed internet connection or taking the shortest route to anywhere, we are very time conscious.

"Teach us to make the most of our time, so that we may grow in wisdom."
Psalm 90:12

We often get upset when people waste our time by being late or by creating trivial distractions.

If you get upset when people waste your time, how do you think God must feel when we waste His?

In spite of God's constant exhortations and commands to be about His business and work while there is still light, we get caught up in time-wasting trivial pursuits. We waste time and energy that might well be better spent on growing in our relationship with God through prayer and meditating on His Word, serving others, or doing those things for which God gifted and created us before we were ever born.

A quick time study of how much time and energy we devote to TV, movies, and recreational pursuits versus the time we devote to God and ministering His love to others through fellowship and service will most often be a sobering reminder of how wasteful we are with God's time.

One hour a week is weak. Abiding is full-time responsibility if we are to live our lives faithful to the Great Commandment and Great Commission.

When the Holy Spirit comes to live within us to empower us to make a difference for God by the way we live our lives, how should we respond?

"See then that you walk circumspectly, not as fools but as wise, redeeming the time, because the days are evil."
Ephesians 5:15, 16

Once the day is spent, there is no getting back the wasted hours. When we stand before the judgment throne, we will see our wasted time and energy burned away in God's presence.

How much better to see an abundance of God-glorifying and pleasing good works remain and hear our Lord's "well done, good and faithful servant"!

Father, give me a sense of urgency about using the time You have given me wisely and to Your glory. Amen.

Lord, You Are _____

Forgive Me For _____

Thank You For _____

Needs of Others _____

Personal Needs _____

Answered Prayers _____

A Bird in the Hand

"But those who wait on the LORD will find new strength. They will fly high on wings like eagles. They will run and not grow weary. They will walk and not faint." Isaiah 40:31 NLT

Birds have long been used as symbols and figures of speech. The state bird of Florida seems to be the "early bird" as seniors come to take advantage of "early bird" dining specials.

"You have seen what I did to the Egyptians, and how I bore you on eagles' wings and brought you to Myself."
Exodus 19:4

The chicken is still referred to as the "gospel bird" in many southern church circles as millions have been fed to preachers as the favorite menu when they came to dinner.

Scripture abounds with symbolical representations of birds. The Holy Spirit is described as a dove. The eagle is often used to describe God's power and protection. Jesus likened himself to a mother hen wanting to gather the children of Israel under His wings. God's provision for us was illustrated by His eye being upon even the sparrow.

The truth is that when we become birds in the hands of the Almighty we come under the shelter of His wings and have access to the same power that lifted the children out of Egypt and raised Christ from the dead.

Through the blood of Jesus, we are lifted up into a newness of life where we become secure in the Sovereignty of God and His wonderful promises.

We can even go through the deep waters of pain and suffering sheltered and sustained under the wings of The Eagle.

"Then, together with them, we who are still alive and remain on the earth will be caught up in the clouds to meet the Lord in the air and remain with Him forever."
1 Thessalonians 4:17 NLT

There is absolutely no reason for us to wander aimlessly lost in the jungle of sin. We can become a bird in the hand of God who will someday fly away to the Promised Land on eagle's wings or on the wings of a snow white dove.

Father, keep me under the shelter of Your wings as I put my future and my hope in Your hands. Amen.

Lord, You Are _____

Forgive Me For _____

Thank You For _____

Needs of Others _____

Personal Needs _____

Answered Prayers _____

Blest Be the Tie That Binds

"For you are all sons of God through faith in Christ Jesus. For as many of you as were baptized into Christ have put on Christ." Galatians 6:26

Intra-Christian quarrelling is one of the devil's favorite tools for impeding the Great Commandment and Great Commission. The time and energy Christians spend tearing down other Christians, denominations, or churches could and should be so much better spent on building up the kingdom of God instead of trying to tear it down.

"Behold, how good and how pleasant it is for brethren to dwell together in unity!"
Psalm 133:1

We are told to "pursue the things which make for peace and the things by which one may edify another" (Romans 14:19).

God is not a respecter of denominations. He is not nearly interested in where you worship as in Whom you worship! All who believe in Jesus Christ as their Lord and Savior are brothers and sisters in Christ and members of the church triumphant no matter to what denomination they belong.

The freedom that is ours in Christ is also a freedom to enjoy Christian liberty in our understanding of things that are neither condoned nor condemned in Scripture.

There are many tenets of faith about which devout, Bible-believing Christians can have different understandings and the scriptural authority to support them.

To dismiss others who don't agree with your beliefs concerning Baptism, infantile Baptism, the Lord's Supper, etc., as nonbelievers or people who don't believe the Bible gives rise to the kind of hypocritical glory that is an abomination to God.

"And have put on the new man who is renewed in knowledge according to the image of Him who created him, where there is neither Greek nor Jew, circumcised nor uncircumcised, barbarian, Scythian, slave nor free, but Christ is all and in all."
Colossians 3:10.11

We are all going to have to give an account of our faith and beliefs to God personally and individually. No church or individual can give this for us. We had best live out our own salvation with fear and trembling instead of trying to work out everyone else's.

Father let me be bonded in love with all who are trusting in the blood of Jesus for their salvation. Amen.

Lord, You Are _____
Forgive Me For _____
Thank You For _____
Needs of Others _____
Personal Needs _____
Answered Prayers _____

The Seriousness of Sin

"Now the LORD observed the extent of the people's wickedness, and He saw that all their thoughts were consistently and totally evil. So the LORD was sorry He had ever made them. It broke His heart." Genesis 6:5, 6 NLT

Sin is not a very popular subject these days. No one seems to want to be reminded of theirs, and many seem to live as if sins really do not matter. With cheap grace and forgiveness on demand, what's the big deal?

The big deal is that sin is serious to God. Our sins break His heart and have often made Him sorry He ever made us. He has already had to destroy the world once because of sin. He has already chosen to die in order to free us from the bondage to sin that brings us death and destruction.

"But, there is a problem—your sins have cut you off from God. Because of your sin, He has turned away and will not listen anymore." Isaiah 59:2 NLT

God is a God of love and forgiveness. He is always more willing to forgive than we are to be forgiven when we take sin seriously, confess, and repent of it. When anyone equates God's love and forgiveness to mean that we have a license to sin with impunity from punishment or consequences, they are making an equation for disaster.

To receive God's wonderful gift of eternal life, we must receive Jesus Christ with a broken heart and contrite spirit that convicts us of our sin and makes us realize our need for a Savior. We must always remember that God's love of sinners does not mean that He does not hate sin.

"For God did not spare even the angels when they sinned; He threw them into hell, in gloomy caves and darkness until the judgment day." 2 Peter 2:4 NLT

When we receive Jesus as our Savior, we also receive the Holy Spirit who comes to live in our hearts and give us the power from on high to take sin seriously and to avoid falling back into it.

We need to be as broken hearted about sin as God is when it is committed by us or by others. We must never entertain it as a welcome guest, coexist with it, and give the impression to ourselves or to others that it doesn't matter.

Father, help me to take sin seriously. Amen.

Lord, You Are _____

Forgive Me For _____

Thank You For _____

Needs of Others _____

Personal Needs _____

Answered Prayers _____

House of Mirrors

"Now we see things imperfectly as in a poor mirror, but then we will see everything with perfect clarity. All that I know now is partial and incomplete, but then I will know everything completely, just as God knows me now."
1 Corinthians 13:12 NLT

Many fun houses and carnivals have a house of mirrors which distorts your real image into all sorts of weird shapes and sizes.

"Oh, that my actions would consistently reflect your principles!"
Psalm 119:5 NIT

We often look at ourselves or others --- Sometimes we have the most difficult time of all in seeing ourselves as we really are.

Sometimes we tend to have an inflated view of ourselves and our importance, and we like ourselves too much. At other times, we don't like ourselves very much and can't stand to look at ourselves in a mirror.

The differences between who we think we are, who we actually are, and who we would like to be are sometimes too wide to fully understand and impossible to reconcile.

The purpose of our life on this earth is to accurately reflect who God says we already are in Christ and to reduce the distortions caused by the sins that continue to mar our image as we live out our lives being conformed into the image of Christ and becoming imitators of Christ by the power of the Holy Spirit living within us.

As reflectors of God's love, we are called to shine in the beauty of His light and let His light shine through us so that others will see the image of Christ through us and be drawn to the light of salvation.

When we see ourselves as God sees us – unconditionally loved, forever forgiven, and fully pleasing in His sight because of Jesus – this reality increases and the distortions decrease. When we appropriate God's image of us as our self image by faith, we will know the peace and security that only this God-inspired image can afford.

"And all of us have had that veil removed so that we can be mirrors that brightly reflect the glory of the Lord. And as the Spirit of the Lord works within us, we become more and more like him and reflect his glory even more."
2 Corinthians 3:18 NLT

Father let others see Christ living in and through me as I grow into His fullness by the power of the Holy Spirit living and working within me. Amen.

Lord, You Are _____

Forgive Me For _____

Thank You For _____

Needs of Others _____

Personal Needs _____

Answered Prayers _____

Seeing God's Friendly Smile

"'No, please accept them,' Jacob said, 'for what a relief it is to see your friendly smile. It is like seeing the smile of God!'" Genesis 33:11 NLT

Jacob had good reason to believe that his brother might kill him. He had cheated him out of his birthright through trickery and deceit. No wonder he was so relieved to see Esau's friendly smile.

> **"Or, you may fall on your knees and pray—to God's delight! You'll see God's smile and celebrate, finding yourself set right with God."**
> **Job 33:26 MSG**

How many times have you deserved and expected the worst and been relieved to receive something good instead?

We experience relief when we see that reassuring smile from a spouse that extends forgiveness in a quarrel or signifies that the quarrel is done.

The smile of reconciliation and forgiveness lets us see God's friendly smile in these lives of those who reconcile and forgive.

What a relief it is to see a refund check instead of a demand for additional taxes when we open a letter from the Internal Revenue Service.

How blessed we feel when we see God making even our enemies be at peace with us.

The realization that we are sinners, utterly lost and condemned by our sin, can fill us with great fear and apprehension when we confess and seek God's forgiveness and salvation through Jesus Christ.

What relief it is to know we will see God's smile when we "come fearlessly into God's presence, assured of His glad welcome" (Ephesians 3:12b NLT).

> **"Do not fear, little flock, for it is your Father's good pleasure to give you the kingdom."**
> **Luke 12:32**

God did not create us for His misery but for His joy and pleasure. Jesus did not come into this world and die to make us miserable. It was His father's "good pleasure" to give us the kingdom of God with all its rights and privileges through Him.

May we all know the joy of God's smile upon us as we lead lives fully pleasing to Him and fruitful in every good work.

Father, may I find the smile of Your pleasure in every area of my life. Amen.

Lord, You Are _____

Forgive Me For _____

Thank You For _____

Needs of Others _____

Personal Needs _____

Answered Prayers _____

God's Pocket of Prosperity

"Let them shout for joy and be glad, who favor my righteous cause; and let them say continually, 'Let the LORD be magnified, Who has pleasure in the prosperity of His servant.'" Psalm 35:17

We have a deep-pocket God. He owns the world and everything in it. He has pleasure in our prosperity.

"Always remember that it is the Lord your God who gives you power to become rich, and He does it to fulfill the covenant He made with your ancestors."
Deuteronomy 8:18 NLT

Unfortunately, most of God's children have not handled prosperity well. They became self absorbed and proud, and they went carousing with other idols. Many today have a tendency to forget God in their prosperity and become wise in their own conceits, seeing no need of God.

Although God allows both the just and the unjust to reach into His pockets, there are certain promises He makes to those who are obedient. He is also "a rewarder of those who seek Him" in the material realm.

God asks us to test Him in our giving of tithes and offerings and to be generous to those who are generous to Him.

God blesses us with material abundance so that we can be generous and bless others.

We need to ask ourselves whether God can trust us with material prosperity and whether it would be a blessing or curse to us. It is when we are found faithful with little that He can trust us with more.

God's deep pockets are available to supply our every material need. He supplies them the best when He is our true treasure.

"Yes, you will be enriched so that you can give even more generously. And when we take your gifts to those who need them, they will break out in thanksgiving to God."
2 Corinthians 9:13 NLT

We should never try to pick pocket God. His deep pockets of material prosperity can best be accessed as a by product of seeking first His kingdom and His righteousness. Prosperity must never become the treasure we seek or the God we worship.

Father, let any prosperity of material riches be the byproduct of the prosperity of my soul which I have in and through Jesus Christ. Amen.

Lord, You Are _____

Forgive Me For _____

Thank You For _____

Needs of Others _____

Personal Needs _____

Answered Prayers _____

Unforgettables

"For God is not unfair. He will not forget how hard you have worked for Him and how you have shown your love to Him by caring for other Christians, as you still do." Hebrews 6:10 NLT

Our lives are filled with unforgettables. We all have people, places, and events carved into our memories. The richer our lives, the more unforgettable memories we will have.

"I recall all you have done, O LORD; I remember your wonderful deeds of long ago." Psalm 77:11

Some memories of parents, brothers, and sisters will never be forgotten.

Most of us have been blessed with that special teacher or two who impacted our lives and entered our memory hall of fame.

Our first day of school, graduations, weddings, and memorable jobs, will often be remembered.

Memories of failures, sins, bad choices, and blown opportunities sometimes leave scars that never completely heal. The more we can be like God and remember these sins no more, the happier we will be. We should never harbor a memory hall of shame.

It is especially important that we forgive and forget everyone for anything they have ever done to hurt us so that we can know the totality of God's forgiveness.

God has given us the revelation of who He is, what He has done, and what He is going to do. He gives the indwelling presence of the Holy Spirit to help us always remember His great love and promises.

Hebrews 11 is often referred to as God's hall of faith, where the extraordinary feats of ordinary people God used to build His kingdom will never be forgotten.

"And do not bring sorrow to God's Holy Spirit by the way you live. Remember, He is the one who has identified you as His own, guaranteeing that you will be saved on the day of redemption." Ephesians 4:30 NLT

We need to be ever mindful that everything we do that glorifies God and accomplishes His purposes is recorded in our book of life and will not be forgotten by God.

Father, help me to leave some unforgettable good memories for those I leave behind. Amen.

Lord, You Are _____

Forgive Me For _____

Thank You For _____

Needs of Others _____

Personal Needs _____

Answered Prayers _____

November 17   Read 2 Timothy 2, 1 Chronicles 29:10-20

Look Out Below

"The LORD doesn't make decisions the way you do! People judge by outward appearance, but the LORD looks at a person's thoughts and intentions." 1 Samuel 16b NLT

Icebergs should remind us of the fact that when we look at people what we don't see is always much more than what we do see. We need to look below the surface to find what's really happening. This is why it's often a mistake to base our opinions of people on outward appearances or first impressions.

"I know, my God, that you examine our hearts and rejoice when you find integrity there. You know I have done all this with good motives, and I have watched Your people offer their gifts willingly and joyously."
1 Chronicles 29:17 NIV

That God would choose the young and inexperienced David mystified everyone. When we look at the ordinary people through whom God chose to do extraordinary things we should remember that "The eyes of the LORD search the whole earth in order to strengthen those whose hearts are fully committed to Him" (2 Chronicles 16:9).

We are often drawn to others because of their appearance, their talent, or their accomplishments. In the world, we have heard "clothes make the man," "you are what you eat," etc., and we are drawn to success by the world's standards.

The character beneath the outward appearance is what matters to God, and it should be what matters to us.

"Pursue faith and love and peace, and enjoy the companionship of those who call on the Lord with pure hearts."
2 Timothy 2:22b

When we examine ourselves, we need to examine the honesty of our thoughts and intentions. Do we have a heart for service or for lip service? Are we walking in our ways or God's ways? Would God not be ashamed to be called our God?

The integrity of our heart should be the top priority in our lives. We must always remember that God will strengthen and sustain the heart that is right with Him no matter what suffering or discipline we must endure.

Father, by the power of the Holy Spirit, guard my heart that it always be found faithful to you. Amen.

Lord, You Are _____

Forgive Me For _____

Thank You For _____

Needs of Others _____

Personal Needs _____

Answered Prayers _____

Why Do We?

"But why do you judge your brother? Or why do you show contempt for your brother? For we shall all stand before the judgment seat of Christ." Romans 14:10

Being "wise as a serpent and harmless as a dove" or having a discerning spirit has nothing to do with being critical.

A critical or judgmental spirit is nothing other than a conscious or unconscious attempt to make ourselves look better by trying to make others look worse. It is hypocritical glory at its worst, and we should seek to avoid it at all costs, because the cost is always going to be highest to us.

"This is what the LORD Almighty says: Judge fairly and honestly, and show mercy and kindness to one another."
Zechariah 7:9 NLT

A critical or judgmental spirit brings a harshness and cruelty to our lives that should have no place in the life of a child of God and follower of Jesus Christ.

We often see this evil spirit casting its worst spells in disagreements and quarrels within local churches and national denominations. It often shows up in quarrels between denominations. Many love to make fun of or take cheap shots at other believers who have different understandings.

Before we judge or are critical of others, we need to ask what is going to happen to us when God judges us the way we judge others. Anyone who thinks that he or she is without sin and does not say, do, or believe anything that God could criticize is deceiving themselves.

"For with what judgment you judge, you will be judged, and with the measure you use, it will be measured back to you."
Matthew 7:2

Just as God withholds forgiveness from those who refuse to forgive, He will withhold mercy from those who are not willing to be merciful instead of judgmental and vindictive.

Although we must sometimes "speak the truth in love" as the Holy Spirit uses us to convict an erring brother or sister in Christ, we must never fall into the trap of speaking in a cruel, critical, and judgmental manner with any motive other than love.

Father, do not let a critical spirit find a dwelling place in my heart. Amen.

Lord, You Are _____

Forgive Me For _____

Thank You For _____

Needs of Others _____

Personal Needs _____

Answered Prayers _____

Doing a FF

"The wise shall inherit glory, but shame shall be the legacy of fools."
Proverbs 3:34

The fast forward button on the record or video player is a handy tool for getting to the favorite part of a song or video.

"For the vision is yet for an appointed time; but at the end it will speak, and it will not lie." Habakkuk 2:3

Doing a fast forward to where we will be, what we have accomplished, and what we will be leaving behind will sometimes serve to give us a better perspective on our lives and help us to make changes while there is still time.

What will people be saying about you at your funeral? What would you like for them to be saying? Where did you waste your time? How did you store up rewards in heaven?

When we see the past from the perspective of our advanced age, we can usually think of things we could have done better, things we could have done and didn't, and things we didn't do and should have. When we move our hindsight 10, 20, or even 50 years ahead, we can seek to address these things so that we will have better answers when we get there.

Like it or not, we are all living a legacy we acquired from our parents and others, and we are all going to leave a legacy in the hearts and minds of those we leave behind.

As nice as it may be to leave a material inheritance to our loved ones when we die, how much better to leave a legacy of love and a life of faith lived in love for those we leave behind.

Along with our salvation, this is the legacy Jesus Christ left us. There is no higher calling than to become an imitator of Jesus.

"Let your roots grow down into Him and draw up nourishment from Him, so you will grow in faith, strong and vigorous in the truth you were taught. Let your lives overflow with thanksgiving for all He has done." Colossians 2:7

We all need to lead a life worth living so that we can keep on living through the lives we influence while we are here.

Father, keep me ever mindful of who I am, where I am going, and what I will leave behind to Your praise and glory. Amen.

Lord, You Are _____

Forgive Me For _____

Thank You For _____

Needs of Others _____

Personal Needs _____

Answered Prayers _____

The Key to Excellence

"I discipline my body like an athlete, training it to do what it should. Otherwise, I fear that after preaching to others I myself might be disqualified." 1 Corinthians 9:27 NLT

There is a common thread that is found in any successful pursuit of excellence. Sooner or later, it boils down to discipline.

"Through these proverbs, people will receive instruction in discipline, good conduct, and doing what is right, just, and fair."
Proverbs 1:3 NLT

The ranks of college dropouts are filled with bright people who were so bright they could breeze through high school without developing the discipline of study required at the college level, and they flunked out.

A closer look at almost any overnight sensation will reveal the hours of disciplined practice and training that went into perfecting their talent or skill.

There are no shortcuts to fame and fortune without exercising discipline and self control.

When children are allowed to grow up without learning the disciplines of neatness, orderly habits, obedience, and respect for others, they will have a whole lot of catching up to do if they are ever going to excel at anything.

The discipline of discipleship is a road less traveled. The longsuffering, patience, love, kindness, and self control required to become an imitator of Christ are too high prices for many. Although the yoke is easy and the burden light, old habits die hard.

Only the grace of God dispensed by the supernatural power of the Holy Spirit can supply the discipline required to be transformed from sinner to saint as we die to sin and become alive in Christ.

God's desire for all of His children is moral excellence. The sooner we develop the prescribed pattern of behavior lived out by Jesus, the sooner the discipline of discipleship will become our standard of conduct for our new life in Christ.

"So make every effort to apply the benefits of these promises to your life. Then your faith will produce a life of moral excellence. A life of moral excellence leads to knowing God better."
2 Peter 1:5 NIV

Father, help me to excel in the discipline of discipleship through the power of the Holy Spirit. Amen.

Lord, You Are _____

Forgive Me For _____

Thank You For _____

Needs of Others _____

Personal Needs _____

Answered Prayers _____

Finding Happiness

"Now godliness with contentment is great gain. For we brought nothing into this world, and it is certain we can carry nothing out." 1 Timothy 6:6

Happiness is not something you can buy. It does not come in a bottle, gift wrap, or ribbon. You can't eat it, smell it, or store it. It is not found in riches, places, or pastimes. Happiness is a state of mind. It is a state of well being and contentment. It is a blessing from God.

"Happy is the person who finds wisdom and gains understanding. For the profit of wisdom is better than silver, and her wages are better than gold."
Proverbs 3:13 NLT

Every American is brought up and taught about "life, liberty, and the pursuit of happiness." Unfortunately, the message has been skewed to mean "life, license, and the pursuit of pleasure" for too many people.

The liberty or freedom from bondage to sin does not mean the license to sin. "If it feels good, do it," "no blame, no shame," and "everyone's doing it" are catch phrases designed to catch the unsuspecting and hold them in the darkness of their understanding, totally separated from God – the only source of true happiness.

Confusing pleasure or success with happiness causes us to pursue self gratification instead of God glorification, and we will never experience true peace and joy when we are living separated from God.

Like it or not, God owns us. Our life and time for now and forever is subject to His sovereignty and His good and gracious will.

We may be enjoying what we perceive to be the good life apart from God and see no need for Him. Our darkened understanding will keep us wandering aimlessly lost, often not even aware of it.

"You love Him even though you have never seen Him. Though you do not see Him, you trust Him; and even now you are happy with a glorious, inexpressible joy."
1 Peter 1:8 NLT

When we live our lives seeking happiness apart from its only source, we are going to eventually come up empty. We are never going to know the love of the Father or ever enter into the joy of the Lord which defines real happiness.

Father, help me to remember that true happiness comes from You. Amen.

Lord, You Are _____
Forgive Me For _____
Thank You For _____
Needs of Others _____
Personal Needs _____
Answered Prayers _____

God is Not A Kill Joy!

"Always be full of joy in the Lord. I say it again—rejoice!" Philippians 4:4

Contrary to a widespread misconception, God is not a kill joy! He does not come lying in wait to pounce on us and punish us when we do wrong.

"The commandments of the LORD are right, bringing joy to the heart. The commands of the LORD are clear, giving insight to life." Psalm 19:8

He has made plans not to harm us but plans to bless us and give us a future and a hope.

God "loves us dearly," and He wants His very best for us. He gave us His very best – Jesus Christ– to die for our sins so that we would not have to die. Jesus did this for "the joy that was set before Him."

Jesus came that we might have life in all its fullness and especially the fullness of His joy.

In Christ, we have the joy of God's presence, the joy of His salvation, His forgiveness, and His love. He even promises to turn our mourning into joy. When we think of how much joy our children give us, we should be reminded of how much joy we give God.

Have you ever heard of anyone not finding joy in bearing the fruit of God's love, joy, peace, longsuffering, kindness, goodness, faithfulness, gentleness, and self control?

God's boundaries are not to kill our joy but to increase our joy in every area of our lives. He knows what will harm us and seeks to protect us from the harmful influences of our flesh, the world, and the devil so that we can do life God's way in the fullness of His joy and all-surpassing peace.

"Command those who are rich in this present age not to be haughty, nor to trust in uncertain riches but in the living God, who gives us richly all things to enjoy." 1 Timothy 6:17 NLT

Father, may I never look upon obedience to You as a hindrance but rather as a conduit of living in the fullness of joy that can only be found in You. Amen.

Lord, You Are _____

Forgive Me For _____

Thank You For _____

Needs of Others _____

Personal Needs _____

Answered Prayers _____

November 23   Read Matthew 10:7-40, Psalm 33

The Fear Factor

"There is no fear in love; but perfect love casts out fear, because fear involves torment. But he who fears has not been made perfect in love."
John 4:18 NLT

Even the strongest of the strong and bravest of the brave have or will experience fear. Whether it is of someone or some thing, there will be those times when we get that sick feeling experiencing or thinking about it.

"Let all the earth fear the LORD; Let all the inhabitants of the world stand in awe of Him."
Psalm 33:8

Scripture after scripture gives example of those who feared and failed yet overcame and those who failed to fear and were overcome.

Failing to fear should be the biggest fear of all. Those who insist on going through life in their own strength without the fear and reverence of the Lord are doomed and will find out only too late what they missed.

When we fear someone or some thing more than we fear God, we are failing to put God first in our lives and will often suffer the consequences.

God has given us the power to cast out all fear by the power of the Holy Spirit that is living within each of us. As we grow in the fullness of Christ and the perfection of His love, we will find that perfect love casting out more of our fears and giving us the peace and security that only the fear and reverence for God can provide.

We can find strength and comfort in recalling God's grace and mercy of the past and His never failing promises for the present and future.

God has not called any of us to a fear free life of ease and comfort. He has called us not only to ministry but also to rejoice in any persecution, pain, or suffering we may be called upon to endure as we live lives faithful to the Great Commandment and Great Commission.

"And do not fear those who kill the body but cannot kill the soul. But rather fear Him who is able to destroy both soul and body in hell."
Matthew 10:26 NLT

Faith in Jesus Christ is the only remedy for overcoming the greatest fear of all. He died on the cross to take away the fear and sting of death.

Father, help me to always fear You more than anyone or anything and find my strength and courage in Your mighty power. Amen.

Lord, You Are _____
Forgive Me For _____
Thank You For _____
Needs of Others _____
Personal Needs _____
Answered Prayers _____

Reign Over Me

"The law of Moses could not save us, because of our sinful nature. But God put into effect a different plan to save us. He sent his own Son in a human body like ours, except that ours are sinful. God destroyed sin's control over us by giving his Son as a sacrifice for our sins." Romans 8:3 NLT

Life is all about control. It is against our prideful nature to be controlled by anyone or anything, yet the quality of our lives for now and forever is and will be determined by who and what's in control.

"Don't sin by letting anger gain control over you. Think about it overnight and remain silent."
Psalm 4:4 NLT

When we insist on letting our flesh and sinful nature control our lives, God will get out of the way and let nature take its course.

It is unbelievable but true that many will refuse God's control, yet they will allow dope or alcohol, pride, anger, envy, or lust to take control of their lives and determine how they will spend them and end them.

The bondage of our flesh to our sin nature blinds us to the reality that there is no real freedom and no real, lasting happiness apart from submitting to the Reign of God over our lives and the way we live them.

The way that seems right to us by nature is the way of death and destruction. We must call out and reach up to God to find the Way, the Truth, and the Life that is ours in Jesus Christ.

We are all born with a propensity to be our own worst enemies and one of the devil's best friends. God, in His mercy, has provided a means of escape to give us friendship with and life in Him and death to our lives controlled by sin.

"Do not let sin control the way you live; do not give in to its lustful desires."
Romans 6:12 NLT

Our new life is based on our faith in Jesus Christ as Lord and Savior and living out that faith by submitting to the sovereign reign of God through obedience in a close and personal relationship with Jesus.

Why, oh, why would anyone choose to live in a desert of depravity and despair controlled by their flesh and all its weakness when God offers to take control and lead all who will receive Him by faith into the green pastures by the still waters of His love, grace, and mercy?

Father, thank you for that all-surpassing peace and joy that is mine in submitting to Your control and sovereignty. Amen.

Lord, You Are _____

Forgive Me For _____

Thank You For _____

Needs of Others _____

Personal Needs _____

Answered Prayers _____

High Risk, High Reward

"For God is not unfair. He will not forget how hard you have worked for Him and how you have shown your love to Him by caring for other Christians, as you still do." Hebrews 6:10

Scripture is full of examples of God's risk takers. All of the patriarchs, Rahab the prostitute, King David, and all of the apostles are heroes of the faith because they had the faith to risk it all for God.

"But without faith it is impossible to please Him, for he who comes to God must believe that He is, and that He is a rewarder of those who diligently seek Him."
Hebrews 11:6

"No pain, no gain" has become a trite response to the rigors or hardships of training or participating in athletic endeavors. It should be a battle cry of faith in action for those who sense the call of God on their life.

Like it or not, we are living in a high risk world. We face the risk of accidents in the home and out daily. Circumstances over which we have absolutely no control can wreak havoc upon us at anytime.

The fear factor is always trying to discourage and hold us back. It is only when the Holy Spirit gives us the strength to live by faith in God and His promises and not by sight that we can ever muster enough faith to get out of our comfort zones, into the battleground of life, and into the war that is raging all around us.

The fear of the consequences for not doing God's business until He comes should override any concerns we might have about the fear of failure in risking the life and resources God has given us with which to be risk takers and kingdom builders.

God's favor and eternal rewards clearly rest with those who suffer and who labor for the cause of Christ. Our faith should be a living, growing, pro-active pursuit of fulfilling God's purposes for which He created us. God rewards and blesses His risk takers.

"He said, 'That's what I mean: Risk your life and get more than you ever dreamed of. Play it safe and end up holding the bag.'"
Luke 19:26 MSG

Father, give me the perfect love that casts out all my fears and reservations so that I might be a risk taker for You and Your kingdom. Amen.

Lord, You Are _____

Forgive Me For _____

Thank You For _____

Needs of Others _____

Personal Needs _____

Answered Prayers _____

Are You A Catalyst?

"Dear brothers and sisters, I close my letter with these last words: Rejoice. Change your ways. Encourage each other. Live in harmony and peace. Then the God of love and peace will be with you." 2 Corinthians 13:11

Like it or not, we are all catalysts or agents of change to those around us.

"Put all your rebellion behind you, and get for yourselves a new heart and a new spirit. For why should you die, O people of Israel?"
Ezekiel 18:31 NLT

People within our families, schools, churches, jobs, or other spheres of influence where God chooses to place us might well be influenced by our actions.

The call of God to all is not only a call to salvation or a call to change. It is also a call to be a catalyst or agent of change to others.

The wonderful peace and joy that is ours in Christ is not something to be hidden; it is something to be shared through both the Great Commandment and Great Commission.

When we receive God's love, grace, and mercy through our vertical relationship of faith in Jesus Christ, we are commanded to pass on this love, grace, and mercy to others through a horizontal relationship with all whom God chooses to put in our lives.

When people see the change that a right faith relationship with God has made in our lives, we will become catalysts for change in their lives as we disciple them to become disciples.

The testimony of a life well lived in Christ is still the most powerful witness God uses to call others unto Himself. The testimony of a professing Christian who does not walk the walk is probably the biggest roadblock to faith for others who know him or her.

"'I'm sending you off to open the eyes of the outsiders so they can see the difference between dark and light, and choose light, see the difference between Satan and God, and choose God."
Acts 26:17a MSG

When we let God's love shine in us and God's truth live through us, we will become catalysts for Christ.

Father, let me be a stumbling block to no one but a catalyst for Christ to everyone. Amen.

Lord, You Are _____

Forgive Me For _____

Thank You For _____

Needs of Others _____

Personal Needs _____

Answered Prayers _____

Holy Marinating

"Meditate on these things; give yourself entirely to them, that your progress may be evident to all." 1 Timothy 4:15

Every good cook knows the secret of marinating. This is the process of soaking meat in an ingredient to add flavor and tenderize.

"I ponder every morsel of wisdom from You, I attentively watch how You've done it. I relish everything You've told me of life, I won't forget a word of it."
Psalm 119:15 MSG

God's Word is the means through which the Holy Spirit marinates us. When we soak up the commands, encouragements, warnings, and other truths of the Bible into our hearts and souls, we experience the added zest and joy of living and the tenderness of Spirit that can come only by the grace of God through our new birth in Christ.

When the Word of God takes root in our hearts by the power of the Holy Spirit, our hardness of heart is tenderized by our conviction of our sinfulness and need for a Savior.

This tenderness leads us to God's throne of grace where we receive our wonderful gift of salvation by confession and repentance.

The hour we first believe is the instant we receive the righteousness of Christ in God's sight and the indwelling presence of the Holy Spirit who begins the marinating process of conforming us into becoming in reality what we have already become theologically.

As we soak up God's truth and let it marinate in our hearts, we will begin imitating Christ in the way we think, the way we pray, and the way we live our lives. Christ in us as our hope of glory will become the reality of our life as we receive the grace to live fruitful, God-pleasing lives that honor God.

"Meditate on these things; give yourself entirely to them, that your progress may be evident to all."
Philippians 4:15

When we hold every thought captive in the marinating chamber of our souls, we will begin to see God's purposes and will for our lives more clearly, and we will begin to taste and see how good God really is.

Father, help me to know the joy of holy marinating through Your Word. Amen.

Lord, You Are _____
Forgive Me For _____
Thank You For _____
Needs of Others _____
Personal Needs _____
Answered Prayers _____

The Trustability Index

"Those who listen to instruction will prosper; those who trust the LORD will be happy." Proverbs 16:20

We all rely on or trust something or someone every day of our lives.

"For the word of the LORD holds true, and everything He does is worthy of our trust." Psalm 33:4 NLT

In seeking happiness, people put their trust in money, prestige, peers, education, appearances, pleasure, a bottle, or a pill. "I will be happy if, when, or why whatever I am trusting in kicks in."

In seeking physical security, people put their trust in their own strength, their spouse, an arsenal of weapons, burglar alarms, or watch dogs.

We trust our schools, our governments, our stock brokers, doctors, employers, and other entities to meet our needs.

If we were to assign an index number based on the reliability of all of these factors, we still couldn't come up with a high trustability index.

The simple truth is that there is no happiness and no security apart from God.

People will often fail and disappoint; popularity and prestige will often wane. The booze or dope will eventually kill you. Your arsenal of weapons will often cause someone you love to get killed more often than they will protect you.

Our schools are teaching wrongs as rights; our government is not nearly as trustworthy as it should be. Stockbrokers sometimes break us; doctors sometimes kill us. Our strength starts failing almost as soon as we acquire any, and there is always someone stronger.

God is the only one who scores 100 on any trustability index. When we consider Who He is, what He has done and continues to do, and that He has kept or is keeping every promise He has ever made, how can we not trust Him?

"And God, in His mighty power, will protect you until you receive this salvation, because you are trusting Him." 1 Peter 1:5 NLT

When we can say with all sincerity that we are happy and secure because of who we are Christ and our trust in His promises, we will forget about putting our trust in the wrong people, places, and things.

Father, may my trust always be anchored in You and Your Word. Amen

Lord, You Are _____

Forgive Me For _____

Thank You For _____

Needs of Others _____

Personal Needs _____

Answered Prayers _____

Gilding the Lily

"As we have said before, so now I say again, if anyone preaches any other gospel to you than what you have received, let him be accursed." Galatians 1:9

The beauty of the lily is for all to see. It needs no embellishment or gilding. The Good News of eternal life through faith in Jesus Christ also is beautiful in itself and needs no gilding.

"I will be like the dew to Israel; he shall grow like the lily, and lengthen his roots like Lebanon." Hosea 14:5

Ever since the Good News was proclaimed, people have been trying to gild it by adding conditions to God's unconditional love and teaching.

Today's prosperity gospel attracts millions with the mistaken idea that God wants us all to be rich and enjoy good health and good fortune all the days of our lives, and all we have to do is "name it and claim it." When this doesn't happen, people are told it's because they didn't have enough faith, and they are left holding the bag of unfilled expectations from a misunderstood God.

The Apostle Paul had mountain-moving faith and plenty of good works but prayed for healing which was never received in this life. The disciples were not issued Rolex watches. They did not live in the lap of luxury nor did anyone else of record who picked up their cross to follow Jesus.

The prosperity gospel should be proclaiming the prosperity of the soul that is ours through being justified through faith in Jesus Christ. Living richly means a whole lot more than being healthy, wealthy, and wise by the world's standards.

God does want us to prosper. He is the Giver of every good and perfect gift of every kind. He does love and promise to bless cheerful givers. He has also told us that in this world we will have much trouble and that if we are going to share in His glory, we must share in His suffering.

"Yet true religion with contentment is great wealth." 1 Timothy 1:6 NLT

When we find prosperity for our souls in the all-surpassing peace and joy of the Lord, we have found the ungilded lily in all its beauty.

Father, keep me ever mindful that Your all-sufficient grace is more than enough to satisfy my every longing and supply my every need. Amen.

Lord, You Are _____
Forgive Me For _____
Thank You For _____
Needs of Others _____
Personal Needs _____
Answered Prayers _____

The Big Tent

"Yes, I think it is right, as long as I am in this tent, to stir you up by reminding you," 2 Peter 1:13

Political parties like to often brag about having big tents under which many people with many differing views and agendas can unite. This principle of inclusion is also one of the basic principles of the Christian faith.

"Then the cloud covered the tabernacle of meeting, and the glory of the Lord filled the tabernacle." Exodus 30:34

The fellowship of believers that comprise the body of Jesus Christ is about as inclusive as you can get. Rich or poor, sick or well, black, white, yellow, or red will all find room at Jesus' big tent.

This big tent is open to all, not on the basis of who you are or where you come from, but on the basis of Whose you are and Who you worship in spirit and in truth.

Although this tent is the oldest in existence, it is also the strongest and most durable. It has survived fires, heresies, and attacks of every kind from within and without because it was made to last till the end of life on this planet.

It takes a big tent to hold all of the children of a big God.

All who seek shelter from the storms of life will find refuge and strength here. All who labor and are heavy laden will find rest

"That is why the earthly tent and everything in it—which were copies of things in heaven—had to be purified by the blood of animals. But the real things in heaven had to be purified with far better sacrifices than the blood of animals," Hebrews 9:14 NLT

for their souls. All who come to this tent with a broken spirit and contrite heart will never be refused admission or cast out.

This is a tent without walls. God is not a respecter of persons or denominations. All who are trusting in Jesus Christ alone for their salvation can come into God's tent assured of a glad welcome.

Father, thank you for giving the security of Your love in Your tent of grace. Amen.

Lord, You Are _____
Forgive Me For _____
Thank You For _____
Needs of Others _____
Personal Needs _____
Answered Prayers _____

God's Straightjacket

"Take My yoke upon you and learn from Me, for I am gentle and lowly in heart, and you will find rest for your souls. For My yoke is easy and My burden is light." Matthew 11:29, 30

When we think of a straightjacket, we immediately conjure up visions of mentally or emotionally disturbed people being restrained by a straightjacket.

"I have restrained my feet from every evil way, that I may keep Your word."
Psalm 119:101

Too often, many have a negative view of God's straightjacket. Many assume that God is a kill joy and wants us to wear a straightjacket to keep us from enjoying life. Some reject His call to salvation when it comes because they are afraid of what they might have to give up.

The worst straightjacket is the one we all wear as the curse of our inherited sin nature. This straightjacket keeps us in bondage to sin and restrains us from ever enjoying the freedom from death and sin that is ours through faith in Jesus Christ.

God knows us better than we know ourselves. He knows what is best for us and what will give Him the most glory and us the most joy. His ways are so much higher and so much better than ours; we dare not question or go against them.

God has set boundaries of obedience for all who would enjoy the abundant life to the utmost and experience the blessings that can only be obtained through obedience.

God's straightjacket is really a "straight" jacket which allows us to walk in the straight and narrow way of righteousness, holiness, and obedience without which we will never see God.

Abide in Me, and I in you. As the branch cannot bear fruit of itself, unless it abides in the vine, neither can you, unless you abide in Me."
John 15:4

So many ways that seem right to us are ways that will lead to misery, pain, sorrow, and even death. How much better to seek God's way as the way that leads to life in its fullest now and in eternity.

Father, thank you for giving me Your straightjacket of love. Amen.

Lord, You Are _____

Forgive Me For _____

Thank You For _____

Needs of Others _____

Personal Needs _____

Answered Prayers _____

Churchianity

"For they have betrayed the honor of the LORD, bearing children that aren't His. Now their false religion will devour them, along with their wealth." Hosea 5:7

"Righteousness and justice are the foundation of Your throne; mercy and truth go before Your face." **Psalm 89:14**

Webster's defines churchianity as "the usually excessive or sectarian attachment to the practices and interests of a particular church."

The scribes and Pharisees of the New Testament were masters at practicing churchianity. Jesus described them as a "brood of vipers" and "white-washed tombstones."

Today, we have many professing Christians who are practicing churchianity instead of Christianity.

Individual members and pastors get so caught up in building up followings, increasing numbers, constructing buildings, and other personal agendas that building up the body of Christ becomes a lost or secondary agenda. When Jesus returns to some churches, instead of being able to say "See how they love one another," He will have to say, "See how they quarrel and argue with one another."

We have seminaries brainwashing students that their job is to defend the faith and traditions of a particular faith rather than to equip the saints to make disciples and grow in their personal relationship with the Living Lord.

Too many churches are in a "maintenance mode" of ministering within, instead of reaching out to seek and save the lost.

The tradition wars of how we should worship often totally distract the real importance of Whom we should worship.

When the Great Commandment and Great Commission take a back seat to churchianity, there is going to be hell opened up for many people. Confucius or some other wise person once said, "He who makes religion his god, will not have God for his religion."

"How terrible it will be for you experts in religious law! For you hide the key to knowledge from the people. You don't enter the Kingdom yourselves, and you prevent others from entering." **Luke 11:53 NLT**

Father, help me to always keep the main thing the main thing in my life, my home, and Your church. Amen

Lord, You Are _____
Forgive Me For _____
Thank You For _____
Needs of Others _____
Personal Needs _____
Answered Prayers _____

Clean-up Costs

"But if we walk in the light as He is in the light, we have fellowship with one another, and the blood of Jesus Christ His Son cleanses us from all sin." 1 John 1:7

The cost of cleanup and repairs for hurricanes and other natural disasters often reaches astronomical proportions. The total costs incurred and still being spent for Katrina will never really be fully known.

"'Come now, and let us reason together,' says the Lord. 'Though your sins are like scarlet, they shall be as white as snow; though they are red like crimson, they shall be as wool.'"
Isaiah 1:16

All builders have a fixed amount for clean up costs after a building is completed.

Disposable paper plates, napkins, cups, and tableware are often used to save the clean up costs after a big picnic or party.

Many sins would never have been committed if the sinners had considered the clean up costs they would incur.

There is often no clean up possible. Lungs damaged by cigarette smoking can never be fully cleaned.

Lives lived in the muck and mire of sin can never be cleaned up except by the grace of God.

Jesus' death on the cross for your sins and mine was the highest clean-up cost ever paid, but God loved us so much that He thought we were worth it.

When the blood of Jesus cleanses us of all unrighteousness, we are cleansed indeed. We are not only cleansed, but we are given a white robe of righteousness that will keep us clean in God's sight spiritually while we struggle to clean up our lives physically by the power of the Holy Spirit living within us when we receive Jesus Christ as our Lord and Savior.

The Holy Spirit comes not only to live within us to comfort, strengthen, and guide us in all truth but also to keep us clean through daily confession and repentance until Jesus calls us home.

"For he who lacks these things is shortsighted, even to blindness, and has forgotten that he was cleansed from his old sins."
2 Peter 1:9

Are YOU using your daily clean up service?

Father, let me bathe in Your ocean of grace daily so that I may stay clean. Amen.

Lord, You Are _____
Forgive Me For _____
Thank You For _____
Needs of Others _____
Personal Needs _____
Answered Prayers _____

Read Luke 18:23-30, Luke 14:28-33 — **December 4**

How Much is Your Overhead?

"It is dangerous to make a rash promise to God before counting the cost."
Proverbs 20:25

Overhead is the cost of doing business apart from the cost of any product sold or service rendered.

**"So no one can become my disciple without giving up everything for me."
Luke 14:33**

On a personal level, our overhead is our cost of living each day. Some of us have a very high maintenance overhead, especially when we try to validate our worth by the kind of car we drive, the house in which we live, and the clothes we wear.

On a spiritual level, we are also told to count the cost.

If we honestly count the cost of our sins, we will often find the price is too high. Guilt, shame, loss of life, loss of self respect, jail, or other consequences often make whatever perceived pleasure we derive simply not worth the cost.

The cost of discipleship may be even higher, but the benefits are beyond measure. We must be willing to surrender our time, talents, treasures, pride, friends, worldly pleasures, loved ones, and even our lives to take up our cross and follow Jesus.

Most of us struggle with giving up all to follow Jesus. We hold on to many areas of our lives until the Holy Spirit takes control and gives us the strength and desire to exchange the old for the new as we experience the transforming power of God through our new birth in Christ.

We have to be willing to give it all up in order to find the all-surpassing peace and joy that Jesus promises. This often gives us a quality of life for now and forever that will more than compensate us for any temporary pains or losses.

God's peace includes godly contentment that can actually cut our overhead expenses as we base our worth not on what we have but on Whom we have.

**"But when the man heard this, he became sad because he was very rich."
Luke 18:23 NLT**

Jesus counted the cost and deemed us worth his death. Can we do any less than deem Him worth more than any cost of living for Him? His promise to supply our every need will more than cover our overhead costs.

Father, make me ever willing to take up my cross and follow Jesus no matter what. Amen.

Lord, You Are _____
Forgive Me For _____
Thank You For _____
Needs of Others _____
Personal Needs _____
Answered Prayers _____

December 5   Read 2 Peter 1, Jeremiah 13:23-27

Can a Leopard Change His Spots?

"Through the Spirit, Christ offered Himself as an unblemished sacrifice, freeing us from all those dead-end efforts to make ourselves respectable, so that we can live all out for God." Hebrews 9:15 MSG

Many things are impossible for man, but nothing is impossible for God. God could change the leopard's spots if He chose to do so, but He has much more important spots to confront.

"Can a leopard take away its spots? Neither can you start doing good, for you always do evil." Jeremiah 13:23b NLT

Every child born of woman comes with a nature that will blemish with spots of sin throughout their life. Our just and holy God, who created us for fellowship with Him, positively hates sin but loves us. Through the ages, He has done everything possible to bring His children into a close, personal, and holy relationship with Him.

God's children have fallen off the wagon of holiness into the muck and mire of every imaginable sin. They have been so bad that God has had to destroy the world by flood, destroy Sodom and Gomorroh by hail and brimstone, and allow the apples of His eye to fall into the hands of the Babylonians all because of their wickedness.

Finally, in His love and mercy, God ordained a wonderful plan of salvation where our sin spots would be covered, and He would see them no more. He sent His only Son Jesus to live a perfect life and become the perfect, unblemished sacrifice to remove the sin spots from our record by covering them with the perfection and righteousness of Christ.

"They will receive the wages of unrighteousness, as those who count it pleasure to carouse in the daytime. They are spots and blemishes, carousing in their own deceptions while they feast with you." 2 Peter 1:13

When we receive Jesus Christ as our Lord and Savior by faith, we see our spots of sin exchanged for fruit of righteousness that allows us to live lives fully pleasing to God and fruitful in every good work by the power of the Holy Spirit living within us.

No one has to go through life spotted worse than a leopard by sin. They can all be washed away by the blood of Jesus through confession, godly sorrow, true repentance, and faith in Jesus Christ.

Father, thank you for cleansing my spots with the blood of Jesus. Amen.

Lord, You Are _____

Forgive Me For _____

Thank You For _____

Needs of Others _____

Personal Needs _____

Answered Prayers _____

Jaywalkin' to Jesus

"There is a way that seems right to a man, but its end is the way of death."
Proverbs 14:12

It doesn't take a nuclear physicist to realize that you can't jaywalk to God. With the sin traffic in the world today at an all-time high, the chances of getting across the road of life to heaven safely are zero or less.

"But I have my eye on salt-of-the-earth people— they're the ones I want working with me; men and women on the straight and narrow these are the ones I want at my side. But no one who traffics in lies."
Psalm 101:7 MSG

Imagine trying to walk across the busiest interstate expressway in the world at rush hour. Here comes 18 wheels of lust at 80 mph; right beside it is a van loaded with greed. If you dodge these, there is a convoy of envy and pride bearing down on you at break-neck speed. The Anger express is coming right at you. Addictions and abuses are flying down every lane.

Jesus knew that we could never make it safely across to the other side without a pedestrian crossing and a map to show us where to cross.

Jesus and His blood is our bridge over troubled waters, and He has given the Holy Spirit and His Word to guide us safely through the traffic of sin.

There are no shortcuts from death to life. Jesus is the only way we can safely reach the other side. He has cleared the traffic of sin to give us an overpass made of grace and fueled by faith. To all who will call upon His name, He gives the power to become the children of God and joint heirs of an eternal home in heaven.

"You can enter God's Kingdom only through the narrow gate. The highway to hell is broad, and its gate is wide for the many who choose the easy way."
Matthew 7:13 NLT

Before we risk trying to cross over on our own, we had best remember that there are no shortcuts and no jaywalking. Jesus is the only way to eternal life with he Father. All other ground is sinking sand.

Father, may I never try to jaywalk on You. Amen

Lord, You Are _____

Forgive Me For _____

Thank You For _____

Needs of Others _____

Personal Needs _____

Answered Prayers _____

December 7   Read Mark 8, Isaiah 43:1-7

Getting in the Swim

"So they picked up Jonah and threw him into the sea, and the sea ceased from its raging." Jonah 1:13 NLT

Whether we are talking about swimming socially, financially, spiritually, or physically, there are always risks attached to "getting in the swim."

"When you go through deep waters and great trouble, I will be with you. When you go through rivers of difficulty, you will not drown!"
Isaiah 43:2 NLT

When we get out of our natural element, we make ourselves vulnerable to attacks by sharks or alligators either literally or figuratively. We need to be aware of the dangers lurking below the surface.

We need to be careful about with whom we go swimming. Peer pressure and seeking the approval of others can often lead to drowning our character or self respect in a sea of grief and remorse.

Money sharks abound in our world of instant easy credit and can have us swimming in debt so deep that we struggle just to tread water.

In the journey of life, we may often find ourselves swimming in seas of loneliness, bitterness, doubt, and despair.

The shipwrecks of life come in many ways and for many reasons. We can be sailing along without a care in the world and suddenly find ourselves thrown overboard, swimming for our lives.

Many of our shipwrecks are the consequences of bad choices we make in disobeying God and trying to sail out of the harbor of His will. Jonah found out quickly that it doesn't pay to disobey.

"The disciples woke Him up, shouting, 'Master, Master, we're going to drown!' So Jesus rebuked the wind and the raging waves. The storm stopped and all was calm! Then He asked them, 'Where is your faith?'"
Mark 8:24, 25 NLT

When we are up to our necks in alligators or find ourselves swimming in shark-infested waters, it is so good to know that we have a lifeguard who will rescue us and pull us into the lifeboat of His mercy and grace. He is always just a prayer of confession and repentance away.

Father, let me swim in the safety of Your ocean of love. Amen.

Lord, You Are _____
Forgive Me For _____
Thank You For _____
Needs of Others _____
Personal Needs _____
Answered Prayers _____

Do or Done Religions

"For by grace you have been saved through faith, and that not of yourselves; it is the gift of God, not of works, lest anyone should boast." Ephesians 2:8, 9

Christianity is the only living faith. All religious leaders except Jesus are dead.

"For I know that my Redeemer lives, and He shall stand at last on the earth." Job 19:25

There are no other bodily resurrections documented and witnessed as historical facts.

How liberating it is to base our assurance of eternal life on what Jesus Christ did on the cross for us rather than what we must do to earn eternal life.

All other religions are based on doing in order to earn God's favor rather than believing that Jesus earned God's favor for us.

The observance of the disciplines of any faith are all essentially good things. We should all love others, pray frequently, observe the holy days, and pursue righteousness because God commands and promises to bless us when we do these things.

The difference is that all others do these things to earn God's favor while true Christians do them because of what God has done in Christ.

It is sad indeed that so many professing Christians will give the wrong testimony when asked about the reason for the hope that is in them. "I'm a good person...I go to church...I have been faithful to my wife...I give to the poor" are common answers given even by professing Christians when asked why God should let them into heaven.

Anyone who bases their hope of heaven on how good they have been instead of how good Jesus is are setting themselves up for a big disappointment. God's standard for entering His eternal rest is perfection, and no one other than the perfect Lamb of God who knew no sin has ever been good enough to fulfill God's standard.

"Can we boast, then, that we have done anything to be accepted by God? No, because our acquittal is not based on our good deeds. It is based on our faith." Romans 3:27

Father let my life be a celebration of praise for what You have done for me through Jesus Christ. Amen.

Lord, You Are _____

Forgive Me For _____

Thank You For _____

Needs of Others _____

Personal Needs _____

Answered Prayers _____

Leanings

"Trust in the LORD with all your heart, and lean not on your own understanding; in all your ways acknowledge Him, and He shall direct your paths." Proverbs 3:5, 6

We all have leanings. We may find ourselves leaning toward a particular candidate, career, or decision. We might even be leaning toward God.

"Trust in the LORD and do good. Then you will live safely in the land and prosper." Psalm 37:3 NLT

The difference between life and death, heaven and hell, joy and sorrow is often made by the way we lean.

When we lean on our own understanding, we are leaning on the slippery slope of self-centered living in the flesh and bearing the consequences of committing the sins of the flesh.

Pontius Pilate was "almost persuaded." The rich young ruler was leaning. The road to hell might well be paved with "leaners" who turn their back after Jesus softly and tenderly calls them to repentance and a new life in Christ.

When our leaning towards Jesus becomes trust and obedience, we become endued with power from on high to die to our sin nature and become alive in Christ. We are given a new nature that bears the fruit of righteousness which promises rich blessings instead of consequences.

There are uncertainties in life that we are never going to understand. We are called to walk by faith and not by sight. Some things can only be understood by the power of the Holy Spirit working in us, Who guides us into all truth and writes God's law in our hearts.

Jesus came into the world, and God's chosen people knew Him not because they were leaning on their own understanding. He comes to us in Spirit and in truth. He can find us only when we remove the scales of blindness caused by our human understanding and lean on the everlasting arms of Jesus.

"And may you have the power to understand, as all God's people should, how wide, how long, how high, and how deep His love really is." Ephesians 3:18 NLT

Father, may I find and understand You with the wisdom and spiritual discernment that only You can give by grace through faith. Amen.

Lord, You Are _____

Forgive Me For _____

Thank You For _____

Needs of Others _____

Personal Needs _____

Answered Prayers _____

Deceitfulness

"Blessed is the man to whom the Lord does not impute iniquity, and in whose spirit there is no deceit." Psalm 32:2

It all started in the Garden of Eden. Eve was deceived into disobeying God by the deception of a false promise that she would become as wise as God and that she surely would not die.

"Who may ascend into the hill of the LORD? Or who may stand in His holy place? He who has clean hands and a pure heart, who has not lifted up his soul to an idol, nor sworn deceitfully,"
Psalm 24:2, 3

Since this time, every child born of woman has been born with a heart that "is deceitful above all things. Who can know it?" *(Jeremiah 17:9)*

We often deceive ourselves through justification, rationalization, blaming others, and denial. *(Does "I just want to be happy"... "I deserve it"... "The devil made me do it"... "I can handle it"... "I don't have a problem" sound familiar to you?)*

Satan has never quit deceiving. He will deceive us to keep us from turning to God, to cause us to doubt God and our salvation, and to tempt us to fulfill the pride and lust of the flesh. He is a slippery snake with a slippery tongue and absolutely no conscience. The truth is not in Him, except to twist and deceive.

Perhaps worst of all, Satan has infiltrated Christ's church with his agents who are wolves in sheeps clothing perverting God's truth and trying to lead us astray.

Today's world is a hot bed of manipulation through deception. Advertising tries to deceive us into equating good times with good beer and tries to get us to measure our worth by our beauty, our cars, or other possessions.

The "if it feels good, do it" and relative truth mentality would deceive us to believe that what God calls abominations are perfectly fine.

We must stay anchored deep in the truth of God's Word and continually pray for wisdom and spiritual discernment so that we will not be deceived. We must guard our hearts. ("Above all else, guard your heart, for it affects everything you do." Proverbs 4:23)

"But evil men and impostors will grow worse and worse, deceiving and being deceived."
2 Timothy 3:13-17

Father, help me guard my heart through the power of the Holy Spirit. Amen.

Lord, You Are _____

Forgive Me For _____

Thank You For _____

Needs of Others _____

Personal Needs _____

Answered Prayers _____

Full Confidence
"Since this new covenant gives us such confidence, we can be very bold."
2 Corinthians 3:12 NLT

Walking by faith instead of by sight is not always easy. In fact, it is downright impossible without the supernatural power from on high. This power is the result of God's grace working in and through His Word to give us the understanding of the hidden treasures of wisdom and knowledge.

"The Sovereign LORD, the Holy One of Israel, says, 'Only in returning to Me and waiting for Me will you be saved. In quietness and confidence is your strength,'"
Isaiah 30:15a NLT

When we realize that Christ was almighty God in the flesh and that we are united with Him and all His fullness when we receive Jesus as our Savior, we will know God by knowing Jesus.

We grow into the fullness of Christ by growing in our knowledge of and friendship with Him through His Word. The blessed assurance of whom we are and what we have in Him gives us the confidence we need to persevere and endure through whatever may come our way.

We cannot claim the promises of God without knowing what they are and how to claim them. As we grow in His fullness through growing in His Word, we get our knowledge and strength from God.

The mystery of Christ in us being our hope of glory will be a reality as we live out our lives in the fullness of Jesus' peace and joy in the mighty power of God.

"My goal is that they will be encouraged and knit together by strong ties of love. I want them to have full confidence because they have complete understanding of God's secret plan, which is Christ Himself."
Colossians 2:2 NLT

The blessed assurance that we have been redeemed by the blood of the Lamb will fan the flames of our faith into the full confidence that nothing can ever separate us from the love of God that is ours in Christ Jesus.

Father let my confidence in You grow as Your fullness grows within me. Amen.

Lord, You Are _____

Forgive Me For _____

Thank You For _____

Needs of Others _____

Personal Needs _____

Answered Prayers _____

New and Improved

"But you are a chosen generation, a royal priesthood, a holy nation, His own special people, that you may proclaim the praises of Him who called you out of darkness into His marvelous light." 1 Peter 2:9

Walk down any supermarket aisle and you will find "new and improved" tags on many of the products you see. I would suspect that TIDE has been made new and improved at least 50 times during the past 60 years.

> **"He has given me a new song to sing, a hymn of praise to our God."**
> **Psalm 40:3 NLT**

Making things look, work, or perform better is the life blood of almost every successful business. After all, we have to have some reason to buy that new car or computer; otherwise, we would just keep the old.

God's plan for all His children is to improve us by washing away our sin and making us new creatures in Christ.

Jesus not only makes us new through a new birth in Christ, but He also sends a helper (a.k.a the Holy Spirt) to help us look, work, perform, and be better everyday in every way by molding and melding us into the likeness of Christ.

The old self-centered, flesh-driven attitudes become Christ-centered fruit as we live out our lives in the power of Christ in us through the Holy Spirit.

Best of all, as new and improved children of God, we are the heirs of the new and improved covenent of grace God has made.

Because Jesus Christ lived the perfect life and died on the cross as the perfect sacrifice to fulfull the righteous demands of the law, we can look forward to living forever with Him in the heavenly home He has gone to prepare for us.

In the meantime, we have become new and improved priests who no longer have to make blood sacrifices for sin but can now make sacrifices of praise and thanksgiving to God for the great things He has done.

> **"'This is the new covenant I will make with my people on that day,' says the Lord. 'I will put my laws in their hearts so they will understand them, and I will write them on their minds so they will obey them.'"**
> **Hebrews 10:16 NLT**

Father, thank you for making me a joint heir with Christ in Your wonderful, new and improved covenant of grace. Amen.

Lord, You Are _____
Forgive Me For _____
Thank You For _____
Needs of Others _____
Personal Needs _____
Answered Prayers _____

The Swamp of Sin

"These were his instructions to them: 'You must always act in the fear of the LORD, with integrity and with undivided hearts.'" 2 Chronicles 19:9 NLT

Alligators are thriving and increasing in Florida. More and more attacks are being recorded, and more and more gators are

"This is what happens to those who live for the moment, who only look out for themselves: Death herds them like sheep straight to hell; they disappear down the gullet of the grave," Psalm 49:13 MSG

having to be killed because they have lost their fear of humans. People feed them, show them off, and think they are like pets, and this is how they lose their fear.

Sin is also thriving and increasing not only in Florida but around the world. Satan and the forces of evil are feeding it to us relentlessly and frequently; we are in danger of losing our fear of it.

As we pursue the pleasures of the world and the flesh, we are encouraged to do anything that feels good and live guilt and regret free. As we do this, we harden our hearts and dull our God-given consciences to the point where we die in our sins and suffer the torments thereof.

When we lose our fear of sin, we are losing our fear of God and all hope of being reconciled to Him through faith in Jesus Christ.

When we lose our fear of sin, we become proud of it instead of ashamed of it, and we will never have the conviction and godly sorrow to die to sin. Instead, we need to confess and repent so that can become alive in Christ.

"It wasn't so long ago that you were mired in that old stagnant life of sin. You let the world, which doesn't know the first thing about living, tell you how to live. You filled your lungs with polluted unbelief, and then exhaled disobedience." Ephesians 2:1 MSG

We need to maintain our fear of sin and reverence for God. We need to flee temptation just like we would flee an alligator coming after us.

Although we may be up to our necks in the alligators of sin, we have the sword of the Spirit and shield of faith to help us through the swamp.

Father, help me to keep the swamp of sin drained so that I won't become "gator bait." Amen.

Lord, You Are _____

Forgive Me For _____

Thank You For _____

Needs of Others _____

Personal Needs _____

Answered Prayers _____

Taking Things for Granted

"Everything in the world is about to be wrapped up, so take nothing for granted. Stay wide-awake in prayer. Most of all, love each other as if your life depended on it." 1 Peter 4:7 MSG

We often take too many things for granted.

> "Now I'm alert to GOD's ways; I don't take God for granted. Every day I review the ways He works; I try not to miss a trick."
> **Psalm 18:21 MSG**

Numerous marriages have gone bad because one partner takes the other for granted and fails to communicate or even consider a spouse's needs, concerns, or expectations.

It is easy to take good health for granted until we experience the effects of illness, pain, or injury firsthand.

Our jobs, the honesty, dependability, and sincerity of others, our prosperity, or success should never be taken for granted.

We live in a world filled with uncertainties, never knowing from one day to the next what tragedy may strike or trouble may come.

Life itself is something we should not take for granted. We could wake up tomorrow in heaven or hell without being able to make amends or say goodbye.

We need to always hope for, but never assume, the best, to be wise as serpents and harmless as doves, and pray daily for wisdom and spiritual discernment in knowing whom and what we can trust.

We need to enjoy and appreciate every blessing and be mindful of the Source.

There are some things we can take for granted. We can be sure of God's faithfulness and sovereignty. We can be sure of His unconditional love and forever forgiveness. We can be sure of His promise to work all things for our good and His glory when we have received Jesus as our Savior and make Him the Lord of our life.

> "Make sure you don't take things for granted and go slack in working for the common good; share what you have with others. God takes particular pleasure in acts of worship—a different kind of 'sacrifice'—that take place in kitchen and workplace and on the streets."
> **Heb rews 13:15 MSG**

Father, help me to anchor deep in the certainty that You are Whom You say and that You will do what You say You will do. Amen.

Lord, You Are _____

Forgive Me For _____

Thank You For _____

Needs of Others _____

Personal Needs _____

Answered Prayers _____

Casual is Not Cool to God

"So then, because you are lukewarm, and neither cold nor hot, I will vomit you out of My mouth." Revelation 3:16

As much as God hates hypocrisy and legalism, He probably hates casual Christianity even worse. God will not be mocked, and He does not wink at sin.

"Expose all who drift away from Your sayings; their casual idolatry is lethal." Psalm 119:118 MSG

Preachers used to literally preach the hell right out of people, or at least people right out of hell, by warning of the seriousness of sin and judgment that awaits us all.

Too many want "feel good" sermons and sugar-coated varnish that glosses over sin and trivializes it as no big deal. After all, everybody's doing it, so it must be all right. We do not like to be reminded of the reality of death and the wages of sin.

There appears to be a widespread belief that you can do or believe anything as long as you're sincere, and our freedom in Christ somehow gives us freedom from the authority of God's clear instructions regarding morality and how we should be living our lives in and for Him.

If parents do not take sin seriously, neither will their children. If parents take their faith casually, so will their children, and the covenant will be twice broken and almost impossible to restore.

Too often, we are satisfied to have Jesus as a casual acquaintance instead of developing a close and personal relationship through prayer and abiding in His Word that will make Him our bestfriend for now and forever.

"Knowing the correct password—saying 'Master, Master,' for instance—isn't going to get you anywhere with Me. What is required is serious obedience—doing what My Father wills." Matthew 7:21 MSG

We like Christians who are religious but not too religious and a God who we can define by our standards, instead of the clear and complete standards revealed in His Word.

The question we should all be asking is how casual was God in hating sin so much that He sent His Son to die to pay the penalty for ours.

Father, help me to always remember that Your grace is free but not cheap, and there is nothing casual about Your hatred of sin. Amen.

Lord, You Are _____
Forgive Me For _____
Thank You For _____
Needs of Others _____
Personal Needs _____
Answered Prayers _____

Read 1 Peter 4, Psalm 119:27-32

The Rest of the Story

"My brethren, count it all joy when you fall into various trials." James 1:2

Paul Harvey has entertained and blessed millions of listeners during a

"Make me understand the way of Your precepts; so shall I meditate on Your wonderful works."
Psalm 119:27

distinguished lifetime career in radio broadcasting telling "The Rest of the Story." These behind-the-scenes tidbits have shed much light on interesting people, places, and things.

As believers, we should all spend more time dwelling on the rest of the story of Jesus. Too many of us, too often, only get it half right.

We love to relish knowing Jesus as the Son of God and Savior of the world and to claim all of the blessings our faith in Him brings.

It is great to know the blessings of abiding and the abundant life we have in and through Jesus when we receive Him as our Savior. We too often forget to dwell on His call to also share in His suffering and to pick up our cross and follow Him where ever, whenever, no matter what.

The way of the cross is a wonderful way of finding peace and happiness through a close and personal relationship with God through faith in Jesus Christ. It is also a way of pain and suffering that we are all called to endure with perseverance by the all-sufficient grace of God.

"The Rest of the Story" is that the way of the cross may well be a way of pain and sorrow that we may have to bear as we journey through the hills and valleys of this life. We should never be surprised when bad things happen but rather learn to rejoice in all our circumstances because of whom we are and Whom we have in Christ

The "Best of the Story" is that we will never have to bear or suffer through anything alone once we have received Jesus as our Lord and Savior. We will receive His all-sufficient grace, and He will be our help in time of trouble.

"Instead, be very glad— because these trials will make you partners with Christ in His suffering, and afterward you will have the wonderful joy of sharing His glory when it is displayed to all the world."
1 Peter 4:13 NLT

Father, keep me ever mindful of the rest of the story. Amen.

Lord, You Are _____
Forgive Me For _____
Thank You For _____
Needs of Others _____
Personal Needs _____
Answered Prayers _____

The Tables of Blessings

"You prepare a table before me in the presence of my enemies; You anoint my head with oil; my cup runs over." Psalm 23:5

God's tables of blessings are bigger than the biggest of any Chinese super buffet. The key to enjoying them is in understanding what they are and how to get them.

"For I will look on you favorly and make you fruitful, multiply you and confirm My covenant with you."

Leviticus 26:5

We need to know that God is a God of blessings. He loves to give good gifts to His children. No good thing will He withhold from those who love Him.

God's table of general blessings is poured out upon all people. He makes the sun to shine on the just and the unjust. Even bad people enjoy blessings of good health and prosperity from a good God.

God's blessing of eternal life is a blessing of believing. This is a free gift offered to all. This table always has a few extra chairs available anytime for all who call upon the name of the Lord to be saved.

God has set a table of obedience blessings reserved for those who hear the Word and obey it. He is a rewarder of those who seek Him. He keeps wonderful promises to those who obey.

God also has a table of blessings reserved for those who ask.

Many of the best tables are tables of spiritual blessings. You can't buy happiness, all-surpassing peace, strength to cover your weaknesses, joy, or ever-present help in time of trouble. A forever life with Christ is the greatest blessing.

God does not cut corners at His all-you-can-eat physical blessing table. We are all millionaires when it comes to counting our blessings of health and a sound mind for being a dwelling place to invite the Holy Spirit.

"Now when one of those who sat at the table with Him heard these things, he said to Him, 'Blessed is he who shall eat bread in the kingdom of God!' Luke 14:15

The greatest blessings are reserved for those who find their joy in giving instead of receiving. Just as God's love is a giving love, we are even more blessed by giving to others.

Father, help me to always come to Your tables of blessings with joy and thanksgiving and multiply them all by thanksliving. Amen.

Lord, You Are _____

Forgive Me For _____

Thank You For _____

Needs of Others _____

Personal Needs _____

Answered Prayers _____

Strikeout Records

"Since we've compiled this long and sorry record as sinners (both us and them) and proved that we are utterly incapable of living the glorious lives God wills for us, God did it for us." Romans 3:23, 24 MSG

In baseball circles, home-run records are a much discussed benchmark for

"Lord, if you kept a record of our sins, who, O Lord, could ever survive?"
Psalm 130:3 NLT

many players. Reggie Jackson and Willie Stargill are rememberd by baseball buffs for their home-run hitting prowess. Not nearly as many people remember that they are career strikeout leaders.

Thomas Edison, arguably one of the greatest inventers of all time, had some 900 inventions that didn't work. He was also arguably the greatest strikeout leader.

We need to understand that we are all going to strikeout from time to time in the game of life. Satan is going to continually throw us curves and fast balls.

The question is not if we strike out but when we strike out. How do we respond? Reggie Jackson, Willie Stargill, and Thomas Edison responded by hitting home runs, and we should strive to do the same.

We are all power hitters when we step up to the plate in the power of the Holy Spirit. We have been endued with power from on high to give us the strength to overcome or persevere through every failure or weakness.

The same resurrection power that raised Jesus from the dead can raise us up from the pits of sin, death, and destruction into the abundant new life of peace and joy that is in Christ.

"He canceled the record that contained the charges against us. He took it and destroyed it by nailing it to Christ's cross."
Colossians 2:14 NLT

Best of all, God doesn't operate on the three-strikes-and-you're-out rule. He doesn't even keep a record of strikeouts. Failure is never final with God, and the Holy Spirit is ever ready to help us hit a home run to heaven through faith in Jesus Christ.

Father after all my strikeouts have been buried at the cross , may the home run of righteousness remain when I stand before You. Amen.

Lord, You Are _____
Forgive Me For _____
Thank You For _____
Needs of Others _____
Personal Needs _____
Answered Prayers _____

Low Ego Emission

"All of you, clothe yourselves with humility toward one another, because, God opposes the proud but gives grace to the humble." 1 Peter 5:5b NIV

A leading car manufacturer advertised their car as having low ego emission. In this era of high ego emission, any status symbol of humility is a welcome relief.

"The humble will be filled with fresh joy from the LORD. Those who are poor will rejoice in the Holy One of Israel."
Isaiah 29:19 NLT

In the worlds of entertainment, sports, and business, corporate CEO's big egos are supported by big salaries and product endorsements that exceed the gross national product of some countries.

When we let our egos validate our self worth, we will find ourselves driving status symbol cars, going deeper into debt for prestigious neighborhoods and clubs, and will run the risk of choking any real and meaningful relationship with God through faith in Jesus Christ.

We see high ego emission preachers and worship leaders flashing Rolexes and jetting around the country in their own twenty-million-dollar ministry jets. It's almost as if the prosperity gospel demands that those who preach it flaunt it with their personal lifestyles and "perks."

Billy Graham and Mother Teresa modeled the humility of Christ with such low ego emission that the world was disarmed by the transparency and simplicity of their lives and deeds.

As professing Christians, we are all called to be imitators of Christ, who humbled himself by dying a criminal's death on the cross.

We are called to die to our egocentric selves and live Christ-centered lives fully pleasing to God and fruitful in every good work.

The sooner we understand that life is not about us but about the One who created us for His pleasure and His purposes, the sooner we will realize that high emission egos have no place in the kingdom of God.

"But those who exalt themselves will be humbled, and those who humble themselves will be exalted."
Matthew 23:12

Father, do not let me pollute the genuineness of my faith or sincerity of my love with high ego emissions. Amen.

Lord, You Are _____

Forgive Me For _____

Thank You For _____

Needs of Others _____

Personal Needs _____

Answered Prayers _____

Falling Out of Love

"Restore to me the joy of Your salvation, and uphold me by Your generous Spirit." Psalm 51:12

Falling out of love with Jesus seems to be a much too prevalent and widespread occurrence these days. It is heartbreaking to see those who once were so in love with Jesus turn their backs on Him.

"So I will restore to you the years that the swarming locust has eaten, the crawling locust, the consuming locust, and the chewing locust, My great army which I sent among you."
Joel 2:25

The question of whether someone who was truly saved can ever be lost is a matter of debate and division among theologians. Most of those who say you can't, say that if you do, it is evidence that you were never really saved in the first place.

The parable of the sower and the seed gives a lot of insight into how people fall out of love with Jesus. The buzzards of doubt and despair, the rocks of hard knocks, and the thorny weeds of deceitfulness of riches and desire for worldly pleasure all take their toll. We will all lose our battles with the world, the flesh, and the devil if we fail to anchor deep in our faith and put on the full armor of God.

There seem to be many people who want to blame God for a failed marriage, the untimely death of a spouse or loved one, or any major disappointment or problem incurred in life.

We all must realize that walking by faith instead of by sight means rejoicing inspite of our problems and disappointments.

"Dear friends, even though we are talking like this, we really don't believe that it applies to you. We are confident that you are meant for better things, things that come with salvation."
Hebrews 6:9

Above all, we must guard our hearts and never let them become hardened by bitterness or resentment when disappointments come.

For any who may have fallen out of love with Jesus, please remember that He has not fallen out of love with you and stands at the sheepgate ready to welcome you back any time.

Lord, You Are _____

Forgive Me For _____

Thank You For _____

Needs of Others _____

Personal Needs _____

Answered Prayers _____

December 21   Read Jude 1:20-25, Psalm 65
Living it Down by Living it Up
"Those who say they live in God should live their lives as Christ did."
1 John 2:5 NLT

"What joy for those you choose to bring near, those who live in Your holy courts. What joys await us inside Your holy Temple."
Psalm 65:4 NLT

We all have probably had some embarassing moments which we have felt we would never live down. Because of our faith in what Jesus Christ did for us on the cross , we will never have to worry about living anything down.

When we receive the new birth in Christ, our lives become all about "living it up." This means that we must rise above our circumstances, weaknesses, and disappointments and begin "living it up" in the joy of the Lord as we begin growing into the fullness of Christ.

When we receive Jesus Christ as our Savior, we are freed from the dominion of sin and bondage to the flesh that keeps us tied down in the muck and the mire of sin.

We become free to rise to the throne of God's grace and mercy covered by the righteousness of Christ.

We become free to live up to our adoption as sons and daughters of the Living Lord and live fruitful lives fully pleasing to Him.

Sanctification is the life-long process of living up to the image of Christ by being made holy and and growing in our faith as He sets us apart for His use.

As we begin living up our faith by living it out in the fullness of Christ, we experience the blessings of Jesus' joy, friendship with Jesus, answered prayers, and the awareness of God's love and His will.

"Live in such a way that God's love can bless you as you wait for the eternal life that our Lord Jesus Christ in His mercy is going to give you,"
Jude 1:21 NLT

Once we have tasted the peace and joy of abiding in Christ, we will never want to live back down in the depravity of the flesh. Our lives will become a living sacrifice of praise and thanksgiving to God for what He has done for us through Jesus.

Father, help me to "live it up" by lifting You up daily by glorifying You in all that I say and do. Amen.

Lord, You Are _____
Forgive Me For _____
Thank You For _____
Needs of Others _____
Personal Needs _____
Answered Prayers _____

Fragrance of Faith

"Just as lotions and fragrance give sensual delight, a sweet friendship refreshes the soul." Proverbs 27:9 MSG

The fact that Body washes, colognes, perfumes, and aftershave lotions are a multi-billion-dollar business throughout the world is proof that people want to make themselves attractive to others by smelling good.

"And the Lord smelled a soothing aroma. Then the Lord said in His heart, 'I will never again curse the ground for man's sake,' Genesis 8:21a

There is a fragrance that is sweeter than anything that comes in a bottle or spray, and it will make anyone more attractive to themselves and to others. This is the sweet fragrance of our faith in Jesus Christ as Lord and Savior.

When the Holy Spirit comes to live within us, the sweetness of our spirits is evidenced by the fragrance of the love, joy, peace, longsuffering, kindness, goodness, faithfulness, gentleness, and self control which we shower on others.

When we bathe in the ocean of God's love and forgiveness, the stench of our sin is washed away, and we become transformed by the renewing of our minds. Our lives become a sweet fragrance of praise and thanksgiving to God.

The more we abide in Christ through His Word, the more His friendship refreshes our souls and empowers us to refresh others.

One of the nicest things we can say about anyone is that they have a "sweet spirit." We are drawn to those who show the evidence of their holy transformation by bearing the fruit of a sweet spirit.

And now I have it all—and keep getting more! The gifts you sent with Epaphroditus were more than enough, like a sweet-smelling sacrifice roasting on the altar, filling the air with fragrance, pleasing God to no end." Philippians 4:18 MSG

The fragrance of our faith should perfume the world around us with our joy, peace, faith, hope, and love. We will become like a breath of fresh air that refreshes better than any scent manufactured by man.

Father, let the fragrance of my faith be like a sweet aroma that draws others to You. Amen.

Lord, You Are _____

Forgive Me For _____

Thank You For _____

Needs of Others _____

Personal Needs _____

Answered Prayers _____

Who Needs Him?

"God blesses those who realize their need for Him, for the Kingdom of Heaven is given to them." Matthew 5:3 NLT

More and more people are deciding that they don't need God. The world is singing odes to the power of self and the importance to doing it our way. We've got everything we want, so who needs God?

"But I would feed you with the best of foods. I would satisfy you with wild honey from the rock." Psalm 81:16 NLT

The fear of divine retribution has all but vanished in an anything-goes, relative-truth world. After getting by with sinning mightily without the sky falling, the brakes are off and moral meltdown is in full sway.

Many seem to be getting along better without God than those who confess their faith in Him. Many come to God as their personal Santa Claus, and they cut and run when He doesn't deliver the goods for which they ask.

In His longsuffering and patient kindness, God often puts up with a lot of guff before manifesting His total power and total control of the world in which we live and everything in it.

Sodom and Gomorrah saw no need of God and were totally destroyed. God swept away the entire human race who thought they didn't need God in the flood. When given the choice of eternal life or his riches, the rich young ruler decided that he didn't need God as badly as He loved His riches.

The heartbreak of seeing those we love rejecting the faith of their heritage and breaking God's covenant chain of blessings is a hard cross to bear.

"And human hands can't serve His needs—for He has no needs. He Himself gives life and breath to everything, and He satisfies every need there is." Acts 17:25 NLT

It is a sobering thought for those who see no need of God to remind them that the time is coming when they are going to need Him, and they would be wise to seek Him while and where He may be found.

Father, by the power of the Holy Spirit, let the desire to know You become a desire to need You in the hearts of all. Amen.

Lord, You Are _____

Forgive Me For _____

Thank You For _____

Needs of Others _____

Personal Needs _____

Answered Prayers _____

Friend of Sinners

"And I, the Son of Man, feast and drink, and you say, 'He's a glutton and a drunkard, and a friend of the worst sort of sinners!' But wisdom is shown to be right by what results from it." Matthew 11:19

Those hell bent on taking Christ out of Christmas in our schools, our workplaces, and the world at large should take note of the reality of what a friend everyone has in Jesus.

> **"Friendship with the LORD is reserved for those who fear Him. With them He shares the secrets of His covenant."**
> **Psalm 25:14 NLT**

The millions of merchants who depend on the Christmas season to put them in the black for the year know what a friend they have in Jesus.

The atheists, civil libertarians, and secular humanists who are trying to eliminate Christ should realize that their freedom to try to eliminate Christ is allowed only by the permissive will of God, which gives them the free will to disregard, ignore, and disobey plain truth.

If Jesus were not the friend of sinners, none of us would be enjoying our gift of salvation through faith in Him. He could just as easily have ignored us as we tend to ignore the poor and downtrodden among us.

Jesus was born for the express purpose of making saints out of sinners. He has reconciled us with God because of our faith, and He is conforming us into His image by drawing us into a close and personal friendship with Him.

What other friend sticks closer than a brother to keep us beside the still waters and to restore our souls? What other friend loved us enough to die so that we would not have to die? What other friend fills us with the incredible peace and joy of the Spirit and the comfort of God's love?

> **"So now we can rejoice in our wonderful new relationship with God— all because of what our Lord Jesus Christ has done for us in making us friends of God."**
> **Romans 5:11 NLT**

As believers, we have the wonderful gift of friendship with God and the high privilege of being joint heirs of all His promises for this world and the next.

We should be "promise seekers" as we pursue our friendship by abiding in Christ through abiding in the Word.

Saints and sinners alike should rejoice in "what a friend we have in Jesus"!

Father, help me to realize what Christmas really means. Amen.

Lord, You Are _____
Forgive Me For _____
Thank You For _____
Needs of Others _____
Personal Needs _____
Answered Prayers _____

All Wrapped Up for Christmas

"My gifts are better than the purest gold, my wages better than sterling silver!" Proverbs 8:19 NLT

Gift wrapping is a multi-billion-dollar business. The care and talent so many put into wrapping their gifts knowing that the wrappings will be torn to pieces and discarded in the trash does not diminish the effort and expense put into gift wrapping.

"They will come home and sing songs of joy on the heights of Jerusalem. They will be radiant because of the many gifts the LORD has given them," Jeremiah 31:12a NLT

We need to let Christmas be a poignant reminder that we too should be wrapped in the "swaddling clothes of the manger" for Christmas.

Unfortunately, many of us may get so wrapped up in ourselves and all of the distractions of gift shopping, swapping, and wanting, we may diminish the real meaning of Christmas.

If we would put as much thought into the greatest gift we could ever have received being given to us on that first Christmas as we do into what we are going to buy, to whom we will and will not send cards, decorating the tree and house, etc., we would be getting all wrapped up in the right things.

We need to be all wrapped up in Jesus, whose birth brought us the light of our salvation and whose death means that we will never have to die for our sins.

Just as the wise men sought Him then, if we are wise, we will continually seek Him and grow into His fullness every day of our lives.

"She gave birth to her first child, a son. She wrapped Him snugly in strips of cloth and laid Him in a manger, because there was no room for them in the village inn." Luke 2:7 NLT

God's desire for all of us is that we become imitators of Christ in every area of our lives. When we get "all wrapped up" in Jesus by abiding in His Word, we will not have to ask "what would Jesus do" because we will remember everything He did and seek to imitate His actions.

May the reality of "Emmanuel – God With Us" be our minds' attention and hearts' affection every year. Merry Christmas!

May I always make room in the manger of my heart for You, Lord. Amen.

Lord, You Are _____

Forgive Me For _____

Thank You For _____

Needs of Others _____

Personal Needs _____

Answered Prayers _____

The Original Super Center

"Buy the truth, and do not sell it, also wisdom and instruction and understanding." Proverbs 23:23

Wal-Mart has developed the super-center concept into a profitable business format by keeping their shopping centers open 24 hours a day, 7 days a week, but they did not invent the concept.

God has been operating an one-stop shopping center that has never closed for centuries.

"The eyes of the LORD are on the righteous, and His ears are open to their cry." Psalm 34:15

Every department is well stocked with an abundance of grace to supply every need.

We can find salvation right down the main aisle that is ours for the receiving. There are rows of comfort stocked with shelves of healing and encouragement.

There is a fountain of forgiveness with a continual flow that never stagnates or becomes polluted with bitterness.

The housewares department is stocked to the brim with items essential for having a happy home. We will find the all-sufficient grace required to live as a family of God in a world of the ungodly.

The produce department has the fruit of the Spirit available at an every day low price. We can find all the love, joy, peace, longsuffering, kindness, goodness, faithfulness, gentleness, and self-control we need to help us fulfill God's law of love.

The clothing department has wedding garments designed to cover all of our sins with the righteousness of Christ.

The outdoor living department features built armor to wear when we go out into the world.

When we go to the checkout counter, we will find a gift certificate with our name written on it so that no further payment is required. Isn't it time for you to do your shopping at the real super center?

"Here's what I want you to do: Buy your gold from me, gold that's been through the refiner's fire. Then you'll be rich." Revelation 3:18 NLT

Father, thank you for keeping Your storehouse of blessings always open for me. Amen.

Lord, You Are _____

Forgive Me For _____

Thank You For _____

Needs of Others _____

Personal Needs _____

Answered Prayers _____

Choosing to Lose

"But if you are unwilling to serve the LORD, then choose today whom you will serve." Joshua 24:15a NLT

The world says that winning is everything. Secular humanism teaches that man should be his own god, and we can all control our own destiny and be all that we can be in our own strength.

"Today I have given you the choice between life and death, between blessings and curses. I call on heaven and earth to witness the choice you make. Oh, that you would choose life, that you and your descendants might live! "
Deuteronomy 30:19 NLT

We don't have to look very far to see how this philosophy has moved forward in the minds of more and more people. As a result, morality and decency have moved backwards. All of the decadence that brought the fall of the Roman Empire is now prevalent among us.

We must choose to lose our life in the flesh and become dead to sin in order to receive the all-surpassing peace and fullness of joy that is ours through becoming alive in Christ and being born again in Him.

Instead of choosing to lose, we choose to win in the game of life by appropriating by faith God's strength to cover our weaknesses and His enabling power to be and to do what we could never be or do on our own.

Without the all-sufficient grace of God, we are doomed to lose out on the greatest joys and true peace and happiness that only come from a close, personal relationship with Jesus Christ.

The real losers are the ones who choose to reject the call of salvation and live in the futility of the flesh wandering aimlessly lost and separated from God.

"Our old sinful selves were crucified with Christ so that sin might lose its power in our lives. We are no longer slaves to sin."
Romans 6:6 NLT

Father, help me to choose to die daily to sin and live a life worth living in the richness of Your grace. Amen.

Lord, You Are _____

Forgive Me For _____

Thank You For _____

Needs of Others _____

Personal Needs _____

Answered Prayers _____

Saving Face

"It's better to be promoted to a place of honor than face humiliation by being demoted." Proverbs 25:27 MSG

Different cultures have different standards for protecting and defending one's dignity and honor. Many church and government officials and many employees are allowed to quit or resign jobs rather than get fired in order for them to save face.

"We can't escape the constant humiliation; shame is written across our faces."
Psalm 44:15NLT

We should all be sensitive and try to preserve the honor and dignity of others by avoiding doing anything that would cause them humiliation or to feel disrespected.

Redemption through the blood of Jesus is one of the oldest and most effective methods ever devised for saving face. When saving grace is appropriated by faith, it becomes a means for saving face for all who lost honor and dignity to the ravages of sin. It can turn shame into fame; it can restore dignity and honor to the defeated and downtrodden.

Peter denied Jesus three times after proudly proclaiming his allegiance and commitment in one of the most famous examples of dishonor and humiliation in Scripture.

Charles Colson and thousands of other convicted felons have had their faces of dishonor saved by the transforming power of Jesus Christ.

We are all going to have embarrassing moments where we fall short of the glory of God and know the humiliation of dishonor and defeat. The good news is we never have to hide our face in shame from God.

"But God has chosen the foolish things of the world to put to shame the wise, and God has chosen the weak things of the world to put to shame the things which are mighty,"
1 Corinthians 1:17

He couldn't love us any more than He does, and He will never love us any less regardless of our conduct and failures. Because we are covered with the righteousness of Christ by faith, God views us as righteous in spite of our sins and moral meltdowns. We will never have to worry about saving face with God.

Father, help me to take my blame and shame to the cross and trade them for the joy of Christ living in me as I seek His face. Amen.

Lord, You Are _____
Forgive Me For _____
Thank You For _____
Needs of Others _____
Personal Needs _____
Answered Prayers _____

We Ain't Seen Nothin' Yet!

"Eye has not seen, nor ear heard, nor have entered into the heart of man the things which God has prepared for those who love Him."
2 Corinthians 2:9

God has given us a good life of pleasure and purpose to live on this earth. The One who made it all also owns it all, and He wants to share it all with us, who are "the apple of His eye."

"For behold, I create new heavens and a new earth; and the former shall not be remembered or come to mind."
Isaiah 65:17

The bond of fellowship with Adam and Eve ended when innocence went out and sin moved in through their disobedience.

Paradise was destroyed, and the good life became the conditional good life based on God's covenants or contracts with His children.Unfortunately, God's children always found a way to invent and worship other gods of their own making.

Sin broke God's heart and became a wall of separation between God and man. There was no good life to be lived.

God's unfailing love and compassion came down to live the good life in the humanity of man in the person of Jesus Christ. He chose to die on the cross to redeem us and to give us a good new life free from bondage to sin and death.

Jesus came that all who receive Him as Lord and Savior will live a good life to the fullest in Him. Although we can expect to share in His sorrow and suffering in this life, we have the Holy Spirit living within us to comfort and strengthen us so that we can endure and persevere through any troubles that come our way.

Best of all, because of what Jesus has done for us, we are reconciled with God and can look forward to having the sinless perfection of paradise restored when Jesus comes back to take us there.

"And God will wipe away every tear from their eyes; there shall be no more death, nor sorrow, nor crying. There shall be no more pain, for the former things have passed away."
Revelation 21:4

No matter what peace and joy we have experienced in this life and no matter how good our lives are here, compared to the joys that await us in heaven, "we ain't seen nothin' yet!"

Father, help me to keep my eye on the future and hope I have in Jesus. Amen.

Lord, You Are _____
Forgive Me For _____
Thank You For _____
Needs of Others _____
Personal Needs _____
Answered Prayers _____

What Are You Worth?

"Once for all time he took blood into that Most Holy Place, but not the blood of goats and calves. He took his own blood, and with it he secured our salvation forever." Hebrews 9:6 NLT

Bankers are always looking at an individual's or company's worth as a means of determining credit worthiness and capacity. The bottom line is what is left after everything you owe is subtracted from everything you own.

"Ho! Everyone who thirsts, come to the waters; and you who have no money, come, buy and eat. Come, buy wine and milk without money and without price."
Isaiah 55:1

As raw materials, our bodies are worth about $5.00 for their physical properties.

Beyond monetary value, we have the concept of worth being the quality of something or the value with which it is esteemed.

Our emotional security and peace of mind is usually based on our self worth or self esteem.

The bottom line for all believers is in knowing that we are worth much to God. As worthless as we actually act sometimes and as fickle and faithless as we may have been, we can live victoriously in the reality of the future and hope that we have in Christ because He thought that we were worth dying for on the cross of Calvary.

As much as we might desire to be a person of worth in the eyes of others and even have our worth validated in our own eyes by our wealth, power, popularity, talents, or accomplishments, none of this can begin to compare with finding our security and significance in knowing that we are significant to God.

"For you were bought at a price; therefore glorify God in your body and in your spirit, which are God's."
1 Corinthians 6:20

When we live out the reality of His love and supreme sacrifice by loving Him and loving others, we are confirming to Him that we were worth it.

When we base our security on whom God says we are, we are free to become all that we can be in Christ.

Father, by the power of Your Spirit, help me to live a life worth living that reflects the price You paid for me. Amen.

Lord, You Are _____

Forgive Me For _____

Thank You For _____

Needs of Others _____

Personal Needs _____

Answered Prayers _____

The Last to Know

"Their eyes are open but don't see a thing; their ears are open but don't hear a thing." Luke 8:10 MSG

Some people are so self centered and self absorbed that they are totally unaware of what's happening even in their homes and marriages. They may ignore or be oblivious to the warning signs of children getting into serious trouble or their marriage breaking up. Often they are the last to know.

"Harden the hearts of these people. Close their ears, and shut their eyes. That way, they will not see with their eyes, hear with their ears, understand with their hearts, and turn to Me for healing."
Isaiah 6:10 NLT

Sometimes our pride makes it difficult, if not impossible, for us to think that we might have been or be wrong about something. We are often totally unaware or the last to know some of the offenses we have given or hurts we have caused.

We often bathe in the river of denial. We are so intent on advancing or protecting our own interests that we are totally oblivious and insensitive to the needs and interests of others and our need for God.

He who knew us before we were even born knows everything we have ever done and everything we will ever do. He is often saddened but never surprised.

Good communication is the key to avoid becoming the last to know. When we take the time to listen, we will learn a great deal about what's going on in the lives of others. We will become more sensitive to their needs and better able not only to help them but to resolve minor concerns and problems before they become major.

"But Abraham said, 'If they won't listen to Moses and the prophets, they won't listen even if someone rises from the dead.'"
Luke 16:31

The only thing worse than being the last to know is never coming to know the love of God that is ours through faith in Jesus Christ.

Millions of people are dying every day doomed to eternal separation from God because they heard but refused to believe or put off God's call to salvation until it was too late.

Father, help me to avoid the heartbreak and surprise of being the last to know by becoming a good listener. Amen.

Lord, You Are _____
Forgive Me For _____
Thank You For _____
Needs of Others _____
Personal Needs _____
Answered Prayers _____

We ask God to give you a complete understanding of what He wants to do in your lives, and we ask him to make you wise with spiritual wisdom.

Then the way you live will always honor and please the Lord, and you will continually do good, kind things for others.

All the while, you will learn to know God better and better.

We also pray that you will be strengthened with His glorious power so that you will have all the patience and endurance you need.

May you be filled with joy!

Colossians 1:9-11 NLT

*(We join the Apostle Paul in praying
this prayer for all who read this book)*